AMERICAN VOICES
Webs of Diversity

ELIZABETH QUINTERO
University of Minnesota–Duluth

MARY KAY RUMMEL
University of Minnesota–Duluth

Prentice
Hall

Merrill, an imprint of
Prentice Hall
Upper Saddle River, New Jersey   Columbus, Ohio

Library of Congress Cataloging-in-Publication Data

Quintero, Elizabeth P.

American voices : webs of diversity / Elizabeth Quintero, Mary Kay Rummel.

p.   cm.

Includes bibliographical references and index.

ISBN 0-13-517807-X

1. Readers—United States.   2. United States—Civilization—Problems, exercises, etc.   3. Pluralism (Social sciences)—Problems, exercises, etc. 4. American literature. 5. College readers.   I. Rummel, Mary Kay. II. Title.

PE1127.H5Q56 1998

305.8'00973—dc21

97-28119
CIP

Editor: Debra A. Stollenwerk
Production Editor: Sheryl Glicker Langner
Design Coordinator: Julia Zonneveld Van Hook
Text Designer: Anne Flanagan
Cover art generated by Steve Botts
Cover design generated by Ceri Fitzgerald
Production Manager: Patricia A. Tonneman
Director of Marketing: Kevin Flanagan
Marketing Manager: Suzanne Stanton
Advertising/Marketing Coordinator: Julie Shough

Printed in the United States of America

10 9 8 7 6 5 4 3

ISBN: 0-13-517807-X

Prentice-Hall International (UK) Limited,London
Prentice-Hall of Australia Pty. Limited, Sydney
Prentice-Hall Canada Inc., Toronto
Prentice-Hall Hispanoamericana, S.A., Mexico
Prentice-Hall of India Private Limited, New Delhi
Prentice-Hall of Japan, Inc., Tokyo
Pearson Education Asia Pte. Ltd., Singapore
Editora Prentice-Hall do Brasil, Ltda., Rio de Janeiro

To all our children

PREFACE

The literature selections in this book combine various aspects of learning and living, chosen for the collection because of the complex thoughts they generate. The problem-posing method comes from Freirian activists (whom we thank) and is powerful because it situates the participant as the activist in the dance between lived experience and new information. The approach is not intended to be a recipe. Every problem-posing classroom will be different because all the interactions spring from the students themselves. The activities we offer are only suggestions. We believe the magic that comes from the combination of reader and reading is the essence of the reader's participation.

Short works of narrative fiction and occasional poetry are points of departure to inspire students to question their assumptions about the way the world works for people who have perspectives and lives different from their own. Each narrative is accompanied by listening guidelines and action suggestions that encourage readers to tie the narrative to their own experiences before reading; to reflect on their own questions as they read; and to consider their assumptions in light of the narrative, suggested readings, and questions posed. As one reviewer commented, "this is classic 'into, through, and beyond' critical pedagogy."

This method encourages what we see as a natural movement from reflection toward action that can be the result of reading literature. We use the method with the teacher educators we work with, and they use the problem-posing process with all ages of students. Maxine Greene (1995) advises, "As we devise curriculum and work on curriculum frameworks, it seems important to hold in mind the prospective, the possible. This means encouraging the kind of learning that has to do with becoming different, that reaches toward an open future—toward what might be or what ought to be" (p. 131).

The problem-posing (Freire, 1973) activities of our methodology are organized into selections of theme webs because they provide a nonlinear framework in which complex information can be connected to students' lives. The theme webs include choices of literature and poetry that represent perspectives on cultural context, language, age, ability, and other complexities that make up social context. Students respond to literature by relating their own experience or choosing other aspects included in the webs to further their reading and background knowledge. They reflect on their own families, the community of their classrooms and schools, and their larger community context. In the *listening* part of the class, we may have an introduction by the teacher that includes social and historical information related to the authors' subject. Then we may suggest reflective journaling by individual students to reacquaint them with their own past experiences and prereading activities for focusing purposes. Then the students listen to the authors by reading the literature selection. In the *dialogue* part, the authors dialogue with the readers through their own voices, students dialogue with themselves as they write responses to the readings, and students dialogue with peers through small and large group discussions. In the *action* part, we encourage questioning. Student questions generate further questions that begin to confront the world outside the classroom. Students may generate suggestions for observation activities in schools and at community events, for interviewing topics, and for individual and collective community action.

In some activities students are asked to read one or more books or longer works of fiction and nonfiction and then summarize them or reflect on their themes. The instructor using the book is encouraged to choose parameters for which activities to use depending on other course responsibilities and students' level of study. We hope, in the spirit of critical pedagogy, that within the objectives and parameters that instructors define according to the course of study the students will have choice in the aspects of their participation. Questions that follow the reading of a longer work are purposely consistent to point out to the students the importance of critical questioning and to reiterate the process regardless of the theme topic and type of information. Questions are also meant to provide a small scaffolding of structure in a loosely structured text.

Students are asked to review research in some of the related action option activities. Again, flexibility is provided so choices can be made according to responsibilities and level of study. Annotated bibliographies are included as suggestions and are in no way meant to be exclusive reading lists. The organization of the book is such that teachers can use the material in an order that fits their particular situation. We stress that community and context are the underpinnings of the pedagogical approach in this book.

Finally, we hope that these stories, the community of scholars in each learning environment, and participation in our broader communities will generate transformation. As Zinn (1994) says, "We don't have to engage in grand, heroic actions to participate in the process of change. Small acts, when multiplied by millions of people, can transform the world" (p. 208).

ACKNOWLEDGMENTS

We would like to thank three education students at the University of Minnesota at Duluth: Kristi Chupurdia, Ann Green, and Rebecca Remer. Their hard work and commitment helped us immeasurably. We would also like to acknowledge the master teachers whose interviews and current practice have inspired and informed our work. Of course, many thanks and much admiration goes out to the authors of the selections who have been so generous with their creative work. Thanks also to Penny Burleson. Finally, we extend a heartfelt thanks to our editor, Debbie Stollenwerk, for her vision, support, and enthusiasm through the years of conception to production.

We would especially like to thank the following reviewers for their valuable comments and suggestions: Carol J. Carter, Central Connecticut State University; Sandy B. DeCosta, Indiana State University; Christian Faltis, Arizona State University; Beatrice Fennimore, Indiana University of Pennsylvania; Samuel Hinton, Eastern Kentucky University; Judith Lessow-Hurley, San José State University; and Francesina R. Jackson, North Carolina Central University.

REFERENCES

Freire, P. (1973). *Education for critical consciousness.* New York: Seabury Press.

Greene, M. (1995). Notes on the search for coherence. In J. Beane (Ed.), *ASCD Yearbook* (pp. 139–145). Alexandria, VA: ASCD.

Zinn, H. (1994). *You can't be neutral on a moving train: A personal history of our times.* Boston: Beacon.

⅃ ACKNOWLEDGMENTS

"Losing Absalom" by Alexs D. Pate. Coffee House Press, 1994. Used by permission of the publisher. © 1994 by Alexs D. Pate.

"In the General Population, in Ordinary Time" by Carol Masters. © 1994 by Carol Masters.

"Luck of the Irish" by Gary Geddes. © 1995 by Gary Geddes.

"Growing through the Ugly" by Diego Vázquez, Jr.

"Culture Clash" by Jim Northrup. © 1993 by Jim Northrup, reprinted with permission of Publisher, Voyageur Press, Inc., 123 North Second Street, Stillwater, Minnesota 55083 U.S.A., 1-800-888-9653.

"Flying Blind" by Gary Geddes. © 1995 by Gary Geddes.

"Ellen Ryan's Braided Rug" by Pat Barone. © 1995 by Pat Barone.

"Taking Miss Kezee to the Polls" by David Haynes. © 1991 by David Haynes.

"Renga" by Kate Hallet Dayton. © 1995 by Kate Hallett Dayton.

"Newsbrief" by Norita Dittberner-Jax. © 1995 by Norita Dittberner-Jax.

"Busted: A Boy's True Tale of Real Life in a Big City Junior High School" by David Haynes. Originally appeared in *Glimmer Train Stories* and is part of the novel *Heathens* (New Rivers Press, 1996).

"The Whispering Cloth" by Pegi Deitz Shea. © 1995 by Pegi Deitz Shea. Reprinted by permission of Boyds Mills Press.

"Rufus at the Door" by Jon Hassler. © 1988 by Jon Hassler. Reprinted from *Stiller's Pond*.

"Southeast Asia, Second Grade" by Roseann Lloyd. First published in *Tap Dancing for Big Mom*, New Rivers Press, 1986. Reprinted by permission of the author.

"A First Day" by Kevin Fitzpatrick. First published in *Down on the Corner*, Midwest Villages and Voices, 1987. Reprinted by permission of the author.

"Lessons from Space" by Roseann Lloyd. First published in *War Baby Express*, Holy Cow! Press, 1996.

"My Slanted View" by Sara Ryung Clement. © by Sara Ryung Clement.

"Spring Concert" by Stephen Peters. Stephen Peters is a writer and storyteller who lives in Minneapolis, Minnesota.

"The Great Circle of These Things" by Tom Peacock. Reprinted by permission of the author.

"Writing Down Secrets" by Sara Mosle. From *The New Yorker*, 1995.

"Lexicon of Exile" by Aleida Rodríguez. Reprinted by permission of the author.

"Reach for the Moon" by Samantha Abeel. Reprinted with permission from *Reach for the Moon*, © 1994 by Samantha Abeel and Charles R. Murphy, published by Pfeifer-Hamilton Publishers, Duluth, Minnesota.

"The Boy without a Flag" by Abraham Rodriguez, Jr. Originally published in *The Boy without a Flag* by Abraham Rodriguez, Jr. (Milkweed Editions, 1992). © 1992 by Abraham Rodriguez, Jr. Reprinted with permission from Milkweed Editions.

"Steps to a New and More Wonderful You" by David Haynes. Originally appeared in *Glimmer Train Stories* and is part of the novel *Heathens* (New Rivers Press, 1996).

"But You Don't Look Chinese" by Demian Hess. © 1995 by Demian Hess. First published in "Sticky Rice: The Power of Community," *Journal of the Asian American Renaissance*, vol. 1 (1995).

"Distant Touch" by Ellen Hawley. © 1995 by Ellen Hawley.

"Sour Rice" by Nhien T. Nguyen. Reprinted by permission of the author.

"Women Like Those" by David Haynes. © 1994 by David Haynes.

"The Peace Terrorist" by Carol Masters. © 1994 by Carol Masters.

"And Say Good-Bye to Yourself" by Susan Williams. Reprinted by permission of the author.

"The World of Chili Peatoad" by Tom Peacock. Reprinted by permission of the author.

"New York City Mira Mira Blues" by Gloria Vando. Reprinted with permission from the publisher of *Promesas: Geography of the Impossible* (Houston: Arte Publico Press—University of Houston, 1993).

C O N T E N T S

Contents   **xi**

Introduction

Think of American culture as a conversation among different voices. . . . The
purpose of education is to recognize the voices.

(Greene, 1992, p. 13)

And the world
is less bitter to me
because you will retell the story.
      (Boland, 1994, p. 50)

My grandmother used to tell stories; she was from the West Indies and she used
to tell a lot of folk tales that her mother had told her when she was growing up.
We would lie in bed together every afternoon and she would tell those stories to
me. Scary stories and ghost stories that taught a lesson about how to behave. . . .
I would ask her to tell them to me again and again. Then my mother intro-
duced me to books and I still have some of the books that she bought for me. She
would read aloud to me and I had favorites that I would bring to her again
and again.

(Brathwaite, in press, p. 166)

Vicki Brathwaite is a reading specialist and elementary school teacher in Brooklyn, New York. In an interview she describes her literacy experiences as circular: her grandmother's stories lead to her work with children; the children sit in circles to read and write; stories appear and reappear; reading leads to writing leads to reading; she belongs to circle groups of professionals who share their literate experiences. The human circle of literacy is a central metaphor for her. As Metzger (1991) explains, "stories go in circles. They don't go in straight lines. So it helps if you listen in circles because there are stories inside stories and stories between stories and finding your way through them is as easy and hard as finding your way home. And part of the finding is the getting lost. If you're lost, you really start to look around and listen" (p. 104).

In this book we discuss a problem-posing teaching method using literature that reflects our assumptions about teaching and learning. This method, which is non-linear and uses the wisdom passed on in story, explores ways of encouraging a natural movement from reflection toward action, which can be the result of reading literature. Maxine Greene (1995) advises, "As we devise curriculum and work on curriculum frameworks, it seems important to hold in mind the prospective, the possible. This means encouraging the kind of learning that has to do with becoming different, that reaches toward an open future—toward what might be or what ought to be" (p. 131).

RATIONALE

As teacher researchers, we believe that all of us must consistently reflect on our work and our convictions. This constant clarification of our own values and action in all areas of pluralistic work with students is the ongoing aim of education. We see this clarification as Freire (1985) does when he defines *conscientization* (based on the Portuguese word *conscientização*) as "the process by which human beings participate critically in a transforming act" (p. 106). We see our classrooms as communities of learners that reflect characteristics of the larger communities from which the students come and the global community where we all struggle to live together peacefully. We use this problem-posing teaching method as a way to facilitate student choice and generative work that is integral to students' lives. We suggest literature selections and thematic activities that focus on issues of human diversity, including the nature of culture, race, ethnicity, class, gender, language, the social construction of at-risk populations, ableness, aging, and changing configurations of family in a problem-posing format (Freire, 1973). Literature is effective for our purposes because story is not only the way people learn but leaves the complex issues in teaching, as in life, intact. Therefore, the danger of stereotypical oversimplification is minimalized.

This problem-posing approach is often described as critical pedagogy. We believe that there is a strong connection between critical pedagogy and using literature in teaching because a natural outcome of reading literature can be transformative action. We believe this natural outcome is not causal but that metaphors enriched by reading and other creative activities structure our thinking, our understanding of events, and consequently our behavior (Lakoff & Johnson, 1980). Many experiences can give rise to metaphors. More surely than anything else, we are defined by our stories—the cultural myths we hear from our earliest days. At the same time we are defined by the way we "rewrite" the myths we hear. Only when old patterns in our consciousness crumble are new patterns possible.

In a recent study we found that the metaphors coming from literacy experiences provided a mechanism for "remything" (Rummel & Quintero, in press). Living in the twilight of the twentieth century, we are surrounded by the ruins of myths and metaphors that have lost their power to shape and animate our lives. All around us, we hear the cracking of old certainties. Yet in the midst of our confusion and grief, a new mythology is being born. In our end-of-the-century study of teachers' lives, we discovered that all the teachers are midwifing emergent mythologies. They are transforming their school classrooms into mythogenetic zones: places where new myths and metaphors are born. They are vessels through which new mythologies are slowly emerging. The teachers in this study, faced with the need to re-create common mythologies, did so at a young age. This re-creation happened during a critical reading of what they were learning in and out of school. For example, Raúl Quintanilla, who teaches English as a second language, realized as a child:

> We didn't have any heroes to identify with. We didn't have General MacArthur, we didn't have Roosevelt, we didn't have. . . . We couldn't identify with them because we were Mexican Americans. People that they would consider heroes like Jim Bowie and Davy Crockett were white people. To Texas history or American history they are heroes. But if you

look at Northern Mexican history they are not heroes. They are the crooks who kicked people out of areas. In fact the school I went to was Sam Houston Elementary. And they would praise him. We didn't know him so we tried to learn. We didn't really have anyone to identify with, except for the "Cinco de Mayo." We had one person. General Zaragoza. The reason that we identify with him is because he was born in an area of South Texas, which is now Goldeanne, and he was the one that won the final battle. The Mexicans didn't want us because we were Chicanos and Americans didn't want us because they think we're Mexican. So we made this guy our hero. Then John F. Kennedy. He was a hero. (Quintanilla, in press, pp. 262–263)

THEORETICAL PERSPECTIVE

We have based the pedagogy in this book on a theoretical triangulation using critical theory, feminist theory, and autobiographical theory. Freire's work regarding conscientization, which is an important aspect of critical theory and critical pedagogy, is grounded in the philosophical position that all learners are experts in their own reality and must be given the opportunity and skills to be transformative intellectuals. We see this perspective as relevant to all students of human diversity—who come to the task of study with their own experiences and life learnings—in our global society. Giroux (1988) maintains that this quest of the intellectual is helpful for three reasons. First, it defines one's work as an intellectual endeavor as opposed to a mere technical one. Second, it brings to light the conditions necessary for people to combine ideological and practical issues. Third, it legitimizes our roles in combining political, economic, and social interests through daily work.

Not only do critical theory and critical pedagogy stress valuing the life experiences of the learners, but the political and practical situation of learners comes to the forefront of attention: "A critical pedagogy can only be correctly discussed from within a particular 'point of practice'; from within a specific time and place and within a particular theme. This means doing critical pedagogy is a strategic, practical task, not a scientific one. It arises not against a background of psychological, sociological, or anthropological universals as does much educational theory related to pedagogy—but from such questions as: *'how is human possibility being diminished here?'* " (Simon, 1988, p. 2).

Critical pedagogy (Freire, 1985) rejects exploitation of any kind. We, like Brady (1995), believe that three educational issues relating to potential exploitation must also be addressed. According to Brady (1995):

1. Teacher authority can be emancipatory when a feminist pedagogy of place is recognized (schools are institutions based on patriarchal philosophy, goals, delivery systems). Feminist pedagogy recognizes the limits that this contextual reality places upon cooperative, noncompetitive learning, production of knowledge, and social realities.
2. Any discussion of authority must be rooted in identity politics that acknowledges the need for people to represent themselves. This is not to romanticize experiences, but the person must have the opportunity to speak from experience to be responsible for actions in both the ideological and political sense.
3. Feminist authority must provide the conditions for students to gain control of their learning within a place and in a context in which they are not threatened by the implications of what they say. (p. 30)

Brady (1995) points out that, in identifying a politics of difference and identity, literacy is a central mechanism for discussing power, subjectivity, history, and experience. It becomes a way to translate these issues of politics into pedagogy. In this book we ask readers to consider who is looking at whom in a particular story. We ask, "What political, social, and cultural forces are behind this 'looking'?"

Various theories about diverse ways of knowing and the nature of knowledge are being discussed in the context of teaching and learning. Feminist epistemology has influenced our thinking about diversity and human relations. This theory has challenged many tenets of traditional knowledge as it is male-defined and practiced in Western patriarchal cultures (Rogers, 1993). Through this feminist theory the learner seeks to include, rather than exclude, herself or himself in research and interpretation. As Shannon (1993) points out, "feminist theory looks not for what has been excluded, but for what has been silenced" (p. 124). Thus, we use literature that reflects alternative ways of knowing, stories from voices that have traditionally been silenced in the United States. Alternative ways of knowing—alternatives to traditional Euro-American mainstream cultural norms—are persevering in some contexts through the practice of raising children and passing on family cultural traditions.

We encourage students to choose and examine voices in literature through poetry, fiction, and memory (from oral traditions that have been documented), focusing on authenticity of multiple experiences in multiple contexts. Through the process of participating in the activities and readings, and through reflection, we believe the reader is participating in a complex form of autobiographical narrative. This combination of literature and critical theory allows readers to use autobiography as a way to move beyond a neutral conception of culture in discussions of the relationship between schools and families and toward a better-defined conception of culture in a pluralistic, multicultural society (Willis, 1995). The students' participation in this method is autobiographical in the sense, both that the student reader is constantly encouraged to reflect on her or his own experience, and that the authors of the literature are giving us glimpses into their own autobiographies. Personal narrative lets us listen to the voices of the participants—students and authors in their cultural contexts—as they tell about their experiences and explain ongoing efforts at agency and transformation. Bloch (1991) explains that this type of symbolic science "focuses on intersubjectivities that are created through interactions between people, their discourse, and the interpretations of meaning within specific contexts" (p. 97). This relational theory sees experience as central to theorizing and to understanding practice.

Drawing on the notion of moving from reading, to interpretation, to criticism, Appleman and Green (1993) show the value of teaching high school students theoretical perspectives: reader-response, structuralist, Marxist, and feminist critical approaches. When providing students with critical theory, Appleman found that, particularly with feminist and Marxists perspectives, students acquired a critical vocabulary that resulted in insightful interpretations of literature. She also found that, although the students' understanding of these theoretical perspectives remained somewhat superficial, having a theoretical orientation enhanced their confidence in articulating and sharing their responses in the classroom. Our students lead themselves and their peers (in age-appropriate ways) a step farther than classroom response: criticism to action.

It has been reported that students learn political withdrawal from the cynicism of the media, from the pronouncements of their peers, from hesitations passed on by parents and teachers. Some students feel disconnected from anyone not of the same social status and background. Other young adults believe they cannot afford to engage in controversial public issues or stand up for their beliefs. Nevertheless, there is documented evidence that children exposed to social concern often develop an "ethic of engagement" (Loeb, 1995, pp. 40–41).

Mary Tacheny, a primary teacher at Franklin Magnet School in St. Paul, Minnesota, works with Southeast Asian immigrant children and their families. In a discussion about risk, she talks about the problem-posing aspects of her work with first graders:

I think one area that has really helped strengthen me in taking risks in curriculum has been embracing an integrated approach, and interdisciplinary strategies. For example, . . . writing really was a turning point for me. You can incorporate a lot of learning into the writing process and writing strategies just by following the brainstorming, prewriting activities, what your follow up is. You don't have to be "married to a manual," you don't have to take the curriculum and follow every scope and sequence activity. There are things that I can do to put together the objectives that are more appropriate to the needs of the students in my classroom and not let the manual dictate that. It's well worth the risk to go beyond that and to extend curriculum by embracing an integrated approach. For instance, I might be teaching reading and then I'll branch off into a math lesson that came from that reading context. I'm probably not a traditional teacher. I like to do a lot of creative dramatics. I like to give children experiences of leadership within a framework. Where you teach them leadership skills then give them opportunities for leadership. I think my children are just as important as an author. My students write to state senators, they have written to a judge, etc. It is overwhelming the responses they get. I have had a state senator come and meet my class based on their letters. We've been invited down to the Ramsey County Court House by a judge. Whether they are first graders or third graders, they really respond when children write genuinely from their hearts. To give children a voice is a risk because a lot of teachers want control. I think particularly with students at risk, you have to help let them know that it is okay to talk about things or it is okay for them to question because who wants robot kids? If we want to program their answers, forget it. There's no thinking or evidence of that critical thinking process that is the buzz word that we are trying to instill in them. Along with that you have a climate that offers children the opportunity to question, and you have to set up an atmosphere where it's okay to make mistakes. I really applaud kids that are willing to take a risk in not knowing what the outcome will be. (Tacheny, in press, pp. 233–234)

Mary Tacheny's classroom is a positive, real example of a safe and respectful context where the students are able to grow, question, support each other, and take risks. Mary's combination of respect for the learners and knowledge of writing-process techniques provides the kind of classroom that some critics (Lensmire, 1995) aim for and, when they are unable to achieve it, imply that the blame should be owned by the children, the philosophy underlying the method, or the methodology itself.

METHOD

The problem-posing activities of our methodology are organized into selections of theme webs because they provide a nonlinear framework in which complex information can be connected with students' lives. The theme webs include choices of literature selections that represent perspectives of varied lives in terms of cultural context, language, age, ability, and other complexities that make up social context. Freire's (1973) problem-posing format of *listening, dialogue, action* is then used in flexible ways. Students participate in the activities by relating their own experience or choose other aspects included in the webs to further their reading and background knowledge. They reflect upon the community they have entered in general and in field placements, pursue their particular field of inquiry in terms of human diversity issues, and learn from related issues in other participants' fields. This is especially true for issues relating to sociocultural contexts of communities and schools. Freire's dialogue teaching method (1973) reduces student withdrawal and teacher talk in the classroom. A dialogic class begins with a problem-posing discussion and sends powerful signals to students that their participation is expected and needed. As Trueba, Spindler, and Spindler (1989) state, "his model goes beyond mere description, however. It aims to educate people in the skills necessary so that they can de-enculturate themselves individually and collectively—thereby reasserting greater control over their lives as social and historical beings" (p. 97).

Maxine Greene (1995) believes that, by carefully reading and reflecting on literature, students "can tap domains of experience ordinarily obscured or ignored" (p. 132). She goes on: "Again, it takes imagination to engage with literature and other art forms—aesthetic imagination and social imagination" (p. 132). One of the purposes of this book is to encourage the development of social imagination in students. This ability to see the "what ifs" exists not just for individuals to visualize future possibilities for themselves but for transformative action in a much wider context.

REFERENCES

Appleman, D., & Green, D. (1993). Mapping the elusive boundary between high school and college writing. *College Composition & Communication, 44*(2), 191–199.

Boland, E. (1994). *In a time of violence.* New York: Norton.

Bloch, M. N. (1991). Critical science and the history of child development's influence on early education research. *Early Education and Development, 2*(2), pp. 95–108.

Brady, J. (1995). *Schooling young children: A feminist pedagogy for liberatory learning.* Albany, NY: SUNY Press.

Brathwaite, V. (In press). Vicki Brathwaite. In M. K. Rummel & E. P. Quintero (Eds.), *Teachers' reading/teachers' lives.* (p. 166). Albany, NY: SUNY Press.

Freire, P. (1973). *Education for critical consciousness.* New York: Seabury.

Freire, P. (1985). *The politics of education.* Granby, MA: Bergin & Garvey.

Giroux, H. A. (1988). *Teachers as intellectuals: Toward a critical pedagogy of learning.* Granby, MA: Bergin & Garvey.

Greene, M. (1992). The passions of pluralism: Multiculturalism and the expanding community. *Educational Researcher, 22*(1), 13–18.

Greene, M. (1995). Notes on the search for coherence. In J. Beane, (Ed.), *ASCD Yearbook* (pp. 139–145). Alexandria, VA: ASCD.

Lakoff, G., & Johnson, M. (1980). *Metaphors we live by.* Chicago: University of Chicago Press.

Lensmire, T. J. (1995). Learning gender. [Review of Davies, B. (1993). *Shards of glass: Children reading and writing beyond gendered identities.* New York: Hampton.] *Educational Researcher, 24*(5), pp. 31–32.

Loeb, P. (1995, Spring). The choice to care. *Teaching Tolerance, 4*(1), pp. 38–43.

Metzger, D. (1991). Circles of stories. In C. Witherell & N. Noddings (Eds.), *Stories lives tell.* New York: Teachers College Press.

Quintanilla, R. (In press). Raúl Quintanilla. In M. K. Rummel & E. P. Quintero (Eds.), *Teachers' reading/teachers' lives* (pp. 262–263). Albany, NY: SUNY Press.

Rogers, A. G. (1993). Voice, play, and the practice of ordinary courage in girls' and women's lives. *Harvard Educational Review, 63*(3), pp. 265–295.

Rummel, M. K., & Quintero, E. P. (Eds.), (In press). *Teachers' reading/teachers' lives.* Albany, NY: SUNY Press.

Shannon, P. (1993). *Becoming political.* Portsmouth, NH: Heinemann.

Simon, R. (1988, February). For a pedagogy of possibility. *Critical Pedagogy Networker, 1,* pp. 2–3.

Tacheny, M. (In press). Mary Tacheny. In M. K. Rummel & E. P. Quintero (Eds.), *Teachers' reading/teachers' lives* (pp. 233–234). Albany, NY: SUNY Press.

Trueba, H., Spindler G., & Spindler, L. (Eds.). (1989). *What do anthropologists have to say about dropouts?* New York: Falmer.

Willis, A. I. (1995). Reading the world of school literacy: Contextualizing the experience of a Young African American male. *Harvard Educational Review, 65*(1), pp. 30–49.

THEME WEB ONE

The Fabric of Community

Who makes up our communities? What are their customs, values, and modes of communication and collaboration? What are the strengths and barriers of their people? Theme Web I reflects on these questions. Soto (1991) says that "part of our role as researchers is to educate individuals not cognizant of the issues faced by diverse families which on the surface appear to overshadow enriching and positive contributions" (p. 159). Trueba, Jacobs, and Kirton (1990) add: "Educators, especially teachers, need to become aware of the contributions of immigrants and refugees to America in order to inculcate in all students genuine appreciation for the richness of American culture and of immigrants' commitment to the continued existence of democratic institutions" (p. 1).

Sleeter (1991) calls for multicultural, reconstructionist education that creates an active coalition among oppressed peoples and dominant groups. This coalition demands that we name social problems, teach about political and economic oppression and discrimination, and use social action to transform participants' lives (Sleeter & Grant, 1994). We see community as a place of hope for social change. For example, various community action programs, including family literacy programs in diverse communities (Weinstein-Shr & Quintero, 1994), work to use language in ways that heal rather than divide the generations; they concentrate on reestablishing channels for cultural transmission among the generations. In Duluth, Minnesota, a group of Hmong women meeting together in a family literacy class became angry and frustrated when comments from teachers at their children's elementary school revealed that "those parents just don't care. They never come to parent conferences" (Quintero, in press). The mothers were angry because, in spite of state desegregation money's being allocated to the school for translating newsletters and information for families who speak languages other than English, they had received no notification about the parent conferences. They wrote a letter to the principal. The only words in English were "Dear Mr. Smith" (not the actual name). The rest of the letter, which was written in Hmong, explained that it is very frustrating for parents who don't speak English to receive school information only in English. They pointed out that perhaps he could now see their difficulty because he had to go to the trouble to seek out a translator to read the letter. Within two days, the principal called a meeting with the Hmong parents, with an interpreter, and hired a part-time translator to take care of correspondence from school to home and provide interpretations at parent conferences. The work of forging relationships among schools, communities, governments, work places, and homes, of bridging cultures and healing generations, is difficult and requires partnership. While agendas may not be the same, by understanding diversity and negotiating common ground, all players can be strengthened, and our work can take on a new and stronger life of its own.

Many people in communities in the United States have experienced exile in one form or another. Edward Said (1990) explains, "Exile is strangely compelling to think about but terrible to experience. It is the unhealable rift forced between a human being and a native place, between the self and its true home: its essential sadness can never be surmounted" (p. 357). He advises us to explore this world of exile and better understand our own worlds: "Regard experiences as if they were about to disappear. What is it that anchors them in reality? What would you save of them? What would you give? Only someone who has achieved independence and detachment, someone whose homeland is 'sweet' but whose circumstances make it impossible to recapture that sweetness, can answer those questions" (Said, 1990, p. 366).

We believe that there is a magical power of art and imagination that has a definite role in creating a sense of place, a community. This relates to rethinking the narrative of neighborhood and constructing the "poetry of neighborhood," discussed by Crichlow (1995), who describes various maps of a neighborhood drawn by parents and children. We use as an example the story of Donn Morson-McKie, a teacher in the Brooklyn schools, who, as a preschooler, learned literacy skills while she created a fantasy world for herself (Rummel & Quintero, in press).

At the time I lived in a neighborhood where you couldn't go outside and play with other children because it wasn't safe at all. When I had the chance to actually see other children on TV playing and going outside in the sunshine . . . Sesame St. was really fantasy land for me. To be able to go to the store and talk to the people there, that was fantasy. (p. 263)

From her story, we also gain insights into the importance of the media in the lives of young children, for the media gave Donn Morson-McKie a neighborhood.

I remember Sesame Street, Electric Company, Zoom, things like that and getting involved with the singing and acting out of certain things. I was an only child up until I was about twelve years old so since I didn't have anyone at home I would interact with the TV. My mom encouraged me to watch programs like Sesame Street, Electric Company and Zoom and she always tells me that I learned how to read from those programs and a lot of my skills came from those. She would read to me sometimes and then one day I just picked up a book, I believe it was a Dr. Seuss book, and I started reading it to her and she was amazed. I got a lot from those programs. I think it was the fact that I could identify, I saw other children. I loved that blue monster, Grover! I also loved Bert and Ernie because they were pals and I thought it was so funny that they were living together without a mommy. Big Bird was okay but I was a little scared of him. (Morson-McKie, (1996), p. 125)

In addition to giving her a neighborhood, television ("Sesame Street" in particular) taught Donn to read and stimulated her interest in art, in the visual image that would shape her life. Donn's is a story of creation of community. She constructed it with artifacts, objects that helped her create a community for herself: Grover, Cookie Monster, Bert, Ernie, the other puppets, the corner store. Toni Morrison (1987) describes the writing of a memoir as a process of gaining access to interior life—"a kind of literary archeology; on the basis of some information and a little guesswork you journey to a site to see what remains were left behind and to reconstruct the world that these remains imply" (p. 104).

Objects become the generative images in our memories. The objects that peopled Donn's neighborhood and her mind worked in a way similar to how a Schmidt's beer sign in another city worked for Patricia Hampl (1981). Hampl described herself as a young girl looking down on the neighborhood where she was born, telling how an image, an object from that neighborhood, instilled the rhythms that later shaped her writing:

> From the St. Clair Hill I looked down on the West Seventh neighborhood, the name of the area taken from its main street. My park bench was situated so that I saw not only the unremarkable houses of the old neighborhood, but the Schmidt Brewery sign, mounted above the nineteenth-century brick factory, that spelled over and over, like an eternal one-word spelling bee, the name S-C-H-M-I-D-T in neon-red chancel-style letters. I looked down on the old neighborhood as if from an airplane, as if on my way to somewhere more important. I was higher, bigger, more life-size than the toy houses and cars and streets, the miniature twig trees and tiny doll people down there. The only thing approaching my dimension was the brewery itself and its blinking sign. Hypnotized, I watched this sign for hours, for whole seasons. I think I sat there just to watch it. We know our own rhythms, I read years later in Muriel Rukeyser's book, *The Life of Poetry,* "Our rhythms are more recognizably our selves than any of our forms." Yes. And once again, as so many times before and later, the Schmidt sign blinked behind my eyes. (p. 15)

Maxine Greene (1995) describes the roles of imagination: to help create "as if" worlds, to create alternative realities; to synthesize the finite with the infinite, the particular with the universal; and to give the visionary power to transform fear and despair. Within this framework, narrative and storytelling become ways of knowing. Details are the means of connection. Greene (1995) describes how details allow the imaginations of both the teller and the receiver of the story to particularize, to see and hear things in their concreteness. Details overcome abstractions. "The Power of the image is basic to all ideation," she says, showing how the mind grasps objects—leather ball, silk dress—and they become carriers of meaning (1995, p. 129). What language uncovers is the meaning of these objects in a life narrative. In her work with university students, Diane Brunner (1994) expands the meaning of the world of objects by emphasizing the central role of media, film, and art in the construction of image and the connection between these images and the spiritual in our lives. She describes how image making constructs identity through a narrative myth making: "embodied narrative seems to be much more than the articulation of what is understood, more than the framing and understanding of one's experiences, more than play with words. . . . this applies to narratives we read, narratives we write, and narratives we vocalize, and, indeed, even those we think but never vocalize" (1994, pp. 17–18). Brunner (1994) also suggests that those whom society has marginalized create new myths because patriarchic archetypes such as the conquering hero are not universal.

Community ways of knowing that are often misunderstood by outsiders are poignantly described by Robert Coles (1990) as he discusses how Hopi children's way of knowing directly conflicts with both the knowledge and social context of the children's teachers.

> Here, for example, is what I eventually heard from a ten-year-old Hopi girl I'd known for almost two years: "The sky watches us and listens to us. It talks to us, and it hopes we are ready to talk back. The sky is where the God of the Anglos lives, a teacher told us. She asked where our God lives. I said, 'I don't know.' I was telling the truth! Our God is the sky, and lives wherever the sky is. Our God is the sun and the moon, too; and our God is our people, if we remember to stay here. This is where we're supposed to be, and if we leave, we lose God."

Coles asked the child if she had explained those thoughts to the teacher.

"No."

"Why?"

"Because—she thinks God is a person. If I'd told her, she'd give us that smile."

"What smile?"

"The smile that says to us, 'You kids are cute, but you're dumb; you're different—and you're all wrong!'" (Coles, 1990, p. 26)

Other communities reflect strengths that are not always acknowledged. Raúl Quintanilla grew up in a family of farm workers who migrated yearly from Texas to Minnesota. He explains,

My parents lived in Mexico and then they crossed to the United States. I was born right on this side of the border. I have eight brothers and eight sisters. In the summer I would work every day from 5:00 AM 'til sundown. We didn't work during the school year except for weekends. (Quintanilla, in press, p. 211)

He goes on to describe the days in the fields:

Everything was very positive. Your father is there, your mother is there, and your brothers and sisters are there too. You are all working together and your father is saying good things all day, every day for a long time. I didn't know at that time, but it was a close family unit. They talk about supporting a family now with two incomes. With the migrant families we were doing that long ago. (p. 212)

To quote Freire's (1994) *Pedagogy of Hope:* "there is no authentic utopia apart from the tension between the denunciation of a present becoming more and more intolerable, and the 'annunciation,' announcement, of a future to be created, built—politically, aesthetically, and ethically—by us women and men" (p. 91).

For this community theme web, we have chosen literature selections in which several critical aspects of community are presented. These issues are told through story and poetry selections that have all the complexities and drama of real life. We do not want to impose our interpretation of the individual pieces on the reader, but we do encourage listening, dialogue, and action that consider the language of communities, the sense of place existing in communities, cultural conflicts and bridges within and among communities, and the strengths and barriers present in them. We have included stories from authors with varied racial, class, and gender backgrounds and from a variety of contexts.

In the chapter from Alexs D. Pate's (1994) *Losing Absalom*, two characters who have worked together for years show the tremendous gulf in perception that can exist between two members of the same geographic community. The characters' experience avoids oversimplifying the idea of building bridges between cultural communities.

"The General Population, in Ordinary Time" by Carol Masters (1994) shows that the sense of community can arise despite the impersonal, punitive system of a prison. Diego Vázquez, Jr., in the selection from *Growing through the Ugly* (1997) shares the language and community context that he grew up with on the Texas-Mexico border.

Alternative ways of knowing—alternatives to traditional Euro-American mainstream cultural norms—are persevering in some contexts through the practice of raising children and passing on family cultural traditions. Both children and adults experience conflict. In the short story "Culture Clash," from *Walking the Rez Road* by Jim Northrup (1993), the clashes are physical and cultural. This complex dissonance—along with absolute miscommunication—is the theme of the story.

Gary Geddes's (1995) two narrative poems, "Luck of the Irish" and "Flying Blind," show the complexity of history and meaning and illustrate the dissonance between physical imprisonment and freedom of spirit. Another context of loss of potential and misunderstanding exists in the communities of the aged. In "Ellen Ryan's Braided Rug," Pat Barone (unpublished manuscript) shows Ellen's strengths in terms of both knowledge and human wisdom. The loss is that her potential has been discarded.

In the story "Taking Miss Kezee to the Polls" (Haynes, 1991), a young man performing a community service in a southern town learns about himself, an old woman, the politics of his community, and issues of adaptation and accommodation.

Renga by Kate Hallett Dayton (unpublished manuscript) is the story of a support community of people with physical disabilities. It illustrates the importance of imagination and storytelling in both personal and community healing. Finally, in "News brief," Norita Dittberner-Jax (1995) shows us how the images and realities of communities outside our experience are an inseparable part of our world.

REFERENCES

Barone, P. (1992). Ellen Ryan's braided rug. Unpublished story.

Brunner, D. (1994). *Inquiry and reflection: Framing narrative practice in education*. Albany, NY: SUNY Press.

Coles, R. (1990). *The spiritual life of children*. Boston: Houghton Mifflin.

Crichlow, W. (1995). Rethinking the narrative of urban neighborhood: Perspectives on the social context and processes of identity formation among African American youth. Paper presented at a meeting of the American Educational Research Association, San Francisco.

Dayton, K. (1994). Renga. Unpublished story.

Dittberner-Jax, N. (1995). Newsbrief. In *What they always need* (p. 44). Minneapolis: New Rivers Press.

Freire, P. (1994). *Pedagogy of hope*. New York: Continuum.

Geddes, G. (1995). Flying blind. In F. Ringold (Ed.), *Nimrod: International Journal of Prose & Poetry* (pp. 38–39). Tulsa: Arts & Humanities Council of Tulsa.

Geddes, G. (1995). Luck of the Irish. In *Nimrod: International Journal of Prose & Poetry* (pp. 35–37). Tulsa: Arts & Humanities Council of Tulsa.

Greene, M. (1995). *Releasing the imagination: Essays on education, the arts, and social change*. San Francisco: Jossey-Bass.

Hampl, P. (1981). *A romantic education*. Boston: Houghton Mifflin.

Haynes, D. (1991). Taking Miss Kezee to the polls. In J. Agee, R. Blakely, & Welch (Eds.), *Stiller's Pond* (pp. 66–72). Minneapolis: New Rivers Press.

Masters, C. (1994). The general population, in ordinary time. In *The Peace Terrorist* (pp. 73–87). Minneapolis: New Rivers.

Morrison, T. (1987). The site of memory. In W. Zinsser (Ed.), *Inventing the truth: The art and craft of memoir* (pp. 49–61). Boston: Houghton Mifflin.

Morson-McKie, D. (1996). In M. K. Rummel & E. P. Quintero (Eds.), *Teachers' reading/teachers' lives* (pp. 123–138). Albany, NY: SUNY Press.

Northrup, J. (1993). Culture clash. In *Walking the Rez Road* (pp. 99–103). Stillwater, MN: Voyager.

Pate, A. D. (1994). *Losing Absalom*. New York: Berkeley Books.

Quintanilla, R. (In press). Raúl Quintanilla. In M. K. Rummel & E. P. Quintero (Eds.), *Teachers' reading/teachers' lives* (pp. 262–263). Albany, NY: SUNY Press.

Quintero, E. P. (In press). Hmong and Mexican families informing Head Start: Family literacy revisited. In J. Ellsworth & L. Ames (Eds.), *Critical perspectives on Project Head Start: Revisioning the hope and challenge*. Albany, NY: SUNY Press.

Rummel, M. K., & Quintero, E. P. (Eds.). (In press). *Teachers' reading/teachers' lives*. Albany, NY: SUNY Press.

Said, E. W. (1990). Reflections on exile. In R. Ferguson, M. Gever, T. T. Minh-ha, & C. West (Eds.), *Out there: Marginalization and contemporary cultures* (pp. 357–366). New York: New Museum of Contemporary Art; Cambridge: MIT Press.

Sleeter, C. (1991). *Empowerment through multicultural education*. Albany, NY: SUNY Press.

Sleeter, C., & Grant, C. (1994). *Making choices for multicultural education: Five approaches to race, class, and gender*. Upper Saddle River, NJ: Merrill/Prentice Hall.

Soto, L. D. (1991, January). Understanding bilingual/bicultural young children. *Young Children, 46*(2), 30–36.

Trueba, H. T., Jacobs, L., & Kirton, E. (1990). *Cultural conflict and adaptation: The case of Hmong children in American society*. New York: Falmer.

Vazquez, D. (1997). *Growing through the ugly*. New York: Norton.

Weinstein-Shr, G., & Quintero, E. (Eds.). (1994). *Immigrant learners and their families: Literacy to connect the generations*. Washington, DC: Center for Applied Linguistics, Delta Systems.

LOSING ABSALOM

OPTIONS FOR LISTENING

- In your journal describe (draw a web, brainstorm in narrative form, or write about) your personal experiences relating to "neighborhood." You could describe the neighborhood where you grew up or a neighborhood you have lived in more recently. Did you feel that you and the people you lived with were a part of the larger neighborhood? In what ways? If not, why not?

- Continue in your journal and respond: Did you know about or experience any tensions among people in your neighborhood? Did you take any action? Was it by choice or necessity? What strengths allowed you to do it? What were your barriers?

- Think back to a time in your life when you were ill or just waking up from a very deep sleep and you remember dreaming in detail about an actual incident from long ago. Write a few sentences about what you remember. Did the memory bring back old knowledge, questions, or feelings?

- Read the selection and, as you read, write questions that come to your mind. Also, write down any personal connections to the story that emerge in your mind. See the example.

These student-generated questions are to assist the reader to become aware of her or his own questions about life in general and the specific themes and information in the stories. This self-awareness provides a meeting ground for us to connect with lives in the stories that may be different from (or similar to) our own. Because of the importance of this questioning process we will model our questions for the first selection.

Here are some questions we had as we read this selection. We wrote the questions in our journals for the purpose of focusing our thinking and going back later to reflect. Your questions may be very different or very similar; there are no correct questions.

"How could Sy know so little about Absalom and his family after living in the same community for so long?"

"Was Sy asking all these questions because he was simply curious or because he really cared?"

"Which comes first the caring or the knowing?"

"Are many of these differences (in the story) because of race or economics?"

We also wrote that the conversations in the story remind us of conversations we heard during and after the riots in Los Angeles regarding the Rodney King incident. The descriptions of the neighborhood reminded one of us of West Seventh Street in St. Paul, Minnesota, and the other of Ybor City, Florida.

Losing Absalom
by Alexs D. Pate
(from chapter 4 of Losing Absalom)

Absalom felt the wheels rolling under his body. He was being moved again. He liked the shaking rumble under his butt. It was a familiar feeling. For nearly all of his working life he had been a truck driver for Sy Bonansky's bakery.

In the early hours of the breaking day, Absalom would load up his truck with trays of pumpernickel, challah, and other breads, donuts, cakes, and pies. There were six Bonansky outlets, not including the bakery itself. During the day, he maneuvered his truck throughout the city, in the snow, and in the soft asphalt summer to bring fresh baked goods to Bonansky's customers, most of whom were Jewish. After he delivered to the bakery outlets, there was another set of deliveries to independent stores. Altogether he wasn't finished until about noon.

As tired and sleepy as he felt driving to work at 3:45 in the morning, Absalom loved the time just before dawn. The shadows of the city were in retreat, fading into the bricks and cement as he drove along. And no matter what season it was, that time was the coolest, the quietest the city could ever be.

It was strange how the streets in this city of neighborhoods appeared so similar before people began moving around in them. In the waning darkness, the streets were empty shells, washed-out blood and earth colors against a blue-black background. But as the day progressed and people walked out into the world, each neighborhood became a pounding heart.

South Philly clamored with dark-eyed Italians, Spring Garden with Puerto Rican smiles, 52nd Street with slick clothes and the sound of jazz, Fish-shirts rolled up with Marlboros at the shoulder. On the Northeast, where fleeing inner-city Jews had landed.

And in North Philly where the bakery was built, the family-owned business was now just one of the many white islands still floating in the African American sea that surrounded them.

But before dawn, each neighborhood was nothing but concrete and bricks, corner stones and churches, bars and parks. It was the lilt of language and the sweat of culture that defined them.

Absalom wasn't as comfortable on the streets during the day as he was early in the morning. With his truck filled with the smell of fresh baked bread, Absalom was welcomed everywhere he went.

Every morning when Absalom arrived at the bakery, Sy Bonansky would be sitting on the loading dock with a cup of coffee in his hands. Sy nearly always wore the uniform of the bakers—white T-shirt, white baker's pants, and white tennis shoes—even though he had never baked a single cupcake. A bit overweight, with a paunch that put a downward pressure on his pants, he was tall, as was Absalom. His thinning hair was nearly all white.

When Sy was at the University of Pennsylvania he was considered handsome, but time and food had destroyed the few angled contours his face had once had.

Sy had inherited the bakery from his father, who had built it. Sy was twenty-two when his father announced to family and friends that it was he and not either of his two brothers who would ascend the floured throne. Sy had felt the heat from the star that had risen above him. But he had learned the business standing by his father's side, and he worked hard to prove that his father had made the right decision.

"Absalom, my best driver. I cannot have a good day until you get here." Sy greeted him every day with the same salutation. And then he would playfully slap Absalom on his back and ask about his family. And every day Absalom would cart the trays of bagels, pastries, and bread from the kitchen to the loading dock and then into the truck. Sy would literally follow Absalom's every movement, no matter how many times Absalom had to go back and forth from the kitchen to the dock, or even into the back of the truck.

Sometimes this agitated Absalom. He couldn't believe that Sy didn't have better things to do. Sometimes he wanted to ask him, "What the hell do you keep following me around for?" But he never did. He did, however, on occasion abruptly stop walking, turn around, and stare at Sy. Inevitably, Sy would be in mid-stride, his puffy face frozen in curiosity.

"What? What's the matter, Ab?"

Absalom would just stare at him. Not menacingly. He wasn't angry. He just wanted to know why Sy followed him around all the time. Absalom had his suspicions. At first he thought that Sy was worried that he might be stealing food. But there was no reason to do that. There was more than enough surplus at the end of a run. Absalom always brought food home.

After a while, Absalom came to realize that Sy wasn't trying to catch him doing anything wrong. Sy was curious. That's what it was. He had never known a black man before. Never listened to a black man talk about his wife and family. Sy had never even had a conversation with a black man before he met Absalom. And from the first day that Absalom had come to work at Bonansky's as a kitchen helper, Sy had liked him.

He liked the fact that Absalom was so quiet. He never joined in the kitchen banter. Never got into flour fights. Whenever things moved to the raucous, Absalom found a way to disappear. Sy learned later that Absalom never "played around" with white men. Having grown up in the South, Absalom could work with white men but wasn't able to feel relaxed around them. In fact, Absalom found it very difficult to let his guard down, unless the subject was sports, especially prize fighting. If the talk turned to boxing, then Absalom's nostrils would expand like little brown bellows. His face would widen to hold the growing smile. Absalom loved the art of fighting and could and would hold his own in any discussion.

One day as Sy was coming into the kitchen he overheard Absalom talking about Cassius Clay. "Naw, Henry,"—Absalom was going through the motions of sweeping, but he was looking directly at one of the bakers—"if you think Cassius Clay is full of hot air you don't know nothing about fighting. That boy is so fast, he puts so many punches upside the other guy's head that his body just short-circuits. Boom boom boom booom booom." Absalom dropped the broom and jabbed his hand into the air. "And then he's out of there."

As Absalom finished his sentence he looked up and saw Sy. He gulped. But Sy was smiling. He had never heard Absalom say so many words at one time. And that somehow solidified his need to know the man better. It had almost become an obsession. And so Sy had made it a routine to drink his first cup of coffee with Absalom. To get to know his family. To try to understand him. At some point Sy realized that he was really trying to see if a black man was the same as a white man. If the stories and the feelings were the same. Along the way he came to like Absalom.

There were times when Sy's attention was actually pleasant. Absalom loved to talk about his family, anyway. Sometimes Absalom looked forward to their conversations.

He had been working for Sy for eleven years when their conversations reached a new level. He remembered the day it happened because it was two days after Martin Luther King Jr. was assassinated. Two days after angry crowds set fire to stores on Columbia Avenue.

"What's going on in this country, Ab? Colored people burning down stores. Their own homes. Why would a man burn down his own home?" Sy sipped his coffee. Over the years, his voice had disintegrated into gravel.

"A man would have to be pretty angry to do that, Sy." Absalom was stacking trays of rye bread in the truck.

"I've never been that angry," Sy said. "But burn my own house down? I've worked like a damn dog to get that goddamn house. Vera'd kill my ass anyway if I did something like that." He paused and considered his wife standing in her robe bathed in the glow of flickering flames. "What about you? You ever been that mad?"

"I don't know, Sy. I don't know."

"I'm talking about your own house. Okay, so you're upset. It's terrible what's going on. It really is. I know about it. My family didn't have it so good, you know. So I understand. I give every year to the NAACP you know. I've been doing that for at least five years. So I put my money where my mouth is. But set fire to your home? That's crazy. What do you say, Ab, that's crazy, ain't it?"

"It depends on how you look at it. Me, I wouldn't do it. Gwen and I kind of like our house. But I guess if you don't think you got nothing then maybe. . . . I don't know why people do things. I just try to do what I'm supposed to do." Absalom thought about what was going on throughout the country. Tension walked the Main Streets. Anger and fear flowered everywhere.

"That's what I mean. I couldn't see you running around the streets like a crazy person. Burning things down."

Absalom turned away and picked up another tray. He was not incapable of anger. He could explode. Deep inside him there was the potential to step outside his quiet life, strip away the warm smile and the soft voice to reveal just another enraged black man. That rage was there. But it was held in check by good fortune. He had nearly everything he had hoped for.

He was making good money, owned his own house, was married to a woman he loved, and was the father of two children. This was already more than many people had. And yet there was so much that was completely out of his reach. The pictures that flashed on the television of families with new cars, new appliances, roach-free kitchens, and nice green lawns were well beyond his grasp. Even then Absalom knew there were many things he would never experience, never have. He worked too hard to not be angry about that.

In the beginning, when he left his father's farm to join the army, when he came to Philadelphia to work, when he met Gwen, Absalom believed in the promise of America. He wanted what he deserved for being a hardworking American.

It wasn't race as much as it was economics. Yes, he knew very well that there were white people out there who would hurt him. But most of his interactions with them came from the cab of his truck or when he was delivering food to them. Besides, he wasn't angry at them. His anger was for something between him and a sense of self-completion. Was he just one of hundreds of thousands of working slaves?

"Did you see the news last night?" Sy leaned way back into the wall.

"Yeah, I saw it." Absalom knew what was coming next.

"It was shocking, Ab. There were kids out there carrying televisions on their backs. Washing machines. Vacuum cleaners. People just carting what they wanted out of the store. They just busted up the windows and took what they could carry. I couldn't believe it. Why would they hurt the merchants in their own neighborhoods? Some of these people . . . the only reason they are still in the city is because they care about their customers. And what do they get? They get their windows broken and their goods stolen. Those mobs are just criminals. What kind of world is this? I ask you."

Absalom had not only seen the news, but he had driven through the riot-torn area on his way home from work. He had seen the people with new couches on their backs wobbling their way back home. And he had wondered about it. He felt no desire to join them but he understood about it. And until Sy had mentioned it, Absalom had already erased those images from his mind. He had a job to do. Hours to put in. He had learned to leave the pain of his people at home. He had to face white people all the time. He knew no way to hold that pain and do his job at the same time.

And now he was fighting the desire to end his conversation with Sy and get to his deliveries. "It's always been a crazy world."

"How come they won't work, Ab? Like you? How come more of them aren't like you?"

"Like me? What do you mean, Sy? Colored people been working like dogs all our lives. Everybody I know who can find a job has got one. And still it don't seem like nothing changes. How many colored drivers you think there are in this city, Sy? I don't know another colored man who drives a truck. Loaders, yeah, but drivers? Those people are taking that stuff and burning those buildings because they're tired, Sy. Just plain wore out. All those televisions and record players and furniture is stuff they can't get. They see it all around them but they can't get it. What do you expect?"

Sy looked up at Absalom, who was now standing over him. Absalom's smile was gone. For a second, Sy's body tensed. "I know it's not in fashion these days, but hell, Ab, Rome wasn't built in a day, you know. Your people have come a long way. A little patience and some hard work. I mean, there are too many examples of colored folks getting ahead these days. It just takes . . ."

"Time." Absalom had heard enough. "Sy, you know I served in Korea."

"I know, but—"

"There wasn't no buts then, Sy. They shipped my ass right over there. They took my colored butt, no questions asked. But if I want to be treated like a man, I got to have patience. I got to work hard. Where does it say you got to work hard to be a man, Sy? Where?"

Sy could find no words. He's never gotten that close to this Absalom. This Absalom was almost trembling with anger. This Absalom made him feel uncomfortable.

Absalom didn't want to fight with Sy, not at 4:30 in the morning and not about race, but he wouldn't let Sy put black people down. "Listen," he said softly, "I got to be getting out of here, Sy, or else I'll be another colored man without a job."

"Absalom, I can see you're upset with me. Maybe I deserve it or maybe you're just more of a hothead than I thought, but you're still my best employee and as long as I'm alive and you want to be here, you've got a job."

Absalom turned his head toward the loaded truck. What Sy had said almost made him feel happy. And yet he couldn't let Sy see it. To make his point, Absalom punctuated the moment by slamming the rolling back door of the truck closed. He tried his best not to see skin color. He tried not to be angry. He tried to work hard enough to become somebody Gwen could be proud of. That was all he knew.

Sy's body jumped when the truck door crashed down. "Come on, Ab, I didn't mean no harm. You know how I feel about you and your family. I know you're a good man. I just don't understand why everybody's so angry at those of us who are trying to stay down here."

Absalom sighed. Sy never knew when to quit. "The only thing, Sy, is that most of the white people who have businesses down here," Absalom headed for the cab of the truck, "go home somewhere out in the suburbs. They don't have to put up with what we put up with down here no more. It's like everybody's saying just be good and everything will work out. But it's not happening that way, and you know it. Now somebody kills our leader. What do you expect people to do? They're tired. That's all. Folks is just tired."

Absalom climbed into the truck and headed out into the morning with his head cradled in the smell of warm bread.

And now the wheels of the hospital trolley shuttled Absalom through heavy doors that opened like castle gates as he approached. He opened his eyes just long enough to see the pictures of open fields and flowers and abstract shapes hanging on the wall as they pushed him through the halls. And then he felt the wind under his body and the movement of space.

OPTIONS FOR DIALOGUE

- With one dialogue partner discuss the strengths of the characters Absalom and Sy.
- Discuss the barriers each faced.
- Do you both feel Sy ever understood Absalom's world? Do you feel it is possible to really "walk in someone else's shoes" when the experiences are different?
- Discuss your opinions about the previous questions in a group of three or four peers. What aspects of everyone's opinion were the same? Different? What are some things that could lessen Absalom's isolation?

SUGGESTIONS FOR ACTION

- Observe in your field placement site the ways in which two members of the same community are different because of age, class, inclusion, exclusion. Does this make the participants feel secure or insecure?
- Read about "neighborhood" in a culture with which you are not familiar. Make a comparison chart of similarities and differences between the information about this culture and your own.
- View the video "A Class Divided" from PBS's *Frontline* or read the nonfiction book *The Eye of the Storm* by Jane Elliot. Compare the stories you hear from these contexts with the story of Absalom and Sy.

  A class divided [Video]. (1985). W. Peters (Producer and director). Washington, DC: PBS Video. Documents a reunion of Iowa teacher Jane Elliott and her third-grade class of 1970, subjects that year of an ABC news documentary called "The Eye of the Storm." Shows how her experimental curriculum on the evils of discrimination had a lasting effect on the lives of the students.

- How can you support or not support inclusion in your neighborhood or living situation? Why? Make an action plan to take one small step toward this potential change.
- Investigate the academic research regarding "habituation." How do these studies relate to issues of prejudice, child rearing, inclusion, and exclusion?
- Read one of the following books (or one with a related theme):

  Allen, P. G. (1992). *Grandmothers of the light.* Boston: Beacon.
  Through the images that come alive in these tales from Mayan, Aztec, Navajo, and Cherokee sources, among others, the supernatural and the seemingly ordinary join together to form a tapestry of life that is both spiritual and concrete.

  Anaya, R. (1972). *Bless me, Ultima.* Berkeley, CA: TQA Publications.
  This coming-of-age story is about a young boy growing up in New Mexico. His mother comes from one community and his father comes from a very different one in a part of the

country that many people think is overshadowed by similarities. Ultima, the boy's elderly friend and mentor, who comes to live with the family is a *curandera* (a traditional healer).

Morrison, T. (1972). *The bluest eye*. New York: Pocket Books.
This is the story of an African-American girl, Pecola, who believed all her troubles would go away if only she had blue eyes. The story shows the strengths of Pecola, her community, and her family in the context of historical oppression.

Pate, A. D. (1994). *Losing Absalom*. New York: Berkeley Books.
This a story about life and death, family relationships, relationships in neighborhoods, relationships among and between different groups with all the drama of everyday life.

- Answer these questions about your reading:
  1. In a few sentences, summarize the reading(s).
  2. Why did you read this? What relationship to your personal or professional life does it have?
  3. Do you feel an accurate picture of the information was presented? Why or why not?
  4. Which points from the reading did you *not* agree with? Why?
  5. Discuss which information or opinions presented here were new to you.
  6. Discuss any conversation about this subject that you may have had.

- Create a map of a neighborhood. Include objects and artifacts in your sketch. Note (in any creative way) the places where stories developed and connected to the artifacts, the objects and, of course, the people interacting with each other and these objects.

- Listen to an elder from a community near your educational setting describe a nearby neighborhood. As she or he remembers it, what are some of the historical, political, and social events that shaped the changes in that neighborhood?

IN THE GENERAL POPULATION, IN ORDINARY TIME

OPTIONS FOR LISTENING

- In your journal write about communication in your family. Is there a system of rules arising from cooperation and shared respect? Who sets that system up? How does it change? What happens when someone alters or refuses to follow the system?

- Continue in your journals, and describe (draw a web, brainstorm in narrative form, or list examples of) when you were involved with an institution in which you felt trapped.

- In writing, following one of your previous entries about the institution or family situation in which you felt trapped, draw a rough sketch depicting the communication system in that institution or group. What happens when someone alters or refuses to follow the system?

- Regarding that institution, what other (other than communication) systems of human interaction can you identify? List them.

- Read the selection and, as you read, write questions and connections.

In the General Population, in Ordinary Time
by Carol Masters
(From *The Peace Terrorist*)

The building is a disappointment. Squat and spread-eagled over a small ragged plot, the Women's Section is a poor cousin to the fortress next door. The Men's Section, set like a monument on its vast treeless grounds, looms dark and sooty as any urban jail, and wears the bleak spyglass windows of guard towers. The Men's can house four hundred: tiers of cages face a common multi-storied hall. The Women's holds one-tenth that many, although Jen knows it is overcrowded these days, short-term women sleeping in the day room on weekends.

Two wings with opaque windows flank a central square structure, all facing the road; behind these, a longer protuberance juts into the vacant fields. Across the fields, a row of suburban bungalows shield their backs with hedges and moderately expensive landscaping. The Women's could be some sort of small machine factory, or a processing plant. Yes, the latter is what it is: I will be processed, Jen thinks; I will follow the procedures.

Jen's been in jail before, but served only the standard sentence for trespassers, two days on a short-term lock-up, in the company of other activists. Now she'll be with others, the regular prisoners, will eat and drink and talk with them. She is not frightened; what's to fear from boredom, and from doing as you are told in a locked building?

She is, however, depressed.

Jail wasn't part of her plans for this week—or month. Bastard. He didn't have to do it. Sitting up there like lord almighty, yes, you did get the hanging judge, he says. She'd tried to be respectful, even used the word, must respectfully refuse to pay the fine. She'd dressed up for court, squeezed into a dark dress from her secretarial days, nylons, and the heels she wouldn't even wear to church. She'd surrendered the comfort of warm picket-line slacks and sweaters, to look respectable and respectful. In conscience, your honor, I can't pay a fine. Can't, or won't? he asks. The court takes indigence into account. She tells him she isn't indigent, it's a matter of conscience, but she isn't eloquent enough. She mentions that fines do discriminate, but what he doesn't like is that she says she won't buy her way out. Thirty days, he says, contempt of court. But I'm not being contemptuous, she argues. The judge stops listening, motions to the bailiff. She has a minute to talk to Bob; but even her usually supportive husband has a comment about her timing, before he kisses her good-bye.

She wants to take in the outside air—the day crowding down in swollen clouds, dark grays, with a tang of snow. It's been a dry season. Leaves are powder under her feet and the dust from them hazes the sky over Parker's Lake, just across the road. It's been hours since she was outside, free, and an hour of that morning time was spent on the bus downtown, with its tired air. She couldn't sit next to Bob, and the man next to her was so big half of Jen's right hip, no slouch itself, was perched on nothing. She could scarcely read for all the jouncing around. They probably won't give her the book, inside, because it has a hard cover and could harbor something dangerous—drugs, a stick of gum.

Now there is moisture in the wind and on the sides of the grimy van—a smear of soot lines her forearm as she hitches herself down. A few fat flakes of snow fall like raindrops and disappear into the grass.

"Come on." The driver carefully piles her coat, boots, and a grocery bag containing her purse, book, and intake papers into Jen's outstretched arms. Then he unlocks her handcuffs; nothing spills. He puts a hand under one elbow: uncuffed, her arm needs custody, she thinks. She might make a break for it, dash to the lake and spin pebbles onto the singing film of ice and listen to the mystery of it until evening.

In the shower room, she steps out of her clothes and away from her body. Ms. Mackenzie, as the guard's name tag reads, watches her and hands her another grocery bag for her clothing.

"Fold them. They'll have to stay in the bag until they're checked overnight."

Jen focuses on the clock above Mackenzie's head, but listens to the instructions. Her body is obedient, unembarrassed, Jen notes with approval. I'm invisible, she thinks, no, opaque. I'm here but my body tells her nothing; the guard can't see inside me. Jen can still do three deep knee bends without trembling. Lifting her hair so that Mackenzie can peer behind her ears, though, is more intimate. Abruptly Jen is inside her nakedness, and sees the pale hairs on her arms stand with the goosebumps.

At dinnertime, the lights flicker. The televisions, three of them in a large and small day room, and in the dormitory hall, have been tuned to warnings all afternoon.

White letters slide under Alex Keaton's dimples and all through "Jeopardy." A fenced exercise yard is visible from the dining area windows, and it begins to fill with snow, wet and lumpy at first, but soon turning mean and dry, spinning with a shrill wind. The guards are jumpy, those going off work at six wanting to get on the road.

After she has been hurried through the line, Jen has to start a new table, so she doesn't have anyone to practice her icebreaker on. She's going to say, Nice night to be Inside. But by the time other women join her, she's decided against it.

At 5:30 the lights flicker twice. The women exclaim and laugh: something is really happening. The conversation swells until a hasty conference of guards decides it's an emergency, they're going to be short-handed tonight.

"All right, ladies. Room time. Finish up, clear your plates. Last table, stand, take your dishes."

Guards Parris and Bordman, two male guards assigned under the new Equal Opportunity rules, come and stand by the scraping table as the women stack their plates. "Go immediately to your wing," they say, unnecessarily, Jen thinks. This is unfair; room time shouldn't be for hours yet. She hears the women grumbling, but there's no time for discussion.

She's just begun to eat, so she's swallowing fast. A stout woman at the next table is still hunched over her coffee. She appears to hear nothing. She has just come in tonight, and has the stunned, sullen inattention of a newcomer, except that she draws away more noticeably from contact. One hand is taped, and one brown cheek is purplish black from bruising.

"Jones," Parris addresses her. She doesn't look up.

"Jones! Up, now!" The woman starts and gives him a sidelong glance. "I ain't finished my coffee." She's nervous but belligerent; she lowers her head to blow on the cup, admittedly still steaming. Jen thinks maybe this is the way to be, stand your ground.

Parris jerks his head at Bordman, who comes to second him.

"Come on, Betsy. You don't want more trouble."

Jen's the last in line at the trash bucket, scraping her plate, so she sees what happens next. Betsy panics and wraps her plump legs around her chair, so it comes along when the men attempt to hoist her. The chair screeches, then clatters to the floor as they scoot her along.

Bordman is half laughing; he's muscular and the woman isn't really offering much resistance, just yelling, "no, no, you got no right!" It's only twenty feet down the hall to the first cell, which is a separation cell.

That night, the banging begins. Bordman and then Parris move to Betsy's door to yell, or to try to talk reasonably to her, by turns. She'd better shape up or she's in separation through Thanksgiving. Sounds of objects hitting the floor, and Bordman's laugh, carry down to Jen's cell. She flattens her face against the ten-inch opening in the steel door, but she can't put her head through, and the angle's wrong. She's three cells down, on the same side. A few minutes later, she can just see a barricade the guards put up to shield the patrols from flying objects. Jen can't imagine what could be left in the cell to throw. Her own cell has no movable furniture except the desk chair and bedding; bed, desk, and sink are bolted to the floor or wall, as is the steel mirror, which rather pleasantly masks her wrinkles and flaws. For a while she imagines Betsy dismantling her cell tile by tile to toss at the hallway.

Then Betsy begins knocking. She starts off with a string of insults, names for the guards, focusing on their weight problems: blubberbutt, blimpo, or other physical characteristics, which Jen thinks could do wonders for her own vocabulary. A few people on the wing shout to cool it, mama, you in bad trouble, but Betsy's sounds come only wilder and sadder. Through the gradual quieting of other noises on the cellblock, Betsy bangs on the wall or the door. She doesn't stop. She continues a regular, sometimes muffled, sometimes hollow pounding that goes on and on, a patient, hopeless, defiant sound that quiets her listeners.

Down the hall, someone calls to the guard but Jen thinks they've left the area. Nobody can be hurt now; the prisoners are all safe in their cells.

Jen's throat aches with wanting to yell something; she finally does, "Please stop!" but her voice is thin and ineffectual. She decides silence and waiting are best. Still it doesn't stop.

Jen couldn't let her babies cry it out. She remembers deciding to time their nighttime fussing after she'd put them down, but she never had done that. The watch hands wouldn't move. Picking up the baby after what must have been only minutes, she'd rock him again. And again. When she'd calmed herself, rocking, the baby slept. Now she doesn't have a watch, anyway. What's the point of taking away our watches? She wonders. We're going to hang ourselves on our watchbands? Swallow them? Tiny ticking machines in our stomachs, marking the moments, timing, doing time. . . .

Five minutes can seem forever, she knows. Probably Jones hadn't been banging that long, but now Jen's head throbs. The trouble is, she can't do anything about this situation. She's powerless. Maybe she can pray for Jones, for Betsy. Concentrating her thought, Jen pictures Betsy in her cell, the extra large pink jogging suit from the clothing room pushed back on her thick arms, her face, sweaty and heavy with fatigue, her wide-fingered black hand fisting a shoe—it must be a shoe—knocking it against the door. Jen tries to imagine the creator of Betsy calming her, stopping her impossible protest and bringing peace and quiet to the rest of them.

But the noise doesn't stop. Jen is dismayed to feel her resentment turn to something uglier; she thinks specifically of breaking Betsy's wrist. God isn't anywhere, and Jen's heart hammers faster than Betsy's noise. Breathe, she tells herself, breathe; she'll be okay, you'll be okay.

The next morning she approaches Mackenzie, sitting by herself at the end of the wing hall. All the cell doors are open, including the separation room, which is empty. In fact, Betsy had been at breakfast queening over a crowded table of African-American dormitory women who talk low and fast, giggling like conspirators.

Dormitory is a misnomer; the women do not sleep in one room, but have individual cells containing one cot, one student desk, one chair, and one hook. The dormitory wing is identical to Jen's, except that the cells do not contain their own toilets or washbowls, which are in a common lavatory on one end of the wing. Besides not having to sleep three feet from a toilet, the advantage of the dormitory is that the women are not locked in their cells but only into the wing, during the night.

Mackenzie tells her that Betsy is a long-termer, not a newcomer as Jen thought. She's been in long enough to have had a day pass for a family emergency, except that she took three weeks. They had to bring her back.

"Is that how she got the bruises?" Jen believes she's overstepping her bounds, but the question presses at her. She wants to redeem her uncharitable reactions of last night, if only for herself. She doesn't remember when the knocking became the rhythm of her own heartbeat, but she fell easily into sleep, and slept well.

Mackenzie is curt. "No. Family, I think. The health officer saw her. She's all right."

Betsy is more than all right, she's back to work in the laundry room. They can hear her, as a nervous line of weekenders deposit bedding inside the laundry room door, one by one, and bustle back to their stripped cells to clean them.

"In the *whites*, bitch! You separate them now." Jen hears a querulous defensive answer and scornful, "Sheeit!" from Betsy. Mackenzie looks toward the laundry door but doesn't move.

"You check your job yet?"

Jen had forgotten. "Oh, right." It was part of the intake instructions; she was supposed to check the job chart posted outside the kitchen door, right after breakfast.

Mackenzie gives her a brief smile. "First day." She consults a clip board on her lap. "Okay. Soon as you're done, go back to your cell and strip your bed. We're moving you into the dormitory."

Jen is alarmed, but wants to keep the mood light. "Okay. Is this a promotion?"

Mackenzie narrows her eyes. "Not exactly. We like to keep the one wing for short termers, DWIs, weekenders. You're technically with general population."

Technically. Encouraged, Jen thinks she can try to be political. "You know why I'm here?"

But Mackenzie closes down. "Everybody knows. But listen to me. Nobody thinks they should be here, you understand? My job is to take care of your needs. I don't ask anybody why they're in, it don't matter. And I don't care. I do a better job that way. And you, you will too, understand?"

Jen nods, and moves away. All this and lectures, too. Does that mean she should keep her mouth shut? Everybody knows, nobody cares? They must think she can handle herself in the dormitory, but what does that mean?

The chart says Jen is supposed to mop the day room. The mop buckets are already taken, or so Betsy tells her when she looks into the laundry room. So Jen begins to straighten *True Confessions* and *Plain Truth* magazines in the day room, where she will have a vantage point on the laundry room door. When she reaches the lower shelves, she pulls a chair over to them and sits down, trying not to look too comfortable. But Mr. Ward, the cook, pokes his head in from the kitchen and beckons to her. "What are you supposed to be doing?"

She stands up. Respectful, always respectful. "Mopping. Buckets are gone."

He turns away. "Wait for one."

She sighs and turns back to the magazines. "Not here!" he yelps.

Ms. Mackenzie comes in from the hall as Jen tries to leave the day room. "So what's going on now?"

Mr. Ward lights a cigarette.

"I'm waiting," Jen says, patiently, glancing at the cook; he's waiting, we're all waiting, she thinks, for my next words. "For a bucket."

She thinks she says it patiently; but Mackenzie steps in very close. "There are three buckets in the laundry room. You take one, you mop this room and the kitchen, you return the bucket, clean it out, and you do not get written up again today."

There are indeed three full buckets in the laundry room, returned in the last thirty seconds like magic. Betsy's broad back is turned to the door, and she's humming as she gathers warm towels and bedspreads into her arms from the dryer. "Any special one I should take?"

Betsy looks around. "Not my business." Then as Jen is hauling the full pail and wringer into the hall, she adds, "Sugarbabe you supposed to get *clean* water if you do the kitchen!"

Jen flushes; my god, the ptomaine kid. That water definitely had seen clearer days. Betsy points her to the floor drain and to the shelf where the detergent and vinegar are kept. She also points out that girl scout isn't in her job description.

Jen awakes. When had she fallen asleep? It must have been before the television in the dormitory hall had gone off at lights-out, because the last sounds she remembers are gunshots from some police story, the third in a row, Jesus, didn't they get enough of that in their real lives? But we have to miss the ten o'clock news, after lights-out, so at least we miss that violence, she thinks. Jen couldn't have heard about the latest demonstrations, either. Well, maybe it was for the best. Night after night, she had been so tired. The slogans still echo in her head, louder here against the background noise, the constant television. No more killing, no more war, U.S. Out of El Salvador.

She twists away from the sudden glare. The flashlight circle sweeps down her body and disappears. A few seconds later, she hears a groan and curse from next door. Guard rounds. Is it near morning? No light from the window. More people die just before dawn than at any other time. That's probably a myth, but her body is indeed stiffening, cramping. It's so cold. She sits up, far enough to reach her day clothes on the hook above the bed and pulls them down over the covers. The extra weight helps a little; the warmth spreads and soothes her. She won't think of Bob, not yet. After all, she was used to turning down the thermostat at night, used to cold sheets they kicked at, laughing, daring each other to be first inside. The first could be charitable and warm the other's side before sliding over. How often had she been the charitable one?

Jen wonders how many women in here put themselves to sleep warming their hands between their thighs, timing it between guard rounds, how often? Most, she supposes, but she doesn't want to, not now, it's too sad. She won't cry.

The next night is worse. The cells are no longer cold, though; men have been on the wing tinkering with the heat system, and the furnace blasts through with ancient dust and metallic-smelling air. Because of the repair work, the prisoners have had no room time during the day, and have been packed into the day room and told to watch television quietly. Jen's eyes itch from all the television and from the cigarettes, but she's just not tired. She hasn't had a job all day except to clean ashtrays, which took maybe ten minutes. She tried to talk to Patrice, a bright forger with a coke habit, about Jen's work publicizing Contragate, and the evidence about U.S. guns traded for Contra drugs. Patrice's eyes widened, but she countered with a fantastic rumor about Administration marijuana ranches. Jen worried, "Well, maybe that's a little exaggeration, but . . ."

"Just say no, ha!" Patrice shook her head and wandered off.

Now too warm, the cell smells of stale smoke and Lysol. She decides to open the window, a lower casement that pulls inward and opens directly on a steel mesh screen and the November air. As she kicks back the latch, a rustle outside and a sudden shadow make her jump. Someone is standing by the window! The whir of a dozen pair of large wings reassure her: Canada geese rise in the moonlight and settle twenty feet away, silent but standing in profile to her. Their two lookouts pace between the window and the flock, wary. As she crouches to see them better, cold fresh air washes her shoulders. The lake must still be open, or maybe the geese will winter here; she hopes so, they'll be something to look at. In a few seconds they are still again, nestled near some low shrubs, though the lookouts are open-eyed and standing erect.

The wall beside her brightens. "Hey! Close that window! Those windows stay closed at night!"

Jen knows that is not a rational rule, and if she had the energy, she might be assertive about it. But the light plays on her nightgown until she closes the window, so she does it quickly and slips back into bed.

The cell is already becoming stuffy again. She throws off the blanket. Hot rooms at night give her nightmares, and she feels the uneasiness of a bad night coming on. If only her thoughts would line up obediently to be sorted and processed, she would sleep better. She has a civilly disobedient brain.

If only she hadn't argued with her friend Anne, so many months ago, Anne might come to see her. Who would come, on visiting days? Most people would think a month wasn't so long; she could take it. You had to be ready to take consequences, just a little piece of your life, that's all. For your friends. Not that she was doing this work for Anne, or for some religious principle. It was closer than that. Of course it was selfish, sure, it was her own children who made her look at weapons and weaponmakers with the sick dread she held for rapists or molesters. And then she looked long and hard at pictures of the Salvadoran and Nicaraguan children, this decade's victims, those beautiful dark eyes, and the blood.

But Anne, how could she? Maybe she didn't want to be a church counselor any more, but applying to Federal Munitions, in Human Resources? Human she said. She said Jen didn't give her credit for thinking out her decision. Of course I did, Jen thinks. I wanted Anne to tell me why, some misbegotten ministry to the affluent? A good company, Anne said. A death factory, Jen said. Are you going to pay my rent? Anne asked. Oh, shit.

Is that what the women in here want to know, too? Jen wonders. Who's going to pay the rent? Is Jen supposed to have the answers?

Limp pale toast for the third morning, white bread, of course. The oranges run out before Jen's turn in line, and she's given canned peach slices, five of them half afloat in the viscous liquid like lean goldfish. She says so to Vivian, a six-foot tall, red-haired, red-elbowed Louisiana girl who generally has empty chairs around her at mealtime. She leans into people, angry or needy, absorbing others' space like a sponge.

Vivian's smile broadens bony cheeks and her eyes gleam; everything on her face is on fire. "Yeah they look like fish! Lookit," she elbows Patrice, in line behind her, "my fish!"

"Watch it!" Vivian's tray hits Patrice's and a glob of syrup spills just into a splash of sunlight on the formica table. Bits of peach pulp shimmer, and Vivian is enthralled. "Hey, tiny fish. Minnows!"

Patrice snorts and turns away, but Jen smiles. Vivian says, "Hey! I'm gonna write a poem about fish. You know we got a typewriter? You know how to type?"

Jen agrees to type the poem about fish for Vivian's boyfriend. It will pass the time.

The dormitory telephone system works by consensus; Jen approves. She knows the value of self-regulation and flexibility. But it takes her three days to learn she has to interrupt an established order and insert herself into a time slot convenient to her neighbors.

She asks Chris if she can talk next; Chris tells her Betsy is next; she asks Betsy, and Betsy refers her to Vivian. Vivian says Patrice is next but Patrice is on kitchen duty until 7:00, so maybe Jen can be on the phone list if Vivian can get on the phone by 6:30. The first nights Vivian can't. Betsy hooks her sturdy ankles around her chair legs beside the phone and suggests cheerful immovability for nearly twenty-five minutes. Vivian is next, but when Jen comes to check on Vivian's progress a few minutes later, Betsy is again sprawled on the chair in earnest conversation, her head down.

The next night Jen believes she will wait in the hall near the phone and insist on her turn. Guard Bordman sends her back to her cell. Then she hits on the plan of lurking in the washroom across the hall, and she is in luck. When Vivian finishes her call and is on her way to Betsy's cell to fetch her, Jen grabs the receiver and quickly dials. On the third ring, Vivian and Betsy pass, scowling.

"Hi, honey," Jen says to the still ringing phone, and mouths to Betsy, "I'll tell Patrice when I'm done." She is very pleased with herself. But Bob isn't home.

On the fourth day of Jen's incarceration, she and Vivian attend a GED class in parenting, conducted by a social worker from the country. Vivian is not a mother, but the topic is What is abuse? What is discipline? And Vivian carries the scars from her mother's discipline. Besides, the craft today is making place cards for Thanksgiving, with heavy use of glue and glitter, and Vivan's long bony fingers become graceful in picking bits of glitter from the table and her pants legs.

"I'm gonna put a border around this one, but I'll leave a home for someone's name."

"Who, Viv?" the social worker asks. None of them will be home for Thanksgiving, but they can send the cards home.

Vivian shrugs.

Jen will send hers to Bob. She'd finally reached him; he's decided to drive down to visit their son at school for the long weekend. But he says, hang in there. She wonders what the alternative is.

None of the women think hitting children is the best discipline, although they admit to having done it under duress.

"What about adults?" Betsy enters the room, late, with piles of clothes for the women there. She wants to describe her recent fight with her husband.

"He thinks he can yell and smack me around, he's got another thing coming. I took the extension cord, it was one of those big jobbers, thick, like my thumb, what you call 'em . . ."

"Utility, uh, heavy duty, those orange ones?" Jen wants to make an accurate contribution to the conversation.

"Maybe, and I reared back and flung it like a lasso; it got him around the neck." She put her own thick hands on her throat and stuck out her tongue to show how it was, him spitting and trying to yell.

"Sure Betsy," Patrice says, "and what's he do to you?"

"What could he do, he's busy trying to breathe and unfasten that cord, his hands was so tied up . . ."

"Oh you tie him up first," Vivian remarks.

"You shut up girl. You so smart why's your ugly face in here?"

The social worker interrupts, tries to bring them back to children. Since Jen is new, she asks her gently, "What about you, Jen? What do you think?"

Jen frowns. "No, of course I don't think you should punish by hitting." She pauses, remembering. "But you can hurt them other ways too." Then she has no idea how to go on.

"Do you want to tell us?" the worker prods.

She doesn't, really. "Oh, the worst thing maybe is ignoring, not paying attention when they need it, or getting so wrapped up in your own pain . . ."

She probably won't see these women again in her life. She has their attention; it's something.

"It was a long time ago. Davey, my son, he was still in diapers, but running around. My husband was addicted, and they had just released him, and I couldn't manage." She looks around, and sees heads nod. "I swallowed a bunch of his pills.

Davey was playing in the next room, but I couldn't think about him, I wanted someone to take care of *me*."

She stops. It's too complicated to explain about her husband, the death of that marriage and wanting to die. "It was a lot of years ago. Things are better now."

But the social worker asks her to finish. "So what happened?"

"Right after I did it, I stuck my finger down my throat, threw up. All over my in-laws' Aubusson carpet. That was one of the *best* things I ever did."

The five women in the room are staring at her. Betsy hoots. "And now last week you throw blood all over the senator's carpet. You still messy, Jen."

They do know. Jen laughs, "Housekeeping was never one of my strong suits."

After the social worker leaves, they talk about worse things and drugs. Patrice has been careful around the social worker because she wants her children back and the lady is going to write a letter for her to the court. Now she explains to an admiring circle how she passed the last urine test she had, with her little daughter's pee funneled into a balloon. The balloon was tied and tucked into Patrice's skirtband. Her deft fingers weave the story in her lap, how she maneuvered the neck of the balloon into the specimen bottle, slipped the tie onto her finger, and filled the bottle. "The only hard part," she laughs, "is holding back your own pee."

Chris tells about being a cocaine cardiac. "My heart stopped, must of been almost a minute! Ma had called 911, they worked on me when I was out, and they said my heart stopped. I was in County a couple weeks, they say I'll never be able to coach again."

Chris is a tiny Hispanic woman of twenty who volunteers in a girl's program as a basketball coach. She moves as though she's been choreographed, and still has the tight muscled legs of an athlete, but she's restricted from heavy cleaning. Dancing with a broom, she begins to cough, a wheezy kitten sound.

"It's the needle, huh?" Riva asks her. "Crack?" She is afraid of needles herself, because of AIDS. Riva's a cab driver who has been intercepted at the airport and, through an unfortunate error in baggage handling, was discovered to be transporting an illegal substance. She's heavy-set, with the cool light and shadows of the moon in her pretty, pitted face. Her complaint is that she had to double up in the Minneapolis jail with a well-publicized prostitute who does have AIDS. "You know, maybe she has an open sore and there I am sick, with this eczema." Her bare arms are still inflamed. "I yelled all the first day, but you think anybody listens?"

The women nod; they know the disease isn't spread by touch but they leave Riva a lot of space.

That night Jen sleeps soundly, except that an old classroom teacher comes in, shaking his head at her honors paper. "Hang it up," he says to her dream self. "This is new work," she insists, but her paper is messy, covered with hen tracks and scratching out, dirt. She tries to grab it from him before he can see the drops of blood coursing down the margin.

The next day is Thanksgiving. Special visitors, The Prince of Peace Singers, have come and gone with their Sunday dresses, high hair, and heels clicking back down the corridor, through the gate. The building is quieter, but the dinner has an anticlimactic air. Some of the women have a pass for the day and will be brought back by van from downtown. Jen is late for the meal; for some reason there was no call to dinner. She'd been reading and no one came to call her from her cell.

She turns from the steam table into the dining area; with the reduced population, only the back half of the long room is set up and lit. At the last table, though, she sees an empty chair. She makes for it and puts her tray down. Riva blocks the chair with her arm.

"You can't sit here," she claims, "we're saving a place for Betsy." Jen looks around the table, uncertainly; maybe they'd make room if she pulled up another chair. One or two women look worried but no one moves. Vivian grins, "Hey Betsy'll raise a ruckus, we don't save her place."

It's true. Betsy always sits here, in the last chair, by the window. The dining room is oppressively quiet tonight; even Betsy's table seems subdued. Outside, a tree branch beside the window scratches at the glass, like a dog asking to be let in.

Jen carries her tray to the darkened section and sets it down. She walks to the other end of the room and turns on all the switches. Parris, standing by the door, looks around at the sudden light, but doesn't move or say anything. They could have pulled up another chair, Jen thinks, they just didn't want me there.

It's too much. She doesn't belong here, not even here. There is nothing she can give to these women, to ease the weight of their lives, their desperate needs.

At least there's a box of Kleenex by the light switch and she has her back to the rest of the women. She blows her nose, but the tears keep forming and falling and she has to put a hand on the counter for support. When Jen had come out of prison the first time, she called Anne, her former friend. She had asked Anne if she thought Jen was a fool. Anne decided to be pastoral; she said, only in the way we're called to be fools. Maybe Jen doesn't believe in the calling part anymore; for sure, she feels like a fool. She can't stop the tears.

Then heavy arms come around her from behind, despite the stringent rules about touching one another, and a head is laid against hers. A soft mouth brushes her ear. "Hey girl," Betsy says, "Don't worry about it. Everybody cries in here. There's a lot of shoulders—so many shoulders you wouldn't believe it."

OPTIONS FOR DIALOGUE

- In groups of three or four participants, respond to the story from a community perspective.
    1. Describe what is portrayed about the prison system.
    2. Describe the unspoken systems within this, such as power relationships among women.
    3. What are the communication patterns within each system? Who has the right to speak and be heard?
    4. Where do the women's family communities intersect?
    5. What are the political, social, and cultural forces that are affecting the women in this story? How does the perspective of the narrator affect what she sees in the other women?

SUGGESTIONS FOR ACTION

- Make a map of this story from a community perspective. Use a color key to indicate where there is support for individuals and lack of it.
- Make a similar map of the community in your social service placement or in another place where you work.

- Read different examples of diaries, letters, or poetry written from a person in exile. Here are some possibilities:

  Rigoberta Menchu (from Guatemala)
  Anna Akhmatova (from Russia)
  Nelson Mandela (from South Africa)
  Malcolm X (from the United States)
  Paulo Freire (from Brazil)
  Milan Kundera (from Yugoslavia)

Write a summary of what you learned and how this information relates to this literature selection. Report to your class.

- Create an imaginary dialogue with one of the persons just listed in the form of a song, poem, painting, or drama or create a dialogue between one of these prisoners or exiles and the one enforcing that imprisonment or exile.

LUCK OF THE IRISH

OPTIONS FOR LISTENING

- Visualize a scene from your personal experience in which there are contrasts—sensory, ethical, emotional. Write a few paragraphs describing your memory.
- Read the poem, listen for the contrasts, and write down any questions and personal connections that emerge.

Luck of the Irish
by Gary Geddes

(from Awards 17: Nimrod International Journal of Prose and Poetry)

A day off from politics. No
polluted villages, jailhouse confessions;
only the shops in West Jerusalem
and, with luck, hotdogs, a couple of beers,

and an ice-cream cone. I tell John
about meeting an Arab poet in Marrakesh
in 1970, with whom I could communicate
only in broken French, making up for what

I didn't know by coining compounds,
like the Anglo-Saxon phrase whale-road,
a kenning for sea or ocean. That encounter
wound up at an ice-cream parlour too,

not far from the medina. Ice-cream
and hot places, thermal yin-yang. As a kid
in Vancouver, my favourite outing
was a trip to the dairy, where you could get

a small scoop of Arctic Ice Cream for a dime
or half a brick for twenty-five cents.
As the cooling flavours teased my throat
and made my forehead ache, Larry Flynn

worked in the warehouse out back
or organized shipments and accounts
in the office. I was seven, my mother
was dying but I did not know it yet, and life

seemed pretty good. My health was okay.
I weighed sixty-seven pounds, Larry's
exact weight at fifteen when he was transferred
to Lager IV. *Die Fir Lager,* nicknamed

"the hospital," specialized in helping
the sick and handicapped shuffle off
their mortal coils. Malingerers
were infected with typhus and rallied

to join the no-longer-marching saints
piled high in connecting sheds.
Larry ran from building to building
in search of his brother, shifting corpses

whose skin had a translucent hue
and stretched thin as bat-wings. Once,
in response to his calls and frantic
rummaging, an arm rose faintly

from the mountain of the doomed
and rocked slowly back and forth, a pale
flower or metronome marking time,
as if to say: Stand by me, 78850

I am not yet dead. Instead of going to fight
in Palestine, Larry began life again
in Vancouver, feeding ovens
in an Italian bakery, scrubbing the killing floor

of the Alberta Meat Market with its sections
for hanging, scalding, eviscerating, chilling, cut-up
and processing. Eventually, he graduated
to grinding organs and guts for fertilizers,

dogfood. While I weigh the relative merits
of twenty-five flavours, Larry
is in the freezer backstage at Arctic Ice Cream
arguing with his brother and friends

in management about the ethics
of changing his name from Freeman to Flynn.
He toys with a flashlight in the dim interior
of the vault, cupping the beam

in his palm, watching the warm blood
pulse and circulate. I couldn't take my eyes off him
as he related these experiences at a workshop
in the Vancouver Art Gallery, twelve teenagers

intent on his stories and body language, his
disconcerting smile and apologetic tone,
the amount of water he consumed, surviving
again the ordeal that will not be denied.

Our place of meeting was a courtroom
in its previous incarnation, the raised
platform and dark wood panelling
still intact. The flavour I'm just finishing

is rum and raisin. A Japanese trade mission
mounts the cobbled Jerusalem street, its parade
of male dancers and kimonoed women
distributing glossy leaflets in Hebrew and English

only. The label on the manufacturers's brochure
says WOMEN SWEAR. A whole culture
lost in the translation. Rather than confront
racism in his old firm, Larry retired

early. A hand rises from the judicial bench
to guide us or conduct our requiem.
If Mengele jerks his thumb
towards the bathhouse, we'll be saved.

OPTIONS FOR DIALOGUE

• Go back to your visualized scene. Create a rough sketch of the scene. On your
sketch mark the places where stories could occur. With a partner, choose one of
your possible stories and create two characters for it.

GROWING THROUGH THE UGLY

OPTIONS FOR LISTENING

- In your journal describe (draw a web, brainstorm in narrative form, or just write) your personal concept of "home." What forms of languages were used there? What made you comfortable? Made you laugh? Made you furious? Made you nervous? Made you sad? Did your home reflect the broader community in which you were located? If yes, in what ways? If no, in what ways? In what ways did family members relate to the community where you lived?
- Continue in your journal and respond: Did you leave home at any point in your life? Was it by choice or necessity? What strengths allowed you to do it? What were your barriers?
- Read the selection, write the questions that arise as you read, and note any personal connections to the story.

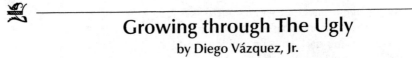

Growing through The Ugly

by Diego Vázquez, Jr.

from *Growing through the Ugly*

When I was six, I knew things. I knew the sound of strangers when they approached from behind. I knew you could eat potatoes with the skin if they got washed real good. Not so with jícama. If you eat jícama skin, it jangles the feel of the earth onto your tongue for days and days. I learned this from my grandmother, mi abuelita, Nana Kika.

Nana Kika sold tortillas de maíz and two choices of tamales all day, every day of the week, at the Mercado Bustamante on Calle Paisano in El Paso de Tejas. Six was an important age for all of her grandchildren because it marked our first trip to the mercado to help her work. Our abuelita was famous. Nana Kika would amplify a lecture on the importance of keeping our lengua in working order, insisting, "The best hope for keeping your mother tongue intact is in this marketplace." In my early Mexican Spanish, I always defined lengua as "beef tongue for dinner." La Doña Kika Soldano did not want our tongue boiled and lost in the puffy steam of this caldron de los Estados Norteños.

From the day I turned six until three months before I reached the small age of fourteen, my El Paso home was with her. Her three-story yellow house was a little rumbly sometimes because the Southern Pacific ran right off the backyard. It wasn't really a backyard. Maybe fifty feet, and one tree separated the back door from the railroad tracks. When cousins or friends came over to play they usually stayed in front of abuelita's "big yellow bird cage." Except for me. I was always drawn to the backyard. The adults would warn me not to lead any of their offspring toward the tracks. "Don't be playing on those tracks when you hear the trains coming." Then, of course, they would offer any one of numerous stories about a small child becoming a bundle of blood on the rails.

Nana Kika was gentle and great. My old skinny grandmother, with the eyes of a rain-charged mudslide and the hair of a snowstorm, had the tall sense of an old Ponderosa with broken limbs all about her. La Señora Kika Soldano was the Ponderosa loggers would leave stand after a clearing.

For years, abuelita appeared to me as the tallest woman on earth. My head reached her waist. She was just under five feet, seven inches tall but she towered over all her grandchildren. I was frail, with cream skin and round eyes like my mother. The dry mood of my darkness came from a lost father. Nana Kika was my father's mother. Whenever I walked with granny, I would hold her hand, believing she could see beyond the horizon. Beyond the dirt crusted Rocky Mountains.

I must rely on legend to transcribe my name. My real name is Bernadino Soldano Dysyadachek, Jr. But I've been Buzzy Digit since I was a child. The exact moment it began is lost for me. Abuelita Kika used to ask how many Juniors could one family stand. It is said my favorite books as a child were about cats. Children's books called cats "pussies." When I said "pussies" it came out "boosie." My older cousins, who were farther along in their command of this New World english, played on it. Boosie became pussey, busy, boogsie, booze, boozy, Buzzy. My mother's Chicago-Polish last name was a burden to all. They took Dysyadachek and turned it to Dissachikie, Disastick, Digitstick, digs shit, dig it, Digit. . . . My cousins were kind. They decided against calling me a pussy that digs shit. They invented Buzzy Digit. Because my mother was from the Windy City, I decided my real birthplace was Chicago. A Chicago Chicano, Buzzy Digit.

Abuelita Kika was also a diplomat. When I claimed to be her favorite grandchild, she would smile and lift the gentle, dusty importance of my desire into a look in her eyes that would send me into storms of joy. In private, she assured me of my most favorite status, though I was never able to get her to confirm this in public. All my cousins, who were direct descendants of Satan and not worthy of Nana Kika's affection, also considered themselves her favorite.

My abuelo, my grandfather the baker, died of a heart attack when I was three. Nana Kika often spoke of the gentle heart of her Don Pablo, her huge baker macho de hombre who had seeded her with nine children. He was struck at the panadería, his bakery, a few minutes after midnight as he prepared to bake bread for a November Wednesday morning in an old West Tejas smelting town. I don't remember abuelo, but his bakery and his land became a legacy that survived all the debts his sons piled up against their inheritance.

The wars of inheritance raged as soon as abuelo was put into the ground. Nana Kika had four sons who served this country during la Segunda Guerra. Only two saw combat. One died three days after coming home from Nazi Europe. The other, my father, came home with malaria and the horror of the siege on Guadalcanal. He saved himself from those horrors by abandoning his familia—all the familia, his two little girls, his tiny boy, and a disbelieving wife.

Two versions of my father's disappearance evolved. The first, and most prevalent, blamed his duty as a Marine medic on that island as having permanently stolen his soul. At family gatherings, an uncle or auntie would pat me on the head and whisper sorrow for my terrible fate. I was good for tips, too, because they would stuff money into my little palm, telling me his return from la Guerra had affected him in ways no one could know. They insisted it was not his lack of love for me that caused him to run, but rather the toll of too many bodies he could not fix. The terror this caused his inner world could not be mended.

The second and least talked about version of my daddy's fugitive status involved our almost-teenaged cousin, Gloria. She was the first grandchild, the oldest cousin, an epileptic. Exactly one year after my grandfather died, my father took Gloria to her swimming lesson at the downtown Y. The sun rose, promising to cover the desert with more heat. In the early morning, my dad gave Gloria the ride to her final swimming lesson. He drove away with the top down on his latest "demo," a red Chevy Bel Air. Sixty-seven minutes after Gloria waved goodbye to my dad, Auntie Margie received the call that would affect all our lives for the rest of time. The young swimming instructor cried to my dearest tía, "Everyone thought Gloria was holding her breath under water. She was in the shallow end of the pool and all the other girls were doing the same thing. The others kept coming up for air, thinking Gloria was just ahead of them in going back under. They thought she was winning." When the instructor witnessed a color of purple contrition on our Gloria's face, it was already too late. The small puddle of chlorinated water had poured a flood into the territory of a young girl's life. The water forced itself into her lungs without waiting for her seizure to stop. The water took Gloria as a gift. Our oldest cousin, almost a teenage girl, had been taken back. Gloria had become an angel.

Only one time did I hear Nana Kika mention my dad in the same breath with talk of Gloria's death. Only one time did I hear her say she thought it was the one ride that destroyed him. All the other excuses for his abandonment centered on the war. The second big war. I became a believer of the drowned version.

They say my mother is beautiful. But she abandoned me after my daddy ran, her brave heart broken and saddened. I only recall her screams. Once, some crazy ghost screaming from an abandoned graveyard made her slice the skin on my head with a jab from a broom handle. I locked myself in the bathroom and cried while my head dripped blood onto my hands. When she finally opened the door, the blood had dried. She told me it was nothing and not to say anything to Nana Kika. In most pictures, she has eyes that look like the desert green of small lizards. Abuelita said they were the deepest green she had ever seen. They were eyes that made people feel as if they were looking into the center of the ocean.

My grandmother spoke softly of my mom and dad. "Mi'jo, they were so pretty, O, pretty together. But the war ruined him. Tu padre signed up with those Marines without telling anyone. At seventeen, he was already filling prescriptions for Hidalgo's pharmacy. He told the Marines he was going to be a doctor so they made him a medic. Y tu mamá, mi hijito, tan hermosa, and so strong."

"But, abuelita, if she was so strong, why did she hit me and where is she now?"

"When your daddy ran away, she left with a Mexican painter from Chihuahua. After that, she met some writer, or poet, from Chile and they went back to his home in a place called Temuco. The last we heard was her letter telling us of a place called Antofagasta. It is the place on this earth where the sun is always the toughest. She said you will be sent for when they get settled."

"They" included my two older sisters. My mother pleaded with Nana Kika that girls needed to be with their mother much more than a boy did. Granny never turned away a child and this is how I came to live with her. I was one of many cousins who would ask Nana to be my mother.

I had a favorite dream during my first year of school. It gave me a second chance at choosing a mother. In waking, I told myself that since the first one was lousy, the next one would not have to be so pretty that her eyes need to be green. *I just want her eyes to see me when she looks at me. That will be fine. She can wear short dresses. I want her to walk with me. If she wants to hold my hand, I will let her. She can touch me in public. She can be old, like thirty-three. She can have dark hair, short ears, crooked nose, and wide soft lips. Her breath will be from the heart of a strawberry. And when I sleep, she will kiss me. If I wake from broken dreams, she will let me sleep with her. I can lay my head on the inside of her thighs, or her belly, or on her breast like I used to when I could put my lips on her nipples. She will let me sleep on her buttocks if I want. She will take me like the ocean returning to gather all its stranded creatures. Her skin can have sand in the pores, but her eyes will remain clear. She won't hit me with crazy broom handles when I cry. I promise to choose a mommy who will tell me it is not necessary for tears because she knows how to be funny. We will laugh at men's jokes. And, because she wants me to grow protective of her, she will tell me about men. Then, she will let me warn her about things she already knows. As the night gets darker, she will let me be her child.*

When I was six, I knew things.

OPTIONS FOR DIALOGUE

- With one dialogue partner discuss the strengths of the narrator, Nana Kika, and any of the other characters.
- Discuss the barriers they faced.
- Write in your journal about a place or a context or situation in which you didn't fit in or feel at home. In what ways do you think you felt like any of the characters in the selection?
- Discuss that experience of not fitting in with a group of three or four peers. What aspects of everyone's situation were the same? Different? What would have helped you in your experiences of isolation? What are some things that could lessen the narrator's isolation?

SUGGESTIONS FOR ACTION

- Observe in your field placement site the ways in which language is used. Which languages? Spanish, English, Hmong, Vietnamese? Formal language or informal language? Nonverbal language? Is language used as a marker for age, class, inclusion, exclusion? Does the language used make participants feel secure or insecure?
- Go back to the journal entry in which you described (drew a web, brainstormed in narrative form, or free-wrote) your personal concept of home. Answer the previous questions about language in the context of your description.
- Read *Friends from the Other Side/Amigos Del Otro Lado* (1993) by Gloria Anzaldúa, illustrated by Consuelo Méndez. San Francisco: Children's Book Press. Choose from the following listening, dialogue, and action activities.

OPTIONS FOR LISTENING

- In your journal write about how you describe or define your racial/ethnic identity. What is important and not important to you about this aspect of yourself? If it is important, why? If unimportant, why not? Is your ethnic identity tied to a particular place? In what ways?
- How did you learn about your racial/ethnic identity? What are your earliest memories? What was fun or painful as you learned about these aspects of your identity? What do you remember about peers' ideas of newcomers' identities? Write about this.
- In your notes, create an idea web around the word *borders.* What are your personal connections with the concept of borders?
- Read the story.

OPTIONS FOR DIALOGUE

- In your groups, discuss anything from this story that relates to your career preparation, work, reading, or other personal experience. What did you learn from this story? What do you feel is the most important learning in the story? Share these ideas with a partner. Do you agree or disagree? What other questions do you have about any other aspect of the story?
- Share how you agree or disagree with your parents' or friends' views about race and ethnicity. If you disagree, how did you develop your own ideas? If you are a parent (or plan to be one), what do you want to teach your own children?
- What would our country be like if we had no borders, if anyone who wanted to live here could do so?
- Who is a *curandera* (healer) in your background? Is the healer male or female? Old or young? Tell your group a story about a healer in your family.

SUGGESTIONS FOR ACTION

- Have you ever had to fight personally against a large social system (for example, a university, school administration, or governmental office)? Tell about it in writing or as an oral story.
- Read about home and community in a culture with which you are not familiar. Make a comparison chart of similarities and differences between the information about this culture and your own.
- View the PBS video segment from the Macneil-Lehrer News Hour (MLNQ703, July 5, 1993) regarding bilingual, bicultural Cuban Americans in Miami, Florida. Compare the stories you hear from these interviews with the narrator's experiences in this story.
- In any current work that you are doing in your community, what voices do you culturally support or not support? Why? How can you change this? Discuss a plan of action with a colleague also involved in this work.
- Review the research of Lily Wong Fillmore regarding immigrant children and families in our country who experience "English only" schooling and no support for home language. How does this information relate to the story?

Wong Fillmore, L. (1990). *Latino families and the schools. California perspectives: An anthology.* Los Angeles: Immigrant Writers Project.

Wong Fillmore, L. (1991). When learning a second language means losing the first. *Early Childhood Research Quarterly, 6*(3), 323–347.

CULTURE CLASH

OPTIONS FOR LISTENING

- In your journal describe a situation in which you felt you were discriminated against. What was the context (where were you; what was your relationship to the person or people who were the perpetrators—a situation of employer/employee, adult/child, teacher/student, peer/peer)? Was there misunderstanding because of lack of information? Was there an obvious example of stereotyping?
- Ask a partner to define *conflict* and listen to the message that person is conveying.
- Ask another partner to give her or his definition of *culture.*
- Read the selection, write any question that you think of, and note any personal connections.

Culture Clash
by Jim Northrup
(from: *Walking the Rez Road)*

Luke Warmwater and his old lady Dolly were riding down a gravel road on the reservation. Luke and Dolly were on a ride because they had the gas.

It was ricing season, but the lakes were closed so they could rest. The wind was combing the tangles out of the rice. They were glad because they knew they could harvest the next day.

Down the road they saw someone shambling along.

"A way day," said Luke, pointing with his lower lip.

"Ayah," agreed Dolly. "That's your brother, the one they call Almost, isn't it?"

"Yah, I wonder what the hell he's doing around here," wondered Luke.

From the way he walked, Luke knew Almost had been on a drunk. There was nothing unusual about that. What was unusual was the bloody washrag he held against his head.

Almost got into the car and said, "Hey, brother, you got a smoke?"

As Luke handed him one, he began complaining and explaining. He was complaining about the cut on his head and explaining how it happened.

"This gash must need thirty-seven stitches. How about a ride to the hospital?" Almost said.

"No problem," said Luke, "put your seatbelt on—we're now riding in an ambulance."

"That old girl broke her frying pan over my head, you know, one of those cast iron ones. I knew I shouldn't have gone home yet," Almost moaned. "Sure, I've been on a drunk, but she was laying for me when I got home. She used that frying pan for something besides fry bread."

"We went ricing yesterday," Luke said.

"That bonk on the noggin did nothing to improve my hangover. She was yelling about that skinny Red Laker I passed out next to. I got out of there before she really got mad," Almost continued.

"We got 150 pounds of rice at Dead Fish Lake yesterday," Luke said.

He began the ritual of "Rushing Him to the Hospital." He felt good about driving so fast. He was on a genuine mission of mercy and he could bend and even break the traffic laws.

Luke's old car was holding up pretty good on the high speed run. "She'll need a quart of oil by the time we get there," he said.

The cops sitting at the edge of town eating donuts didn't know of Luke's mission of mercy. All they saw was a carload of Indians weaving through traffic.

Donuts and curses flew through the air as they began one of their own institutions called "High Speed Chase."

One cop was screaming on the radio about the chase. The other was trying to keep track of all the laws that were being broken.

"Hey, all right, we got an official police escort," said Luke when he saw the red lights in his mirrors.

By the time Luke's escort had grown to three city squads, the deputies were coming to join the chase.

The ambulance came sliding into the hospital parking lot and stopped by the emergency room. Dolly got Almost out of the car and helped him into the building.

Luke drove over to where you're supposed to park and began congratulating himself on the successful run to the hospital. His troubles began when the cops got to the parking lot. They were excited about the chase.

"What's wrong with you, driving like that?" yelled a cop as he came running up to Luke.

"I wanna see your license!" screamed the second cop as he tried to wrestle Luke to the ground.

"Good, he's gonna resist arrest," said the first cop as he drew out his nightstick.

"My brother, Almost, is . . . ," Luke got out before a nightstick glanced off the side of his head and shut him up.

Luke gave up trying to explain and just began to fight back. He was holding his own and even took one of the nightsticks away. He threw that thing up on the roof so they'd quit hitting him with it.

The balance of power shifted towards the law and order as more cops piled into the battle. Pretty soon Luke was sitting on the pavement, a subdued and handcuffed Indian. There never is an easy way to end these things, he thought.

The cops jerked Luke up on his tiptoes and marched him into the emergency room. Luke's head needed some doctor attention after all those nightsticks. They laid Luke down on the table next to Almost.

"Matching stitches," growled Luke to his brother.

"Anin da nah," said Almost and then shut up when he saw the cops and cuffs.

There was something ironic about the whole situation, but Luke couldn't figure it out as the doctor stitched the brothers up.

The cops took Luke to jail. On the ride, Luke saw the ripped uniforms and lumps on the cops. That would explain why they put the cuffs on so damned tight.

Luke was pushed into his usual cellblock and he checked himself over for damages. It was good to get those cuffs off.

A cop came in and handed Luke his copy of the charges. In addition to traffic charges, there was one for theft of city property. They couldn't find the nightstick he threw away.

The cellblock door clanged open and Almost was pushed in.

"We gotta stop meeting like this," sighed Luke. "What they got you for?"

"Disorderly conduct, and of course resisting arrest," said Almost.

"We'll go to court this afternoon," calculated Luke.

"When I got out of the hospital, the cops were still outside. They must have been mad yet because when I offered to drive your car home, they attacked," said Almost as he rubbed his cuff damaged wrists.

So Almost went to jail, the car went with the tow truck, and Dolly went visiting relatives to raise bail money.

She got back to the jail as the brothers were being taken to court.

"Got you covered," she said as she flashed the bail money.

Luke grinned hard at her.

In court, the brothers Warmwater pleaded not guilty and demanded a jury trial. A new court date was set and the matter of bail came up.

Luke got up and addressed the judge.

"Your honor, I hate seeing you under these conditions. I've been here before and as you may recall, I've always showed up on time for court.

"Ricing comes only once a year. The harvest is good this year and my old lady, Dolly, is finally learning how to make rice, I'm sure you know how important to the Indian people the rice crop is.

"The reason I'm telling you all this is because I'd like to request a release on my own recognizance."

"Request granted," the judge said as he gaveled the case down the court calendar.

As long as he had the judge's ear, Luke got brave and said, "Oh, yeah, your honor, all that stuff is true for my brother too."

The judge cut them both loose. They walked out of there free ricing Indians. They used the bail money Dolly raised to rescue the car and to buy that quart of oil they needed.

They dropped Almost off at home. His old lady was kind of sorry about hitting him. When he promised to buy her a new frying pan, she forgave him. They began making preparations for ricing the next day.

Luke and Dolly continued their ride down the gravel on the Reservation. Down the road, they saw someone walking.

"A way day," said Luke, pointing with his lower lip.

"Don't you dare stop, Luke Warmwater!" said Dolly.

OPTIONS FOR DIALOGUE

• In a group of three or four peers, list specific examples of cultural conflict that you found in the story.

- In this same group draw a graphic representation that illustrates which characters understood each other.
- Discuss a positive aspect of Indian culture that may have been misunderstood as negative.

SUGGESTIONS FOR ACTION

- Draw a chart showing the lines of communication at your practicum site. Where are the lines supported by the institutional structure or by the persons involved? Where are the lines broken by the institutional structure or by the persons involved?
- Observe and document examples of nonverbal communication among participants in your practicum situation or in another working situation. Analyze the data and select a way to share the information with someone or some group who is involved in this work.
- Interview a person who is a single parent. Does this information reveal cultural conflict (in the sense that this informant represents a culture other than the "All-American family," with Mother, Father, two children and a dog), misinformation, and lack of sensitivity and support? What do you see as implications of this information for your chosen work?
- Read one of the following books or one with a related theme:

   Danticat, E. (1994). *Eyes, breath, memory.* New York: Soho.
   This novel is set in Haiti and New York. Sophie Caco, the narrator, a child of rape, comes to the United States at the age of twelve to join her immigrant mother, whom she has never known.
   Danticat, E. (1995). *Krik? Krak!* New York: Soho.
   This is a collection of short stories about life in contemporary Haiti and Haitian refugees in the United States.
   Erdrich, L. (1986). *The beet queen.* New York: Holt.
   A tough yet empathetic novel exposes the loneliness and craving that keep people separate even when their lives intersect.
   García, C. (1992). *Dreaming in Cuban.* New York: Ballantine.
   This novel is about Cuba, García's native country, and three generations of del Pino women who are seeking spiritual homes for their passionate, often troubled souls.
   Høeg, P. (1994). *Smilla's sense of snow.* New York: Dell.
   This is a mystery novel on one level and at the same time a story about relationships, multicultural issues, and science.
   Matthiessen, P. (1991). *In the spirit of Crazy Horse.* New York: Viking.
   A solidly documented history of the U.S. government's oppression of American Indians. The account brings in issues from the early nineteenth century and weaves in modern events leading to the fighting at Pine Ridge Reservation and the trial of Leonard Peltier.
   Northrup, J. (1993). *Walking the rez road.* Stillwater, MN: Voyageur.
   This is a book of short stories by Ojibwe writer Northrup.
   Urquhart, J. (1994.) *Away.* New York: Viking.
   This is a novel about an Irish family's memory storehouse of politics and nation, myth and artifact, dreams and losses.
   Vizenor, G. (1990). *Interior landscapes.* Minneapolis: University of Minnesota Press.
   Gerald Vizenor writes about his experiences as a tribal mixed blood in the new world of simulations; the themes in his autobiographical stories arc lost memories and a "remembrance past the barriers."

Answer these questions about your reading:

1. In a few sentences, summarize the reading(s).
2. Why did you read this? What relationship to your personal or professional life does it have?
3. Do you feel an accurate picture of the information was presented? Why or why not?
4. Which points from the reading did you *not* agree with? Why?
5. Discuss which information or opinions presented here were new to you.
6. Discuss any conversation about this subject that you may have had.

- Review the research by Carl Grant, Christine Sleeter, James Banks, Valerie Polakow, Cornel West, Edward Said, Henry Trueba, George and Louise Spindler, or Trinh T. Minh-ha. All address issues of cultural conflict and adaptation. Relate the information from one or more of these researchers to the story. Relate the information to your current work or community contexts.
- Attend a cultural celebration of any form. Pick a communicative format (a story, a poem, an essay, a series of photographs, and so on) for explaining your interpretation of how the celebration reflects the strengths of the community of people.

FLYING BLIND

OPTIONS FOR LISTENING

- Write a few reflective sentences in your journal about any factual information you know about a Middle Eastern country or culture. Write about a relationship (a close friendship or an acquaintance) you may have had with a person from the Middle East. Write a few sentences about what you learned by knowing that person. (Factual or opinion learnings are important.)
- Read the following poem; write down personal questions and connections.

Flying Blind
by Gary Geddes

(from *Awards 17: Nimrod International Journal of Prose and Poetry*)

Hisham Ahmad meets us for lunch
at a restaurant in Bethlehem. Like John
he is blind; even has a Ph.D.
from the States and a job to go back to
in Michigan. He's become critical
of his homeland, though he's back
for a year to do research and refurbish

domestic relations. The place is empty
except for us, two blind Arabs and
a sighted minority consuming chicken

shishkebabs. Four hands scuttle across
platters, up the sides of glasses
like spiders or bottom-feeders anxious
to see what is there. Rough palms

navigate culinary reefs meticulous
as metal detectors. We departed
the University of Bethlehem in a rush,
after disgracing ourselves at a seminar
in the English Department, where a plump
brother of the Church was chairing
a session built around an academic paper

entitled "English for the 21st Century."
We endured what we could, an hour of fake
Platonic dialogue, only to be told the purpose
of English study is to help us communicate,
adapt, think critically, use technology
that is available, and work in a multicultural
setting. Christ, I whispered loudly to John,
given Vatican support for this dump,
does it surprise you the article is written
by someone with the surname Pope?
My visually-challenged friends have scarfed
most of the chicken and ordered seconds
of bread, which they take unbuttered
in the Arab fashion. Though we insist,

Hisham is fastidious about paying his share
and making connections at Deheishe,
the refugee camp where he lives with parents
and blind brother. Vitamin deficiency
and contaminated water are responsible
for their condition. While the brother
tells us about being tortured and imprisoned

by the Israelis, Hisham grows uneasy
and starts interrupting, imposing his own
interpretation on events. I'm mesmerized
by the story and the absolute stillness
of the teller, no light emanating
from his dead eyes. If the animus is not visible
in the eyes, where does it hang out

in these nosey, brash, interrogating hands?
Without benefit of a doctorate
or the gospel according to Carol Pope,
the brother tells us how urine, excrement,

and blood circulated freely in the undersized cell
where he could neither stand nor lie down,
how he was punched in the back and kidneys

as he clung to the side of the jeep.
Anger and self-pity are completely absent
from his account, which doesn't stop me
indulging a little guilt about my own
complicity. That's when I hear him
call it the central experience of his life. Prison
gave him meaning a purpose,

made him part of the intifada. John is so moved
he has to leave the room. Two brothers,
so differently educated, wave to us
as our car noses the open-sewer
dirt-track into Bethlehem proper, the little town
lying mute and doggo like language itself
before the spectre of a 21st century.

OPTIONS FOR DIALOGUE

- Talk with a partner about your response to the poem and finish these statements:
  This poem is about. . . .
  It reminds me of. . . .
- Both you and your partner should relate anything from the poem to your personal lives.
- Poets believe that truth or meaning lies in details. What sensory details in this poem convey meaning about a human situation?

SUGGESTIONS FOR ACTION

- Think of meeting a person whose story has meant a great deal to you in your own life. Write a story or poem describing that meeting.
- Interview someone who has lived or worked in Palestine.
- Read the writings of Edward Said.
- Research the media for articles on Palestine. Whose voices are heard in the media on the issues? Whose are not heard? What are some ways of hearing the silenced voices?

ELLEN RYAN'S BRAIDED RUG

OPTIONS FOR LISTENING

- Answer the following questions in your journal: have you ever been in a nursing home or other type of care facility for elderly people? What was the environment like? The physical surroundings? The emotional atmosphere? Try to remember specific details about the setting. What was your personal reaction? (If you have never personally been in such a facility, write about a movie you have viewed or an article you have read that described such a context.)

- Read the selection, write any questions that come to your mind, and note personal connections.

Ellen Ryan's Braided Rug
by Pat Barone

Because of dropping the phone when her children called, which alarmed them, or scalding her foot with boiling milk, or breaking her ankle on wet flagstone. Each evening she recites these reasons. Each morning, as soon as she opens her eyes, she is startled to find herself in St. Clothilde's, so startled she forgets her dreams.

Before, when she lived alone, she enjoyed going to bed after a good Katharine Hepburn movie—at two in the morning sometimes—then sleeping late to make up for the way she woke all night to lie in bed thinking about her dreams. They populated her mind, the way the children used to fill the house. In her dreams, it was all plaids, coal fires, boots, mittens, hot soup, hands reaching for platters on the table. But all in slow motion, with their voices no longer asking anything of her. For of course, even inside the dream, she knew they were all grown up, all married but Nora.

Something has happened to her dreams in this place. Maybe the smells drive them away—pine disinfectant to cover the urine. The old cooking smells of chowder and stew—all gone. That's what that woman whose house burned down said she missed the most—the smell of her home. It was really the smell of her family. You could make all the jokes you wanted about people bathing too little, but you didn't mind the way your own smelled—your own little one's diapers, your husband's sweat. The dreams know. What's familiar about this place to start them up? Nothing.

So she is surprised and pleased to wake this morning with the tail of a dream in her hand—something brightly colored and very familiar. She lies still with her eyes shut, trying not to lose the image or the feeling it gave her of being home. A braid, curving—a spiral getting bigger in someone's hands. The rug she made for the dining room—of Mike's blue shirt, Alanna's red felt circle skirt, Maureen's wheat jeans. She is glad to wake on her own today—a good half a hall before her breakfast tray, by the sound of it. If she lies very still, perhaps more of the dream will come back to her. But no, just a picture of her own hands, with their ropey blue veins, braiding.

Maybe that was all it was. But someone said something. . . . Was it in her dream, or perhaps down the hall at the nurses' station? She gives up trying to keep her dream, and, from an old habit of curiosity, listens to the ward.

In a place like this, if something has to go, she'd rather her eyes than her ears. You get more information just listening. At the nurses' station, some sort of ruckus. . . .

"Where did you get the ivy?" That sounds like Mrs. Olsen, the charge nurse.

"It's mine now; I'm going to keep it. Where are you taking me?" It's Lillian Schneider, who isn't getting forgetful—at least Ellen *thinks* not—but instead, just likes to stir up a little excitement.

"It's Edna's; it's her roommate's." That was Ronnie, the aide.

But where did Lillian think she was going with Edna's plant? Back home? Did it remind her of a plant she used to tend? Ellen was only able to keep one of her ivies, and the Shamrock Nora brought her from Cork maybe fifteen years ago. The ficus in the ten gallon white ceramic tub, the fig tree she inherited from her own mother and re-potted every five years without fail, and kept healthy for fifty years—she had to give to Alice. Too tall for the low ceilings in this place with their cork acoustic tiles.

"Are they paying enough attention to your needs, Ma?" Nora had asked on her last visit. Ellen said that if anything—too much attention to her, on their schedule, not hers. Well, you take the good with the bad. No coffee any more. Has a bad effect on the Parkinson's. It was Sanka now. Oh well.

An irritable push at her door. "Up and at 'em, Ellen!" Ronnie stoops to put the door stop down. Dark sweat patches on her shocking pink uniform—under her arms and between her shoulder blades. She pushes her hair back from her forehead.

Ronnie always holds the arms too high, thinks Ellen, struggling to put her hands into the sleeves of the house dress, which, because of the humidity, sticks to the hump on her back. ("Didn't the doctors know anything about calcium in your day, Ma?" asked Nora.)

Despite the hurry-up mornings, she knows Ronnie likes her. Once she overheard her say to another aide, "That Ryan! She's got a lot of spirit." And when she added, "See how her neck moves in and out of the collar of her dress like a turtle?" Ellen knew Ronnie meant it fondly. She meant she admired the way that Ellen wasn't going to let her new funny way of walking stop her: Her path is unpredictable, a result of the Parkinson's disease. She seems to overshoot herself, and must rest between each cluster of hurried little steps forward.

"Morning, morning," says Ellen to the other two "ambulants"—Lillian and Edna, who are waiting at the table in the day room for Ronnie and their breakfast trays.

"Hey, Ellen," replies Edna Rombeau. Always "hey," never "hi," because she'd grown up in Mississippi. She pats the table, a chipped wooden circle, at the place next to her. Ellen thinks, as she always does, that the table looks odd across from the stainless steel and formica of the nurses' station. It seems out of place in this place. Is it from someone's attic or backyard?

Lillian says, "It's going to be hot. But I still want to go outside." She looks meaningfully at Ronnie.

"Don't look at me," Ronnie says as she puts the trays in front of the three old women. "I have to take two patients to a self-help class. After breakfast trays, I go off the ward for a while."

"Like a bomb," Lillian says and she winks at Ellen.

"Besides," continues Ronnie, "you can't go out until Physical Therapy repairs your leg brace again."

She leaves to get Tillie Napsen, who must be strapped into her wheelchair so she doesn't fall forward into her scrambled eggs and farina. She likes to feed herself, but it's slow going. With her right side paralyzed, she has to use her left hand. Tillie doesn't take her last bite until the others are halfway through "Search for a Brighter Day." No one but Edna is really paying attention to the querulous voices from the T.V.: "When I was just a little girl, I used to think something wonderful would happen to me," says the doctor's deserted wife.

"When I was a little girl, I used to think," Edna says to no one in particular.

Ellen knows what she means, but she doesn't say so. People suppose you're getting senile if you say you have difficulty making your thoughts follow one idea. But really, it was more a matter of having a whole life time there at your elbow, just waiting, the way she used to have a basket of colored yarn remnants to make sweaters for the grandchildren. She never knew what color she was going to pull up from the basket. And it wasn't her eyesight—she didn't *want* to know; it was more of a challenge to take what came to hand and add it to the pattern as if she'd intended to follow black and white herring bone with purple all along.

What *was* the pattern in the dream? For just a moment, she sees her rug whole—but all the colors are blurred. It tries her to remember, so she thinks instead of the things she made, some finished, worn and given to St. Vincent De Paul forty years ago.

It always took her a while to find out what the final design was going to be. Now that she's too squirrelly to manage the needles any more—since they changed her dosage—it was her life that kept coming up, unraveling from one part and then another: For no reason she's been thinking of the rabbits they used to breed behind the house and that makes her think of Nora's science fair project at St. Bede, and that makes her think . . . and so on. Is she supposed to put it all together, see what it all adds up to? A life. And no complaints, she tells herself. Out of old habit, she focuses on the people around her.

"See you in a little while," says Ronnie to the lounge as she takes away Tillie's tray. She forgets to remove the bib, and by the end of "Search for a Brighter Day," Tillie manages to tug it out of the metal clothespins attached to her robe. She smiles, and folds it in half and half again—all with one hand. Then she shakes it out, folds it diagonally, loses the crease, frowns, folds it again, and then she rests.

Lillian gets slowly to her feet, and is all out of breath by the time she stands. She used to smoke a pack and a half of Camels a day, and she's heavy. ("180 pounds and still growing strong," she complains, "with all the starch here.") She seems to be polishing the floor with her feet as she shuffles, using her quad cane, over to the nurse's station. "Is someone going to take us out today?"

Mrs. Olsen is doing charts, and doesn't even look up. "Who's going to do the B.M. board today?" she asks Ronnie and Megan, the other aide.

"I have seven bed baths," says Megan.

"Oh, all right," Ronnie says.

Lillian raps her cane against the bottom of the counter. "Who's going to take us out today?"

"Don't get your underwear in a bundle." Ronnie is in a good mood. Ellen overheard her tell Megan that her new boyfriend drove her to work. Ronnie grins at Lillian. "Tell you what. I'll wheel you out after I come back from self-help."

"I can walk if you walk with me."

"Oh no you can't. Not that far. Not until they do something about your new leg brace."

Lillian returns to the lounge and sits next to Ellen on the couch. Ellen feels fidgety. She misses her knitting. Instead of looking at "The Price Is Right," she watches

Tillie, who never waits for a by-your-leave from the aides, but, instead, heads down the hall in her wheelchair, pulling herself slowly along the waist-high molding, from door to door, with her one good arm. Her bad leg (surprisingly shapely) is uncovered to mid-thigh. She always rests by the linen supply closet before tackling the door to the clean utility room. When the aides can't find her, she's in a dead end by the elevator. As she can only go in one direction, someone has to wheel her back.

Ellen herself is known to the staff as a traveler. "Ma, we've been waiting for you almost forty minutes," Nora complained when she came to visit with her brothers, Tim and Brian, the twins and eldest of Ellen's nine children. "And the staff couldn't even find you. We almost had to leave without seeing you. Where did you go?" Well, that was a little hard to explain. Ellen just stopped for directions along the way. There's the coffee shop, the gift shop, and the beauty parlor, which she likes the best to visit. She used to do hair herself and enjoys seeing the new cuts, and just talking with the beautician who specializes in "soft waves for seniors—none of those bowl-shaped afros just because some girls think you're too senile to talk back!"

There's enough of those who are too senile to talk, Ellen thinks, much less make any sense. Some of them still prowl the halls. Hope someone stops me making a nuisance of myself when it comes to that.

On the lounge T.V., housewives jump up and down. "They make me dizzy," Lillian says.

"That contestant's dressed up like the wallpaper in here," Edna says, "too much orange and green, dontcha know."

"Why are they all trying to get their hands in his pocket? We used to know what *that* meant." Lillian chuckles, and taps Ellen's arm with her magazine. She points to a picture of a movie star—which one, Ellen can't see—"Nobody has any morals any more."

Just then, Tillie's youngest sister, Agnes Napsen, who has recently come back from her trips to Lourdes, Fatima, and the Holy Land, comes to get Tillie for stations of the cross in the garden.

Both aides are now back in the nurses' station getting ready to do vitals on their halls. Mrs. Olsen snaps at Ronnie: "Mind your aseptic technique!" (Whatever that is.)

So no one sees what Tillie is up to but Ellen. As her sister pushes her by the nurses' station, Tillie pulls out a silver flask like a fancy ironing sprinkler, and liberally douses the staff with water. "Bless yourselves! That's from Lourdes!"

"Oh, I'm *so* sorry," apologizes her sister. But Tillie continues to sprinkle, so she ducks her own head and quickly pushes her into the elevator.

"That holy water was too good for you, I should have saved it for those who really need it," says Tillie, as the door closes.

"Well," says Mrs. Olsen, wiping her eyes, "this is no worse than last week when she thought Father Burns was trying to get into bed with her."

Old Ruth Mayron says, "Ain't it awful?" But she is not referring to Tillie. That's what she always says. If Edna had seen Tillie get Mrs. Olsen all wet, Edna would be laughing right now. But Edna is all eyes for the T.V., and Ellen doesn't even feel like telling her. She admits she feels a little low today, and almost has to agree with old Ruth, who turns to Edna and says, "It's awful, just awful." After surveying the room, old Ruth adds, in a surprised tone, "I don't know anybody here, do you?"

Edna's pale blue eyes look a little unfocused, like she just woke up. "I don't know anybody either," says Edna, who usually winks at Ellen any time old Ruth says her usual. This time she doesn't. Well, I don't either, thinks Ellen, not really, not in a place like this.

She turns away from Edna, determined to be diverted by a visitor, who comes into the lounge with her little girl, and picks up a *Ladies Home Journal.* Waiting while her mother is in PT or something. The way the girl stretches her none-too-clean blue-jeaned legs in front of her reminds Ellen of Nora. Is the girl here just out of duty? Is she bored, or maybe even angry about having to visit her mother? Maybe she has a grudge against her mother for the way she was raised. Though the generations shouldn't live together— that's trouble—maybe she feels guilty for not taking her mother in. But the girl's face doesn't give anything away—just like Nora's face.

Old Ruth has gotten her wheelchair locked into her portable swing tray. She can only rock a little—not enough to disengage herself. Unlike Edna, Lillian, Ellen herself, or even Tillie—she never looks to the others for anything.

Still Lillian calls out to the nurses' station, "We need some help over here!"

Nobody pays any attention, or perhaps they don't hear her.

The young mother, seeming a little embarrassed, looks up from her magazine. "Should I. . . ?" She bends down by the wheelchair, is about to lift up the footrest, but hesitates. She almost tiptoes when she goes over to the nurses' station. "Excuse me, but one of the old ladies has her wheel chair all mixed up with her tray. . . ."

Mrs. Olsen twists her mouth, doesn't look at the visitor, but stomps into the lounge where she tips back the chair and kicks the tray out of the way.

The young woman sits back down with her magazine opened to "Can This Marriage Be Saved," while the little girl crawls under her legs.

Edna leans forward. "Aren't you a pretty little girl." The child presses closer to her mother. "What do you call your toy horse?" Edna persists.

"It's not a horse. It's a 'My Little Pony.' Her name is Moonbeam."

"Children always like me," Edna says. Then her face puckers. "My daughter lives in Gulfport," she tells Ellen for what seems like the hundredth time. "I haven't seen Jason and Jenny for. . . ."

"I used to be a little girl," Old Ruth says to the child.

The young woman looks up from her magazine. "Don't bother these ladies."

"Oh, she's no bother. We like to see children," Ellen tells her.

The little girl's dark hair falls forward in a dense fringe over her eyes as she pushes her pony along the floor. She makes it climb up Mrs. Mayron's wheelchair, murmuring to it all the while.

The old woman puts out her hand, touches the little girl's arm with one finger. "I used to be a little girl." The child stares at her. Mrs. Mayron nods, then makes a hissing sound, "Sssssssss shuh sssss shuh," like a tea kettle just starting up, thinks Ellen, but she knows what's coming from old Ruth.

The child starts, and covers her ears, when the old woman wails higher and higher.

"What's wrong with her, Mommy?"

"Oh, she's just old," her mother says, and glances nervously up at the nurses' station before going back to her article.

Edna exchanges a look with Ellen, and Ellen feels better. Maybe Edna's more like herself now, maybe she can make it as far as the coffee shop.

As suddenly as she began crying, old Ruth stops. She decides to leave. It takes her a full two minutes to cross in front of the T.V. Her arthritic hands turn each wheel so slowly that no one can see the Coke commercial.

Megan, passing with the compress cart full of steaming towels, stops her before she gets to the door. "You just wait for me, Ruth, I'll come get you next."

"I want to go home."

"I said I'll take you back to your room in a little while."

"I want to go home!"

"I want to go out! I want to go home!" Lillian shouts, pounding her cane, a big grin on her face.

Edna blinks, looks at Ellen, and then calls out, in her tremulous voice, "I want to go. . . . I want my home back!"

Old Ruth looks at the others and says, "Ain't it awful?" In a higher voice: "I want to go home!"

Ellen feels excited. But she holds on to the thought: No sense in complaining about something you can't do anything about.

Mrs. Olsen, heel toe, heel toe, (fast for her) clicks right over to the lounge, puts her hands on her hips and says, "What's all this I hear? *This* is your home, and this very afternoon you're going to the Holy Land. . . . I mean going to see slides of the Holy Land." When no one says anything, she says, "Megan! Come over here and tell the ladies about the program." Megan has a puzzled frown on her face when Mrs. Olsen continues, "Remember—Miss Napsen is giving a slide show of the Holy Land this afternoon at 3:00. You and Ronnie should start getting the residents into the lecture hall about 2:30."

"Hokay," Megan says, watching the charge nurse return to her chair. She shrugs her shoulders, rolls her eyes, and says, "That's all folks!"

On the lounge T.V., housewives jump up and down. Just like our "demonstration," on ward Two-East thinks Ellen.

Lillian hoists herself to her feet again as soon as she sees Ronnie begin to chart in the nurses' station. "When are you going to take me out?" she asks. But Ronnie, her face red, looks down at her chart.

Mrs. Olsen doesn't reply to the doctor's curt reminder to turn the bed-bound patients more frequently, and she brushes past Lillian, her stethoscope bouncing on her bosom.

"When do I get to go out?" Lillian calls after her.

Ellen gets up, feels for her cane, and jerks forward slowly, so she can stand next to Lillian. She is surprised to hear herself saying, "Won't anybody listen to us?" Her eyes fill with tears.

All of a sudden she remembers what the voice—Nora's voice—had said in her dream. It was: "We don't need any more of your rugs."

Overhead, on the PA, a voice says something that sounds like: *Dr. Arlette, Dr. Arlette, you're wanted in Paradise Two.*

OPTIONS FOR DIALOGUE

- Discuss these questions with a partner: what were the strengths of Ellen Ryan? What were the barriers she faced? What would you say to her if she were a relative or a very close friend?
- Think of the community of nursing home workers and residents in the story. Whom did the staff serve in the story? How? Who, in this community, had the right or opportunity to speak? Who has the right to know? Who does the questioning? Who feels safe to speak? Who listens?

SUGGESTIONS FOR ACTION

- Choose a person in your practicum or work context and discuss with a friend who is not in this class two of this person's most obvious strengths. What were two of the most obvious barriers for this person? What was a barrier that was hidden or indirect but nevertheless an obstacle for this person?
- Read one or more of the books for children and young adults that are listed here.

    Creech, S. (1994). *Walk two moons.* New York: Harper Collins.

    Thirteen-year-old Sal journeys with her grandparents from her new home in Ohio to Idaho, where her mother recently moved. Sal tells the story of Phoebe, a friend whose mother has disappeared. But as Phoebe's story unfolds, so does Sal's, and Sal renders a powerful account of her struggles to understand her mother's departure.

    MacLachlan, P. (1991). *Journey.* New York: Delacorte.

    Mama has packed her suitcase and gone away, but 11-year-old Journey won't accept the fact that she isn't coming back. His family tries to make things easier for him.

    Spinelli, J. (1990). *Maniac Magee.* New York: Harper Collins.

    Maniac runs and reads, although he never attends school. He changes other people's lives with books, either by reading from or by teaching the printed word.

    1. Discuss the strengths of some of the characters. Relate something factual and something attitudinal from both the book and "Ellen Ryan's Braided Rug" to your own personal experience (or to that of a friend or family member whom you are close to).
    2. Discuss two issues that were addressed both in the book for children or young adults and in the story of Ellen Ryan. Did you feel the information was presented convincingly in both?

- Critically view and analyze the film *My Left Foot.* Describe the intergenerational interactions and the interactions (including support and barriers) between the main character and his communities.
- Review academic research that describes intergenerational family literacy projects. How are the supports, both formal and informal, developed to empower the participants?
- Consider the ways your own attitudes discount older people? Create a letter that would develop or renew a meaningful relationship with an older person.

TAKING MISS KEZEE TO THE POLLS

OPTIONS FOR LISTENING

- Watch "Given a Chance," a video from the PBS War on Poverty series.
- Write personal responses in your journal. Please consider which information was not new to you? How do the political, social, and cultural issues of the civil rights movement relate to your own life? In what ways have voting rights and educational and social service programs changed as a result of this movement? Which information was new to you? How does this information relate to your present and future work?
- Read the selection, write any questions that you think of, and note personal connections.

Taking Miss Kezee to the Polls
by David Haynes
(from *Stiller's Pond*)

The rubber band "plinked" as I popped out the next three by five card. It said Miss Xenobia C. Kezee, who had voted faithfully in every election since 1925—local and national—was "in her 80's," a lifetime resident of St. Paul, and had lived at 887 Dayton for thirty-five years. She was a Democrat, although independent and opinionated. Her polling place: Hill Elementary on Selby. A college roommate, John—now Pastor John—who organized this "get out the vote drive" cautioned me that Miss Kezee would be ready to vote at 1:00 P.M. She expected promptness, courtesy, and cooperation. He would hear about it, and there would be consequences if she were in any way disappointed. Anything for the cause: I rang her doorbell with minutes to spare.

"Who is that and what you want? If it's you damn kids again I'm calling the police."

"Looking for a . . . Miss Kezee? I came to take her to vote."

"Stand over so as I can see you in my peephole. Who sent you?"

"Pastor Thomas from the church. You do remember that it's election day, Miss?"

"Hell, yes. Thomas didn't say nothin bout sendin no man. He usually send one of the sisters."

"Maybe you should call him."

"And maybe you should close your fresh mouth and stop givin orders." She opened the door. "You sit yourself down while I finish fixin up. I got me a gun back here. I'll blow your black ass to Mississippi if you tries anything, you understand me, boy?"

"Yes, ma'am."

This was not what I expected.

She scurried like a nervous squirrel around the visible areas of her house looking for valuables to hide from my pilfering hands. She was as thin as a willow branch and from the side curved like a question mark, her wrinkled face and hands the color of an old penny. Tied across her head were two silvery braids. She hustled back to her dressing area.

"What's your name, boy," she shouted from somewhere. I imagined her loading her gun.

"David Johnson, ma'am."

"You related to them Johnsons over on Iglehart?"

"No, ma'am. I don't know of them."

"Can't stand them fools, no how. Now, as I'm rememberin I ain't seen you up to the church neither. Let's see, you from around here? Seems like I know you."

"No. I originally come from St. Louis."

"St. Louis, huh." She popped her leathery-looking head around the corner like a turtle in order to get a better look at me. "I married me a man from down that way must be going on thirty years back. You familiar with some Huey's?" (Before I could say "no"), "Ornery nigger. Put his ornery butt out a here twenty-five years ago. A lazy dog. How you like my house, sugar? You don't see no dust, do you?"

"No, ma'am." But there was a dusty smell: like trunks of old books. The maple dining area was polished to a high luster. My fingers stroked velvety thistles and brambles that snaked upholstery on a comfortable couch and overstuffed chair. Heavy draperies drawn against the afternoon sun matched in a flowery blue. Doilies saddled the arms of the seating and strangled the tables like spider's webs, and the wide mantel of a little used fireplace carried framed pictures—so many that, one face blended into another in nightmarish collage. "Everything is beautiful. You have a lovely home, ma'am."

"You don't see no dust, do you. You let me know if you do. I got me a girl comin in to help me out—this little yella gal what live next door. She as lazy as the day is long. You let me know if you see any dust and I'll take care of the heifer. And don't you be 'ma'amin' me. You call me 'Miss Kezee' like other folks do. You got that, boy?"

"Yes. . . ." It was getting late, and I had two yet to get to the polls. "Are you about ready, Miss Kezee?"

She emerged from the back of the house wearing a fire-red wig, pink knee socks and a faded dress with tiny roses on it. "You in a hurry, sugar? Miss Kezee don't need no rush. You like this wig? I got me two more, not countin my church wig." She was chewing; one rumpled cheek blown up like a rusty balloon.

"You look very nice."

"Let's go, then." I held the screen door while she locked a half dozen dead bolts.

"Take Miss Kezee's arm while we walkin to the car, sugar."

"Afternoon, Miss Kezee," a round, dark woman fanning herself called from the porch next door. "How you feelin today?"

"Feelin just a little poorly today, May Ellen. Got a touch of this summer cold. You tell that Tonia she done a good job this week and I'll be payin her when my check come."

"Don't you worry bout that now. Looks like you got a new gentleman friend. Go on for yourself, girl." She waved a hand at her.

"I'm on my way to vote. Best be gettin your own self down there stead of messin in other folks' business."

"All right, then, Miss Kezee. You all have a nice trip."

She sputtered to herself as I let her into the car. "Ignorant, bit-ass, triflin gal. Bitch wouldn't vote if you paid her. All she got is baby on the brain. Done had a baby by every man in town—got five or six of em. Come in every color, they does."

"Now, you don't know that, Miss Ke. . . ."

"She got one bout your color. Maybe that's where Miss Kezee seen you before, huh?" She laughed like a coughing fit. "What kind of car this be, sugar?"

"It's a Dodge Colt."

"Sure is uncomfortable. Make a life there."

"J. J. Hill is on Selby, Miss Kezee."

Her look said, "Is you crazy?" I made a left.

"Left again and go on down here a ways on Marshall towards Central." She hummed quietly to herself and did double-takes at everyone on the street. "Who that?" she'd mumble.

"Stop!" she hollered at the top of her antique lungs. "Pull it over right here, darling. How you roll this window down?"

I showed her. We were stopped in front of a ramshackle vegetable stand on a vacant lot. An old couple like crows guarded a table of half hearted melons and pathetic tomatoes.

"Mattie! You got any kale today? Or spinach?"

"We bout out of everything today, Miss Kezee. Check back on Saturday."

"Uh huh." She waved and cranked the window arthritically. "Damn! Can't get nothing fresh. But, you like donuts, don't you, sugar? Make a right up here on Lexington."

"We should be gettin to the polls. We wouldn't want them to run out of ballots, would we?"

"Don't get an attitude, darlin. Miss Kezee don't vote without donuts. Another right up at University."

She hummed some more—noisy, tuneless songs—while I tried to figure out how to pay John back for this "little favor." She spit an oily wad into a napkin or rag she'd fished from my glove compartment.

"You keep your eyes open, sugar, and let me know if you see any hos out there on University so as Miss Kezee can give a little piece of her mind. Walkin the streets day and night like they owns it. And look up here. You see this dirty movie mess up here on the corner. That's the problem. They only put this here in the colored neighborhood. Can't even walk down here to the store no more."

"Don't get yourself too worked up now. . . ."

"Lord, look who comin out of . . . Miss Henry's neph . . . Stop! . . . Roll this window down!"

"Miss Kezee, I'm driving!" She got it halfway down by herself as we cleared the intersection.

"Get your black ass away from that nasty stuff before I call your mama and. . . ."

"Miss Kezee, please!"

"What you hollerin for? Donut place just up the next block." Miss Kezee's wig sat crooked on her head where she tried to force it out the car window. She bounced around like a sack of laundry as I turned into the steep and rutted parking lot.

"You come on in case they try to get smart with Miss Kezee. You may have to knock some heads for her."

There were only three or four trays of donuts left from the morning rush. A pimply faced high school-aged white boy gave us a friendly can-I-help-you. She stared him down.

"What you got fresh back there?"

"All our donuts are made up fresh daily, ma'am."

She looked at me over her glasses with a see-what-I-mean look, pointing the fire-red wig in the clerk's direction.

"These here chocolate cullas fresh?"

"Yes, ma'am."

"Better be. Give me four. No! Not that one. This one here with all the chocolate. How bout these long ones? They fresh?"

"Yes, ma'am. All our. . . . "

"Better be. Give me four. Uh huh. You getting the idea now. Why ain't child this age in school?"

"This is a work-study pro. . . ."

"These chocolate cake fresh?"

"Yes, ma'am. . . ."

"Better be. Give me four. That's an even dozen. You want anything, sugar? Pay up, then, and let's get to votin. Miss Kezee don't have all day."

I was in shock; I glared at her.

"Go ahead! Pay him!"

Good thing I'd brought some extra cash. I paid and Miss Kezee snatched up her box of donuts, clutching them to her chest like her own newborn baby. "Have a nice day," the clerk chirped.

"If these donuts is stale you go back in there and beat his ass, you hear." She whispered, I thought, loud enough for him to hear.

"Miss Kezee, I didn't expect to. . . ."

"Used to be when you went in them places it was 'Auntie this' and 'What y'all want in here.' You know what I'm saying. I can't stand them."

I dropped it and drove toward the polling place.

"You want some of these donuts, sugar?" Miss Kezee stuffed herself with chocolate which smeared her face. She wiped her hands on my vinyl seats.

"Bastard didn't put no napkins in this box. Have we got time to go back so you can rough him up?" She coughed her laugh again.

"No, ma. . . ." I caught myself just in time, and laughed with her. "I think I will have one of those." They were already half gone.

"Who we voting for today, baby?"

"This is the primary election for the general elections in the fall."

"You must think I'm crazy or something. I asked: who are we voting for today? We!" (Oh, that we.)

"Don't know that there's a recommended candidate as such. None of them seem like they're interested in our issues much."

"Haven't been a good one since Mr. Humphreys—H.H.H.! At least it seems that way to me. Voted for him for years. Is you married . . . how old is you, twenty-five, thirty?"

"Twenty-eight, and no."

"Why not? Can't find you one? I got a few little gals up to the church be interested in making a home with you." A damp, sincere hand gripped my arm.

"No, thank you, anyway, Miss Kezee." (I'd met John's parade of future homemakers on more than one occasion.) Miss Kezee hummed to herself and looked at the neighborhood.

"Things be changing fast. New houses. New people. Seems like I don't hardly recognize it no more. Sad." She nodded off to sleep.

"Miss Kezee, time to go in and vote." I shook her arm. This time her wig had slipped forward on her head. A drizzle of drool interrupted the chocolate beard she'd smeared on her chin.

"Just a second, sugar." She wiped with a perfumy handkerchief. "Do I look okay, baby? Might be some eligible mens in here of a certain age, if you know what I mean."

"You look fine. I'm eligible, aren't I?"

"What you want with a man with a cheap ass car like this here? Open the door for Miss Kezee and help her in."

"Good afternoon and who have we here?"

We have an old black woman who will cuss your condescending white self out if you keep it up, I thought to myself. Miss Kezee was unusually quiet. Leaning her weight like a sack of potatoes on my arm, she didn't answer.

"This is Miss Xenobia Kezee, here to vote," I said. Miss Kezee looked down from my arm to her shoes and back.

"Honey, is this your usual polling place?" The worker shouted as if to a small child. No answer from Miss Kezee. "Your granny's hard of hearing, huh? Is this where she votes normally, or is this her first time?"

"Miss Kezee has voted in every election for over fifty years."

"Oh yes, here we have her . . . on Dayton? Do you know . . . does she know how to use the booths?"

Since before you were born, I answered in my head. "She'll be fine," I said instead. I walked Miss Kezee to the booth.

"How we doin, sugar?" she whispered.

"You can't go in there with her." Miss Loud-Mouth masked her contempt with saccharine. I waved my hand at her in disgust. From within the booth I heard cursing and hurrumping; damn crooks-fools-cheats. Miss Kezee ambled out all weak and lost. I grabbed her arm and headed for the exit.

"See you in November, granny. You tell your granny I'll see her in November, okay?"

"Fuck you, too." I half-said over my shoulder.

Miss Kezee brightened up and lightened up considerably by the time I'd closed the car door.

"Sugar, Miss Kezee don't approve of no swearing. I'm a church going woman. Besides, ain't much good in saying what can't be heard, what with that meek whispering you does." Once again her dry hack.

"You were awfully quiet in there, Miss Kezee."

"Gotta give folks what they spect, baby."

"It's the nineteen-eighties, Miss Kezee. Nobody expects anything. Things have changed."

"Have they, sugar?" she snapped, and silently eyed me the two blocks back to her house where, in her parlour, she seemed remote—out of range.

"You sit a spell. I be right back." Moments later she returned wigless and wilted.

"You still here?" and then immediately, "I kindly thank you for all your troubles today, Mr. Johnson. I can't offer you no money."

"I wouldn't think of taking it. I enjoyed myself. Guess I should get my other two now."

"I won't be keeping you." She opened the door. "Thank you again." She gripped my arm.

I squeezed the wrinkled hand. "Goodbye, now, and take care."

"Sugar, I was one of the first, you know." And she closed and locked the door behind me.

I looked at my address: two blocks away. Spying a chocolate stained seat, I wiped it off with a forgotten, perfumy handkerchief.

OPTIONS FOR DIALOGUE

- In small groups, please discuss what were Miss Kezee's strengths? What were Mr. Johnson's strengths? What were Miss Kezee's barriers? What were Mr. Johnson's barriers?
- In this relationship, how did the age differences complicate the interactions? Which issues are related to cultural roles regarding age, gender, and position? How did the age differences enrich the relationship? What did Mr. Johnson learn?
- Discuss both characters' use of language that is considered insensitive and unacceptable in most cases. Discuss the issue of who can and cannot use labels.

SUGGESTIONS FOR ACTION

- Make some telephone calls or conduct some interviews to find out who votes and who doesn't vote in your community. Investigate why this is the case.
- Interview a person involved with voter registration. Arrange to accompany that person on a half day's activities. What did you learn?
- Interview a high school civics teacher regarding issues addressed in this section. What does this teacher teach? How are the priorities of the larger community reflected in the teacher's priorities for lessons?
- Interview an elder about the changing roles among age groups, genders, and ethnic groups in your community.
- Read one of the following books or a book with a related theme:

    Anzaldúa, G. (1987). *Borderlands*. San Francisco: Aunt Lute.
      Anzaldúa writes in a lyrical mixture of English and Spanish. Some of her essays and poems are about migrant workers, memories, the Aztec religion, and oppression of people who are culturally or sexually different.

Castillo, A. (1993). *So far from God.* New York: Norton.

This novel is set in the town of Tome, New Mexico. It tells the stories of Sofi and her four daughters.

Cisneros, S. (1991). *The house on Mango Street.* New York: Vintage.

Esperanza Cordero is a sensitive young Mexican-American girl eager to climb the social ladder, not in terms of money and reputation but with regard to her minority status as an ethnic female.

Haynes, D. (1995). *Somebody else's Mama.* Minneapolis: Milkweed Editions.

This story is about a modern African-American family. All the strengths and humor involved are realistically portrayed as the narrator tells the story of living with her mother-in-law.

Answer these questions about your reading:

1. In a few sentences, summarize the reading(s).
2. Why did you read this? What relationship to your personal or professional life does it have?
3. Do you feel that an accurate picture of the information was presented? Why or why not?
4. Which points from the reading did you *not* agree with? Why?
5. Discuss which information or opinions presented here were new to you.
6. Discuss any conversation about this subject that you may have had.

- Write a short skit based on two characters you've met in your life who illustrate the difficulties and the richness of their relationship in some of the same ways addressed in the story. Perform the skit for the class and discuss the implications.

RENGA

OPTIONS FOR LISTENING

- Choose one of these topics to free-write about in your journal:

1. Think of a way in which imagination helped you overcome a difficult situation. Is imagination/art (in a broad sense) important in your life now? How? Is there a way in which imagination has helped you connect with others?
2. Have you ever found a group of people who gave you support when you needed it by listening to your story? Free-write about this experience. What did it mean to you at the time? Now?

- Read the selection and note personal questions and connections.

Renga
by Kate Hallett Dayton

It started in an art class. Drawing, really. They called it sumi-e. Brought to the States in the 60's by Gary Snyder, Allen Ginsberg and the Beat Generation. Somewhere she'd read that Snyder spent the summer in a forest lookout making sumi-e paintings. Only after she read Pico Iyer's *The Lady and the Monk* did she decide she wanted to try some lessons. She didn't know the stories she heard would change her life more than the art form. She couldn't learn it from a book any more. Some Buddhist method. The teacher painted goldfish. There was plenty of time to talk while they worked.

Kobe came to the first class, her right eye covered by a black patch and her right jaw slack, the muscles in her cheek hollow. She was deaf in her right ear, she said, so they had to speak up. As it happened, there were three deaf people in the group. John used a cane and, at seventy, was the oldest.

On the second day, Kobe dispensed with the eye patch. She wanted to be accepted for who she was now, she said. Kobe, not Beth. She had shoved her short, dark hair under a yellow beret because the pool doors were locked that morning and she couldn't swim laps. She sat down next to John.

Jean, recently deaf in her left ear, began to talk about her patients. She worked as a physical therapist at Abbott Northwestern. She had helped a man whose Trans Am climbed a tree. He'd been out too long. Slowed his thinking, she said. Patients like him had helped her understand her own deafness.

What happened?

An inner ear infection, she said. She had learned to lip read only recently.

Moni asked if she could lip read for Kobe, too.

Misunderstanding, she said she wouldn't be able to read Kobe's lips. She turned to face the younger woman and asked how she had gotten that beautiful face.

Plastic surgery, Kobe answered, assuming Jean wondered about the repair of the damage and the damage itself.

A miracle, no question, John said quietly.

A road grader backed into the Austin Healey she was riding in, Kobe said.

God.

No, Pierre, she said. She had waited two hours for the ambulance. First they sent a helicopter, but it couldn't get in close enough. They had to go back and send an ambulance up.

All that time you waited, John said.

How could you do it? Moni asked.

Do what?

Lay there and wait.

Practice. Years in the ashram. The discipline saved my life. Focus. One focus. I could hear this meadowlark singing on the mountainside and I held on to that voice. I still do.

Where were you?

Chama River Valley near Abiquiu, New Mexico. A spiritual place. Monasteries. Mosques. Penitente adobes. Ashrams.

Pierre charged up behind a road grader perched on an impassable curve. He tried to pass.

I've driven the Colorado Gorge between Taos and the National Forest at night, Moni said. One lane. No room to pass. A pick-up driver parked on the ledge at the curve so I could inch past on the inside.

That's just like Pierre, Kobe said. He loved to hang out on the edge. This time the grader backed into the passenger side. She said it all matter-of-factly. Without bitterness. She couldn't jump, she said. The back was piled too high with luggage. She was right next to the drop off. Pierre couldn't see the guy backing up just as he tried to streak past. Kobe was silent for awhile.

So, where's the guy now? Moni asked.

Switzerland, Kobe said. He wasn't injured. Things were already over between them. That's probably why he was driving so fast. They wanted to get away from each other.

So, he just took off?

Moved on, she said. It was over between us anyway and this really freaked him, she said. She had stayed in the Albuquerque hospital for six weeks. It was really harder in the hospital than on the mountain side. No birds.

Only six weeks, Jean repeated, incredulous. You recovered fast. Some patients take months. . . .

When she met her mother in the airport, Kobe said, she couldn't stop crying. She hadn't seen her face since the bandages had come off. Her sister saved the situation, though. She said. "You're beautiful, Beth, like one of Picasso's women."

OPTIONS FOR DIALOGUE

- In your journals compare what is happening in "Renga" to your responses to one of the questions in the listening section. What does the Picasso reference mean? How do you feel about it?
- Share your responses in a group of four. How are your responses similar? Different?

SUGGESTIONS FOR ACTION

- Think about the ways in which the need for imagination/art and storytelling/listening is nourished in your practicum or in another situation in which you work. Discuss this in your group. How could these needs be better satisfied? Make an action plan based on your conversations.

NEWSBRIEF

OPTIONS FOR LISTENING

- Reflect on your being very moved (either positively or negatively) by an event that occurred in a community far away from your own present time and place. What happened? Why were you so affected? Were there people or events in your life that in some way connected you to this event? Describe how you were affected.
- Read the poem and write down your personal questions and connections.

Newsbrief

by Norita Dittberner-Jax

(from *What They Always Were*)

I read yesterday's paper that
in the Sudan, the refugees are so weak
they can't fight off the hyenas
plucking at the bodies of their dead
relatives. I only wanted a quick
once-over to keep myself informed.
I have a bridal shower to give,
a hundred things to clean and hide.
Emergency food has been sent
to the region, but most of it is not
reaching the refugees because of
the political situation. Everyone
is coming, my sisters and cousins,
ten nieces, not counting the bride;
I've ordered the centerpiece,
tulips and hyenas. Neither officials
of the Sudan nor neighboring Ethiopia
could be reached for a comment.
If the news account had been more abstract,
the shower would be perfect,
right down to the mints. As it is,
I'm planning a quieter celebration
because of the death in the family.

OPTIONS FOR DIALOGUE

• Explain to a partner something about what you wrote in the listening section. Relate both of your stories to the poem.

SUGGESTIONS FOR ACTION

• Conduct a media analysis: watch local and national television news broadcasts and read the front page and editorial of a daily newspaper for one week and write a report detailing your findings. Draw conclusions about the role of the media in the development and maintenance of social norms in terms of "us and them." Some things to note as you analyze the news might be who is in the news? How often are they represented? How are they portrayed? Are opposing forces in a conflict not considered casualties? Are the human situations of people from communities far away played down in terms of importance?

Schools: Mirrors of Hope

It is important to communicate to young people that the world is an unfin-
ished task. . . . An object, classroom, neighborhood, street, field of flowers shows
itself differently when encountered by different spectators. . . . the reality of
that object or classroom or neighborhood or field of flowers arises out of the sum
total of its appearances.

(Greene, 1992, p. 13)

Amerian society, as reflected in the schools, is a collage of strengths and barriers, voices seldom heard and voices heard more often. This section of the book presents for reflection the voices of authors expressing their schooling experiences. Their stories are windows into the experiences of students—experiences that are often not discussed or addressed. We hope the reader will be convinced of the potential of all students and learn what needs of children and families must be addressed by the schools.

The stories in this section also give us a picture of both some very effective teachers and some whose work we should question. We believe that the literature reiterates three important truths. First, all students and their families are an integrated entirety that schools must consider rather than planning just for "the second grader" or "the ninth grader." Second, teachers' beliefs and their life experiences cannot be separated from what they do in the classroom. Third, true multiculturalism is a combination of what someone believes and what he or she does—what action the person takes. Outstanding teachers and schools exemplify a pluralistic stance, an ever-expanding interest in and acceptance of many students' families, cultures, and differences.

FAMILY STRENGTHS AND THE SCHOOLS

We envision schools that will reflect the strengths of families. School contexts often reproduce mainstream society's biases regarding race, ethnicity, class, and gender. We concur with Swadener and Kessler (1991) when they point out that there is a relationship between "what we teach in school and the unequal outcomes of schooling based on social class, race, language or dialect, and gender" (p. 87). Polakow (1993) vividly points out how public schools are "a mirror reflection of public perceptions of the poor" (p. 107), thus perpetuating the tragic misconception of minority and poor children. Yet schools "can also be a place for change. As teachers learn to read children's texts more critically, they will help children learn to be resisting readers and writers of their own and other texts and explore through language new metaphors and structures that challenge" (Kamler, 1992, p. 32).

How do teachers and schools become aware of families' strengths and their desires, visions, realities, and repertoires? Greene (1986) notes, "I think of how little many teachers know about their students' diverse lives and thinking processes, how little they can know because of the paucity of dialogue in the classroom space" (p. 80). We can all listen to children and students as they tell us about their families. Children in schools are often vocal about their connections to their families. For example, one child expresses it in a poem describing "the day I was born." This child's fantasy about her birth uses the power of metaphor to connect herself, her family, and her world (Quintero & Rummel, 1995, p. 109).

On the day I was born
The sun shown
Bright n' high.
The birds started singing.
My mom and dad
Started to cry
'Cause they were so happy
I came.
On the day I was born
All the land animals
Started to gather
All around my room
To see me.
The rivers flowed
More than ever.
It rained
But after that
A beautiful rainbow appeared.
And my mom and dad
Said the rainbow was perfect
And so am I.
They said I made their lives happy.
On the day I was born
I made the sun show bright.
And made my mom and dad cry.
On the day I was born
Everyone was on my side.

LINGUISTICALLY AND CULTURALLY DIVERSE STUDENTS

The resilience of children and families from immigrant and minority communities is dramatic. In a family literacy class in El Paso, Texas, Arturo, age 5, and his mother, Ms. Montoya, were a family team that exemplified family strengths and educational priorities.

Arturo lived in central El Paso with his mother, father, 10-year-old brother, 19-year-old sister, and 21-year-old sister. The closeness of the family was an interwoven tapestry of both social context interactions and cognitive literacy development interactions. Often in literacy class he mentioned activities that he enjoyed doing with his brother and sisters. He made Valentine cards for his mother and father. Ms. Montoya reported in two separate parent interviews that she tells Arturo stories *every* morning. She also reported that she reads aloud from the Bible daily and that her home is "una M" (a library). Both Arturo and Ms. Montoya talked about the two sisters who are honor students at the University of Texas at El Paso. The tradition of literacy in the home and in the family seems to be taking root in Arturo and his brother, who are always on the honor roll at their elementary school. One day, Ms. Montoya reported that different family members read and reread Arturo's library book (*What Makes Day and Night*) the previous night because he didn't understand the concepts. Both Arturo and Ms. Montoya explained which family member said what to explain the phenomena of the Earth's rotation and revolution. The familial cohesiveness—both emotionally and interactively—in support of literacy and learning in general seems to contradict some research regarding the correlation between formal education for mothers (a high school diploma) and school success for their children (Stitcht & McDonald, 1989).

Ms. Montoya had only six years of formal schooling in Mexico. Yet her *biblioteca* (library) in her home, her literacy practices with her children, as well as her own habits show no lack of academic support. Furthermore, the academic success of all four children—those in elementary school and those in high school and the university—contradict the myth that, unless mothers obtain a high school diploma, children will not succeed in school. Weinstein-Shr (1992) cites research that discusses the Montoya's family strengths. The research indicates that when families participate in a variety of literacy activities, including home language literacy and activities in which children read to parents (Tizard, Schofield, & Hewison, 1992; Viola, Gray, & Murphy, 1986), the literacy development of the children is enhanced.

Related to home language literacy is the issue of home language use and how this affects schooling. Unfortunately, much of the available information about language, the literacy of non-English–speaking people, and the best schooling programs for these students is false. Students and their families who speak languages other than English can and should continue to nurture their home language while their English acquisition is in progress. The languages and literacies enrich each other; they do not prohibit the students' becoming fluent and literate in English. Urgency in teaching English to non-English–speaking children and concern about postponing children's exit from bilingual programs are unfounded according to linguists Hakuta and Snow (1996). There is no evidence that native language instruction holds students back, as proponents of "U.S. English only" claim.

Conversations for many bilingual children often take place in both languages. For example, during a lesson in a bilingual family literacy class in which the theme was "friends," the teacher asked Arturo, "What is a friend? Do you have a friend?" Arturo answered in English, "Next door house. Ruly." His mother explained, in Spanish, that Ruly is Raúl, a neighbor. When the children were asked to draw a picture of their friend, Arturo's mother commented with a laugh to Arturo as he drew, "No lo está viendo con mucha misericordia" (he isn't doing this with much mercy). She then guided, "No, Arturo, con un sólo color" (no, Arturo, with one color). Arturo asked his mom, "The shirt?" His oral code-switching ability occurred naturally in his interactions with his mother.[1] While she is not bilingual, she does have useful receptive code-switching ability, which served well in these interactions with her son and provided constant support for his Spanish language development.

---

[1]Definitions for code switching vary across the literature; the definition used here may correspond to what others call code shifting, code alternation, language alternation, or language mixing.

Lily Wong Fillmore (1991), a researcher in second language learning and early education, spearheaded a nationwide research project regarding the effects of inappropriate early education efforts to teach very young children a second language. The findings of this study show that not only do most of these children lose their first language in the process but there are tragic losses in family communication. Cultural values and traditional child-rearing principles are not communicated. Give-and-take conversations, which are the backbone of relationships, cease to exist. Wong Fillmore (1991) contends that "teachers and parents must work together to try to mitigate the harm that can be done to children when they discover that differences are not welcome in the social world represented by the school. Parents need to be warned of the consequences of not insisting that their children speak to them in the language of the home" (p. 345).

June Jordan (1987) speaks of this empowerment through language: "If we lived in a democratic state, our language would have to hurtle, fly, curse, and sing, in all the common American names, all the undeniable and representative participating voices of everybody here" (p. 30). Our goal is to encourage the development of schools where all the participating voices are heard.

The Montoya family's example is one of many in family literacy proving that culturally and linguistically diverse parents do participate in the education of their children. It is also another family that disproves the myth perpetrated by some school personnel that, because culturally diverse parents often do not attend school functions, meetings, or special classes, they don't care about their children. All parents care. Yet parents often do miss school events. Why? Because all families have problems that keep them from attending some events consistently. Drug abuse, child and spouse abuse, and extreme poverty—to the point of not having running water, heated shelter, warm clothes, or food—are some of the problems faced by families. Additional problems are lack of transportation, cold weather, and illness in the immediate or extended family.

It is important that the family's voice be part of the dialogue so that we "hear different voices tell their stories about how they experience education or schooling" (Bloch, 1991, p. 106). This brings to mind Delpit's (1988) research about codes of power. All children must have the opportunity to validate their own cultural experiences and learn mainstream culture's code upon which so much of school success is based. As Delpit (1988) has pointed out, persons with less power in societal arenas, including schools, are very aware of that power's existence. Furthermore, children and families who are not participants in the culture of power have shown over and over again that, when the rules of a culture are explicitly pointed out, acquiring power comes easier.

BARRIERS FOR SOME STUDENTS

Rigid classrooms are not limited to poor children; they cut across the socioeconomic spectrum and all age and grade levels. Goodlad (1984) has documented the predominance of teacher talk and lack of choice and decision making in elementary and secondary classrooms across the country. This becomes even more damaging when applied to the teaching of poor children. Polakow (1993) documents research delineating the ways in which poor children receive a class-based education that focuses on drill and rote learning and emphasizes mechanical skills. In these classrooms children who are different or poor, many of them bright, lively, and talkative, are constructed as impaired when they disrupt rigid classroom routines that permit neither time nor space for imagination, for transformation of what they are taught.

Lisa Delpit (1995) says,

> I believe that teaching the skills and perspectives needed for real participation in a democratic society is one of the most revolutionary tasks that an educator committed to social justice can undertake. It is only through such education that we can hope to create a truly just society where the most disenfranchised of our citizens can gain access to the political power needed to change the world. (p. 41)

THE TEACHERS AND THE PEDAGOGY

In a recent study (Rummel & Quintero, in press), we found that we can learn from teachers' life stories, their literacy teaching, and their personal uses of literacy. We investigated the effects of this reading on teachers' lives and explored how reading affects our becoming effective authors of our own lives. The interviews showed us that teachers had some common approaches to pedagogy consistent with and expanding upon the characteristics of "teacher as artisan" (Casey, 1993). They all exhibited a belief that it is their responsibility to find ways of engaging all their students in learning activity. They accepted responsibility for making the classroom an interesting, engaging place. They persisted in trying to meet the individual needs of the children in their classes, searching for what worked best for each student. In short, they continually searched for better ways of doing things.

Tracy Montero's Teaching Story

In her description of her use of resources, Tracy Montero gave us an outstanding example of the pedagogical practices that are based on beliefs shared by all the teachers in our study.

We've got an open library. We're uncomfortable with reading centers, Manny and I, because we feel like, what do you do for the kids who slip through the cracks? But we also use the traditional approach of pulling kids out on a needed basis. We may do the mini lesson which is focused on a skill or reader response to a book or anything that is related to reading that we feel is important that day. It may be with a partner or questions like, "How did this make you feel?" or "Did you notice the periods?" or "Were you able to read with voices?" or "Wasn't this a great story because. . . ?" or mini lessons about five to ten minutes in length. After that we have our reading time when kids have the rest of the forty five minutes or so to be into reading baskets. Those change weekly; they choose them on Friday and our library is entirely organized by theme so we have an animal bin, a transportation bin, seasons and holidays and poetry bins. While kids are in those baskets, Manny and I will pull kids out; I've got half the class and he's got the other half.

Some days I'll pull out one child who really needs help on one skill for that day and sometimes I'll pull out two or three. We'll read books and talk about it and meanwhile the other kids are in their reading baskets also responding in a reading log. It wasn't always an hour long. We started for ten minutes of reading and then we worked ourselves up. They really run it themselves. They've got their reading logs which they respond to and sometimes they don't and that's okay. We are not very structured in the sense that we tell them exactly what to do or how. It is sort of open-ended so that everyone has the chance to accomplish what he/she wants to do within that reading. (Montero, in press, pp. 109–110.)

Another example of teachers' continual search for what is best for their students is the involvement of students in learning that transcends curriculum, textbooks (often), and achievement tests. None of the teachers talked about testing as a measure of success. Rather, they are predisposed to emphasize students' efforts in defining success. These teachers see protecting and enhancing students' involvement in learning activities as their highest priority. If they run into a problem in doing this, they find ways around it. They are able to generate practical, specific applications of theories and philosophies; at the same time, they are able to see the whole picture. Day by day, these teachers are working hard to make schools better. Their teaching is an act of love, like that described by Hannah Arendt (1961):

> Education is the point at which we decide whether we love the world enough to assume responsibility for it and by the same token save it from that ruin which, except for renewal, except for the coming of the new and the young, would be inevitable. And education, too, is where we decide whether we love children enough not to expel them from our world and leave them to their own devices, nor to strike from their hands their chance of undertaking something new, something unforseen by us, but to prepare them in advance for the task of renewing a common world. (p. 196)

Cochran-Smith (1991) urges teachers to have the self-confidence to take risks in order to "teach against the grain." The teachers we interviewed showed us many ways in which we as teachers can be resistant and take risks for the ultimate goal of improving learning situations so that our students can become transformative intellectuals. Critical pedagogists strive for becoming what Giroux (1991) describes as "teacher as intellectual":

> If teachers are to take an active role in raising serious questions about what they teach, how they are to teach, and the larger goals for which they are striving, it means they must take a more critical role in defining the nature of their work as well as in shaping the conditions under which they work. In my mind, teachers need to view themselves as intellectuals who combine conception and implementation, thinking and practice. (p. 19)

Mary Tacheny's Teaching Story

The teachers in our study showed critical thought and continuing study and became resistant teachers. They also were committed to creating an optimum learning environment in the classrooms. This environment includes the language and the social and emotional environments that are also connected to the intellectual environment. Mary Tacheny, a teacher in St. Paul, Minnesota, described the strength and acceptance of her first-grade classroom community.

One thing I have noticed about kids with different backgrounds and diversity is that there isn't a lot of judging. I have seen a lot of empathy grow in children. They rally around each other when someone is low or has had a bad point and the kids are kind of like, "don't mess with my people, we're all in this together." They are good buddies. I had one boy talk about this story from Cambodia. He was talking about how his mother saw

one of her children killed and there was nothing she could do and she had to keep run-
ning with the baby or she might die, too. This is not something the kids would have seen
even on TV. The different ways that the kids respond! Diversity is something I wish that
every school had. Even when you are talking about counting. Children come at it from
so many different ways. If they are counting in another language they naturally start
sharing their language. If you happen to be reading a book with a cultural background
and a child has connections they show a lot of ethnic pride. I think diversity lends itself
to hopefully, someday, erasing prejudice. We should all realize that we have a lot of things
in common and that we all have past histories. What we bring to the present and where
we want to be in the future are parts of who we are but I think we are parts of each other's
stories now. (Tacheny, in press, pp. 226–227)

Vicki Brathwaite's Teaching Story

In the section introducing Theme Web I, we discussed our belief that story is central
in classrooms of transformative teachers. These teachers sit in circles to read and write;
stories appear and reappear; reading leads to writing leads to reading. The human circle of literacy is a central metaphor for Vicki Brathwaite. She told us:

My grandmother used to tell stories; she was from the West Indies and she used to tell a lot
of folk tales that her mother had told her when she was growing up. We would lie in bed to-
gether every afternoon and she would tell those stories to me. (Brathwaite, in press, p. 163)

Vicki belongs to circle groups of professionals who share their literate experiences.
She nurtures her own literacy, and this becomes nurturance for her students. The following story describes a support group of readers/writers/teachers.

Some of the people who were in that original group have since gone on to other jobs so it
wasn't easy for us to meet here in school. So we decided that we would have a book group
and we formalized it, we called it Brown Women and we meet once a month at each oth-
ers homes. That has continued for about eight years now. At first we started reading a list
of black fiction; we do read some nonfiction. Then we started reading multi-ethnic women
such as Amy Tan. Really everything! We just bring out critiques from the Times, or from
Essence Magazine or what we have heard, everything! We keep notebooks, write journals,
we sit around the table and say what we are going to read next and from that. There are
about fourteen members and it is not only a time to talk about books but it is like a sup-
port group talking about life and being social. I think all of us agree that Beloved *by Toni*
Morrison is our favorite. Another favorite is A Lesson Before Dying *by Ernest Gaines.*
It is a social kind of thing. We look forward to it. (Brathwaite, in press, pp. 168–169)

In Vicki's description one sees a literacy community forming. As Keen (1988)
says, "stories open us up to the stories of others, as common and singular as our own.
They are the best way we have found to 'overcome loneliness, develop compassion and
create community' " (pp. 46–47). Not surprisingly, Vicki is always searching for books
that will help her students feel pride in their own identity and heritage and learn about
diversity and the complexity of American society.

My students like reading about people in other cultures, different countries and their popula-
tions and landmarks. Animals are always a favorite; dinosaurs are a hit and whales too. In-

sects are real big. Another favorite book is The Piñata Maker. *It is a Mexican nonfiction book; it is a photo/essay of master pinata maker and it is in English and Spanish. The children love that book. They like books from their experiences. Children who are bilingual love books that are written in both languages and speak of their experiences from their native country. Asian children love to identify with* Omi Wong *and other Asian books. Children love to identify with books and solve problems through characters in books. Children just love to be read to and I think adults do too. You have no behavior problems when you really speak from your heart about, "I'm reading this to you for a purpose and I want you to find out what this character does and says," and you ask if, from their real experience, they can relate to it. It sort of invites them into the book regardless of how you are going to share it with them. You have to catch children's attention. I mean, if you have a tv next to you and you want to read to them, what are you going to do? You have to be real and correct.* (Brathwaite, in press, pp. 170–171)

Raúl Quintanilla's Teaching Story

As we have said, the literature in this section informs us about the metaphors the authors have for schooling. We believe we have much to learn from these metaphors. Metaphors structure our thinking and understanding of events and consequently our behavior (Lakoff & Johnson 1980). Clandinin (1986, p. 142) found that the verbal imagery of teachers often clusters around metaphors such as "planting a seed" or "making a home" and that these metaphors reveal the "complex coalescence of personal and professional experience and of theory and practice." Munby (1986) attempted a concordance of related imagery to see how teachers use metaphor to construct their professional world and how metaphor studies could aid understanding of teachers' professional knowledge. The metaphors and beliefs that drive teacher artisans give them a sensitivity to the needs of the child within a particular social context. This awareness of the importance of social context leads them to look at methodology differently. It directs the professional choices that they make.

The images of schooling found in the stories and poems in this book reveal authors' experiences as students. Likewise, this literature gives us insight into the metaphors held by teachers. In our teacher interview study (Rummel & Quintero, in press), teachers' life metaphors took on generative importance. For example, as a child, Raúl, who is now a teacher in St. Paul, Minnesota, saw the sun as a light leading to meaning. He now follows this metaphor through his reading and teaching.

I had a teacher in seventh grade, because we were really poor and everything, she gave me a set of encyclopedias. The old ones. Real small. I just wanted to know everything. It reminds me of the Hmong students now. Like I taught seventh and eighth grade last year. If they have nothing to do they will get a dictionary and they will just read the words. I don't know if they are comprehending but they just like looking and looking. The visual aids. (Quintanilla, in press, p. 204)

Bill Simpson's Teaching Story

Another way of thinking about the sources of knowledge for teaching concerns communities that may inform our knowledge base, cultures that may exist in harmony with one another or clash and cause tension for the teacher (Gee, 1992). Comparing and contrasting personal metaphors with institutional metaphors might be a useful means for preservice teachers to develop alternative ways of thinking about teaching and for considering the ethical implications of holding one or another conception of teaching. It is very important to understand that these personal metaphors are life metaphors arising out of early language experiences fed by experience with books and media. It tells us that these generative metaphors must be uncovered. "It is difficult for me," Maxine Greene tells us, "to teach educational history or philosophy to teachers-to-be without engaging them in the domain of imagination and metaphor. How else are they to make meaning out of the discrepant things they learn?" (1995, p. 99). We would extend the importance of imagination and metaphor to all preservice and inservice methods classes.

The story Bill Simpson told in his interview is a strong example of the power of metaphor fed by early literacy to affect both personal life and teaching. From his reading as a child Bill developed a metaphor of life as adventure. For him it nurtured the sense of "what is out there, what I can reach if I try," which is described by Maxine Greene (1992). Through the language of reading Bill was able to begin to live adventure and to bring dreams into being for himself and his students.

Bill's life and teaching exemplify a pluralistic stance. His love of adventure has led him, first through books and then in actual experience, to an ever-expanding interest in and acceptance of many cultures and differences.

And I always lived in this life of reading and then began to live the adventure even when I wasn't reading. And I still do. Now books kind of lead me to places. A book led me to a really fascinating place this summer. To northern Russia. I had been there before but I went again to go on a kayaking trip. This book I read two years ago called They Took My Father *was a story of Finnish people from the iron range moving back to Russia in the nineteen thirties during the depression. They got into Russia and found out it wasn't the place that it was claimed to be and then the border was closed and they couldn't leave. So they lived their lives in Russia as U.S. citizens from Minnesota. It just blew my mind that up to 10,000 people had done this. So I found a way to get to that area. It was a wonderful adventure. It was like a Tom Sawyer adventure; every day was a new episode. So books do that for me; they lead me places.*

Every summer I take a trip to the Arctic. Way up north in Canada to the High Arctic. The special thing about that area is the remoteness. I like cold weather. I like the Inuit people. Mainly, it is the last true wilderness left on earth. I love that you can go a month and never see a sign of a human being. I need that. I have read much of the Arctic literature, all of the explorers. (Simpson, in press, pp. 48–49)

Bill used the metaphor of life as adventure to open up wider worlds outside his experience through reading. He actively engages in photography. This art making is clearly a part of both his self-nurturance and his teaching as he presents slide shows and brings his students in contact with students from other countries. In our interview study (Rummel & Quintero, in press), art and literature are parts of the self-nurturance of each teacher and also become ways in which children are nourished. The path that leads from the school into the broader community flows directly from literacy-enriched metaphor and art. "It takes imagination to engage with literature and other art forms," Greene (1995, p. 141) tells us. "Encounters of this sort push back the boundaries. . . . They locate learners in a wider world, even as they bring them in closer touch with their own actualities."

Bill Simpson's connections among reading for self-nurturance, adventuring, and work for children become global:

We started a sister city in Ginger, Uganda with Stillwater. Then we started a special school project with our school and a school in Uganda. There are three thousand students in this school and no books. So a friend of mine started this program. This month the community and schools in Stillwater are bringing in their favorite new books. And also fifty cents for postage. And then we are shipping them to Africa. So my goal is to go over there and visit this school. It would be nice to set up some kind of exchange program with students. (Simpson, in press, pp. 51–52)

For many of the teachers we studied global perspectives, in a concrete and complex sense, bind academics with the affective influences they and their students have on each other. They would agree with Tracy Montero, who said:

I like to know about people in other cultures. I think that they need to be surrounded by maps just to let them know the world view; that there is something else out there besides the little place where you live. I think kids like to know about other places and other people. (Montero, in press, p. 109)

Research indicates, however, that achieving this global perspective and multidirectional interaction between academics and sociocultural dynamics is difficult. Will teachers in the cultural context of the schools do what has to be done in order to live in their culture? As society (and therefore the school) becomes more multicultural, the demands for pluralistic and multicultural teaching become greater. Lily Wong Fillmore (1990) comments on the importance of the teacher role in society: "The teachers are cultural and linguistic bridges connecting the worlds of the home and the classroom; they facilitate the children's entry to school by building on what the children have learned in their homes" (pp. 5–6).

Pamela Russell's Reading Story

The teachers in our study are also global in their reading interests. Their reading is characterized by the absence of a negative, limiting political correctness, and they are courageous and deliberate in their choice of books—some from newer ethnic writers, some from a more traditional canon. For example, David Haynes, an African American who writes novels centered on African-American characters, is an English major who shares Shakespeare with fourth-grade children in St. Paul. Bill Simpson, whose favorite author is Barry Lopez, reads Doris Lessing and Cristina García. Vicki Brathwaite, whose favorite author is Toni Morrison and who searches for all available multicultural literature for her students, talked also about reading the Narnia chronicles with third-grade children in Brooklyn. These teachers know what they like and need, and they read for those purposes. West describes this wide-ranging attitude: "We listen to Ludwig Beethoven, . . . Stevie Wonder or Kathleen Battle, read William Shakespeare, Anton Chekhov, Ralph Ellison, Doris Lessing, . . . Toni Morrison or Gabriel García Marquez,—not in order to undergird bureaucratic assents or enliven cocktail party conversations, but rather to be summoned by the styles they deploy for their profound insight, pleasures and challenges" (West, 1990, p. 31).

Pamela Russell, a primary teacher in Brooklyn, exemplifies this in a story from her own reading history:

I loved Judy Blume. I just devoured everything that she has. Because I went to a parochial school, I was there from K–8 and they were sort of like, "Okay, we have to be careful what we give the kids to read." But I remember I had one teacher, Mrs. Gallager, who was a very liberated woman and she put some of Judy Blume's books in our reading area. We had a rug where you could lay down and I would just read those Judy Blume books. There's another author, Louise Maryweather, and she has this book, Daddy Was a Number Runner. *Just the title of that book enticed me. It is about a young woman of color who is coming of age and growing up in Harlem. Her experiences were so different and I was just so curious. The book had curses in it and so I wanted to read it. It was just a beautiful story and it is one that I've gone back to and read as an adult. As an adult, I worked for a publishing company and Judy Blume's book,* Wifey, *came out and I couldn't wait to get that book and when I worked for the publishing company I found out that she was one of their writers. They had this room where books were all stocked so I went in and got all of her books. I couldn't wait for her to write another adult book but she didn't. She was one of my favorite authors.* (Russell, in press, p. 67)

Pamela shows what Cornell West advises:

The most desirable option for people of color who promote the new cultural politics of difference is to be a critical organic catalyst. By this I mean a person who stays attuned to the best of what the mainstream has to offer—its paradigms, viewpoints and methods—yet maintains a grounding in affirming and enabling subcultures of criticism. Prophetic critics and artists of color should be exemplars of what it means to be intellectual freedom-fighters, that is, cultural workers who simultaneously position themselves within (OR ALONGSIDE) the mainstream while clearly aligned with groups who vow to keep alive potent traditions of critique and resistance. (West, 1990, p. 33)

Pamela is using her honesty, strength, and skill to encourage this in her students. As Greene (1988) maintains, "the growing ability to look at even classical works through new critical lenses has enabled numerous readers, of both genders, to apprehend previously unknown renderings of their lived worlds" (p. 129).

The teachers quoted in this chapter and other outstanding activist teachers want for their students the awakening that they themselves have experienced, the awakening described by Barry Lopez (1990) at the end of *Crow and Weasel:*

"I will urge my children to do what I have done," said Weasel. "Whether they are young men or young women, I will urge them to go."

"That is new thinking for you," said Crow.

"Our journey, seeing different ways of life, has made me wonder about many things," said Weasel. They stood in silence together, their breath rising in a fog.

"One day perhaps my son will travel with your son," said Weasel. "They will return and the people will listen to what they have to say. And then their children. It will go on like that, and that way our people will look into the heart of wisdom."

Crow pondered his friend's words. . . . "Imagine our daughters," he said. "Traveling." (p. 79)

READER-GENERATED PROBLEM POSING ABOUT SCHOOLING

We hope the literature chosen for this section helps the readers in their "traveling." For the Schooling Theme Web, we have chosen selections in which several critical aspects of schooling, teachers, and learners are presented. These issues are told through the story and poetry selections—not often the format of schooling discussions in the media or the academic press. We maintain that, with the help of the authors of the literature, the reader can reflect on the issues surrounding teaching and learning in a profound way. Again, we do not want to impose our interpretation of the individual pieces, but we do encourage listening, dialogue, and action that consider the student as an individual who is part of family and community. We create the context for readers to pose questions and encourage consideration of the strengths of students and their families and the barriers they face daily. We also believe the literature presents some human and soulful aspects of teachers not often captured in other reports.

The short story *Busted: A Boy's True Tale of Real Life in a Big City Junior High School* by David Haynes begins this section because of its themes: strength of family, the failure of school personnel to acknowledge or support these strengths, and the effects of this failure on a gifted African-American adolescent. "There is probably a big sign over my head that says, 'It's all his fault.' It has a big red arrow pointing in my direction at all times," the narrator begins his story.

The Whispering Cloth is the text from a picture book written by Pegi Deitz Shea, illustrated by Anita Riggio and with illustrations of stitching by You Yang. It tells the story of Mai, a Hmong girl living in a refugee camp in Thailand, who learns from her grandmother how to use her imagination to affirm and transform her life through art. The story has much to tell us about children learning in their families and the creative strength of the human spirit.

Rufus at the Door (1991) by John Hassler gives us a vivid example of "a village raising a child" and the destructive effects of labeling on children and their families.

Following this story, four poems convey different images of schooling. In "Southeast Asia, Second Grade" by Rosann Lloyd and "A First Day" by Kevin Fitzpatrick, we hear the voices of teachers learning from their students. "My Slanted View" by Sara Ryung Clement gives us the critical perspective of a high school student, and "Lessons From Space" by Rosann Lloyd is written in the voice of a young child. Both poems describe beliefs about school.

Spring Concert (1995) by Stephen Peters tells the story of a 13-year-old boy whose father is moving to a different part of the country and of a teacher who has no connection to the real lives of her students. *The Great Circle of These Things* by Tom Peacock calls attention to the cultural conflict resulting from a school's unwillingness to validate alternative ways of learning within families and cultures.

Writing Down Secrets first appeared as a *New Yorker* article by Manhattan teacher Sara Mosle. In it she weaves her own story with the stories of her third-grade children. She gives her students the opportunity to use journal writing to give voice to their own realities in terms of culture, social issues, and cognitive development, and she responds to their writing, creating an ongoing dialogue in which she becomes the learner. In "Lexicon of Exile," a poem by Aleida Rodríguez, we focus on issues of language in schooling and, through language, bringing the home into the place of learning.

The next selections were taken from *Reach for the Moon,* a book that is a collaborative effort of high school student Samantha Abeel, watercolorist Charles Murphy, and English teacher Roberta Williams. We present the voice of Samantha, who struggled with learning disabilities and for whom school was a nightmare until she discovered her unique talents, and the voice of her English teacher, who gives us a way to define the concept of teacher. Samantha's poem, "To a Special Teacher," illustrates her metaphors for the empowering teacher.

Finally, the short story *The Boy without a Flag* by Abraham Rodriguez, Jr., provides a link between this section of the book (which focuses on schooling) and the next—the theme web on family. This story brings together many of the issues uncovered in this section, especially the conflict between learning valued by school personnel and learning that occurs in the family. The story makes vivid the negative effect of this conflict on children who are caught between school and family cultures and brings us full circle to the discussion at the beginning of the section.

REFERENCES

Abeel, S. (1993, 1994). Samantha's story: Finding the key to learning [and] To a special teacher. In *Reach for the moon.* Duluth, MN: Pfeifer-Hamilton.

Arendt, H. (1961). *Between past and future.* New York: Viking.

Bloch, M. N. (1991). Critical science and the history of child development's influence on early education research. *Early Education and Development, 2*(2), pp. 95–108.

Brathwaite, V. (In press). Vicki Brathwaite. In M. K. Rummel & E. P. Quintero, (Eds.), *Teachers' reading/teachers' lives* (p. 166). Albany, NY: SUNY Press.

Casey, K. (1993). *I answer with my life: Life histories of women teachers working for social change.* New York: Routledge.

Clandinin, D. (1986). *Classroom practices: Teacher images in action.* London: Falmer.

Clement, S. R. (1995). My slanted view. *Sticky Rice, 1*(1), 11.

Cochran-Smith, M. (1991). Learning to teach against the grain. *Harvard Education Review, 61*(3), pp. 279–310.

Deitz, P. (1995). *The whispering cloth.* Sherman, CT: Boyds Mill.

Delpit, L. (1988). The silenced dialogue: Power and pedagogy in educating other people's children. *Harvard Education Review, 58*(3), 280–297.

Delpit, L. (1995, Winter). Teaching for social justice: An activist forum. *Democracy & Education,* pp. 10–24.

Fitzpatrick, P. (1988). A first day. In *Down on the corner* (p. 10). Minneapolis: Midwest Villages & Voices.

Gee, J. P. (1992). What is literacy? In P. Shannon (Ed.), *Becoming political* (pp. 21–28). Portsmouth, NH: Heinemann.

Giroux, H. (1991). The politics of postmodernism: Rethinking the boundaries of race and ethnicity. *Journal of Urban and Cultural Studies, 1*(1), 5–38.

Goodlad, J. (1984). *A place called school.* New York: McGraw-Hill.

Greene, M. (1986). Reflections and passion in teaching. *Journal of Curriculum and Supervision, 2*(1), 68–81.

Greene, M. (1988). *The dialectic of freedom.* New York: Teachers College Press.

Greene, M. (1992). The passions of pluralism: Multiculturalism and the expanding community. *Educational Researcher, 22*(1), 13–18.

Greene, M. (1995). Notes on the search for coherence. In J. Beane (Ed.), *Toward a coherent curriculum: The 1995 ASCD yearbook* (pp. 139–145). Alexandria, VA: ASCD.

Hakuta, K., & Snow, C. (1996). The role of research in policy decisions about bilingual education. *NABE News, 9*(3), 1, 18–21.

Hassler, J. (1991). Rufus at the door. In J. Agee, R. Blakely, & S. Welch (Eds.), *Stiller's Pond* (pp. 336–342). Minneapolis: New Rivers Press.

Haynes, D. (1996). Busted: A boy's true tale of real life in a big city junior high school. In *Heathens* (pp. 33–44). Minneapolis: New Rivers Press.

Jordan, J. (1987). *On call.* Boston: South End Press.

Kamler, B. (1992). *The social construction of gender in early writing.* Paper presented to the American Educational Research Association, San Francisco.

Keen, S. (1988). The stories we live by. *Psychology Today, 22*(12), 46–47.

Lakoff, G., and Johnson, M. (1980). *Metaphors we live by.* Chicago: University of Chicago Press.

Lloyd, R. (1987). Southeast Asia, second grade. In J. Moore & C. Waterman (Eds.), *Minnesota writes: Poetry* (p. 146). Minneapolis: Milkweed Editions/Nodin Press.

Lloyd, R. (1996). Lessons from space. In *War baby express* (pp. 40–41). Duluth, MN: Holy Cow!

Lopez, B. (1990). *Crow and weasel.* New York: HarperCollins.

Montero, T. (In press). Tracy Montero. In M. K. Rummel & E. P. Quintero (Eds.), *Teachers' reading/teachers' lives* (pp. 106–120). Albany, NY: SUNY Press.

Mosle, S. (1995, September 18). Writing down secrets. *New Yorker,* pp. 52–61.

Munby, H. (1986). Metaphor in the thinking of teachers: An exploratory study. *Journal of Curriculum Studies, 18*(2), 197–209.

Peacock, T. (1995). The circle of things. Unpublished story.

Peters, S. (1995). Spring concert. Unpublished story.

Polakow, V. (1993). *Lives on the edge.* Chicago: University of Chicago Press.

Quintanilla, R. (In press). Raúl Quintanilla. In M. K. Rummel & E. P. Quintero (Eds.), *Teachers reading/teachers' lives* (pp. 203–218). Albany, NY: SUNY Press.

Quintero, E., & Rummel, M. K. (1995). Voice unaltered: Marginalized young writers speak. In E. B. Swadener & S. Lubeck (Eds.), *Children and families at promise: The social construction of risk* (pp. 97–117). Albany, NY: SUNY Press.

Rodriguez, A., Jr. (1992). The boy without a flag. In *The boy without a flag* (pp. 11–30). Minneapolis: Milkweed Editions.

Rodríguez, A. (1996). Lexicon of exile. *Progressive, 60*(2), 39.

Rummel, M. K., & Quintero, E. P. (In press). *Teachers' reading/teachers' lives.* Albany, NY: SUNY Press.

Russell, P. (In press). Pamela Russell. In M. K. Rummel & E. P. Quintero (Eds.), *Teachers' reading/teachers' lives* (pp. 59–71). Albany, NY: SUNY Press.

Simpson, B. (In press). Bill Simpson. In M. K. Rummel & E. P. Quintero (Eds.), *Teachers' reading/teachers' lives* (pp. 233–234). Albany, NY: SUNY Press.

Sticht, T. G., & McDonald, B. A. (1989, January). *Making the nation smarter: The intergenerational transfer of cognitive ability* [Executive Summary]. San Diego: Applied Behavioral and Cognitive Sciences.

Swadener, E. B. & Kessler, S. (1991). Introduction to the special issue. *Early Education & Development, 2*(2), 85–94.

Tacheny, M. (In press). Mary Tacheny. In M. K. Rummel & E. P. Quintero (Eds.), *Teachers' reading/teachers' lives* (pp. 233–234). Albany, NY: SUNY Press.

Tizard, J., Schofield, W., & Hewison, J. (1992). Symposium: Reading collaboration between teachers and parents in assisting children's reading. *British Journal of Educational Psychology, 52,* 1–15.

Viola, M., Gray, A., & Murphy, B. (1986). *Report on the Navajo parent child reading program at the Chinle Primary School.* Chinle, AZ: Chinle School District.

Weinstein-Shr, G. (1992). Learning lives in the post-island world. *Anthropology & Education Quarterly 23*(2), 160–165.

West, C. (1990). The new cultural politics of difference. In R. Ferguson, M. Gener, T. Min-ha, & C. West (Eds.), *Out there: Marginalization and contemporary cultures* (pp. 19–38). New York: New Museum of Contemporary Art; Cambridge MA: MIT Press.

Wong Fillmore, L. (1990). Latino families and the schools. In *California perspectives: An anthology.* Los Angeles: Immigrant Writers Project.

Wong Fillmore, L. (1991). When learning a second language means losing the first. *Early Childhood Research Quarterly, 6*(3), 323–347.

BUSTED: A BOY'S TRUE TALE OF REAL LIFE IN A BIG CITY JUNIOR HIGH SCHOOL

OPTIONS FOR LISTENING

- Go back to when you were 14. Reflect on and write about some things you liked about your immediate family. What do you remember hating about your family? If you could ask family members some questions now about that time, what would the questions be?
- What do you remember about the atmosphere of your junior high school? Write some details about classmates, teachers, and the physical environment.
- Listen to the message a television commercial is conveying about, and to, young teens. Write down the details that support your impressions as well as any critical questions you have.
- Listen to the message a television news report is conveying about, and to, young teens. Write down the details that support your impressions. What questions would you like to ask the producers of the program?
- Read the selection, write any questions that you think of, and note any personal connections.

Busted: A Boy's True Tale of Real Life in a Big City Junior High School
by David Haynes
(from Heathens)

I hate my life. I hate school, I hate all teachers, I hate St. Paul. Some days I hate my mom and dad and Verda. I especially hate Mr. Smutts and Ione's little boy Butchie, who is a sick mental.

There is probably a big sign over my head that says "It's all his fault." It has a big red arrow pointing in my direction at all times.

Here is an example. I am walking down the hall of Hennepin Junior High School. It is hell on earth here and that is not an exaggeration. The toilets are always overflowing, the food is rancid, and Troy Jackson told me that he saw a rat in the boys locker room carrying off someone's tennis shoe, and I believe him because he is one of the few people here who is not a dweeb. It was in the middle of second period and I had just gotten to school because Marcus who is my dad did not get out of bed in the morning to go to his own job until almost 9:00 because he says he is tired, but really he is depressed because LaDonna who is my mom is in jail. So I was late too, though it was not my fault as you can see. Mr. Smutts, who is the assistant principal and who is known to be real mean and hateful, stops me in the hall.

"What's your name, young fella?"

I do not like being called things like young fella. Please, remember that. Thank you.

I put up my hands. I figure there is less chance they will shoot if you just throw up your hands. Mr. Smutts is wearing a suit which has more colors in it than they have flavors at Baskin Robbins. He is a white man who is one of those white men who is all the same color. He is the color of Cheerios. He is probably wearing that suit so he does not fade into the walls. In response to what is my name I say, "Huh?"

"You come with me," he says.

So, I am under arrest. Do not let anyone tell you that you have Constitutional rights if you are twelve, because it is not true. You might as well live in Russia or one of those kinds of places.

I keep my hands up in the air and he puts his hand on my shoulder to walk me to the office. I know the way.

Please, do not ever touch me, thank you, not unless there is something crawling on me like a black widow spider, and especially not if you are the white principal of the junior high.

He takes me in a room which has chairs all around a table. There is going to be a meeting or something here, you just know it.

"Sir," I say, in my most weak and serious type voice. I can use this voice on my grandma Verda and she will give me cash or anything else. "Sir, can I ask you a question?"

"Put your hands down first," he says.

I drop my hands which slam down on the table because they have gone to sleep on me. Sometimes I lay on my back on my bed at home and just hold my arm up over my head and see how long I can keep it there. It hangs there almost like it was hanging from a string until it feels dead and like it isn't even attached to me anymore. Then it comes slamming down hard like it did just now and the blood comes rushing back in, all tingly and stuff. "Excuse me for living," I say.

"There's no excuse for your ilk," Smutts says, which is pretty much uncalled for, wouldn't you say, and ought to be reported to someone but a person wouldn't even know where to begin since, as we all know, they are all in it together.

"Forget it," I say, and he tells me to sit over there with the rest of them. The rest of them are Demetrius, LT, Tony J. and Cool. They are sitting in four chairs in front of a chalkboard. They are probably the four toughest people at Hennepin. You would not want to mess with them, even if you were the assistant principal. Marcus, who is my dad and who is also a teacher, says that when LT was in sixth grade he kicked out the ceiling tiles in the bathroom, touched a live wire and shorted out the electricity in a ten block area of St. Paul. Marcus said that LT said it only stung a little bit. Needless to say these are not the people I hang with. They all got on their shades and are dangling toothpicks from their mouths and snapping their gum. They are all leaned back with their feet up, casual. They could be at home watching "Yo MTV Raps." They all have on Raiders caps and lots of black clothes. It means they are in a gang or something even if this is only St. Paul and they would have you believe there are no problems here of any kind if you watch the news on TV. Just look around this room. Me I am wearing a Vision Wear shirt and a really loud pair of jams. I stick out like dog doo in a snow bank.

Smutts slams down his fist. "Get those feet down. Get those glasses off. Sit up in those chairs. Now." Me, who was already down, off and up, have to put my hands on my knees to keep them from shaking. Next to me I notice the Wild Bunch seem to be shaking just a little bit too.

"You youngsters are in some serious trouble here, and I mean serious. We're talking police. I suggest your attitudes reflect it." Cheerios man has his hands clasped behind his back and is walking back and forth like a duck, his head bobbing up and down with each step. He's one of those popeyed dudes too. I'm trying to remember who it is he reminds me of.

"On this piece of paper you are to put down the full names and phone numbers of whatever adults claim to be responsible for you. Do it now. I suggest no foolishness."

Well, I guessed I was in quite a spot then, because unlike my brothers in crime, whose mothers were probably at this minute at home watching the soaps, that is unless they were down at the bank cashing the welfare checks or standing doorwatch at some crack house, my life had recently gotten more complicated. First we have Marcus, who is supposed to be a teacher over at the Hawthorne School, which is apparently according to him and others, as much of a hell as this hellhole and is also full of a lot of crazy retards like Butchie Simpson the mental pervert who lives next door to me and whose mother has the biggest set of headlights I have ever seen. I know all about Hawthorne school because I actually went there for a month last year and it was so awful that I threatened to become bulemic if Marcus and LaDonna didn't get me out of there, and I actually had to drink four glasses of salt water and throw up on the Domino's Pizza to get them to believe me. Which was okay because we were all getting sick of Dominos anyway seeing as we have to have it twice or three times a week because Marcus gets too stressed out to cook and LaDonna claims to not understand really how the oven works even though Ione has given her lessons on a regular basis for as long as I can remember. Ione is a good cook, too, if you can stand the fact that she has to say a twenty-five minute prayer before each meal and then has to ask her husband Mitch how his day was. Mitch is a park ranger in Como, and he has to tell down to the last detail how his day was, including the exact number of squirrels he saw and how many didn't have tails. And Butchie who is only a couple of years younger than me and still plays with G.I. Joe, chews up his food and opens his mouth for me to see it and makes all kinds of perverted faces at me that make my skin crawl. I would not put up with this at all, but Ione is about the best cook there is. Even her meat loaf is good. I just eat right through the prayer and stuff. There's plenty. Who knows what

Marcus and LaDonna eat. Sometimes school is so bad it is all Marcus can do to lay there on the couch and have LaDonna rub his feet. They lie there and eat bon-bons. They act like rich people except they don't have enough money. If Smutts calls Marcus and tells him I'm in trouble he will just have his usual anxiety attack and then he will do something like have the secretary go watch his class while he lays down for a few hours. And then there is LaDonna, who is a real estate agent, so she says, but she cannot be called because she is what Grandma Verda refers to as "temporarily incarcerated," which just means her butt is in jail for either attempted fraud or for putting a hex on the judge. I was there in court and I couldn't figure it out. All I know, it was a pretty good show. And even if I did know the number of the Shakopee Women's Detention Center, I would not be giving it to Smutts. Right now *The Young and the Restless* is about to start. LaDonna has special dispensation from the prison head doctor who says she is not to be disturbed during her favorite story because doing so would cause "undue psychological stress." She told me on the phone, LaDonna did. She also says the joint is chock full of chumps and anyone who couldn't work the angles out there was a pathetic wimp and a loser. And not that you'd want to let these people know that your mother is in jail anyway, especially since they would not understand, nor probably be very interested in the fact that she is basically a good person who has always had trouble balancing her checkbook and can be a little overdramatic at times.

Which leaves Marcus' mother, Grandma Verda, who would have what Marcus calls a "conniption fit" if she got the call. She will blame the whole thing on the fact that I am a "poor unfortunate child with immature, irresponsible parents." She will have me down in custody court as fast as her fully-equipped Cadillac Coupe d'Ville with cordovan leather seats, automatic windows and fully animated computerized dashboard can get us there. I will end up court-ordered to live in her house, which I like to refer to as "plastic slip cover city." It's a big white house over on Portland Avenue. Grandma puts coasters under the porcelain dogs. She is a little crazy. Besides, I can't remember the code for Tuesdays. It is either ring two times, hang up, ring two times, hang up, then call, or ring once, hang up, ring twice, hang up, then call. Otherwise Verda doesn't answer. It could be Mormons calling.

Just when the paper gets to me, I remember it is Ione's day off. Ione, whose whole name is Ione Wilson Simpson, is also a Pentecost lady, and she teaches at the Mid North Bible College out in the sticks somewhere, but because today is Tuesday and she only teaches on Monday, Wednesday and Friday she will be home, and just like LaDonna, sitting in front of *The Young and the Restless*, except Ione will have her big behind perched on an exercise bike so she can continue to get compliments from Marcus who is always saying crude things to Ione like telling she ought to put curb feelers on her hips and how her big hooters are enough to make any man want to go out and fight for his country. Either he is trying to make her blush or he really does think she has a "nice ass" which is what he is always telling her. Good old Ione. She parades around with all this hair on her head and a pair of cat eye glasses on a beaded chain. She'll come get me. I write her name down and her number and put the word guardian in parentheses. Cheerios takes it without looking and gives it to a woman out in the hall.

"Gentleman," he says. "A case of sexual misconduct has been reported to me this morning."

"Oh, man," some of the boys down the way mumble.

"I have reason to believe one or more of you is involved."

Oh, great, and what is this? Line up the usual suspects. Me? Ali Phillip Hank Aaron Gabriel (yes, those really are all my names for reasons which ought to be apparent). I am a person who has helped old ladies across the street without even having a scout uniform. (What a pack of wusses those guys are.) Yes, I do own and use my skateboard, but I always yield to pedestrians and never ride in front of cars. How did I get in the police line-up. Is snoring in class a crime? Is having a fashionable haircut? I look down the row: here I am like a goldfish in a barrel full of sharks.

"At the time of the incident you young men were found in the hallway, without passes. If any of you would like to step forward and own up to your behavior, you would be showing a lot of maturity and saving the rest of us a lot of grief." Smutts gives us all a look he thinks will melt stone. He thinks his beady eyes will squeeze a confession out of this crowd, but I know for a fact several of us here have lied our way out of tougher spots than this. I raise my hand.

"Uh, sir."

Smutts leans up with interest. He gets ready to take notes.

"What exactly is sexual misconduct?" I mean for all I know one of these guys is as perverted as Butchie, who punishes his G.I. Joes when they are bad by washing their non-anatomically correct private parts with Brillo pads.

Smutts leans back and puts his hands behind his oat-colored hair. He purses his lips. "Fair enough," he says. "One of our female students claims she was touched inappropriately by a black male student. She said it happened in the hallway."

The brothers down the way exhale, shake their heads, sigh. "That's dog," Cool says.

I start to raise my hand and say, "Uh, sir," and I figure I'm gonna ask him what exactly touched inappropriately means. Was she like patted on the head? Did someone pick her nose and dig in her ears? I decide not to because I figured I was in enough trouble anyway, and, besides, when Cheerio dude said "touched inappropriately," everyone in the room knew he meant Tony J. Tony James has the fastest hands in Ramsey County. He practically has a permanent hand-shaped maroon-colored bruise on his face, he has been slapped so many times by all the girls he's felt on, and that is every girl who doesn't have a hair pick with a sharp point on it. If Smutts or any of the rest of them had done something about him in the first place, we wouldn't be sitting here playing the People's Court.

I sure don't want to look down there at Tony, because that would be like giving him away or something, but I can see out of the corner of my eyes that LT, Cool, and Demetrius are doing the same thing: Looking at him and not looking at the same time. Tony J., he is stone cold. Even though he is looking at his feet I can see his eyes shining a little bit like he is proud of himself that he is a human dog who can't even keep his hands to himself, and furthermore has gotten a whole bunch of innocent youth such as myself into a lot of unnecessary trouble they did not need at the time.

"We have all day," says Smutts. "Your parents are being notified of this incident even as we speak."

Well, Demetrius, who was always big and bold anyway and who all the girls think is real handsome, except for those girls who don't like him because they say he is too black, which he is very, (though it is always the girls who are as black as he is saying that kind of stuff) he says, "You can't call my mama, cause I ain't done nothing," and then I hear a round of me neithers from the other guys including Tony J., so I say something too.

"I didn't do nothing," I say, which is just the sort of bad English to send LaDonna and Marcus and Verda and Ione into orbit, and yes, I do know better, and I only said it that way so we could have sort of a brotherhood thing here. (Although as I think about it, I'm not sure why I want to be one of these particular guys, especially since one of them is a well-known sex criminal. But I did it anyway. I figured if you are going to be thrown in with the guys you are probably expected to talk like them too.)

Smutts just about pops a vessel, as Marcus always says he himself is about to do. There's one thing that drives these A.P.s crazy is the "You can't call my mom" bit. Don't ever tell them what they can or cannot do. He slams his hand down on the table. He seems to enjoy that part.

"Listen up, son," he says. (These guys are always calling you son or mister. Unless you are Marcus, please, don't ever call me son, thank you.) "I'll be the one who decides what I do and don't do as long as I'm assistant principal of this school." He's got his finger all pointed in Demetrius' face, and then he flattens his hand and slams it down one more time. "I hope I made myself clear."

Some boys say, "Yes, sir," but I just roll my eyes. Like I'm gonna give him the satisfaction of a response.

And it's then, just then, he says something such as, "All you punks are alike." Or something like that. Then he goes on with a speech about how long he has been around and what all he's seen and how every time this and that and some other. Most of which I don't hear because I am still stuck back on the "all you punks" part. I'm thinking, which punks? All seventh graders? Anyone without a hall pass? Hell, no. What he means is me and these four dudes and then anyone else he can lump in with us. What he means is black folks.

Smutts finishes up with, "and I hope you boys will just keep that in mind," then he gets up and goes to the door. "I'll let you know when we get the mamas up here. Then we'll see some action."

So there I am sitting with the boys and Demetrius looks at me. He laughs and says to the other dudes, "Well, we know he didn't do it." Like I was born with flippers or something and couldn't get a feel if I tried. But the boys don't laugh too long because LT says to Tony, "You just need to go on and admit what you done."

Tony slides down in his chair some more and pulls his hat over his eyes some more. He grins. He looks tougher than ever. He thinks he's really got by with it this time. All that toughness won't help him one bit, because what I can see that he can't see is old Smutts out there pulling back the curtain so as this new girl can point her finger right at him.

He was the one just like I knew he was.

Well, that would be that, seeing as how they got their man and justice was done. Except for one thing. At the very moment Smutts goes to escort us innocents out of the office, here comes storming in Grandma Verda and Ione. Just as I expected, Grandma is in the middle of a conniption fit, grabbing at her clothes and her hair and hollering, "Oh, my goodness. Oh, my poor sweet grandbaby."

"This women here would be the boy's grandmother," Ione says to Smutts. He probably has this figured out by now seeing as how Verda has locked me in a bear hug and is sobbing and carrying on.

"Oh, my goodness," Grandma is saying, and this is such a scene that I bet I am the only one noticing that Ione has got all her Pentecost hair rolled up in Tropicana orange juice cans and tied with an old Smurf's scarf.

"Mr. Smutts," she says. "I am Dr. Ione Wilson Simpson. Just what has the boy done?"

Smutts does not notice the curlers because he is too busy looking at Ione's butt. She is wearing very tight exercise pants the color of swimming pool water. Marcus says those pants drive men wild—brings out the beast in them. Ione always tells him to hush.

It's just then I can remember who Mr. Smutts reminds me of. He is like Barney Fife on Andy Griffith they show on TBS. Even though it was in black and white you just know that Barney was all the same color, too.

Ione says, "I got a call from a girl here. Evidently there has been some sort of a problem."

"Mr. Smutts . . ." says Ms. Marsden. Ms. Marsden is the little secretary woman.

"I went and got this boy's grandma and we came right over."

"Mr. Smutts, she hung up on me before I even got out the first sentence."

"Thank you so much, Ms. Marsden," Smutts says. He herds us into his office. Grandma sits down holding on to me.

"Oh, my goodness. Oh, my goodness," she says.

"We've just had a little misunderstanding," Smutts says. "It's all been settled." His upper lip is sweating and I can tell he is trying to get his looks over his desk at Ione.

"They accused me of trying to get a feel off of this girl," I say. Grandma goes limp, leaving me to sort of ooze out of her arms.

"Sweet Jesus," she says.

"Mr. Smutts," says Ione, "I can assure you that this is the finest Christian family I know. The boy's father is a respected educator, and I have just this morning talked to his mother from her cell where she has told me she is recommitting herself to the life and teachings of Jesus Christ. You have my personal word as a Doctor of Evangelical Studies that this young man was not feeling on anything."

"Mrs. Wilson, is it?"

"Dr. Dr. Ione Wilson Simpson. Dr." Ione straightens her back which makes her chest pop out even more. Smutts is bug-eyed. Grandma is sort of moaning into a handkerchief.

"We've handled this matter expeditiously, following routine procedures. These sorts of things happen in the course of the school year."

Grandma starts to come around. It usually takes her a little longer, but I can see she's done enough of her show. I can also see she is having some sort of a brainstorm. Whenever this happens her eyes sort of focus on the ends of her nose and she gets real quiet. You can almost see the little wheels turning in her head. She puts her hanky away. (She always has a hanky ready for a tragedy like this.) (There is, of course, always another tragedy ready and waiting.) She stuffs the rag back in her purse and leans up towards Smutts. "What made you suspect my grandson in the first place?" she asks. She is real suspicious. She might be crazy, but she is nobody's fool.

Smutts gets this indignant look on his face. "Every building in St. Paul has its operating procedures manual. As an administrator. . . ."

Ione interrupts. She is standing with one hand on the desk and aiming a finger at Smutts. He cannot stop looking at her body. Marcus tells Ione that she has the best balumbas north of Chicago, and right now they are aimed right up in Smutts' face. "Don't play jargon games with me *Mr.* Smutts. I have degrees in English literature and Religious Educational Studies from the finest Christian universities in North America. I expect. . . ."

Then Grandma interrupts her. "You," she points to me. "Out in the hall. Now."

So I go out and close the door. I always get asked to leave when the good parts start, such as when LaDonna and Verda really get into it. But I am not beneath listening at the door and I have learned excellent eavesdropping skills. I can't hear too much now, but I can look in there by pulling the curtain back. Old Verda and Ione both are giving him the old one-two. They are both ranting and raving and waving their arms at him at the same time. Smutts looks like he is sitting on a bed of nails and some of them are working their way inside. He is looking down at his hands and wringing them. He tries to stand up and say something every now and again, but Grandma sits him right back down. Every once and a while I can hear words like "heathens" and "NAACP" and my name. That little secretary woman tells me to sit down. I just look at her. I figure from now on I'll sit if and when I want to.

Ione opens the door. "Come on in now, precious."

They are looking sweet and calm like they have been in here having a tea party and reading passages from the Bible.

"I just want to make sure Ali understands our rule about hall passes," Smutts says.

"He understands," Verda and Ione say together.

"Very well," the big Cheerio says. He is being real sheepish now. He is all sweated out under the arms. I know he is shamed. "I'm sorry if there was a mix-up," he says.

"Very gracious," says Ione sarcastically.

"Humph," says Grandma, walking out. "I'm taking him home with me for the rest of the day," she says. Smutts sort of raises his hand as if to dismiss us. He won't even look at us.

I sit in the back of Ione's Lincoln, hands behind my head, planning my unexpected day off. I stretch out on the back seat. A couple of Butchie's G.I. Joes are tied together naked on the floor of the car. Grandma and Ione aren't saying anything. I figure maybe we will go to the White Castle, but then I remember that White Castles give Grandma the belches. So, I think maybe we will go to Mickey D's. But we just turn up Portland. As we pull up by Grandma's house she turns around and looks at me. She looks at me with a hard serious look. The kind of look I usually see her give to Marcus and LaDonna when she is asking them to please, for her sake, get a divorce. It's like she is mad, but it's not that. She has got something on her mind.

"Don't ever let them put you in a room like that again. Just get up and leave. You understand me?"

"Yes, Ma'am." I say.

"Now tell sister Ione 'thank you' and go on up to the house."

I sit on the screen porch waiting in the sun where it is warm. Ione and Verda talk for twenty minutes. Finally, Verda gets out. Ione honks the horn and pulls away.

Plastic slip cover city isn't so bad sometimes. Especially when Marcus and LaDonna aren't here to fight with Grandma. All day long Verda is fixing me my favorite snacks such as Rice Crispy Bars and Country Time Lemonade. She lets me lay up on her couch and watch television. She puts a sheet over the slip covers so I won't get the plastic dirty, but that is better anyway than laying on plastic, which sweats and sticks to you even on a cold day in April.

At four o'clock it is time to go home and find some dinner for me and Marcus. I kiss Grandma goodbye and she gives me five dollars for being a good boy. I ride my skateboard all the way home and don't stop for the lights or anything.

OPTIONS FOR DIALOGUE

- Discuss some strengths of the main characters of the story. Be sure to include the narrator, Marcus, LaDonna, Mr. Smutts, Grandma, and Ione.
- Discuss some incidents, ways of interacting, and assumptions about people by other people that made you mad. In what ways did these assumptions lead to certain behaviors or actions?
- Discuss some suggestions about how various characters in the story could have been supportive of the students.
- Discuss an incident in which you feel a teacher made some incorrect assumptions about you or a friend of yours. What happened? Why? How did you handle it then? Would you do anything differently now?

SUGGESTIONS FOR ACTION

- Develop some interview questions about school to ask a 13- or 14-year-old student. Find someone you would like to interview. Ask that person for permission to do the interview and conduct it. Summarize your findings and report to the class.
- Secure permission to visit a middle school or junior high school. Do an informal survey of the physical environment. What is the general condition of the building. Is it inviting? Does it look and feel friendly and safe? What are the details in the environment that make you feel that way? What information is posted on the walls? Is student work displayed? In what form? Are notices to students displayed? What is the nature and the tone of the notices? Are you approached by any security people? What did they say to you? What was their nonverbal message to you? Write up a report in the form of a newspaper article and distribute it to your class.
- In the same school (perhaps on another occasion) do an informal survey of the social environment. Are students talking to each other in the hallways, in the cafeteria, outside the school building? Can you overhear some conversations? Is what you hear predictable or are you surprised at either the content or the intention of some of the conversations? Summarize your findings in a way that would make an effective presentation to the counselors of that school.
- If you are working or have worked with children, which ones naturally appeal to you? Why? Which ones make your work problematic? Analyze your response to this question. In what ways do you need to change your attitudes toward children? Make an action plan to initiate this change.

- Read *Becoming Political,* edited by Patrick Shannon. In what way is teaching a political act? Show your understanding of "teacher as political activist" through a project that you can share with others.
- Review research in one of the following books and summarize what you learn, relating the research in some way to "Busted" and to your own work:

Kohl, H. (1994). *"I won't learn from you" and other thoughts on creative maladjustment."* New York: New Press.

Ladson-Billings, G. (1994). *The dreamkeepers.* San Francisco: Jossey-Bass.

Lee, V. E., Winfield, L. F., & Wilson, T. C. (1991, November) Academic behaviors among high-achieving African American students. *Education & Urban Society, 24*(1), 65–86.

Spindler, G., & Spindler, L. (1982). *Doing the ethnography of schooling.* New York: Holt, Rinehart, & Winston.

Read the following story and choose from one of the listening, dialogue, and action activities.

Garden, N. (1993). Parents' night. In *Am I blue? Coming out from the silence.* New York: HarperCollins.
    This is a collection of short stories about gay, lesbian, and bisexual life.

OPTIONS FOR LISTENING

- In your journal reflect on a time during your youth when you felt supported (emotionally, physically, politically, or otherwise) by your parents or some other family member. Were you surprised by this support? Did you doubt that this support would be there? Why or why not? Describe the situation.
- Think of a time in your high school years in which you or someone you knew were discriminated against because of beliefs about sexual preference. Who were the perpetrators of the discrimination? What did you or the person who was discriminated against do? Would the situation come up today if you were in high school now? Why or why not? Write about this incident and give plenty of details about the historical/political/social context of the setting.
- Make a list of all the gay-bashing terms you have heard recently. Next to the terms, list the place (the setting) where you heard them.
- Read the selection.

OPTIONS FOR DIALOGUE

- What were the strengths of Karen's mother, Karen's father, Karen, Roxy, Ab, and Mac?
- What was difficult for each of those characters?
- What ways were the students in the story supported by the school?
- What are some other ways the school could have supported the students?

SUGGESTIONS FOR ACTION

- Write a comparison of two lunch-line related incidents in a high school: in each situation you are in line waiting to make your salad, and you hear a student making derogatory remarks about gay and lesbian people to another student nearby. There are other students and staff who overhear the remarks. Describe the two different school contexts in terms of how the incident is handled. What is said? What is done? Read both stories to your class. Which describes the school where the class members hope to work? How will they help promote this atmosphere?

- Invite a panel of three people who are willing to come to your class and tell their coming-out stories. Ask them to discuss how they planned to tell their parents, how they actually told them, and how the parents reacted.

THE WHISPERING CLOTH

OPTIONS FOR LISTENING

- In your journal describe something—an object, a series of photographs, a collection of materials that tells something of your family's stories. What have you learned about yourself by thinking about this storytelling treasure?
- Write about an experience you've had with a grandparent or other elder in which that person taught you something. How did this person teach you? What was the process? Did you learn a skill, a craft, or something less tangible? What did you learn about yourself in the process of this interaction?
- Describe an out-of-school educational experience. Where were you? Who, besides yourself, was involved in the teaching and learning? How was this learning experience different from many of your in-school learning experiences?
- Read the selection, write down any questions that you think of, and note any personal connections.

Glossary

Hmong (mung)   people originating in the mountains of southwestern China more than 4,000 years ago and populating the hills of northern Vietnam, Laos, and Thailand. About 200,000 Hmong refugees now live in the United States.

Pa'ndau (pah NOW)   a Hmong word meaning "flowery cloth." It is an embroidered tapestry that may include traditional patterns, images of wildlife and plants, or a story. In the United States quilting is a similar folk art.

Paang mahk (pang)   a Thai word meaning "very expensive" or "too expensive." In Thailand, people negotiate the cost of most foods and services.

Baht (bot)   Thai money. One baht equals about 4 cents. The traders paid 400 baht—about $16 dollars—for Grandma's pa'ndau. Such pa'ndau now sell in the United States for at least $50.

Mekong River (MAY kong)   originates in southwestern China, courses south through Laos, and forms a long length of the border between Laos and Thailand. It continues south through Cambodia and Vietnam and empties into the South China Sea. Communist soldiers in Laos regularly ambushed Hmong refugees who tried to cross the Mekong to Thailand.

Foreword

Refugees, such as the Hmong people featured in "The Whispering Cloth," are people without a homeland. Often facing death because they look different from other people or have different beliefs, refugees flee their countries looking for a better life. Unfortunately, it may take them many years to find a country that will accept them.

"The Whispering Cloth" takes place in Ban Vinai, a refugee camp near Chiang Khan, Thailand. The camp has housed Hmong since 1976. Using deadly gas, poisoned nails, and ground and air strikes, the Communist government has driven the Hmong out of Laos for fighting alongside American soldiers during the war in Vietnam and Laos.

Ban Vinai closed completely in 1995. Tens of thousands of refugees were moved to other camps and eventually repatriated to Laos against their will. Many Hmong children may never know freedom.

The Whispering Cloth
by Pegi Deitz Shea

After Mai's cousins moved to America, Mai passed the days with Grandma at the Widows' Store, watching the women do pa'ndau story cloths.

She loved listening to the widows stitch and talk, stitch and talk—mostly about their lives back in Laos, and about their grandmother's lives in China a hundred years ago.

All Mai could remember was life inside the refugee camp, where everyone seemed to come and go but her.

"Mai!" came Grandma's crackly voice. "Put Cousin's letter away. The words will disappear if you read them one more time. Come help me with the pa'ndau borders."

"But I don't know how."

Grandma threaded a needle and wrapped her hand around Mai's. "Push the needle up through the cloth," Grandma instructed. "And poke it back in when it has gone the length of a grain of rice."

For many weeks, Mai practiced stitching, stitches that were short and straight, ones that looped inside others, ones that twirled into long strands, and stitches that looked like dots.

"Beautiful," praised Grandma, amazed at Mai's skill. "You are ready to go on."

Grandma then began drawing herbs and animals on the pa'ndau borders for Mai to embroider. By the end of the hot season, Mai was drawing and stitching her own border designs—vines of milky jasmine, bursts of purple orchid, palm trees plump with papaya.

"Hurry and finish, Mai," Grandma said one day. "The traders will be coming soon from Chiang Khan."

"How much will they pay for the ones I helped on?" Mai asked, knotting her last stitch.

"Twice as much as the others," Grandma bragged. "You sew even better than your mother did when she was alive. And her pa'ndau were prized throughout the hills."

"Paang paang! Paang mahk!" The traders complained when Grandma demanded 500 Thai baht for her pa'ndau. But when they saw the fine detail of the borders, the traders agreed to pay 400 baht—twice the usual price.

"Keep stitching, Mai," Grandma said when the traders left. "And we'll fly from this camp before the rabbit breeds again."

Mai's hands went back to work on the borders. But her eyes and ears were drawn to the tribal stories the women stitched inside the borders. Every time the wind rippled the pa'ndau hanging at the Widows' Store, Mai heard words in the air.

"Grandma, I want to do a whole pa'ndau myself," she said finally. "Can you give me a story?"

"If you do not have a story of your own, you are not ready to do a pa'ndau."

Mai tried for days to think of a story she could stitch. But all the good ones were already whispering around her.

One night, Mai's fingers cramped so much that she couldn't sleep. Grandma lay down on the mat beside Mai, enfolded her, and rubbed her hands.

Grandma's soothing made Mai remember how she had slept when she was little, snug as a banana in a bunch. Snug . . . with her mother behind her, her father in front of her. Mai's lower lip began to quiver.

"I want my mommy and daddy," she cried softly.

"I know, I know . . .," Grandma said. "Call to them, Mai. Call their spirits with the words in your fingers."

Mai closed her eyes and tried to picture her parents. Flashes, noises, smells bombarded her. A story was erupting in her head—a story she could stitch. . . .

Little Mai slept between her mother and father, who were very beautiful even though blood dripped from their heads.

Grandmother put Mai in a basket on her back and ran through the paddies to the riverboats.

Soldiers fired. Bullets whistled over the people's heads and made rings in the brown Mekong.

On the other side of the river, soldiers in different clothes took them to a crowded village inside a tall fence.

People stood in long lines to get little bags of rice and dried fish.

Mai grew taller. She passed the days watching the blacksmiths make knives and tools. Sometimes she pounded balls of silver into flat sheets for the jewelry maker.

She helped Grandmother grow chilies and coriander.

Mai searched for empty glass bottles. When she put them upside down in the ground around her hut, they sparkled.

This is how Mai lived for many years.

Mai finished her pa'ndau as the rainy season was ending. "Grandma, how much will the traders pay for my pa'ndau? Enough to fly to America?"

Grandma ran her fingers over the needlework. Then she took the pa'ndau by the corners and held it up to the breeze. She turned her head so that her good ear grazed the stitches.

After a long time she whispered, "The traders will offer nothing."

"Nothing?" Mai cried in frustration.

"The pa'ndau tells me it has not finished its story," Grandma replied. "But I have nothing to tell."

Grandma squinted, pushing yellow through the eye of the needle. "There is always more thread."

Mai grabbed her pa'ndau and ran through the muddy lanes of brown huts all the way to the camp border.

There, rainwater gushed freely through the barbed fence and joined a stream beyond.

Mai stood in the water and let it wash over her feet. She stared out past the fence for a long time. Then she sat down on the bank and began to stitch.

One day, Grandmother and Mai flew inside an airplane. They glided softly above boxes of land to a village where homes were big as mahogany trees.

Mai and her cousins built men with white crystals, swam in curling salt water, read books with beautiful pictures.

And at night, Mai snuggled with Grandmother in a yellow bed with a silky roof.

Many days later Mai rejoined the women at the Widows' Store and showed them her finished pa'ndau.

"It is very fine," Grandma said, "I like the bed with the roof."

"How much will the traders give me?"

"It is worth much. . . . What do you think?"

Mai picked up the pa'ndau, but the wind blew it back against her. The short, rough stitches of her father's hand stood up from the cloth to stroke Mai's chin. She tried to speak, but the smooth stitches of her mother's cheeks hushed her lips.

"Mai?" Grandma nudged her. "How much?"

"Nothing," Mai whispered, clutching the story cloth.

"Nothing?"

"The pa'ndau tells me it is not for sale."

OPTIONS FOR DIALOGUE

- Discuss with a partner: why wouldn't Mai sell her weaving in the end?
- How does this story relate to you or your work?
- Talk about the teaching and learning dynamics here in terms of this out-of-school educational experience.
- Discuss other examples of history being passed on through art forms? What do you think about the effectiveness of this way of passing on history?

SUGGESTIONS FOR ACTION

- Interview an elder about something (an object, a story, a song, for example) of a family tradition that is not for sale.
- Interview a person who has a connection—personal or through family—to Southeast Asia. What information can you learn about history, politics, the social structure of communities, and the ways in which people gain an education (formal or informal)?
- After interviewing or working with a person from the Hmong culture write a poem about that person's strengths. One preservice education student, Sean Beaverson, wrote this poem:

My Trouble Is My Hmong

Frustrated at trying to understand quotation marks
you manage to tell me, correct everytime,
who says what.

Who was it that told you you did not know much?

I ask how to say hello in hmong, you tell me and laugh at my attempt.
I am unable to repeat such a simple phrase.

I ask you to read, comprehend and deal with the sentences in your grammar book.
You read without trouble.
You understand without the help from your "english" teacher
You struggle, and finally manage to deal with quotations.

How do you say thank you in Hmong, I ask.
you laugh at my inability to say two words.

You who are told you don't know watch me as I leave, you look and smile
and say, "Thank you Sean. Be back next Thursday?"

For True.

SmB

- Research library archives for periodicals or journals that give you historical stories of Southeast Asian people during the second half of the 20th century. Report back to your class and ask classmates to relate your report to Mai's story.
- Review the research by Henry Trueba, Lila Jacobs, and Elizabeth Kirton in the book *Cultural Conflict and Adaptation: The Case of Hmong Children in American Society.* Relate the information to "The Whispering Cloth." Then relate the information to your current work or to community contexts.
- Review "Southeast Asian Refugee Parents: An Inquiry into Home-School Communication and Understanding" by M. Blakely in *Anthropology and Education Quarterly 14*(1), 43–68.
- Attend a Southeast Asian cultural celebration of any form. Pick a communicative format (a story, a poem, an essay, a series of photographs, and so on) for explaining your interpretation of how the celebration reflects the strengths of the community of people.

RUFUS AT THE DOOR

OPTIONS FOR LISTENING

- In your journal describe a person you remember from your school days who had some special needs. What was the person like? Were you comfortable being around this person? Why or why not? Did the people who came into contact with this person support or just tolerate him or her? Did anyone make life more difficult for this person? In what ways?

- Write about an experience you've had with a person who has special needs. What did you learn from this person? What did you learn about yourself?
- Describe an example of a teacher or other person who worked with a person with special needs in a way that you respected. What did the teacher do? Why do you feel he or she was successful? What details gave you information about how the person with special needs felt?
- Read the selection, write down your personal questions as you read, and write down any personal connections you can make to the story.

Rufus at the Door

by Jon Hassler

(from Stiller's Pond)

Each year the ninth and eleventh grades of Plum High School were loaded on a bus and driven to Rochester for a tour of what was then called the insane asylum. The boys' health teacher, Mr. Lance, and the girls', Miss Sylvestri, led us single file through a series of gloomy wards and hallways where we were smiled at, scowled at, lunged at and jeered by all manner of the mentally deficient. I recall much more about my ninth-grade trip than I do about my eleventh. I recall, for example, how the faces of the retarded absorbed the elderly Mr. Lance, how he gazed at them the way we freshmen did, as though he were seeing them for the first time, and yet how he displayed none of our pity or shock or revulsion; his gaze, like a good many of those it met, was intense but neutral. I remember the middle-aged Miss Sylvestri bouncing along at the head of our column and—as though reading labels at the zoo—calling out the categories: "These are morons, class, and over there you have the imbeciles. In the next room they're all insane." I remember my relief when the tour ended, for the place had given me a severe stomachache. As we boarded the bus, Miss Sylvestri turned back for a last look and waved cheerily at a balloonlike face peering out the window of the broad front door and said, "That's a waterhead, class, and now we'll go downtown for lunch."

Mr. Lance drove the bus and Miss Sylvestri stood at his shoulder and delivered an unnecessary lecture about how lucky we were to have been spared from craziness and retardation. She wore a long coat of glistening black fur, and the shape of her tall hat fit the definition, in our geometry text, of a truncated cone. She asked if any of us realized that we had a moron living in Plum.

Pearl Peterson's hand shot up. Pearl was the ninth grade's foremost sycophant. "Henry Ahman," she said. "Henry Ahman is a moron."

"No, I'm sorry, Pearl. Henry Ahman is an epileptic, there's no comparison. Come now, class, I'm asking for a moron."

I knew the right answer, but I kept my mouth shut for fear of losing face with my friends. This was the year a lot of us boys were passing through our anti-achievement phase. We had taken an oath never to raise our hands.

"Please, Miss Sylvestri," said Pearl, "would you tell us again what a moron is?"

Swaying with the traffic, Miss Sylvestri said that morons were a little smarter than idiots and a lot smarter than imbeciles. She said that morons could do things like run errands for their mothers while idiots and imbeciles couldn't leave the house. Sometimes imbeciles couldn't even get out of bed.

The impassive Mr. Lance found his way downtown and parked in front of the Green Parrot Cafe. He looked into the mirror that showed him his whole load, even those of us way in back, and he said, "Chow time." But Miss Sylvestri begged to differ. She said nobody was having lunch until somebody came up with a moron.

My friends and I groaned anonymously.

Pearl suggested the Clifford girl.

"No, I'm sorry, the Clifford girl is an out-and-out imbecile."

Somebody else, a junior, said, "Gilly Stone."

"No, Gilly Stone's problem is polio."

Finally out of hunger—the jolting bus had settled my stomach—I shouted, "Rufus Alexander."

"That's correct—Rufus Alexander. He's very low on the scale but he's still higher than an idiot. He's what you call a low-grade moron."

We were permitted to eat.

At the west edge of Plum, Rufus Alexander lived with his mother in a little house near the stockyards. Rufus was about thirty-five and his mother was very old, yet his hair was turning gray at the same rate as hers. On Saturday afternoons they walked together to the center of the village to shop—the tall, bony faced Mrs. Alexander striding along with her shoulders hunched and her skirts flowing around her shoetops; her tall, grinning son stepping along at her side, his back so straight that he seemed about to tip over backwards. Though he walked fast to keep pace, there was in each of his footsteps an almost imperceptible hesitation, a tentativeness that lent a jerky aspect to his progress down the street and reminded me of old films of the Keystone Kops. Whenever he came to a stop, he always clasped his hands behind his back and stood as though at attention; from a distance, in his long gray coat and white scarf, he might have been mistaken for a diplomat or a funeral director. At home Rufus sat in a deep chair by the front window and listened all day to the radio. Passing the house on my bike, I used to see him there, looking out and grinning. Mrs. Alexander had raised three older sons, but it was Rufus she loved best. He was hard of hearing and mute, though on rare occasions he made guttural noises which his mother took to be words.

In order to go about her Saturday shopping unencumbered by Rufus, who couldn't turn a corner without being steered, Mrs. Alexander would deposit him either in the pool hall or in my father's grocery store. She would look in at the pool hall first, because there Rufus could sit on one of the chairs around the card table, but if she saw that her card-playing son—her oldest son, Lester—hadn't come to town, she would lead Rufus down the street to our store and place him in my father's care.

Not that he needed care. He was content to stand at the full-length window of the front door, looking out. For as long as two hours he would remain there as though enchanted, his hands clasped behind him, his eyes directed at a point slightly above the passing people, his face locked in its customary grin. When someone entered or left the store—Rufus would shuffle backward and allow himself to be pressed for a moment between the plate glass in front of him and the glassine doors of the cookie display behind him, and then as the door went shut he would shuffle forward, keeping his nose about six inches from the glass.

Although our customers were greeted week after week by this moronic face, and although he obscured the cookie display, I don't think Rufus had an adverse effect on our business. Everybody was used to him. In a village as small as Plum the ordinary population didn't outnumber the odd by enough to make the latter seem all that rare. We became, as villagers, so accustomed to each other's presence, so familiar with each other's peculiarities, that even the most eccentric among us—Henry Ahman, who had fits in public; the Clifford girl, who was an out-and-out imbecile—were considered institutions rather than curiosities. I noticed that most of our customers ignored Rufus as they came through the door, while a few, like me, gave him a fleeting smile in return for his incessant grin.

He had an odd face. His round, prominent cheekbones were rosy, healthy-looking, but his eyes were skeletal—deep-set eyes under brows like ledges, blue eyes perfectly round and (I thought at first) perfectly empty. I never saw him—except once—that he wasn't grinning. Though I told myself that this was an unconscious grin, that he probably grinned all night in his sleep, I couldn't help responding to it. Returning time and again to the store after carrying out groceries, I smiled. As an exercise in will power, I would sometimes try to control this reflex. Facing Rufus as I opened the door, I would tell myself that his grin was not a sign of good will but an accident of nature, and I would attempt a neutral stare, like Mr. Lance's, but it was no use. (I could never resist smiling at clowns either, even though I knew their joy was paint.) I asked my father one time if he thought Rufus ever had anything on his mind, if he understood what he was staring at—or staring slightly above. My father said he wondered the same thing himself and had concluded that Rufus was only two-dimensional; there was no depth to him at all. And this, for a time, I believed.

Then one Monday morning—it was around the time of my first trip to the insane asylum—word spread through town that Rufus has another dimension after all. It was said that during a Sunday picnic in Lester Alexander's farmyard, Rufus had flown into a rage. The picnic was attended by scads of Alexanders from far and near, and three or four of his little cousins began to taunt Rufus. They made up a song about his ignorance and sang it to him again and again. He rolled his great round eyes, it was said, and he made a mysterious noise like a groan or a belch (it was not reported whether he lost his grin) and he set out after the cousins, brandishing the long knife his mother had brought along for slicing open her homemade biscuits. Hearing about it, I couldn't believe that anyone had actually been in danger. I pictured Rufus tipping backward as he ran, too slow to catch his quick little cousins; I pictured the knife—a bread-slicer, dull at the tip; I pictured the many Alexander men—strapping farmers all—who could easily have restrained him. But on the other hand, I could also imagine the alarm. I had attended a few of these farmyard picnics, invited by friends, and I imagined how it must have looked to a bystander; the afternoon hazy and hot; dozens of relatives deployed across the sloping, shady lawn; the children shirtless under their bib overalls; the women at the outdoor table, uncovering their tepid hot-dishes and their runny gelatins; the men smoking under the trees;

then suddenly this heightened racket among the children and everyone turning and seeing, to their terror, the youngsters scattering and shrieking (half in fright, half in glee) and Rufus hopping jerkily over the grass, the bread-knife in his hand, the blade glinting in the sun as he thrust it stiffly ahead of him, stabbing the air. As it was told the next day, Rufus's wild mood quickly passed and a half hour later he and the smaller children full of food, lay down together for a nap in the shade. But he had given his brothers and their wives a terrible fright. Rufus would have to be put away, his brothers told their mother. He would have to be taken to the insane asylum.

Never. As long as she lived, said Mrs. Alexander, Rufus would never leave her side. Not once in his life had he disobeyed her; never had he been anything but gentle. How would any of *them* like it, she wanted to know, if they were teased and attacked by a bunch of impudent snips? No, if anyone was coming to take Rufus away, they were coming over her dead body.

And there the matter rested. The three sons refrained from saying what they foresaw. They foresaw the day when their mother would die and Rufus would be whisked off to Rochester.

After the upheaval of that Saturday afternoon, Mrs. Alexander no longer left Rufus at the pool hall, for it was card-playing Lester who had been the first to speak about putting him away. In my father's keeping, then, Rufus was placed each week without fail. Now and then I would glance up from my work and see him there and wonder how it would end. Morons, according to Miss Sylvestri, sometimes died young. Maybe his mother would survive him, and wouldn't that be a blessing? His brothers' secret intention—like all secrets in Plum—had become public knowledge, and I didn't see how Rufus, after all these years of fixed habits and mother love, could adapt himself to the gruesome life of the asylum, particularly now that he had exhibited strong emotion. Hearing of his anger at the picnic, I now suspected that Rufus was capable of perceptions and emotions beyond what my father and I (and probably most of the village) had formerly believed. Now, though his eyes were consistently shallow and his grin steady, I had a hard time thinking of him in only two dimensions. This was a man who knew things, who felt things, I told myself, and therefore if he outlived his mother he was bound to come to grief. I didn't ask my father what he thought about this. I was afraid he would agree.

In the autumn of my junior year, Mrs. Alexander died. Rufus apparently didn't recognize death when he looked it in the face, for although the coroner said she had been dead since midnight it wasn't until the following noon that Rufus went next door and by his moaning and wild look alerted Mrs. Underdahl. No one could say for certain how Rufus, waiting for his mother to wake up, had spent the forenoon, but judging later by the evidence and what we knew of his habits, the village imagined this:

Rufus got out of bed on his own and went into his mother's room to see why she hadn't awakened him, why she hadn't started breakfast. The depth of her sleep puzzled him. He was capable of a number of things; he could dry dishes and dress himself, but he couldn't figure out why his mother lay so late in bed. He put on his clothes and breakfasted on biscuits and milk (or rather cream, for he opened a full bottle and swigged off the top) and he evidently passed the rest of the time listening to the radio. In my mind's eye I see him sitting in his favorite chair by the window, soothed by the voice of Arthur Godfrey. I see him grinning when the audience laughs and grinning when it doesn't. At noon he went back into his mother's bedroom and pulled her by the arm, and when she didn't respond, he tugged harder. He pulled her out of bed and onto the floor. Then, seeing her there at his feet, twisted among the sheets, he perceived something new. A door in his dense thinking opened on an emotion he had never felt before. Not anger this time, but fear. He went straight to Mrs. Underdahl's house and called up the same belching groan he had uttered at the picnic. His great blue eyes were rolling, Mrs. Underdahl later told my father in the store, as though he sensed that this day marked the end of his childhood and now, in his late thirties, he would have to face the world alone—far off from his mother's house, which had been arranged to fit so well his simple needs, far off from his mother's love.

I was one of the altar boys at Mrs. Alexander's funeral. I looked for Rufus among the mourners, but he wasn't there. I supposed, correctly, as it turned out, that he had already been taken to Rochester. At the cemetery it rained. There were dozens of Alexanders standing three-deep around the grave. The little cousins, wearing short pants and neckties, were as antic as ever. While the priest blessed the grave and read aloud the prayers of burial, the cousins shrieked and played tag among the tombstones. Impudent snips, their grandmother had called them.

Six months later my classmates and I were bussed to Rochester for our second look at the unfortunates. Over the years I have tried to figure out why everyone who went through school in Plum during the Lance-Sylvestri era was twice required to pass through this gauntlet of retarded and insane humanity. Surely all of us had been sufficiently impressed the first time by the smells and vacant faces of this dismal congregation, sufficiently impressed by our own good luck at having been spared. One thing we did learn on this second trip—and this may have been the lessons our teachers had in mind (particularly Mr. Lance, who taught it by example)—was how to look impassive in the face of chaos. I had the same pain in my stomach that I had two years earlier, and one of the inmates leaped at and tried to pull off my jacket, but, like most of my classmates, I played the stoic from the time I entered the broad front door until I departed. I acted this way because I was sixteen, the age when nothing seems quite so crucial—especially if freshmen are watching you—as appearing to be above it all; nothing seems quite so clever—if joking would be out of place—as disdain. I discovered that I could be really quite good at looking neutral. The trick was simply to tell myself that none of these crouching, drooling, gawking people were experiencing the misery that visitors pitied them for. They had no knowledge—no memory—of life as it was lived among the normal—life, say, in Plum. Unaware of any better form of existence, they were content. Brainless, they possessed the peace that passes understanding.

But then I saw Rufus. We were boarding the bus when Miss Sylvestri suddenly pointed behind us at the broad front door and said, "Why, that's Rufus Alexander." I turned and saw two men on the doorstep with their backs to us. One was an orderly, the other a tall, white-haired man with a straight spine and his hands clasped behind his back. It was Rufus, all right, and I was surprised—not only because his hair had turned white, but because he had slipped my mind over the winter; I had forgotten that he lived here now. Where had he been during our tour? Outside, strolling the grounds? Or had he been present in one of the crowded wards we passed through, and had a familiar face told him that we were the Plum delegation? Had he tried to follow us out to the bus? The orderly had him tightly by the elbow and was steering him in through the door we had just come out of, but he seemed reluctant to go. Though he didn't struggle, there was a hint of unwillingness in his movements, a hesitation in his step.

This time Miss Sylvestri did not lecture us as Mr. Lance started the bus, but she sat visiting with Pearl Peterson in the front seat on the driver's side. I sat in the back, next to a window, and looked straight at Rufus. The broad front door was now locked and he was standing behind the glass. Our two windows were scarcely thirty feet apart. He didn't look as healthy as he used to. The color was gone from his face and his ledgelike brows were sharper, deeper. While the whiteness of his hair was alarming (in six months it had grown much whiter than his mother's had been), the astonishing thing was the look on his face. He wasn't grinning. His face, without the grin, was that of a much older man, the jaw hanging slack, the cheeks hollow. In his round blue eyes, without the grin, there was something obviously very deep, like yearning. Obvious to me, at least, because his eyes were aimed directly at mine—not slightly above me, the way he used to look at things—and they told me that he had indeed tried to follow us out to the bus; moreover, they told me that mine was the face that reminded him of Plum. I looked away, Mr. Lance shifted gears, and I never saw Rufus again.

OPTIONS FOR DIALOGUE

- There is a similar saying in several cultures—essentially, "It takes a whole village to raise a child." What details from the story reveal ways in which the village was raising Rufus while he lived with his mother?
- Rufus went to the insane asylum. What do you infer about the way he was being raised?
- How does this story relate to what special educators call "the least restrictive environment," which means that a student with special needs should be educated in an environment that is as much like normal as possible?

SUGGESTIONS FOR ACTION

- View one of the following films and relate the information to "Rufus." Give a synopsis and an analysis report to your class:

  My Left Foot
  Rain Man
  This Boy's Life
  What's Eating Gilbert Grape?

- Review the photography and life story of Milton Rogoven, an activist who was brought before the House Committee on Un-American Activities in 1938. He was a casual photographer whose work focused on *The Forgotten Ones* (the title of a 1985 publication).

- Consider the following list of suggestions for improving language related to disabilities and handicaps:

Say . . .	Instead of . . .
child with a disability	disabled or handicapped child
without speech	mute or dumb
developmental delay	slow
emotional disorder or mental illness	crazy or insane
uses a wheelchair	confined to a wheelchair
person with retardation	retarded
person with Down Syndrome	mongoloid
has a learning disability	is learning disabled
has a physical disability	is crippled
communicates with sign	deaf and dumb

Conduct a survey of spoken language in the media. Which language from which list is used more often? Report to your class.

- Review the research of Mara Sapon-Shevin regarding critical perspectives in the field of special education. One of her many articles can be found in Byrnes, D. A. & Kiger, G. (Eds.). (1992). *Anti-bias teaching a diverse society.* Wheaton, MD: Association for Childhood Education International.
- Read one of the following books or one with a related theme:

Cowen-Fletcher, J. (1994). *It takes a village.* New York: Scholastic.
Yemi cares for her little brother, Kakou, at the market while Mama sells mangoes. The story reveals the power of a close-knit community.

Five, C. L. (1992). *Special voices.* Portsmouth, NH: Heinemann.
This is a collection of stories about children with special needs and how their teacher learned to create a classroom environment that enabled them to overcome many of their obstacles.

Hickok, L. (1961). *The touch of magic: The story of Helen Keller's great teacher, Anne Sullivan Macy.* New York: Dodd, Mead.
This is a famous story about great teaching.

Kidder, T. (1989). *Among school children.* New York: Avon.
Tracy Kidder spent nine months in Mrs. Zajar's fifth-grade classroom in the depressed "Flats" of Holyoke, Massachusetts. For an entire year he lived among 20 schoolchildren and their teacher, sharing their joys, catastrophes, and triumphs.

Taylor, D. (1991). *Learning denied.* Portsmouth, NH: Heineman.
Taylor tells the story of a family's clash with special education bureaucracy as Claudia and Pat attempt to help their son, Patrick, in school and then ultimately protect him from the school.

Answer these questions about your reading:

1. In a few sentences, summarize the reading(s).
2. Why did you read this? What relationship to your personal or professional life does it have?
3. Do you feel an accurate picture of the information was presented? Why or why not?
4. Which points from the reading did you *not* agree with? Why?
5. Discuss which information or opinions presented here were new to you.
6. Discuss any conversation about this subject that you may have had.

IMAGES OF SCHOOLING: TEACHERS' METAPHORS

OPTIONS FOR LISTENING

- In your journal create a short metaphor for school. You can begin by making a comparison chart between school and something else (such as a circus, a journey). Begin your metaphor with "school is. . . ." Listen to ideas for metaphors from your group members.
- Read the following four poems with this question in mind: what are the speakers' metaphors for schooling? "My Slanted" View and "Lessons from Space" are written from the point of view of a student. What are metaphors that describe the students' beliefs about school? How do these children see themselves in school? In "Southeast Asia, Second Grade" and "A First Day," what are metaphors that describe the classrooms that the authors are writing about? What is a metaphor that describes each of the writers (both of whom are speaking in a teacher's voice), a view of the classroom, or the school? How do these teachers see themselves in the school? What are differences between the views of schooling held by the teachers and the views of schooling held by the students?

Southeast Asia, Second Grade
by Roseann Lloyd
(from Minnesota Writes: Poetry)

When the art class washes black
over their secret crayola drawings
Blong's Spiderman
pulls a green net across
the watery page. When we write
poems that begin *I Remember*
Blong designs
a Mercedes limousine, the military
detail, exact. In dream
poems, he colors a ship
with two anchors
a ship whose stars and stripes
shine turquoise, orange, and green.
He prints slowly
I'm the one who eats ghosts.
He's the one who searches
all the books for more
designs: a pink brontosaurus grins

and hops, his Arapaho
eagle rises like fire, Norwegian
serpents curl
to bronze, aquamarine, and Spiderman
comes back again
and again without a sound
to my desk, to my lap—
the scraps, Manila, white
paper in sixteen folds.
And I'm the one
with the wide Caucasian face
who stares inscrutable
at the nets that bind. Down the hall
the soldiers' boys, pencils in fists,
grudge out the calligraphy of punishment—
I WILL NOT EXPLODE IN CLASS—
these sentences
knotting inside
one hundred times.

A First Day
by Kevin Fitzpatrick
(from Down on the Corner)

My first day with seventh graders,
I don't know any names.
Breasts are just beginning.
I can't tell boys from the girls—
so it's an old joke—
especially the chubby ones.

Things begin moving: Desks dragging,
tilting; books, pencils dropping;
the lips of a boy in front mumbling.
"Questions?" I ask.
"Oh, I was just singing."
The whole room whirls with hands.

A woman enters.
The clap of her clipboard stills them.
They look down at their hands
like absent-minded owners
scolded at a pet class.
She'll be back, thank God.

Our lesson is *Johnny Tremain,*
when the Bostonians brew salt-water tea.
Too many raise their hands to read—
are they tricking me?—
even slower ones who'll be laughed at.
But they read and read and want to read.

Hasn't the word hooted across the field yet
from the gym teacher, the baseball coach
who nearly played in the majors,
as a boy leaves softball early?
When will the word hoot across the field,
taunting the mild deserter all the way
to his singing drill in the music room?

Hasn't the word come up the row yet
from the sleek night stalker
slouching asleep far in back
as he rubs his eyes to what's on?
When will the word come up the row,
sounding tough as cleats on tile,
that reading aloud isn't cool?

What if it isn't the word, but me?
—a father bringing out heavy books,
helping his children with history
until they drowse forward like drunks
or squirm free pleading,
"You always tell us more than we need!"
—a mother insisting on silverware ways,
literature nibbled with delicate forks.

For now,
the woman with clipboard hasn't returned,
thank God, though we needed her,
as we needed moments of sun,
moments of hands straying toward the ceiling,
and moments like these, just before the bell,
when everyone is following along
as a girl, her face splotched by an old burn,
reads about Johnny Tremain's crippled hand.

Lessons from Space
by Roseann Lloyd
(from War Baby Express)

Astronaut is a foreigner in a silver suit
walking on the moon but Teacher
is our familiar—only one step
away from Mother, the first step out the door.
Teacher, we say, and we can see her hands again
covered with the chalky dust
of our own first grade. We can hear
her voice, insistent, explaining
why and how to as we print
with our fat red pencils—
lower-case s's
fill all the spaces between the sky-blue
dotted lines.

Now we are paying attention
to the front of the room where Ginny Lindstrom
is holding up an orange, representing earth,
and Walter Locke is holding up a lemon,
representing moon. Stephanie Jones gets to hold
the flash light, representing light.
Teacher, we say, we don't get it.
Just try, she always answers, everything
will be O.K. if you will only try.

Now she is mixing bright blue Tempra
which we will apply—*not too thickly*—to our maps
of the seven seas which swirl
around our wobbly pears
of continents, whose names we must also
memorize. *You must learn*
all about the universe. Teacher is moving
about the room, her sleeve is smudged and dusty
like everything else in here, even the solitary
plant that shoots its flat spikes up
in front of the blackboard, which is
also swirling dusty white, like the Milky Way.
After lunch, we put our heads on our desks.
Teacher is reading. She explains the hard parts,
how it is possible in the story
for Harriet Tubman to be underground

and following the stars at the same time.
This is inconceivable as death or the idea of space
having no end.

We turn away from knowledge
and admire our snowflakes, falling across
the glass. We folded white paper and cut them out
yesterday. Teacher says every snowflake
is unique, which means, unlike any other. Teacher
says each of us is a unique individual, special
unto ourselves. It is snowing now, for real.
We can't see the stars at the end of the sky.

If Teacher goes away, who will teach us *how to*
and *why*? How to cut out free-hand
hearts. How to find
the drinking gourd on a starless night.
What is burning in those smudge
pots in the orange groves? What happens
to machines when it's freezing cold?
Why does the T.V. say
blow-up, melt-down, O-rings
out of round? Why
are they looking for freedom up there
in the swirling clouds, in the sky-
blue sky?

My Slanted View
by Sara Ryung Clement
(from Sticky Rice)

I sit in economics class being taught
    or perhaps not.

A video lectures us
on hostile Japanese invasions:
    Nissan
    Honda
    Toyota

            —siphoning off America's jobs and money
                America's lifeblood
            leaving a drained white American zombie
        possessed by Japanese demons.

I sit, and I am not Japanese
   but I am so Asian.

I go home
I find myself Asian-Caucasian.

My Caucasian parents
   their child now
adopted
   their ways.

I am Asian only upon occasion.

Yet
I look at the world with eyes unlike theirs
   —mine do look different
  yes
    and see differently.

Perhaps mine are too sensitive
I squint
   then give my slant on the situation.

A narrow view
True.

I am Asian.

OPTIONS FOR DIALOGUE

- In your groups compare your interpretations of the poems. What metaphors did each of you think of to describe the perceptions of the teachers and students speaking in these poems? Make a list of your metaphors and compare them with those discovered by your group members. How are they alike? How are they different?
- Now compare these metaphors to the personal metaphors that you created before reading. How are they alike? How are they different?

SUGGESTIONS FOR ACTION

- Return to your personal metaphor for schooling. How would you change it after your group discussion? Revise your metaphor with the discussion in mind.
- Ask yourself the following questions about your metaphor for schooling:
  1. How does your metaphor account for the social context of the students?
  2. Is your metaphor distinctive to you or a particular cultural group?
  3. Would it be appropriate for certain other cultural groups?
  4. What are notions about learning, teaching, knowledge, and teacher-student roles that underlie your metaphor?

5. How do parents fit into your metaphor?
6. How might your students' metaphors for the classroom and its related dimensions and for learning conflict with yours? What would be the result?

- After revisions are finished return to your groups and consider the following questions about each of your personal schooling metaphors:

  1. How did your choice of metaphor differ from that of your partner? How would such differences influence your relationship as colleagues in a team-teaching situation?
  2. What are the differences between your metaphor and what you see in classrooms in which you are working?

- Read the following poems by students in one fifth-grade classroom. Consider the metaphors for schooling held by each of these students? How are they alike and different? What could be some of the reasons for the differences among them? How are they alike or different from yours? If you were the teacher, what conflicts could arise from a difference between your metaphor and theirs? What conflicts could arise among the students because of differences in beliefs about school? How would you honor and affirm the experiences that led to these beliefs for all the students?

School is like a jewel handled dagger.
something shiny makes you go grab it.
But when you get there. . .
You find it has an edge.

—Roy

When I'm at school I'm like a . . .
Bike! When I am called down the street
my teacher runs to get me.
When my paint is peeling off
she gives me a new coat.
She fills up tires when they are flat.
When my pedals are worn out
she gets me new ones.
She makes me feel like a Porsche.

—Ken

School is like a piece of pie,
and we are the blueberries,
always trying to stain someone's heart.
We all want to be the ice cream on top—
but I am the crust on the bottom now.

—Jennifer

School is like an ocean beach.
We are the sand,
The bullies are the stones,
The wind is the teacher.

The stones roll around,
Getting us out of place.
The wind comes and
WHOOSH!
We're blown away.
Gone.

—Colleen

School is like the alphabet,
but all mixed up.
The A's and B's are the most important letters.
The D's and F's I try to stay away from.
What would happen if a couple of letters got lost?
I have always been worried about it, about
Whether the alphabet will ever be back in order again.

—Jeff

School is a calendar,
It keeps going on and on.
The teacher is holidays,
The ones that are most important.
The janitor is the last day of the month,
Always the last one, cleaning up after others.
The students are the Mondays,
Always the time something goes wrong.

—Erik

School is like a road system,
many ways to go.
Some cruise easily on the freeway,
others hide on the city streets.
Some race each other on dirt roads,
some run out of gas on deserted roads.
Others stop for hitchhikers,
some only give rides to friends,
and some run out of money on tollways,
and are stuck there for awhile.
I am at an intersection,
not knowing which way to go.

—Tim

- Think about the metaphors for schooling that underlie the other stories in this section. What are metaphors held by the young characters such as the main character in "Busted"? What metaphors are held by administrators like the principal in "Busted"? What are parents' metaphors for schools? What are the conflicts caused by different metaphors representing different beliefs in these stories?

- Read one or more of the following novels that center upon the experience of young people in school. As you read, ask yourself some of the same questions about metaphors for schooling that you discussed in the previous sections. What metaphors are implicit in these stories?

    Childress, A. (1973). *A hero ain't nothing but a sandwich.* New York: Avon.
    This story of a teenage junkie is set in Harlem. It offers an insightful view of schools' attitudes toward troubled kids.

    Cormier, R. (1974). *The chocolate war.* New York: Dell.
    This story is about life in a Catholic high school. Ruled by gangs and teachers who seem almost evil, one student in the school tries to live by a motto even he doesn't understand: "Do I dare disturb the universe?"

    Hentoff, N. (1981). *Does this school have capital punishment?* New York: Delacorte.
    A sequel to *This School Is Driving Me Crazy,* the story of Sam Davidson tells about a likable character with a stormy academic career. While trying to stay out of trouble in his new school, Sam is framed for possession of marijuana.

    Taylor, M. (1976). *Roll of thunder, hear my cry.* New York: Bantam.
    The story tells of the passionate struggle of a black family determined to survive against all odds. It includes an important school scene in which the teacher (who is the mother in this family) is fired for teaching more history about slavery than the textbook represents.

- Ask students and teachers about their metaphors for schooling? How many different metaphors can you find in one classroom? One school? What does this mean for collaboration within the class and within the school? Write, submit, and report on your findings.
- Think of a creative project that will express your metaphor for schooling. It could be made with visual media or music, a poem or a story, a computer program, or a combination. Share it with others in your class.

SPRING CONCERT

OPTIONS FOR LISTENING

- Listen to a partner describe an interest (a hobby, a talent, a pastime) that she or he shares with a parent or other close family member. Then share a similar story with your partner. Write about your own description in your journal.
- Reflect and write about a time in your childhood when you were separated by distance from a parent or close family member. What do you remember about your thoughts and feelings regarding the situation? What are some critical questions you still have about the situation now, years later?
- Listen to a close relative or friend describe their preferences for living in a small community or a large metropolitan area. Write a summary of their thoughts and add some critical personal questions about this topic.

- Remember a school situation in which a teacher went out of her or his way to be sensitive to your changing needs. What did that teacher do? Are there any questions that you would like to ask this teacher now? Write about this.
- Read the selection, write down questions that arise as you read, and make notes of personal connections.

Spring Concert
by Stephen Peters

"Michael," Mrs. Heinemann says to me. "Michael Tressler will please sing his alto part and stop showing off. There are no tenors in this group." I was thirteen here, understand, and I had no nicknames in her presence. I yank my chin back and concentrate hard on singing alto, though when my voice has slipped a gear like this it is no use. This has been happening on and off for weeks, and Mrs. Heinemann's pleas have meant nothing to my willful vocal cords.

"Stay in alto just for tonight, Michael Tressler."

I wear a clean, short-sleeved shirt and a clip-on tie. Carla Rusinsky stands next to me in a strapless red sundress, and her golden hair is combed to one side and battened down with barrettes and left to fall on her bare shoulder. We are both frozen in place, afraid to acknowledge that the backs of our hands are touching. Mrs. Heinemann goes through the windup motion with her willowy arms, and forty seventh-graders lurch off into song again. She flaps her wings at us, mouths our lyrics with all her long face, and I breathe in Carla's lilac perfume until my voice careens back into alto.

"All right, people," Mrs. Heinemann tells us after we've slogged through another of her endless arrangements. "Listen now." She claps her hands and waits for us to settle into attention. "Be back here at ten minutes to eight and line up. That gives you five minutes to comb your hair."

Billy Dreibelbis pushes through the back of the crowd and puts his hands on my shoulders. "Get me out of here, Mike," he says, and we muscle a path toward the door. "Is your voice really doing that, or are you faking it?" he wants to know. Billy sings soprano and, if anything, his voice is only getting higher.

"You can't *fake* that," I tell him.

I shake Billy off in the hallway and go find my father. He is at the usual spot in the lobby, leaning against a post, a paperback book stuffed into his sports jacket pocket, his belly turning the waistband of his trousers back in a neat, white fold. He has the trademark bushy black beard. I am circled and squeezed in his arms. "Where have you *been?*" He kisses the top of my head. "I've been out here *forever.*"

My father has driven sixty miles of Pennsylvania roads from where he lives to see my spring concert.

"The drive over was great," he says. "Everything's blooming its brains out. I kept the windows down all the way to smell it."

He comes to all my concerts and to Parent-Teacher Nights, or he has in the past. Soon he and the bluegrass band he plays for will move to Louisville, Kentucky, and we won't see each other much until I am older. My father was the Original Hippie, the Last Great Beatnik. He and his friends had big plans to make it in the music world. I stand very straight, my shoulders back like a soldier's, thinking it would be better if he didn't hug me here. Since the Louisville announcement, I don't know what to say to him.

"Did you hear us warming up?" I ask.

His eyes look past me, focusing on nothing in particular. I know what he is going to say. "You sounded good." I get a light tap of his fist on my chest. "Really good."

"No, we didn't," I say. "We were practicing those songs because we can't learn them right. Everybody's really mad at her."

He is staring at his right cowboy boot as if something about it is terribly unpleasant. Then, in slow motion, he kicks an imaginary rock or can.

"Why doesn't she make you *smile* when you sing?" he asks for the 500th time. My father is a man given to enthusiasms, and I have very consciously pushed his Mrs. Heinemann-and-the-subject-of-singing button. "That would lift your voices toward some sort of *joy.*" Despite his girth and height, he is sometimes unbelievably graceful, almost dainty. He stands on tiptoe, gesturing with fine long hands, his wrists white, thin, and hairless sticking out of his cuffs. People have turned to see who this raised voice so caught up in itself is. "And why—why, *why*—doesn't she choose simple music and just let you *sing?*" My face signals that his manner is becoming an embarrassment. "After all," he stage whispers, "the whole idea is to make music, to celebrate!"

I agree. We *all* agree. Even Mrs. Heinemann must agree, but I wish he would please shut up.

"My voice keeps cracking," I tell him. "I don't think I can sing my part, but she won't listen to me."

All his considerable weight rests on one leg as he thinks about this. "It's because she's bored with her life, Mike," he sighs. "People need to grow, to move," he says.

I know he hopes I read his mind here. Without saying the exact words, he is trying to explain why he is leaving me again. I feel slightly ashamed of this man I am standing with in the crowded lobby. My friends have started drifting back toward the practice room.

"Are you giving me a ride afterwards?" I ask.

"Sure."

"I'll find you then," I say and leave him.

Everybody has the jitters. We line up on the bleachers, the closed curtain separating us from our audience of murmuring parents. The talk in the cafeteria and on the school bus all week has been that we are not ready for this concert, that we sound awful. Mrs. Heinemann decided five weeks ago we would do all new material. Now, with the stage lights bright and hot on our faces and with Carla's lilac mixing with another girl's rose, Mrs. Heinemann's right hand points in a karate-chop position and counts singers in tiny motions like a good knife dicing vegetables. Every few strokes she stops and waves us closer to one another, and our feet shuffle on the wooden planks. Carla and I try not to touch flesh to flesh. Mrs. Heinemann whispers instructions, holds her right palm up for our attention, points to the left to Audrey Klinger, the accompanist, and to the stage hand who will open the curtain. Both hands come down, we swallow collectively, and Audrey begins playing "Consider Yourself" from *Oliver.*

As the curtain opens, I clasp my hands in front and watch Mrs. Heinemann's flapping wings for the signal to sing. Then Audrey misses a difficult run, gets lost, and we begin in disarray. But I am firmly in alto. We lug together, trying to find our way in the rounds and tempo changes of Mrs. Heinemann's fancy arrangement. Disaster. When it is over, the audience applauds politely, as it does no matter how good or bad we are, and a smiling, oblivious Mrs. Heinemann clicks her high heels to the microphone.

"Welcome to our" this, that, and the other, she is saying. I am looking out at the rows of faces for my mother and father, who will be sitting far away from each other. She goes on thanking people for their contributions, like a little child blessing everyone she knows in her bedtime prayers. I am struck by the sort of comment my father would make: "She is trying to spread the blame for this mess."

At the termination of this speech, Audrey starts the endless, over-moody introduction to "Moon River." The stage lights go down and pale blue ones come up. But not all the blue lights work correctly, and part of the chorus is left in darkness as the stage hands knock around in the back to fix the problem. Our parents chuckle nervously as the light finally comes up. Mrs. Heinemann, unfazed, waves her director's arms at us in a private dance. We are not yet singing. Billy Dreibelbis once suggested that if that introduction were two bars longer she might actually start to fly. My father's beard and receding hairline somehow pop out of the crowd, and I know from how he stretches side to side and up and down that he is looking for me. Once, when I could tell he had found me on stage, he waved. And he kept waving until I acknowledged him by nodding my head yes. I complained about my embarrassment later, but he only shrugged and laughed. "That's the kind of person I am," was all he would say.

We are singing "Moon River" now, and we sound all right. No real enthusiasm, of course, but we manage to hit the right notes. We finish and move from song to song, but we have peaked on "Moon River," and everything else seems to only drag our spirits lower. The program is rigged against our ever soaring. Our parents shift in their seats, losing interest. And there on the stage, at thirteen, I was for some reason struck by the realization that my father was right to escape to something beyond the life of our little town. He was right to pay the heavy price in alienation and hostility I already knew I'd levy for this betrayal. I felt somehow unclean even thinking this at the time, as if *I* were the one walking off to suit myself. But then something happened:

Our program is almost over. The lights are up, and we have just butchered a complicated, disastrous medley. My father is scowling, boiling. I don't even have to look at him; I know how he reacts. Even Mrs. Heinemann seems to have come half-awake to how awful we sound. Her movements are heavier, her mouth has fallen, she closes her eyes as if praying just to get through this evening. She is looking down the barrel of forty angry seventh-graders.

Then Billy Dreibelbis whispers the name of a song we have done well all year, and many of us turn to look at him. He won't look directly at Mrs. Heinemann, but he smiles defiantly. Somebody repeats the title, and then somebody else. Mrs. Heinemann holds her hand up and stares at the floor to quiet us. But dresses rustle and heavy shoes clomp restlessly on the bleachers; more of us whisper the title.

She clicks over to the piano for a conference. Audrey's upturned face nods, and then Mrs. Heinemann comes back across the stage and says the title. Victory. We buck up, hug ourselves, and sing. It is strong, almost desperate singing. I have the sense that we are swaying. When Carla's arm touches mine, I glance into her face and, for one supercharged instant, we sing into each other's eyes. My father's neck almost cranes off his shoulders to get a better look at me. Carla and I edge closer. We are practically holding hands. Our hips are touching.

Then my voice suddenly shifts into a strong tenor, so strong it varooms past the other voices in the chorus and carries out into the auditorium. Somebody, a man, laughs, but I see, I feel, people take special note of me. Mrs. Heinemann's eyes panic, plead. But I can't stop myself. My father's voice climbs inside my head. "Smile, Mike! Smile!"

I smile, lifting both my voice and my face. I imagine the chorus bands together to push me forward. I am filled with a strange sadness and joy, an obedience to inevitability, an overwhelming awareness that the very lining of my soul is now irreparably torn and made visible. My father bounces in his seat; he is waving.

I was thirteen years old here. Changes were taking place in my life that I did not yet understand.

Was he waving me on, or was he only waving good-bye?

OPTIONS FOR DIALOGUE

- Discuss Mrs. Heinemann, Mike, Mike's dad, and Carla.
- Was Mrs. Heinemann sensitive to Mike's voice change? Why or why not?
- What was the turning point that convinced Mrs. Heinemann to listen to the choice of music that the students wanted to sing?
- Discuss Mike's thoughts about Louisville.

SUGGESTIONS FOR ACTION

- Interview a person who grew up in a small town. Be sure to ask about the advantages and the disadvantages to living there. Report your findings to your class.
- Interview a business manager or another person who supervises employees. Ask about the advantages and disadvantages of employees' being from a small town as it relates to the particular work involved in this situation.
- Interview a single parent who is not the custodial parent of his or her children who had to move away from the geographic location where the children live. What were some unexpected positive aspects of the situation? What were the difficulties?
- Read some interviews with well-known musicians in newspapers or magazines. Summarize and report on an artist's thoughts about the relationship between music and young people and society in general. For example, in an interview in the March/April 1996 edition of *Mother Jones,* Bruce Springsteen said: "But kids who are supposed to be invisible and never be heard, who are kicked out of high school, who are losers—they make their way through, generation after generation. Nirvana, Dr. Dre, Pearl Jam. Hell, they weren't supposed to become powerful, but they did." What does that quotation or another of your choosing have to do with our story and your thoughts and discussions about it?

- Read one of the following books or one with a related theme:

  Creech, S. (1994). *Walk two moons.* New York: HarperCollins.
  Thirteen-year-old Sal journeys with her grandparents from her new home in Ohio to Idaho, where her mother has recently moved. Sal tells the story of Phoebe, a friend whose mother has disappeared. But as Phoebe's story unfolds, so does Sal's, and Sal renders a powerful account of her struggles to understand her mother's departure.

  Angelou, M. (1983). *I know why the caged bird sings.* New York: Bantam.
  This is the autobiography of Maya Angelou.

  MacLachlan, P. (1991). *Journey.* New York: Delacorte.
  Mama has packed her suitcase and gone away, but 11-year-old Journey won't accept the fact she isn't coming back. His family tries to make things easier for him.

  Vizenor, G. (1990). *Interior landscapes.* Minneapolis: University of Minnesota Press.
  Vizenor writes about his experiences as a tribal mixed blood in the new world of simulations; the themes in his autobiographical stories are lost memories and a "remembrance past the barriers."

Answer these questions about your reading:

1. In a few sentences, summarize the reading(s).
2. Why did you read this? What relationship to your personal or professional life does it have?
3. Do you feel an accurate picture of the information was presented? Why or why not?
4. Which points from the reading did you *not* agree with? Why?
5. Discuss which information or opinions presented here were new to you.
6. Discuss any conversation about this subject that you may have had.

THE GREAT CIRCLE OF THESE THINGS

OPTIONS FOR LISTENING

- Think back to your high school years. Write about an activity outside of school that you really enjoyed. Where did you do this? Which people were involved, if any? Do you now have a sense of why you enjoyed this so much? Can you see now that you were learning something in the process of doing this activity? What questions do you still have?
- Reflect on a place outdoors where you used to spend time as a teenager. Describe the place in your journal. Was it a rooftop? A vacant lot? A wildlife reserve? A river? Try to capture some details about how you felt when you were in this place. What questions do you still have?
- Try to remember an incident when you were in high school when there was a disagreement between a member of the school staff and one of your parents. What was the issue? What happened? What did you think at the time? What do you think now? Write about this.
- Read the selection, write down questions, and note connections.

The Great Circle of These Things
by Tom Peacock

On most days he would lay in bed and listen to his mother getting up. It was early morning and there were the familiar sounds that signaled the beginning of each day: The sound of her feet padding the floor from his parent's bedroom, the close of the bathroom door and the click of a light switch, the whirring of the bathroom fan, the flush of the toilet. Then there would be a transition to kitchen sounds: The opening and closing of cupboard doors, the running of water, the sounds and smells of coffee brewing. Finally, he would listen as she approached the door to his room. It would open and she would say in her soft and gentle voice, "Ronnie, it's time to get up and get ready for school. You've got about half an hour now so hurry up."

With rare exceptions, this was the way Ron remembered each school day. These were familiar patterns for him. He could not imagine it any other way.

He too would follow familiar and similar rituals each morning of getting up, getting dressed, washing his face and stepping into the kitchen for a quick breakfast. Then he would say good bye and step outside and take the short walk to the old dirt road that made its way down the hill to the main highway. He also left enough time to be outdoors and alone before entering a noisy and boisterous bus load of relatives, neighbors and friends.

He looked back down the driveway to his family's home. It was old and his father had replaced some of the metal windows with mismatched wooden ones he had gotten from summer yard and garage sales. Ron remembered helping him do the carpentry work. Also added was a stove pipe extending from the roof above the living room, which with the exception of summer usually had smoke rising from it. Ron knew the wood stove very well because he was responsible for bringing in firewood from the wood pile. His father would say that everyone in the family had a role to play to keep the house warm, a message that needed repeating whenever Ron was hesitant to haul wood. "I cut the wood, you haul it in and put it in the wood box and your mom puts it in the stove. If a part of that whole process isn't working, the rest breaks down."

His father would say the home was good enough whenever his mother complained about its condition and acknowledged a desire to move into the housing projects the tribe provided for most of its residents. Most of the time these requests were more a teasing, except during the long and cold of winter when she was reminded of the inconvenience by a leaky roof or a drafty house. All of them knew they would never make the move, because his father did not wish to become dependent upon the whims of tribal officials. It was an independence acquired from his own father.

The yard was a collage of old cars and appliances, and it reminded Ron of a television Christmas story about a land of unwanted and broken toys. An old pickup whose transmission had gone years ago sat in one corner of the yard, its blank head lamps greeting anyone entering the driveway. It was filled with old tires, rims, and the parts of several outboard motors. Next to it was a broken Renault Lecar, a nice car in its day. Now it had been recycled for use as a storage shed for an array of alternators, car batteries, a radiator of unknown origin and several kerosene cans. Next to the Lecar was the washing machine his father had gotten for his mother several years ago at a rummage sale in Washburn. It only needed a motor. At an odd angle next to it was an avocado colored clothes dryer, whose belt had broken in the recent past. Most of these things were useful for parts or storage. They served a purpose and only seemed to bother occasional tourists who had their visions of what a reservation was dampened by the modern art of reservation junk.

Next to the home was an aluminum fishing boat on a rusty trailer and next to it were his father's and Uncle Eddie's fishing nets and the grey plastic boxes which held the nets which caught the fish that was their livelihood. All were in perfect working order.

Standing out in the yard in what would seem the greatest irony was a satellite dish, which connected the family to the rest of the world. It was Ron's link to MTV, his father's connection to All Star Wrestling and Nashville Live, and his mother's eyes to the world beyond Red Cliff, Wisconsin. Ron remembered when his father had bought it with the money received from his share in Indian land payment. It even had a remote control. "You have to have your priorities straight," his father would say. Nobody disagreed.

The bus came. It was intimately called the "rez bus" by both Indians and whites alike, because that was its mission—to deliver and return kids from the reservation to and from school. It was always nearly full of kids and almost seemed to dance down the hill each morning. Its door would open and swallow Ron and he would enter a different world, a world of headphones, gum, hats on backwards, jostling and full length of bus conversations.

The bus took him and the other kids on a twice daily tour of the village of Red Cliff. They all knew the journey well. Down the old dirt road to the main highway which paralleled the big lake, Lake Superior, Gitchi Gummee to the elders and few remaining speakers of the Ojibwa language. It would pass the housing projects, which stood stark against the pines and lake in their federally approved blues, yellows and government green pastels. It would careen past the tribal headquarters and the tribally owned businesses, which consisted of a bowling alley, marina and small gaming casino. It would pass other yards, some of which were also decorated with reservation modern art, all with their primary missions complete and awaiting or partaking in other uses. Then it would be off to Bayfield, a short three miles up the highway.

Between conversations with fellow bus mates, Ron would peer out the window toward the lake. He always sat on the lake side of the bus, and either traded places with someone or used his size and demeanor to force others to trade if they were not so inclined. There he would sit and look out to the lake and islands and dream dreams of fishing. The big lake was special to him—special because he wanted to be a commercial fisherman, just like his father and Uncle Eddie, when he became an adult. Since he was a child he had ridden along with them during the summer months and on week-ends to set and pull the fish nets they set around the Apostle Islands. When school was in session this part of his being would become inaccessible, so many times after school he would go down to the docks when the fish boats came in because the men would emerge from the old trawlers with stories of the catch and storms, and of cold, hard work and long hours. Never once, however, did he hear anyone say they were getting out of the business because they didn't like it. It was the manner of their discussions and the look in their eyes that convinced Ron the work was something special. It was a necessary part of their life's journey.

Then the bus would lurch to a stop in front of Bayfield High and he would emerge along with the other kids from the reservation. Most would move in herd like fashion into the school. There was a few minutes of noisy visiting. Then it would be classes, the changing of classes, study hall, lunch, and more classes. Bells would ring. Teachers would try to teach. Students would disrupt teachers. Principals would negotiate disagreements, shoo stragglers to class and pick up gum wrappers.

Each school day he would do this. Get up in the morning, go to the bus, ride the bus, look at the lake, dream, go to school. And in the afternoon the process would reverse and repeat itself. He could not imagine it any other way.

A particular fall evening Ron returned home from school after a typical day. Stepping from the bus he saw his father sitting on the porch making repairs in a fish net. "Them d—— northerns. Every once in a while one of them will end up in a net and they cause one hell of a mess. Just rolling over and over again, tangling and tearing it all to hell."

He set his work down and moved to another subject. "By the way, Ron, are you very busy in school right now? I could sure use you out on the lake for a couple of days. Your mom and I have to go over to Duluth for a couple of days to help Auntie Marilyn move out to Fond du Lac. So we been thinking about heading down there tomorrow sometime and coming back on Friday. She has to be back Friday night because it's her turn to call bingo for the women's group."

This was one of those opportunities no sane tenth grader would ever pass up. A chance to do what he wanted to do and with his parent's permission miss a couple of days of school in the process. A chance to have the house all to himself. It was just too good.

"Sounds like a deal to me. Will Eddie come up and get me in the morning? I might need him to call and wake me up on Friday. Where do you have the nets set?"

His father just laughed and went back to his work. A gut laugh. One that knew exactly what a boy was thinking.

That night Ron was so excited about getting the chance to go out into the lake he had difficulty getting to sleep, and when he finally drifted off he dreamed of the islands and fish, soft wind and the smells of fall.

"Ronnie. Ronnie. . . . Hey, kid, it's time to get up." It was his Uncle Eddie standing over him, a cigarette in his mouth and cup of coffee in hand. He was laughing. "What the hell kind of fisherman do you think you are anyway? We should be out on that lake already."

He was up in an instant, then down the hall to pee. Then out to the kitchen where his mother and father sat drinking coffee. His father dished him out some eggs and fried potatoes and poured him a cup of coffee. His mother reminded him the lunch she'd packed had to last him all day. Uncle Eddie reminded him it was time to get moving. Out the door they went.

It was a beautiful late September morning and the sun sparkled off the lake and made him squint. There was a gentle breeze. He helped Eddie load the net boxes into the old fish boat, "Megan," a name given by a long ago owner. Fishing boat names, once given, were never changed. It was bad luck. Megan fired up and out into the lake they went.

The first set of nets they lifted were out on the south side of Hermit Island, about four miles from shore. To get there they ran the boat along Basswood Island, the closest island to the village of Red Cliff at about a half mile out. From the lake, he could see the fall colors in all their brilliance of yellows and oranges. The wind was gentle in his hair and he looked back toward shore and watched Red Cliff shrink into the shoreline. Wood smoke drifted from many houses. Once past Basswood, they could easily see Hermit, Oak and Stockton Islands. Hermit was a small and beautiful island that he'd explored as a young child, climbing its sheer and red cliffs and swimming from its rocky shore. He remembered walking inland with his father to the abandoned brownstone quarry and seeing an old settler's cabin that was slowly with the years again becoming a natural part of the earth. He wondered what it was like to live there a long time ago. He wondered also about the people who lived in the cabin and of the lives they lived all alone on the island.

"Time to get our butts in gear," Uncle Eddie reminded him. With Megan's hydraulic lifter the 300 foot net came up easily. While Uncle Eddie kept the boat on course, Ron removed and measured the fish and folded the net into the fish box. Lake trout and whitefish smaller than 14 inches were thrown back but the herring were kept regardless of size. Then the fish were put into fish boxes by type. Always the boat was surrounded by noisy gulls, all wanting a taste of the action.

"You know when we go to lift nets over on the other end of Basswood you're going to see them two young eagles swooping down with the gulls trying to get a free handout. It's funnier than hell seeing them do that. They're suppose to just sit in their nest and practice being majestic."

Uncle Eddie knew a lot of what he was talking about and it was one of the reasons Ronnie enjoyed fishing with him. He would get a chance to hear some of his stories. Eddie was one of the few people left who knew the old stories, having learned them from his father and grandfather. He not only knew about the plants and animals that lived on and near the lake, he knew the why of them. For over forty years he had fished these waters and knew its corners and moods. He was familiar with its storms and shifting winds, its gentleness and unpredictability. He had seen several generations of eagles nesting on the south side of Basswood for over twenty years. He knew Hermit Island when the cabin was still standing.

He was a forgiving and good-natured man, easy to tell a joke and poke fun. His laughs were genuine. He had a kind and gentle heart.

"You know them birds and the other animals the old Indians called Elder Brothers because they were here before us. They were the third in creation after the earth and the plants. You know they're special because they know about things before they happen. That's something we ain't too good at yet." He laughed and went on.

"Them young eagles that are always begging for a free meal. They come out to meet us every day because they recognize our boats. A long time ago when the Creator first made eagles he gave them strong wings and the ability to see a long ways. They can be gliding way the hell up there and then come down and pick a fish out of the water just like that."

He made a quick sweeping motion with his arms.

"And the Creator made most of them kind of aloof, like they have an attitude. So to see them begging for fish just doesn't seem right. They beg for them fish and still are uppity." He laughed and lit another cigarette.

Ron knew there was a serious purpose in his uncle's stories. It had something to do with his dismay that others had been feeding the young eagles when the birds should be learning how to fish from their parents. It was something about the fact these two eagles were somehow stooping down to partake in something beneath their dignity. It was the way Ron had learned to interpret stories.

As they passed the rocky outcropping that was the north end of Basswood Island and made their way down its eastern shore between it and Madeline Island, Uncle Eddie told him other stories. One he never tired of hearing was the story about the Great Flood of long ago and how all the animals had helped to create the new earth. Eddie always told the same stories many times and Ron would not know of the reasons for this until years later when it would be his time to tell it to his nephews.

". . . When that sky-woman moved onto the back of that giant turtle she asked the water animals to go down to the bottom of the ocean to get some soil. And the beaver and fisher and marten and loon they all tried to help her get some of that soil but they all came up out of breath. Finally, that old mushrat (muskrat) he tried and he was down there a long time and then he floated up all out of breath. But he had some soil in his hand. And the woman painted the turtle's back with the soil and blew life into it and it spread and became an island as it grew bigger. And she let the big turtle swim away once the island was big enough and soon the island became the home of all the animals. You know that's why us Indians call this Turtle Island. This whole earth, you see, it's Turtle Island."

Soon they reached the south end of Basswood. To the south, Ron could see the city of Bayfield, only two miles away. There most of the other kids his age were in school. It could have been a million miles away. Much farther south at the end of Chequamegon Bay lay Ashland.

As they rounded the island the eagle's nest appeared at its southernmost shores, and two juvenile eagles flew out to meet them and beg food with several hundred noisy gulls. Ron worked and watched them in fascination, these two young eagles not even in their adult colors, their bodies still dark brown and not having the white heads of their parents. They begged food with such grace and dignity. When they found out the Megan and its crew were not going to provide them with a free meal they returned to their nest and sat over the lake and watched the two men work. They practiced being majestic.

They lifted and set three 300 foot nets that day and then returned to the shore. As Megan chugged back toward Red Cliff, Ron hosed out the boat and got the nets ready and fish properly boxed. They brought the catch in and took it down to Severson's fishery to sell. Eddie gave Ron five dollars, a seven up and a small bag of barbecue chips. Honest pay for an honest day's work. When he was dropped off at home it was only 2:30 in the afternoon but Ron was tired and immediately took a three hour nap. He ate popcorn for dinner and watched movies until well past midnight. When he went to bed he dreamed of fish and eagles and turtles and muskrats.

Ronnie. Ronnie. . . . Hey kid, it's time to get up." It was his Uncle Eddie standing over him with a cigarette in his mouth and a cup of coffee in his hand.

"Time to rise and shine, kid," he laughed. "Breakfast in the swamp."

He arose slowly this morning, his body aching from yesterday's work. He spent some quality time sitting on the side of the bed for several minutes, scratching his belly and yawning. Then he got up, padding his feet to the bathroom to pee, then out into the kitchen where his uncle was frying potatoes and eggs. He ate and gulped down two large cups of coffee. He'd need more. It was one of those four coffee cup mornings. They walked outside to a cool and misty late September morning. Eddie's old pick-up coughed and they lurched down the hill to the boat landing.

Megan was fired up. It was an old boat but it purred like a kitten. They loaded the nets into the boat and Eddie reminded Ron he was going to have to settle for his "common peanut butter" sandwiches for lunch. Out of nowhere his uncle said,

"One of them young eagles died yesterday. I heard it last night at the casino."

Ron didn't say anything. It was the way Uncle Eddie had said it and the fact he didn't offer any more of the story. This was the way some of these old Indians say things. They just say something and then people have to think about it for awhile. They rode in silence out to Hermit Island to pull their first set of nets.

After the Hermit nets were lifted and new ones set, they started the journey down the east side of Basswood to its south end. Ron chewed on a peanut butter sandwich and watched his uncle steer the old boat through a small chop and misty day.

"I don't know how that eagle got killed. I've seen it before, though, you know. Some of them make it and some of them don't. Some of them get themselves shot and others get poisoned. Some of them don't come back from their migration. Most years there are eagles in the nest though. Sometimes just one of the young ones make it. Looks like it's going to be one of those years."

And on the journey down the east side of Basswood Island an uncle told his nephew the story about life and the great circle of life, and about the four hills he must climb if he is so lucky to grow to be an old man. It was a story so beautiful and simple and profound that Ron would not consider it important until he was much older—until he himself had climbed the fourth hill.

". . . some of them babies, you know, they don't make it over that first hill."

He reminded Ron about several of his cousins who died as babies and Ron remembered hearing about a baby who froze to death in a car one winter while the mother drank inside Bate's tavern.

". . . and some of them young people they don't clear that second hill. They have lots of energy and most make it over that hill easily but a few don't make it."

Remembered a young cousin who was killed in a car accident several years ago just south of Washburn.

". . . and they come to that third hill and now most of the women and men walk together, although there are some who walk alone. They aren't as frisky as they were when they were here a few years ago but they keep moving ahead."

Ron vaguely remembered Sara, Eddie's wife and his Auntie, who took an evil mix of pills and alcohol.

". . . and some of us, we make it to that fourth hill. The lucky ones." He laughed and lit another cigarette.

"We're old now and it takes a lot of energy to climb that hill and most of us don't make it. The top is always covered in mist. That's our after life. That's where we go when we die."

When they rounded the tip of Basswood only gulls came out to beg for food. One young eagle sat in its nest and practiced being majestic. Uncle Eddie took a cigarette out of his front shirt pocket, crushed it and threw it overboard into the lake.

His mother and father returned from Duluth that night and after his father cooked their dinner his mother went down to the bingo hall because it was her turn to be the caller. The women's group was raising money for the village Christmas party.

The week-end passed.

On Monday morning he lay in bed and listened to his mother getting up: The sound of her feet padding the floor to the bathroom, the close of the bathroom door and whirring of the fan. The flush of the toilet. Then the sound of feet and a transition to kitchen sounds. Finally, she approached the door to his room and said in her soft and gentle voice,

"Ronnie, it's time to get up and get ready for school. You've got a half an hour so hurry up."

After spending some quality time sitting on the edge of the bed he got dressed and went to school. On this day he took a note written by his mother to the principal's office which read:

"Please excuse Ron as we kept him home from school for Thursday and Friday of last week because he was needed out on the lake to help his uncle pull fish nets."

The attendance secretary would not excuse his absence and the school work Ron missed during his absences could not be made up for credit. Ron wouldn't question the decision. He was too consumed with water and islands, turtles and muskrats, eagles and uncles.

He was practicing being majestic.

OPTIONS FOR DIALOGUE

- Discuss the relation between the title of the story and the activities of Ron and his beliefs.
- What was Ron learning from Uncle Eddie?
- What was Ron learning from his school experiences?
- What are some of the school's assumptions about Ron and his family?
- What do you predict that Ron will remember about these years of his life?
- Do you think the school should have excused Ron's absence as described by his mother's note? Why or why not?

SUGGESTIONS FOR ACTION

- Read the following historical accounts and relate the information to Ron's story:

    Quimby, G. I. (1960.) *Indian life in the upper Great Lakes.* Chicago: University of Chicago Press.

    Taylor, I. (1976). *Ojibwe, the wild rice people and Native American contributions to progress.* Shell Lake, WI: Wisconsin Indianhead Vocational, Technical, & Adult Education District Office.

Warren, W. (1970). *History of the Ojibwe nation.* Minneapolis: Ross & Haines (Minnesota Historical Society).

- Review at least three sources of information regarding American Indian sovereignty rights. List all the information that is new to you. Plan a presentation to your class in which you explain the information and relate it to Ron's story.
- Read one of the following books or one with a related theme:

Freire, P. (1994). *Pedagogy of hope.* New York: Continuum.
   This work chronicles the ongoing social struggles of Latin America and the Third World since Freire's landmark publication nearly 25 years ago, *Pedagogy of the Oppressed.*

Erdrich, L. (1986). *The beet queen.* New York: Holt.
   A tough yet empathetic novel exposes the loneliness and craving that keep people separate even when their lives intersect.

Erdrich, L. (1994). *The bingo palace.* New York: HarperCollins.
   Lipsha Morrissey answers a mysterious call to return to his home on the Ojibwe reservation, where he falls in love with and pursues Shawnee Ray Toose.

Kingsolver, B. (1993). *Pigs in heaven.* New York: HarperCollins.
   A humorous and thought-provoking story of the conflict between an adoptive mother and a Native American tribe over the destiny of a Cherokee girl.

Answer these questions about your reading:

1. In a few sentences, summarize the reading(s).
2. Why did you read this? What relationship to your personal or professional life does it have?
3. Do you feel an accurate picture of the information was presented? Why or why not?
4. Which points from the reading did you *not* agree with? Why?
5. Discuss which information or opinions presented here were new to you.
6. Discuss any conversation about this subject that you may have had.

- View the films *Where the Spirit Lives* and *The Raid.* Organize a discussion group relating the information in the movies to some of the historical information you have learned during your work in this section.
- Attend an event sponsored by American Indian people. In writing, reflect on what you have learned.

WRITING DOWN SECRETS

OPTIONS FOR LISTENING

- Reread your journal writings for this class. Find examples of your individual voice in your writing. What specific details and perceptions does your voice capture about your family, school, and community contexts? What specific questions do you ask about your experiences? Underline or list some of these details or questions. Choose some to share with a partner.
- In "Writing Down Secrets" third-grade teacher Sara Mosle used journal writing to help children explore the realities of their lives. In writing these intimations of personal reality are called *voice.* Before reading "Writing Down Secrets" read

the following discussion of voice in writing. When you have finished reading, you may have some critical questions about the information. Please consider the comments and then write down some of your questions.

Each writer, child or adult, has a unique voice that she or he opens to, listens to, and speaks from. Elbow (1981) describes writing with voice as writing into which someone has breathed. Voice, for him, has nothing to do with the words on the page, only with the relationship of the words to the writer: "the words contain not just an explicit message, 'the sun glints down a pathway of ripples,' but also some kind of implicit message about the condition of the writer" (Elbow, 1981, p. 299). The sixth-grade child who wrote the following poem used metaphor simultaneously to create and proclaim who she is. At the same time the poem reveals to us, the readers, her personal stance toward life.

Elbow, P. (1981). *Writing with power.* New York: Oxford University Press.

Life

I'm a heart, pounding in my chest.
I'm a winter breeze, chilling people as they walk by.
I'm a letter, writing to people, cheering them up.
I'm life, coming and going.

More than speech, a writer's voice is distinct, definable, the combination of what you say and how you say it. Voice has as much to do with individual consciousness as it does with the subject of the writing. Who we are determines what we notice; and these things, patterns, ideas, sounds will be apparent in our writing, whether we are conscious of this or not.

Even when the subject is not the self, the self continues to draw individual reality by its perceptions. We write what we notice, and in the process of writing notice more, discover more. Our own voices become stronger the closer we come to what's critically important to us and what unleashes our own emotions. Voice is strong when images are crystal-clear.

Voice also has to do with acts of mind—the questioning, sifting, and connecting process of thought. This is different from experience because it has to do with the process of thinking.

Anna Flanagan (1994) tells us how Kenyan poet Micere Mugo "came to appreciate the political nature of creative writing and poetry as she saw how it enabled her and others to reclaim themselves and give voice to the liberation struggles of the people. . . . Within colonial systems, people are named and defined by those in power. Therefore, the act of seizing responsibility and naming becomes, in Mugo's view, a political act." Mugo says, "Writing can be a lifeline, especially when your existence has been denied, especially when your life and process of growth have been subjected to attempts at strangulation." She views creative writing as a way of breaking what she calls negative silences, "those that are imposed on us, stopping us from articulating ourselves, stopping us from understanding ourselves, stopping us from having dialogue with other people."

Flanagan, A. (1994, June). Kenyan poet sees poetry as political statement. *Council Chronicle,* p. 7.

- Read the selection; note questions and personal connections.

Writing Down Secrets
by Sara Mosle

One morning, in the third-grade class where I taught public school, Shameka was sulking. She had arrived late and empty-handed, in what seemed at first like a defiant mood. "Where's your book bag?" I called from the back of the room. (No book bag meant no books, no pencils, no paper.) She flashed me a bored look, gave an exaggerated shrug, and plopped into her seat. I had more than thirty students in my class and had just got them settled in their morning reading groups when Shameka showed up; I was fenced into a corner by a circle of kids sitting cross-legged on the rug. Then Andrew shouted out, "Hey, Miss Mosle! Shameka's crying!" All heads turned so eyes could look her way. I hated to disrupt the lesson, but what to do? Shameka usually returned such unwelcome attention with a feisty "Shut up!"; her silence made me think her tears weren't trivial. I gave out an impromptu assignment and stepped over the kids' heads to investigate. I crouched down next to her and asked, "Shameka, what's wrong?" But she couldn't, or wouldn't say. As I tried to coax an answer from her, I kept an eye on the kids in the back of the room. Huey had just punched Frederico in the arm. My class was in danger of unraveling.

I was in my third—and, for now, last—year of teaching public school, in Washington Heights, a predominantly Dominican and African-American community that extends some forty-five blocks from Harlem, which ends at about West 155th Street, to Dyckman Street, near the northern tip of Manhattan. The public schools in the neighborhood have some of the most overcrowded classes in the city, and it wasn't until later that day, when I had a free period, that I had a chance to talk to Shameka alone. (Her name, like the names of the other children mentioned here, has been changed.) I took her to an empty lunchroom, the only private spot I could find in the school. She still couldn't talk, but she began to nod or shake her head in response to my questions; this was progress. I tried to pare down the possible causes of her unhappiness, a method that often worked with my students. (By admitting what the problem wasn't, a kid could often acknowledge what it was.) "Is it something that happened at school?" No. "Is it something that someone said?" No. "Are you in physical pain?" No. "Does it have something to do with your family?" Shameka began to cry again: I was getting close. Finally, I asked, "Do you think you could write to me about what is wrong?" She nodded. I ran and got her some paper and a pencil and left her alone for a few minutes.

When I returned, her head lay on the long linoleum-topped table; she had placed the paper and pencil carefully to one side. A single sentence slipped precariously down the page; "I had I DO not have a home but my sister Best frnded home and sha DO not like me."

Huh? Shameka lived a few blocks away, with her mother and several brothers and sisters; I'd walked her home just a few days before.

With the help of the school's social worker, I decoded the note's meaning. Unbeknownst to Shameka, her family had been evicted from its apartment. Her mother, not wanting to take the kids to a shelter, which she regarded as dangerous, had farmed them out among her friends. She hadn't told Shameka what was happening, because she didn't want to upset her until she had found another place for all of them to live. As I talked to Shameka, I realized that, in the absence of an explanation, her imagination had conjured up a far worse reason for the family's sudden dissolution: she assumed that her mother had died.

I used to tell my students, "I can't help you unless you tell me what's wrong." But they weren't accustomed to asking for help, because in their lives help wasn't always forthcoming. Lost toys were often lost forever. A pair of prescription glasses broken in a playground prat-fall and worth a third of the rent might remain broken for months. One kid in my class wept when a button fell off his shirt. (He owned very few clothes, and this shirt was brand-new.) When I produced a needle and thread and sewed the button back on, he grinned at me as though I'd performed a miracle. I suspected that his mother could have performed the same magic, and I turned the incident into a parable: "See? All you have to do is ask for help." But I knew things weren't always that simple. Unlike adults, who have more perspective on their lives, my students often had little idea that the world could be other than what it was for them.

In fact, Shameka's fear about her mother was perfectly plausible. From 1990 to 1992, Washington Heights had more homicides than any other neighborhood in New York. Partly because of the area's proximity to the George Washington Bridge, it has an active—and deadly—drug trade. Suburbanites cross the bridge to buy marijuana, cocaine, and heroin (the current hot drug among the middle class). I've been approached several times by dealers on the street who seemed to assume that because I'm white I must be in the neighborhood to buy drugs. Despite these problems, the neighborhood has a friendly feel. People congregate and socialize on stoops. Milk jugs with the bottoms knocked out are pinned on fences and fire escapes to form basketball hoops. When one boy was murdered, a crossing guard at the school collected more than a hundred dollars from passers-by, in less than an hour, to help his family pay for the burial. Recently, the area has become something of an artists' community: opera singers, actors, and painters have moved in, attracted by low rents and the bohemian atmosphere. Tens of thousands of Dominican immigrants have also poured into this tiny patch of real estate over the last decade, making the neighborhood one of the most densely populated in the city, and creating tensions between Latinos and African-Americans, who have been there longer. The neighborhood has its share of "welfare mothers," but many of my students' parents worked twelve hour days, often at more than one job. They were usually lucky if they earned the minimum wage. Some labored in what sounded like sweatshops, and their children often went unsupervised while they worked. (Fifteen thousand people are currently on the waiting list for child-care programs in the area.) Nearly ninety percent of the kids at the school qualified for free lunches. My students were poor.

Had Shameka not been able to write to me, I might never have discovered what was wrong with her that day. We'd been working on first-person narratives—my students kept daily journals in class. But at first they didn't know how to write about themselves. The skill doesn't necessarily come naturally, as I learned during my first year in the classroom. I would put a topic on the board—"What is your favorite movie?" or "What did you dream last night?"—and my students would invariably groan, "I don't want to write about that!" And who could blame them? Adults don't write in such a void. The purpose of writing—a business letter, a poem, even a bit of graffiti—is to communicate. But in my early, contrived lessons my students weren't writing to anyone.

I asked a friend, Gillian Williams, who was also a first-year teacher, for advice. She told me, "Instead of putting topics on the board, I've started writing back to each kid individually in his or her own notebook." Every morning, students wrote in their journals, and every afternoon, Gillian responded to what they had written with a few lines of her own, asking questions, remarking on their entries, answering questions that her students put to her. The next day, the kids would reply. She had a different dialogue going with each student. She didn't correct spelling or punctuation—she wanted to encourage her students to write freely in this forum, and work on grammar in other lessons. I later learned that this looser method of teaching writing is part of a larger trend in early-childhood education known as "whole language," but Gillian, in the trial-and-error fashion of teachers, had simply devised the approach on her own. I decided to try it in my classroom.

I've never been able to keep a journal. When I start one, the entries usually peter out in a matter of days. Once when I was in the fifth grade, I did keep a diary for several months, but after my older brother found it and teased me about its contents I threw it away. In Dallas, Texas, where I grew up, in the late sixties and early seventies, reticence was a virtue. In those days, the heartland was, in the words of one writer, a "vast non-Freudian America." I learned to read with "Dick and Jane." Rote exercises constituted most of the writing that I did at the public school I attended. The only time I can remember crying in class was when I sat on a tack in the third grade, and I recall the ordeal mainly because of the injustice involved: the teacher unfairly blamed me for the incident.

Another emotion, however, snakes around this memory: unhappiness. Even then, I knew I was crying because of it; the tack had simply provided an alibi for my tears. I seriously doubt whether I could have articulated why I was unhappy then. I don't think it even occurred to me that my unhappiness had a source, although in retrospect it seems obvious: my older sister had died of cancer the year before. The effects of this, however, were so all-encompassing that I thought of her death simply as a fact of life.

I have one sample of my own writing from that period—an account of a trip our family took to Chicago by train over Easter break one year. I was in the third grade— the same age as many of my future students. Here's a typical passage:

I looked out the window. It was fun. Then I went to the room. We were almost to Chicago. Then we went to the lounge. And we looked out the window. Then I sang. Then I looked out the window. Then we were in Chicago.

And so it goes: then, then, then—up to the top of the John Hancock building, through the Museum of Science and Industry, and down the shores of Lake Michigan. What I recall most vividly about that trip now is the giant Seurat painting at the Art Institute of Chicago; back at the hotel, I tried unsuccessfully to mimic his Pointillist style with crayons. But I didn't have the wit, or the know-how, to write about that. And we certainly didn't discuss the recent death in the family, although I was aware that the trip was our family's first since my sister died, and that we were all trying very hard to have fun. I can no longer recall what I thought about my sister's death then, only that I thought about it a lot. I think that in the isolation of our family's silence I regarded her death somewhat selfishly, as something that had happened to me, and to me alone.

My sister's belongings were stored in a closet in the now spare bedroom of our house. It was a kind of shrine. I used to stand in there and stare at the contents: her jewelry box; her clothing; a large get-well card painted by a family friend who was an artist; her sixth-grade notebook, which still contained her schoolwork and smelled of new plastic. Once, while rummaging through her stuff, I came across a small white vinyl diary with a blue heart on the cover and tiny silver-and-green padlock that held it shut. I asked my mom if I could read it. She said "No" in a way that communicated anguish. I immediately assumed that she must have read it herself and discovered something up-setting inside. A few years later, when my brother uncovered my diary, he threatened to reveal some childish remarks I had made about being mad at my mom. I threw the diary away rather than risk her finding it. I can still remember what I was thinking: What if I died? And my mother read my diary? I didn't want to upset her, too.

I became fascinated with my students' journals. As my friend had advised, I encourage the kids not to worry about spelling or grammar but to get their thoughts down, the way they spoke, in "rough draft." I replied to what they wrote. Although my grammar had been better, they were far more expressive than I had been at their age. And I wondered why. It occurred to me as I read their journals that when I was a kid grownups seldom asked me about my life. Children and adults remained strange to one another. I know that I regarded my own elementary-school teachers as creatures from another planet—ageless and not human. My students, however, seemed to view me as far less mysterious. The journals were what bridged the gap. They operated a little like an apartment-house air shaft, providing a common area where we could communicate. Like neighbors leaning out of windows, we exchanged gossip, inquired after family, caught glimpses of one another's lives. They wrote freely, I think, partly because they were also writing to themselves:

I'm feeling smart today Ms. Mosle yo! and one more thing Ms. Mosle I still want more homework.

They sought advice:

Ms. Mosle you said you was going to tell me what to do to help my friend because her mother throw's her out of the house.

They took me to task for perceived injustices:

Why don't you put (me as) the office monitor why did you chang my seat. Just because Marla says that I wana change seats with Colleen doesn't mean that you have to change my seat and your the teacher not Marla or me and anyway I want to go back to the dolphins (table) and my freinds too.

They described events in their lives:

My firends boyfirend died. And she was sad. I herd in the phone tha she was sad. . . . She lives in New Jersey he was seling drugs for 100 dollars and a man came with 50 dollars and sede if he could take a pack and he sede no. So he had a gun and shot him three times in the chest. then he died. I did not go to the funirow.

When one boy's uncle died, I made the mistake of asking, "Are you sad?" He replied:

Why would you akse a question like that? You make me feel sader because my uncle is Dead. I'll get over it Don't remind me any more please? I loves him so much.

Because many of my students were recent immigrants, they sometimes had trouble with idiomatic English. (Certain spelling and syntax errors—for instance, their use of double negatives—consistently reminded me that Spanish was their first language.) Before school one day, I noticed Valentino's mother hovering near her son, and I asked him about it in his journal: "I see your mother every morning. Are you and she close?" Valentino took the question literally, and replied:

Yes becuse sometimes she is cold and I got to grab her a little so she could be a little hot and so she cannot get sick from the wind.

But went on to answer my question:

My mother allways tells me if I'm cold (I) said (just) a little becuse I got a coat. Sometimes my mother where's a jacket cuse she don't have no coat that's why she holds me and my hands too. . . . In winter she holds me real tied (tight) cuse she is cold. Someday she is gonna buy herself a coat so she cannot be cold too much. My mother she gots to hold me cuse she doens't have a coat. She gonna buy a big hot coat for herself.

Valentino's entries were always these little prose poems, full of repetitions, which crescendoed and then culminated in a sly last line. Once, when I asked him about his weekend plans, he wrote:

I'm gonna rent a tape of supernintendo tomorrow afternoon. I'm going to my cusun's house to ride a bike a little bit and its gonna be fun in my cusin's house plus my other friend too. All of them are gonna play with me in the house supernintendo. it's gonna be fun tomorrow. Tomorrow their gonna give me $25 doller and im gonna have $40 dollers tomorrow. I am gonna have a lot of fun. Tomorrow it is my birthday.

I often asked my students about their earliest memories; I had to struggle to recall my own life at their age. I asked Valentino, "Do you remember being a baby? What's the first thing in your life that you remember? How far back does your memory go?" He had an uncanny description of infancy:

A long time ago I used to cry a lot. . . . I used to do things that is too dangurou. My mother always had to give me milk cause I was always hungry. . . . When I was a baby I used to make a lot of noice and cry real hard cause I wanted milk. I used to jump in the bad a lot oo. Sometimes I used to hit somebody by mistake. . . . Sometimes I use glue and knife and stiked it into my nose but my mother took it out. I hide under furniture and under my mother's bed. . . . I used to take toys and throw it in the floor.

Most of my students had no books at home. (Many of them didn't even own crayons.) One day, Colleen began her journal entry this way:

This is a spell:
Double, double toil and trouble,
fire burn and caldron bubble

Eye of newt and frog
wool of bat and toung of dog
Adder's for blindworm sting
Lizzard's legs and owlets wing

for acharm in powerfull trouble
Ike a hell broth boil and bubble

By Me Colleen Acevedo

She had apparently written out the passage from memory. I asked her in her journal where the spell had come from. The next day she replied:

It is from this dictionary and then is Shakespear is all I know. What is the story of Thy Romeo and Juiliat?

I wrote back: "The spell is from Shakespeare. He was a man who wrote plays many years ago. The spell is from a play called 'Macbeth.' It's named for an evil king." This knowledge only excited her further:

I'm right? he did? Where did the name Macbeth come from? I do not know nithing about Romeo and Juliat.

I replied: " 'Romeo and Juliet' is a love story. They love each other, but their parents hate each other and won't let their kids marry. One commits suicide and then so does the other. It's a sad story. Can you tell me a love story?" She responded:

yes I can.

Well is not exactly a love story is my sister who misses the guy she likes and he live in Dykeman (Street) his is 14 years old and my sister is only 12 but still she never forgets him. One day she asked him that she want to go to the movies but she did not know that (the movie was rated R) but she did not care and she went with him. He was kind. . . . he did not did anything bad to her then when my sister came home my mother gave a rusult to my sister that she is grouned for 2 weeks no phone, no raido, and no going outside.

We had been studying cause and effect in class and had been talking about the "results" of characters' actions. Colleen continued:

from that day she was sad and she promised my mother tha she will never Do it again that's my sister love story. Did you like the story? Answer yes or no on the bottom

yes or no

I circled "Yes."

Not all my students were as enterprising as Colleen. It's hard to be resourceful without any resources. Cooped up in their tiny apartments, the kids complained most of being bored. Accounts of some weekends read like the movie listings in *TV Guide*. Daniel described his weekend: "On Satuerday I saw two movies about Keratie First it was (The Last Dragon) then it was a kickboxer and Sunday I saw Hower the Duck and Pee Wee Hermen after that I saw teneg mutie ningja trunle and at ten o'clock I saw Houes partys 2." Daniel's parents weren't supervising their son, because they were working twelve-hour days; his mother also attended school. "She is smart," Daniel wrote. "She goes to school and she allways pass the Test it is good haveing a mother that knows lots of stoff." But for some parents, particularly working mothers, television was the only available child-care option. Daniel often did the babysitting himself; he was responsible for looking after his bedridden grandmother, a task he actually enjoyed. He explained:

She is sick that's why I went to her houes but my little brother made it wrost he was jumping all arounded the houes. I'm going to her house until she gets better but with out my little brother. . . . on Thursday I'm going to buy her medison For she could get better and presnt to cheer her up. We are close but we are closer than that is like glue we are stick.

My students weren't always sweet and nice. Gloria spent several entries impishly describing her skirmishes with her brother: "I hit him in the face so her started to cry." I asked, "Was there any way you could have gotten him to stop hitting you without hitting back?"

Gloria replied:

I hit any way becouse he is a brat. I fight with him a lot becous it get's him mad Pluse I like fighting him it's a lot of fun. . . . he is too much of a crybaby haha. babycryer

I persisted somewhat earnestly: "How would you like to have a sister who hits you? . . . Is there anything that you do with your brother?" She wrote back:

the only relashanship I have withe my brother is rollerskating me and him is good rollershaking but he always crys because me and him always have races and he always loses to much Pluse in the other letter I told you that he is a brat. That little brat.

I had a feeling that I was being baited. I tried a different tactic: "Are you ever bratty? What would your brother say about you if he were writing me?" Gloria responded:

Well I am sometimes bratty but at least I don't cry when they take something away from me.

I gave up: "What do you want to be for Halloween?" Gloria wrote:

I want to be a devil but (my brother) keeps (bugging) me he could be one. So it look like I have to be a angle. But what I realy want to be is a wich and one more thing why did you chang the subject?

She was onto me.

Like the kids of more affluent working families, my students jealously monitored their parents' attention to them. Colleen wrote:

I hated Sunday because when I went to mother work and then when this baby named Michael came he got me so jelous tha he climbed on my mother knees. Of course I missed school.

Indeed, the neighborhood where I taught was not so different from far wealthier communities. There were good parents and bad parents. Penelope's mom made up spelling quizzes and offered her daughter incentives to learn:

I study words when I already studyed the words my mother then she gives me a test and if I get all 40 words right she gives me $5.00. . . . I studyed foolish-big-large-gocery-detective and many hard words.

Some kids went to work with their parents. Renaldo helped his father on weekends and after school at what sounded like a bodega:

Today, I worked with my father waching people if there stealing, and opening boxes. being the cashier and giving chang.

Denny appreciated his father's cameo one weekend:

On Saturday I had a basketball game. they blew us out the score was 7–32 My father was there. This is his first time coming to see me he said I can play(well). . . . Saturday I saw the duncking and shotout (contest). . . . a rookie won they call him baby Jordan! I can't believe that he won because he played agisnst pros.

When one girl's father reneged on his promise to buy her a new coat, she surmised:

I am a little bit angry with him because he said he was going to buy a new coat and dint he always comes up with a lie story he said he had a headace that was just that he dosen't want to spend money.

And a few kids' parents were dead or in jail. These facts would trickle out over time. One kid, William, had transferred to my class several weeks into the year. He was smart, but he never did his homework, and he often picked on other kids in class. I hadn't had much success in talking to him about his difficulties. I asked him what he had done over his Thanksgiving vacation. He replied:

I had a nice Thanksgiving. I ate turkey and rice and ham. I played with me friends I went to see home alone!!! I had a nice thanksgiveing. I went to see my father in jail. I am happy to see him in thanksgiveing.

Beneath what he wrote he drew a picture of a building with a man standing in a window at the top. I asked, "Is this the picture of the jail? How long has your father been there? . . . Will he be there long? Have you visited him before?" He wrote back:

Yes I visited him before a long tie ago and he getting fat and big he look nice. I see my brother and my father I saw my brother on thanksgiveing and we had fun we want to see my father in jail.

Sometimes I wasn't sure how to respond. I tried not to be judgmental: "I bet you miss your father. If you could write him a letter, what would you say?" William wrote, "Dear Dad, I LOVE you. I miss you a lot and I wish you could come out of jail today. I love you, me, mom, brother, and sister." I asked William if he wanted to send his father a real letter, and he said yes. He stayed after school one day, and we made it together, out of construction paper, markers, and glue. He brought his father's address to school the next day, and we mailed his creation. From that moment on, William's behavior changed; he started doing his work and stopped picking fights. He often stayed after school to do homework or just hang out in my classroom while I graded papers or prepared the next day's lessons. And William's father had begun to write to him. William sent his father a valentine and described his father's reply in his journal:

Hi wrote me a ltter sading hi like it he said to write him alot he said he love me and my mother.

During that last year of teaching, I had one student, Drew, who indicated just before Christmas that his mother was ill. Encouraged by my success with William, I asked him if he wanted to make her a get-well card. He nodded, and stayed after school that same afternoon. Drew was a good artist; he decorated his card with a cut-out Christmas tree and freehand drawings of cartoon characters. In his best handwriting, he wrote: "Dear Mom, I hope you feel better. I miss you lots and lots. I hope to see you son. xxx ooo love, Drew." Below this letter he sketched a picture of a woman lying in a hospital bed, surrounded by doctors. When I asked him if he wanted to mail it, he gave me a bewildered look and shook his head. I assumed that his mother was at home and that he would take the card to her there. A couple of months later, another teacher revealed that Drew's mother had died two years earlier; she'd been burned to death by drug dealers.

To this day, I'm not sure why Drew fabricated that story, but I know that there can be shame for a kid in having a dead mother. I occasionally lied as a kid about my sister; friends would come over and ask me who the girl was in all the family photographs and I'd say a cousin, or, incredibly, myself at a younger age; it was easier than trying to explain. At the end of the year, I found the card Drew had made in his desk. Drew, who tore the covers off his workbooks, wadded up assignments, and once scribbled in a brand new library book, had preserved for more than six months the card that he'd made to comfort himself.

Over time, I began to realize how often even young children can feel as responsible as adults do for the people around them. My students wanted to protect their families; they wanted to protect me. "You don't have to walk me home, Ms. Mosle. My block is dangerous," one nine-year-old insisted. It was too dangerous for me but not for him. Another student, Roberto, described the sense of responsibility he felt when his mother fell and broke her leg:

She was trying to walk on her foot with a walker and sometimes I help. . . . she try to go to the bathroom and try to take a bath. Witch is the hard part so I help her to cary the chiar that's so heavy so (I ask) my father to hlep me and I help him sometimes, and (sometimes) he don't want no help so I said ok dad.

He gave me periodic updates on her recovery in his journal:

She's walking a little now and I help mom to walk and I give her wanter oh! . . . and I help her take a bath bursh her teeth help get dressed and help her cook and hlep her do breakfast put on her shoes and sock's and help put on her shirt and puts me to sleep and 8:00.

I wrote, "She is lucky to have such a nice son as you." At one point, he confessed:

I was afraid that mother is going to die but she did'nt die and I was happy and proud of myself and when she came home it was her birthday and I speprail (surprise) her and give her gifts then she went to sleep. thank you for listen.

A few years ago, I finally pried open my sister's diary; I was in my late twenties. I had always assumed that my mother had forbidden me to read it because it contained some revelation that she feared would upset me: a dreadful description by my sister of her cancer or fear of death—or even, perhaps, some damning remark about me. But these, it turned out, were childhood fantasies. My imagination, like Shameka's, had conjured up something far worse than the reality, and after reading the diary I concluded that my mom had never read it herself. I then set to wondering what she might have been afraid of finding inside: Criticism? Descriptions of an illness and suffering that she couldn't prevent or cure? Or just a glimpse of her daughter's lost personality—a loss that she didn't need or want to relive? Maybe my mother, unlike me, didn't need to go searching for clues to who my sister was. (As it happened, I was wrong: I recently learned that of course she had read it, too.)

The diary is, in fact, almost completely empty. The entries begin on September 14, 1969; my sister was ten years old and had just begun the fourth grade. For several months, her entries continue in this vein:

Sept. 19th, 1969 forgot.
Sept. 20th, 1969 forgot.
Sept. 21, 1969 Go to 9:00 church, then 10:50 church (choir). Come home from church. Play Kickball and Soccer with Brian and Jon (Sara, too) Try on clothes. Help mom.
Sept. 22nd, 1969 School (Test) Music Dinner Bed.
Sept. 23rd, 1969 School (test) (orchestra) choir Dinner Bed.
Sept. 24th, 1969 School (Test) play bed.

I had to laugh: my sister's prose style was not unlike my own as a kid. Then, near the end of November, the entries abruptly stop. A few weeks before Christmas of that year, my sister woke up with a sharp pain in her abdomen, and my parents took her to the hospital. She had a malignant tumor on her liver, an almost unheard-of diagnosis in a child her age. On December 21st, she had the first of several operations; I can remember the date because it was on the day after my sixth birthday. Entries don't appear again until the spring, and then there are only three, much like those above; another week's worth when my sister attended summer camp; then there is nothing more until the following June.

I was grateful to learn that my sister's illness hadn't transformed her completely. (At the back of her diary is this list: "BOYS I LIKE: CHRIS B., DALE M., JEFF B.") Only in her last few entries is there any indication that she was ill:

June 16, 1971. Wed. Went to have plasmapharesis blood test. Went have regular blood. Checked in at Methodist Hospital in Houston. Visited with David Mumford. Dr. Crawford and Dr. Eliband dropped by. Granny and Grandpa and Dad came by. Watch TV. Went to bed.

My sister's handwriting reveals a struggle over the spelling of "plasmapheresis." She had obviously encountered something that she didn't want or know how to explain. Does that mean, though, that she didn't understand what was happening to her? I don't know. Nowhere does she mention the chemotherapy, the needles, the catheters, the wig. Reading what she wrote, I understood the desire to back away from these things. (Our family's reticence finally made sense to me.) My sister made her last entry three months before she died:

June 17, 1971. Went to have liver scan. Had biopsy. Laid on my side for four hours.

One afternoon, after my sister's death—I must have been eight or nine years old— I was sitting at my mother's dressing table, trying on her makeup and perfume. Grownups, I think, misunderstand the purpose of playing dress-up. I wasn't pretending to be my mother; I was trying to understand her. In my mind, those bottles and jars contained the secrets of adulthood. As I rummaged through her things, I came across a small cardboard box and opened it. I immediately recognized the contents and their import, and closed the box and put it away. I'd found what I was looking for; I never mentioned the discovery to my mom. Although I'm not sure how, I knew that the lock of blond hair was my sister's, and that it bespoke an enormous unmentionable grief.

I had forgotten this incident until I began to teach. In education classes, I was constantly taught to be sensitive to the obvious differences between my students' backgrounds and my own. But by emphasizing the differences, I think, we sometimes forget that other people's children are like our own. As I read my students' journals, I came to appreciate our unexpected similarities. My students, like my sister, were recognizable children. They, like me, had a secret life that they were yearning to share. Roberto's mother did get well, but some weeks after her accident I asked him in his journal how she was doing. He wrote:

I like to be a doctor and How about she dies before I grow up, and I will tell you when [she] dies. it a secret. . . . it just between us, when my mother dies, am going to take a sissor and cut my mother hair for I won't forget her when she dies. P.S. don't tell nobody. See you soon.

OPTIONS FOR DIALOGUE

• Discuss the following questions in your groups:

1. How does the teacher use writing in her life? Keeping the quote from Mugo in mind, reflect on this question: how is her writing political?

2. How do her students use writing in their lives? How is their writing an example of personal and political empowerment?
3. What does the teacher learn from the students?
4. As you read the writing of these children, what does it tell you about their strengths?
5. What can you learn about the barriers that they face?

SUGGESTIONS FOR ACTION

- Read one of the following articles or another article that focuses on responding to voice in the writing of children:

Rummel, M. K. (1995, Spring). Territories of voice: Social context in poetry for and by children. *New Advocate.*

Rummel, M. K., & Quintero, E. (1996, Spring). Something to say: Voice in the classroom. *Childhood Education.*

Rummel, M. K., & Quintero, E. (1995). Voice unaltered: Marginalized young writers speak. In E. B. Swadener & S. Lubeck (Eds.), *Children and families at promise: The social construction of risk.* Albany, NY: SUNY Press.

- Visit a classroom of children. Ask permission to read some of their writing. What are the aspects of voice that you recognize in the writing? Look for details and metaphors relating to family, school, and community contexts. Write down responses to the writing of children that affirm individual voice. For example, the following is a response to a child's answer on a math essay question: In complete sentences, describe three things you would do if you made a million dollars."

Child answer: "I would construct a hospital in Somalia. I would make a huge wildlife refuge. I would buy a ranch in the country."

Preservice teacher response: "What you wrote tells me that you care about other people and animals. That is a very important quality to have. I, too, worry about the people in Somalia. How would you build a wildlife refuge?"

- Go back to the listening activity at the beginning of this selection. Write a poem, story, or essay about your own voice as it is expressed in your writing and in your life. You could revise journal selections as an example of your voice or create a work of visual art or music instead of writing to share your own voice with the others in the class.
- Read one of the following books written by teachers in order to discover connections between the experiences of the author and the experiences of Sara Mosle, the author of "Writing Down Secrets." What are differences and similarities in the ideas expressed by the authors? How did the author affirm and encourage the development of personal, communal, and critical voice in her or his students? What happened as a result? What did the teachers learn? Compare the experience of the teacher (or the students) in the book to your own. What connections can you make?

Haberman, M. (1995). *Star teachers of children in poverty.* West Lafayette, IN: Kappa Delta Pi.

Kotlowitz, A. (1991). *There are no children here.* New York: Bantam Doubleday Dell.

Kozol, J. (1991). *Savage inequalities.* New York: Crown.

Ladson-Billings, G. (1994). *The dreamkeepers.* San Francisco: Jossey-Bass.

Landsman, J. *Basic needs.* (1993). Minneapolis: Milkweed Editions.

Paley, V. G. (1995). *Kwanza and me.* Cambridge, MA: Harvard University Press.

Sleeter, C. E. (1992). *Keepers of the American dream.* Bristol, PA: Falmer.

- Read published journal selections such as *Life Notes: Personal Writings by Contemporary Black Women* edited by Patricia Bell-Scott. How is this journal writing like that of the children described by Mosle?

LEXICON OF EXILE

OPTIONS FOR LISTENING

- Think of a childhood memory you like to remember. Think of a childhood memory that you would like to forget but cannot. Write in your journal about one of these memories. Please add to your writing some questions you still have about these memories.
- Think of an experience in which you were unable to understand the language with which someone was attempting to communicate with you. Maybe the language was a different language from one you understand, the dialect was unfamiliar to you, or the terms used were simply unknown to you. Write about this. What are some specific questions you have about language, culture, and communication?
- Read the poem; write down any personal questions and connections that come to your mind.

Lexicon of Exile
by Aleida Rodríguez

There is no way I can crank a dial,
scroll back the scenery,
perch *sinsontes* outside my windows
instead of scrub jays and mockingbirds and linnets.

There is no way the brightly lit film
of childhood's cerulean sky, fat with meringue clouds,
can play out its reel unbroken by the hypnotist's snap:
You will not remember this.

There is no way I can make that Pan American plane
fly backward, halt the tanks of the Cuban revolution,
grow old in Guines, smelling the sour blend of rice and milk
fermenting in a pan by the chicken coop.

There is no way I can pull the harsh tongue
from my mouth, replace it with lambent
turquoise on a white sand palate,
the cluck of coconuts high in the arc of palm trees.

The trees fingering their dresses outside my windows now
are live oak, mock orange, pine, eucalyptus.
Gone are the *ciruelas, naranjas agrias,*
the mamoncillos with their crisp green shells
concealing the pink tenderness of lips.

Earth's language is a continuous current,
translating the voices of my early trees along the ground.
I can't afford not to listen.
They find me islanded in Los Angeles,
surrounded by a moat filled with glare,
and deliver a lost dictionary of delight.
A lingual bridge lowers into my backyard,
where the Fuju persimmon beams in late summer
and the fig's gnarled silver limbs become conduits
for all the ants of the world; where the downy woodpecker teletypes
a greeting on the light post and the overripe sapotes fall
with a squishy thud; where the lemon, pointillistically studded
with fruit, glows like a celebration; where the loquat drops
yellow vowels and the scrub jays nesting in the lime
chisel them noisily with their hard black beaks
high in the branches, and the red-throated hummingbird—
mistaking me for a flower—suspends just inches from my face,
deciding whether or not to dip into the nectar of my eyes
until I blink, and it sweeps all my questions into the single sky.

OPTIONS FOR DIALOGUE

- In groups of four please discuss what images in the poem were most dramatic for you? What was the poet trying to convey in terms of feelings and emotions?

SUGGESTIONS FOR ACTION

- View a film with subtitles. Immediately after the film, write down your reflections about the process of the communicative act. Were you sure you were always getting the meaning correctly? Did you trust the subtitles? At any point in the film did you find yourself listening to the unfamiliar language rather than reading the subtitles? Were you getting the meaning in this way as well? How?
- View a film with subtitles but with a different language from the previous film. Repeat the activity. Were your reactions the same? Why or why not?

- Research the history of "English only" legislation in newspaper or congressional archives. Report the findings to your class.
- Review "How Long? A Synthesis of Research on Academic Achievement in a Second Language" by Virginia Collier (1989) in *TESOL Quarterly, 23*(3), 24–37.
- Conduct a survey of class members about "English only" issues. Repeat the survey with a group of students who are not in your class. Report the comparison to your class.

REACH FOR THE MOON

OPTIONS FOR LISTENING

- Choose one of the following questions and reflect upon it in your journal:

  1. Remember a teacher who empowered you. Who was this teacher? What did he or she do to nurture you? What metaphors for teaching or beliefs about teaching might have inspired this teacher? How did this teacher nurture himself or herself in order to keep growing?
  2. Describe the discovery of a personal talent that you have. When did you first begin to recognize this talent? Who helped you develop it? What experiences made you grow? How do you feel about this talent now?
  3. What are further questions you have about teaching and learning?

- The following selections were taken from the illustrated book *Reach for the Moon*. It is a collection of poetry written by Samantha Abeel, a young teenager with learning disabilities. The book is illustrated with paintings by Charles Murphy that inspired the writing. We have included Samantha's introduction to the book ("Samantha's Story"), the reflection written by her seventh-grade English teacher, Roberta Williams, which follows the poems ("Finding the Key to Learning"), and a poem written by Samantha ("To a Special Teacher").
- Read the selections; write down personal questions and connections.

Reach for the Moon
by Samantha Abeel

Samantha's Story

A tree that stands in the moonlight reflects the light, yet also casts a shadow. People are the same. They have gifts that let them shine, yet they also have disabilities, shadows that obscure the light. When I started this project in the seventh grade, I had trouble telling time, counting money, remembering even the simplest of addition and subtraction problems. Yet no matter how hard it was to stay afloat in this ocean of troubles, there was something inside of me, something that became my life preserver—and that was writing.

Seventh grade was a horrible year. I hated school. Every night I would come home and kiss the floor and revel that I had made it through one more day without totally messing up, or if I had, at least I was still alive. Then I would remember that I had to go back the next day and brave through all the same trials. With that thought, the tears and panic attacks grew. Yet one hour of my day was a refuge. Here, there weren't any concepts with numbers, measurements, algebra, or failure. It was my seventh-grade writing class. I had begun to experiment with creative writing in sixth grade, but in seventh grade I discovered how much writing was a part of me and I was a part of it.

To build on this, my mother asked Mrs. Williams, who was my English teacher, if she would work with me by giving me writing assignments and critiquing them as a way of focusing on what was right with me and not on what was wrong. Charles Murphy, a family friend, lent us slides and pictures of his beautiful watercolors. I began to write using his images as inspiration. I discovered that by crawling inside and becoming what I wrote, it made my writing and ideas more powerful.

In eighth grade I was finally recognized as learning disabled. I was taken from my seventh grade algebra class, where I was totally lost and placed in a special education resource classroom. Special education changed my life. It was the best thing that ever happened to me. I could raise my hand in that class, even when being taught the most elementary concepts, and say, "I don't get it." It was the most wonderful feeling in the world. Eighth grade was my best year at the junior high. It is an illusion that students in special education have no abilities. Special education just means that you learn differently. I am so thankful for specially trained teachers who have been able to help me and many other kids like me.

If you struggle with a disability, the first thing you need to do is find something that you are good at, whether it's singing or skate boarding, an interest in science or acting, even just being good with people. Then volunteer at a nursing home or at a day care center; if you love skate boarding, work toward a competition. If it's singing, join a school choir. Even if you can't read music (like me) or read a script, you can always find ways of coping and compensating.

Never let your disability stop you from doing what you are good at or want to do. I have trouble spelling and I'm horrible at grammar, but I was lucky enough to have teachers who graded me on the content of what I had to say instead of how bad my spelling and punctuation were. I was able to use a computer to compensate.

Remember that if you have trouble in school, it might not be because you don't fit the school, it might be because the school doesn't fit you. Be an advocate for yourself. Keep trying. You may not fit in now, but whether you're seven or seventy, one day you will find a place where you excel.

At the beginning of ninth grade we realized that what had started out as an art/poetry project had grown into something more. Because getting the right teachers and having the right educational placement made such a difference in my life, we realized it was a message we wanted to share. LD does not mean "lazy and dumb." It just means you have another way of looking at the world. I hope through my writing and what we have all contributed to this book to remind people that if you're standing in the shadow of the tree, you may need to walk to the other side to see the light it reflects. They are both part of the same tree; both need to be recognized and understood. This is my reflection of the light. Welcome to my book.

Finding the Key to Learning

Have you ever received an unexpected gift? One that not only surprised but changed you? I have, though at the time I didn't recognize it.

Samantha entered my seventh-grade classroom in 1990 as a quiet, shy girl. It didn't take long, however, for her to introduce herself in a compelling way: she wrote. She brought to her assignment insight beyond her years, and her writing showed a gift for imagery and language.

Despite this agility with words and capacity for insight, Samantha struggled with spelling, verb tenses, word omissions, and other technical problems. I learned that these difficulties were insignificant compared to her experience with math. As I got to know her better, I realized that in my classroom, where she excelled, she became a different child from the one who was completely intimidated in her math class. I was determined that my classroom would continue to be a place where Samantha succeeded.

To help with spelling, she used a word processor with a spell-checker. I ignored left-out words and mechanical errors and was flexible about due dates when her school assignments overwhelmed her. These adaptations were a small price to pay for the writing she could produce.

Slowly, Samantha's confidence grew and she bloomed. At the end of the school year, we didn't want to lose our momentum. Her mother, who had come to see Samantha's writing as a lifeline, called me with an interesting proposal. Would I be willing to give Samantha writing lessons?

We chose to structure the summer's writing around the work of an artist we all admired. Charles Murphy knew what it was like to be different, to be constantly discouraged. In high school, he had been denied the chance to take art classes; art wasn't on the college preparatory track. He was eager to encourage Samantha because he empathized with her struggle to pursue what she did well, against great odds.

When we started the project, Samantha had never written poetry, but her imagery-rich language seemed perfect for that medium. We went through boxes of slides of Charles's work and visited gallery openings and shows to see his paintings up close. Insights and images poured from Samantha. She was finally free to express what had been locked inside.

The first time we shared Samantha's writing with Charles, we nervously wondered if she'd got it "right," if what she saw was justified by his own perceptions of his work. Both of these remarkable people deserve praise: Samantha for being courageous enough to share her inner world and Charles for accepting her work seriously, critically, as artist to artist. The poems were a success in every way.

I suspect that many more Samanthas sit in our classrooms: the quiet ones who hide out in the back, the ones who always "forget" their homework or constantly apologize, the ones who cover up by distracting us with their behavior, their language, or their attitude. How many have we missed because we didn't have the right key, didn't know a key existed, didn't even know the door was locked?

I hope Samantha's story provides inspiration for those who are struggling to contend with their disabilities, and also serves as a reminder to educators everywhere. When we look for possibilities and potential in every student, then nurture those qualities, all children become successful learners. The willingness to help them should define the word "teacher."

—Roberta Williams
Traverse City West Junior High School

To a Special Teacher

When the sun rose
from under its misty veil,
you were there to watch,
like the birds over the sea.
When the wind came quietly
and rested in your ear,

you listened, as the earth would at dawn.
When the rain fell,
you reached out with your hands
and let it wash everything away,
like waves as they grasp the shore.
When the plain brown seed was planted,
you could already smell the fragrance of
the flower that was to come,
and you were proud
as a good gardener should be.

Thank you for believing
that there was a flower waiting inside
and for taking the time
to help and watch it grow.
When the sun rose
from under its misty veil,
you were there to watch,
and I am thankful.

—Samantha

OPTIONS FOR DIALOGUE

- What metaphors does Samantha use to describe her empowering teacher? How does she describe herself in the poem? How does Roberta Williams define a good teacher? In what ways is Samantha's experience like or different from the one you described in your journal? Discuss these questions with your classmates.

SUGGESTIONS FOR ACTION

- Visit a classroom in which some children with special needs have been included. Observe each child for a period of time in order to answer this question: what is a unique talent of each child?
- Interview one or more teachers in special education. Ask them to describe some experiences with gifted children who have learning disabilities.
- In your groups compose a definition for the word *teacher.* Compare your definition to that of Roberta Williams, Samantha's teacher.
- Write a poem, essay, or narrative about your experience with a nurturing teacher.
- Create a visual or written metaphor to represent the growth of a child guided by a nurturing teacher.
- Choose an article from *Teaching Exceptional Children,* a journal published by the Council for Exceptional Children. Connect something in this article with the experiences and beliefs of Samantha and her teacher.
- Read one of the following books to see how other teachers have empowered children through writing:

Abeel, S. (1994). *Reach for the moon.* Duluth, MN: Pfeifer-Hamilton.

Calkins, L. (1994). *Writing between the lines.* Portsmouth, NH: Heinemann.

Calkins, L. (1995). *The art of teaching writing.* Portsmouth, NH: Heinemann.

Graves, D. (1983). *Writing: Teachers and children at work.* Portsmouth, NH: Heinemann.

Heard, G. (1994). *For the good of the earth and sun.* Portsmouth, NH: Heinemann.

- Read one of the following books and use it as an inspiration to develop your own voice through journal writing:

Cameron, J. (1992). *The artists' way.* New York: Harper & Row.

Dillard, A. (1989). *The writing life.* New York: Harper & Row.

Goldberg, N. (1990). *The wild mind.* New York: Bantam.

THE BOY WITHOUT A FLAG

OPTIONS FOR LISTENING

- Reflect on a historical or political event that you remember reading or learning about as a teenager. Did you see the event as directly relating to your own history? Did you imagine what it would have been like to be there? Describe this event in your journal. List any questions you still have about this event.
- Write about a conversation you had with a trusted friend during your growing-up years concerning a critical question you had about a patriotic practice or event.
- Try to remember an incident in your childhood in which a parent or other significant adult was giving you some sort of moral lesson. Were you told something to the effect that you should always "do what you know is the right thing to do" and "know that you are a good person"? What happened? Please summarize the situation, the understandings you had as a child, and your current understandings about what was really going on. Write a letter (real or imaginary) to this adult with questions you have about the incident, his or her intentions, and your new (or developing) understandings.
- Read the selection, write down any questions you think of, and note any personal connections.

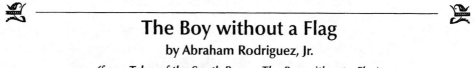

The Boy without a Flag
by Abraham Rodriguez, Jr.
(from Tales of the South Bronx: The Boy without a Flag)

To Ms. Linda Falcón, wherever she is

Swirls of dust danced in the beams of sunlight that came through the tall windows, the buzz of voices resounding in the stuffy auditorium. Mr. Rios stood by our Miss Colon, hovering as if waiting to catch her if she fell. His pale mouse features looked solemnly dutiful. He was a versatile man, doubling as English teacher and gym coach. He was only there because of Miss Colon's legs. She was wearing her neon pink nylons. Our favorite.

We tossed suspicious looks at the two of them. Miss Colon would smirk at Edwin and me, saying, "Hey, face front," but Mr. Rios would glare. I think he knew that we knew what he was after. We knew, because on Fridays, during our free period when we'd get to play records and eat stale pretzel sticks, we would see her way in the back by the tall windows, sitting up on a radiator like a schoolgirl. There would be a strange pinkness on her high cheekbones, and there was Mr. Rios, sitting beside her, playing with her hand. Her face, so thin and girlish, would blush. From then on, her eyes, very close together like a cartoon rendition of a beaver's, would avoid us.

Miss Colon was hardly discreet about her affairs. Edwin had first tipped me off about her love life after one of his lunchtime jaunts through the empty hallways. He would chase girls and toss wet bathroom napkins into classrooms where kids in the lower grades sat, trapped. He claimed to have seen Miss Colon slip into a steward's closet with Mr. Rios and to have heard all manner of sounds through the thick wooden door, which was locked (he tried it). He had told half the class before the day was out, the boys sniggering behind grimy hands, the girls shocked because Miss Colon was married, so married that she even brought the poor unfortunate in one morning as a kind of show-and-tell guest. He was an untidy dark-skinned Puerto Rican type in a colorful dashiki. He carried a paper bag that smelled like glue. His eyes seemed sleepy, his Afro an uncombed Brillo pad. He talked about protest marches, the sixties, the importance of an education. Then he embarrassed Miss Colon greatly by disappearing into the coat closet and falling asleep there. The girls, remembering him, softened their attitude toward her indiscretions, defending her violently. "Face it," one of them blurted out when Edwin began a new series of Miss Colon tales, "she married a bum and needs to find true love."

"She's a slut, and I'm gonna draw a comic book about her," Edwin said, hushing when she walked in through the door. That afternoon, he showed me the first sketches of what would later become a very popular comic book entitled "Slut At The Head Of The Class." Edwin could draw really well, but his stories were terrible, so I volunteered to do the writing. In no time at all, we had three issues circulating under desks and hidden in notebooks all over the school. Edwin secretly ran off close to a hundred copies on a copy machine in the main office after school. It always amazed me how copies of our comic kept popping up in the unlikeliest places. I saw them on radiators in the auditorium, on benches in the gym, tacked up on bulletin boards. There were even some in the teachers' lounge, which I spotted one day while running an errand for Miss Colon. Seeing it, however, in the hands of Miss Marti, the pig-faced assistant principal, nearly made me puke up my lunch. Good thing our names weren't on it.

It was a miracle no one snitched on us during the ensuing investigation, since only a blind fool couldn't see our involvement in the thing. No bloody purge followed, but there was enough fear in both of us to kill the desire to continue our publishing venture. Miss Marti, a woman with a battlefield face and constant odor of Chiclets, made a forceful threat about finding the culprits while holding up the second issue, the one with the hand-colored cover. No one moved. The auditorium grew silent. We medi-tated on the sound of a small plane flying by, its engines rattling the windows. I think we wished we were on it.

It was in the auditorium that the trouble first began. We had all settled into our seats, fidgeting like tiny burrowing animals, when there was a general call for quiet. Miss Marti, up on stage, had a stare that could make any squirming fool sweat. She was a gruff, nasty woman who never smiled without seeming sadistic.

Mr. Rios was at his spot beside Miss Colon, his hands clasped behind his back as if he needed to restrain them. He seemed to whisper to her. Soft, mushy things. Ed-win would watch them from his seat beside me, giving me the details, his shiny face looking worried. He always seemed sweaty, his fingers kind of damp.

"I toldju, I saw um holdin hands," he said. "An now lookit him, he's whispering sweet shits inta huh ear."

He quieted down when he noticed Miss Marti's evil eye sweeping over us like a prison-camp searchlight. There was silence. In her best military bark, Miss Marti or-dered everyone to stand. Two lone, pathetic kids, dragooned by some unseen force, slowly came down the center aisle, each bearing a huge flag on a thick wooden pole. All I could make out was that great star-spangled unfurling, twitching thing that looked like it would fall as it approached over all those bored young heads. The Puerto Rican flag walked beside it, looking smaller and less confident. It clung to its pole.

"The Pledge," Miss Marti roared, putting her hand over the spot where her heart was rumored to be.

That's when I heard my father talking.

He was sitting on his bed, yelling about Chile, about what the CIA had done there. I was standing opposite him in my dingy Pro Keds. I knew about politics. I was eleven when I read William Shirer's book on Hitler. I was ready.

"All this country does is abuse Hispanic nations," my father said, turning a page of his *Post*, "tie them down, make them dependent. It says democracy with one hand while it protects and feeds fascist dictatorships with the other." His eyes blazed with a strange fire. I sat on the bed, on part of his *Post*, transfixed by his oratorical mastery. He had mentioned political things before, but not like this, not with such fiery con-viction. I thought maybe it had to do with my reading Shirer. Maybe he had seen me reading that fat book and figured I was ready for real politics.

Using the knowledge I gained from the book, I defended the Americans. What fascism was he talking about, anyway? I knew we had stopped Hitler. That was a big deal, something to be proud of.

"Come out of fairy-tale land," he said scornfully. "Do you know what imperialism is?"

I didn't really, no.

"Well, why don't you read about that? Why don't you read about Juan Bosch and Allende, men who died fighting imperialism? They stood up against American big business. You should read about that instead of this crap about Hitler."

"But I like reading about Hitler," I said, feeling a little spurned. I didn't even mention that my fascination with Adolf led to my writing a biography of him, a book report one hundred and fifty pages long. It got an A-plus. Miss Colon stapled it to the bulletin board right outside the classroom, where it was promptly stolen.

"So, what makes you want to be a writer?" Miss Colon asked me quietly one day, when Edwin and I, always the helpful ones, volunteered to assist her in getting the classroom spiffed up for a Halloween party.

"I don't know. I guess my father," I replied, fiddling with plastic pumpkins self-consciously while images of my father began parading through my mind.

When I think back to my earliest image of my father, it is one of him sitting behind a huge rented typewriter, his fingers clacking away. He was a frustrated poet, radio announcer, and even stage actor. He had sent for diplomas from fly-by-night companies. He took acting lessons, went into broadcasting, even ended up on the ground floor of what is now Spanish radio, but his family talked him out of all of it. "You should find yourself real work, something substantial," they said, so he did. He dropped all those dreams that were never encouraged by anyone else and got a job at a Nedick's on Third Avenue. My pop the counterman.

Despite that, he kept writing. He recited his poetry into a huge reel-to-reel tape deck that he had, then he'd play it back and sit like a critic, brow furrowed, fingers stroking his lips. He would record strange sounds and play them back to me at outrageous speeds, until I believed that there were tiny people living inside the machine. I used to stand by him and watch him type, his black pompadour spilling over his forehead. There was energy pulsating all around him, and I wanted a part of it.

I was five years old when I first sat in his chair at the kitchen table and began pushing down keys, watching the letters magically appear on the page. I was entranced. My fascination with the typewriter began at that point. By the time I was ten, I was writing war stories, tales of pain and pathos culled from the piles of comic books I devoured. I wrote unreadable novels. With illustrations. My father wasn't impressed. I guess he was hard to impress. My terrific grades did not faze him, nor the fact that I was reading books as fat as milk crates. My unreadable novels piled up. I brought them to him at night to see if he would read them, but after a week of waiting I found them thrown in the bedroom closet, unread. I felt hurt and rejected, despite my mother's kind words. "He's just too busy to read them," she said to me one night when I mentioned it to her. He never brought them up, even when I quietly took them out of the closet one day or when he'd see me furiously hammering on one of his rented machines. I would tell him I wanted to be a writer, and he would smile sadly and pat my head, without a word.

"You have to find something serious to do with your life," he told me one night, after I had shown him my first play, eighty pages long. What was it I had read that got me into writing a play? Was it Arthur Miller? Oscar Wilde? I don't remember, but I recall my determination to write a truly marvelous play about combat because there didn't seem to be any around.

"This is fun as a hobby," my father said, "but you can't get serious about this." His demeanor spoke volumes, but I couldn't stop writing. Novels, I called them, starting a new one every three days. The world was a blank page waiting for my words to recreate it, while the real world remained cold and lonely. My schoolmates didn't understand any of it, and because of the fat books I carried around, I was held in some fear. After all, what kid in his right mind would read a book if it wasn't assigned? I was sick of kids coming up to me and saying, "Gaw, lookit tha fat book. Ya teacha make ya read tha?" (No,

I'm just reading it.) The kids would look at me as if I had just crawled out of a sewer. "Ya crazy, man." My father seemed to share that opinion. Only my teachers understood and encouraged my reading, but my father seemed to want something else from me.

Now, he treated me like an idiot for not knowing what imperialism was. He berated my books and one night handed me a copy of a book about Albizu Campos, the Puerto Rican revolutionary. I read it through in two sittings.

"Some of it seems true," I said.

"Some of it?" my father asked incredulously. "After what they did to him, you can sit there and act like a Yankee flag-waver?"

I watched that Yankee flag making its way up to the stage over indifferent heads, my father's scowling face haunting me, his words resounding in my head.

"Let me tell you something," my father sneered. "In school, all they do is talk about George Washington, right? The first president? The father of democracy? Well, he had slaves. We had our own Washington, and ours had real teeth."

As Old Glory reached the stage, a general clatter ensued.

"We had our own revolution," my father said, "and the United States crushed it with the flick of a pinkie."

Miss Marti barked her royal command. Everyone rose up to salute the flag.

Except me. I didn't get up. I sat in my creaking seat, hands on my knees. A girl behind me tapped me on the back. "Come on, stupid, get up." There was a trace of concern in her voice. I didn't move.

Miss Colon appeared. She leaned over, shaking me gently. "Are you sick? Are you okay?" Her soft hair fell over my neck like a blanket.

"No," I replied.

"What's wrong?" she asked, her face growing stern. I was beginning to feel claustrophobic, what with everyone standing all around me, bodies like walls. My friend Edwin, hand on his heart, watched from the corner of his eye. He almost looked envious, as if he wished he had thought of it. Murmuring voices around me began reciting the Pledge while Mr. Rios appeared, commandingly grabbing me by the shoulder and pulling me out of my seat into the aisle. Miss Colon was beside him, looking a little apprehensive.

"What is wrong with you?" he asked angrily. "You know you're supposed to stand up for the Pledge! Are you religious?"

"No," I said.

"Then what?"

"I'm not saluting that flag," I said.

"What?"

"I said, I'm not saluting that flag."

"Why the. . . ?" He calmed himself; a look of concern flashed over Miss Colon's face. "Why not?"

"Because I'm Puerto Rican. I ain't no American. And I'm not no Yankee flag-waver."

"You're supposed to salute the flag," He said angrily, shoving one of his fat fingers in my face. "You're not supposed to make up your own mind about it. You're supposed to do as you are told."

"I thought I was free," I said, looking at him and at Miss Colon.

"You are," Miss Colon said feebly. "That's why you should salute the flag."

"But shouldn't I do what I feel is right?"

"You should do what you are told!" Mr. Rios yelled into my face. "I'm not playing no games with you, mister. You hear that music? That's the anthem. Now you go stand over there and put your hand over your heart." He made as if to grab my hand, but I pulled away.

"No!" I said sharply. "I'm not saluting that crummy flag! And you can't make me, either. There's nothing you can do about it."

"Oh yeah?" Mr. Rios roared. "We'll see about that!"

"Have you gone crazy?" Miss Colon asked as he led me away by the arm, down the hallway, where I could still hear the strains of the anthem. He walked me briskly into the principal's office and stuck me in a corner.

"You stand there for the rest of the day and see how you feel about it," he said viciously. "Don't you even think of moving from that spot."

I stood there for close to two hours or so. The principal came and went, not even saying hi or hey or anything, as if finding kids in the corners of his office was a common occurrence. I could hear him talking on the phone, scribbling on pads, talking to his secretary. At one point I heard Mr. Rios outside in the main office.

"Some smart-ass. I stuck him in the corner. Thinks he can pull that shit. The kid's got no respect, man. I should get the chance to teach him some."

"Children today have no respect," I heard Miss Marti's reptile voice say as she approached, heels clacking like gunshots. "It has to be forced upon them."

She was in the room. She didn't say a word to the principal, who was on the phone. She walked right over to me. I could hear my heart beating in my ears as her shadow fell over me. Godzilla over Tokyo.

"Well, have you learned your lesson yet?" she asked, turning me from the wall with a finger on my shoulder. I stared at her without replying. My face burned, red hot. I hated it.

"You think you're pretty important, don't you? Well, let me tell you, you're nothing. You're not worth a damn. You're just a snotty-nosed little kid with a lot of stupid ideas." Her eyes bored holes through me, searing my flesh. I felt as if I were going to cry. I fought the urge. Tears rolled down my face anyway. They made her smile, her chapped lips twisting upwards like the mouth of a lizard.

"See? You're a little baby. You don't know anything, but you'd better learn your place." She pointed a finger in my face. "You do as you're told if you don't want big trouble. Now go back to class."

Her eyes continued to stab at me. I looked past her and saw Edwin waiting by the office door for me. I walked past her, wiping at my face. I could feel her eyes on me still, even as we walked up the stairs to the classroom. It was close to three already, and the skies outside the grated windows were cloudy.

"Man," Edwin said to me as we reached our floor, "I think you're crazy."

The classroom was abuzz with activity when I got there. Kids were chattering, getting their windbreakers from the closet, slamming their chairs up on their desks, filled with the euphoria of soon-home. I walked quietly over to my desk and took out my books. The other kids looked at me as if I were a ghost.

I went through the motions like a robot. When we got downstairs to the door, Miss Colon, dismissing the class, pulled me aside, her face compassionate and warm. She squeezed my hand.

"Are you okay?"

I nodded.

"That was a really crazy stunt there. Where did you get such an idea?"

I stared at her black flats. She was wearing tan panty hose and a black miniskirt. I saw Mr. Rios approaching with his class.

"I have to go," I said, and split, running into the frigid breezes and the silver sunshine.

At home, I lay on the floor of our living room, tapping my open notebook with the tip of my pen while the Beatles blared from my father's stereo. I felt humiliated and alone. Miss Marti's reptile face kept appearing in my notebook, her voice intoning, "Let me tell you, you're nothing." Yeah, right. Just what horrible hole did she crawl out of? Were those people really Puerto Ricans? Why should a Puerto Rican salute an American flag?

I put the question to my father, strolling into his bedroom, a tiny M-1 rifle that belonged to my G.I. Joe strapped to my thumb.

"Why?" he asked, loosening the reading glasses that were perched on his nose, his newspaper sprawled open on the bed before him, his cigarette streaming blue smoke. "Because we are owned, like cattle. And because nobody has any pride in their culture to stand up for it."

I pondered those words, feeling as if I were being encouraged, but I didn't dare tell him. I wanted to believe what I had done was a brave and noble thing, but somehow I feared his reaction. I never could impress him with my grades, or my writing. This flag thing would probably upset him. Maybe he, too, would think I was crazy, disrespectful, a "smart-ass" who didn't know his place. I feared that, feared my father saying to me, in a reptile voice, "Let me tell you, you're nothing."

I suited up my G.I. Joe for combat, slipping on his helmet, strapping on his field pack. I fixed the bayonet to his rifle, sticking it in his clutching hands so he seemed ready to fire. "A man's gotta do what a man's gotta do." Was that John Wayne? I don't know who it was, but I did what I had to do, still not telling my father. The following week, in the auditorium, I did it again. This time, everyone noticed. The whole place fell into a weird hush as Mr. Rios screamed at me.

I ended up in my corner again, this time getting a prolonged, pensive stare from the principal before I was made to stare at the wall for two more hours. My mind zoomed past my surroundings. In one strange vision, I saw my crony Edwin climbing up Miss Colon's curvy legs, giving me every detail of what he saw.

"Why?" Miss Colon asked frantically. "This time you don't leave until you tell me why." She was holding me by the arm, masses of kids flying by, happy blurs that faded into the sunlight outside the door.

"Because I'm Puerto Rican, not American," I blurted out in a weary torrent. "That makes sense, don't it?"

"So am I," she said, "but we're in America." She smiled. "Don't you think you could make some kind of compromise?" She tilted her head to one side and said, "Aw, c'mon," in a little-girl whisper.

"What about standing up for what you believe in? Doesn't that matter? You used to talk to us about Kent State and protesting. You said those kids died because they believed in freedom, right? Well, I feel like them now. I wanna make a stand."

She sighed with evident aggravation. She caressed my hair. For a moment, I thought she was going to kiss me. She was going to say something, but just as her pretty lips parted, I caught Mr. Rios approaching.

"I don't wanna see him," I said, pulling away.

"No, wait," she said gently.

"He's gonna deck me," I said to her.

"No, he's not," Miss Colon said, as if challenging him, her eyes taking him in as he stood beside her.

"No, I'm not," he said. "Listen here. Miss Colon was talking to me about you, and I agree with her." He looked like a nervous little boy in front of the class, making his report. "You have a lot of guts. Still, there are rules here. I'm willing to make a deal with you. You go home and think about this. Tomorrow I'll come see you." I looked at him skeptically, and he added, "to talk."

"I'm not changing my mind," I said. Miss Colon exhaled painfully.

"If you don't, it's out of my hands." He frowned and looked at her. She shook her head, as if she were upset with him.

I re-read the book about Albizu. I didn't sleep a wink that night. I didn't tell my father a word, even though I almost burst from the effort. At night, alone in my bed, images attacked me. I saw Miss Marti and Mr. Rios debating Albizu Campos. I saw him in a wheelchair with a flag draped over his body like a holy robe. They would not do that to me. They were bound to break me the way Albizu was broken, not by young smiling American troops bearing chocolate bars, but by conniving, double-dealing, self-serving Puerto Rican landowners and their ilk, who dared say they were the future. They spoke of dignity and democracy while teaching Puerto Ricans how to cling to the great coat of that powerful northern neighbor. Puerto Rico, the shining star, the great lap dog of the Caribbean. I saw my father, the Nationalist hero, screaming from his podium, his great oration stirring everyone around him to acts of bravery. There was a shining arrogance in his eyes as he stared out over the sea of faces mouthing his name, a sparkling audacity that invited and incited. There didn't seem to be fear anywhere in him, only the urge to rush to the attack, with his arm band and revolutionary tunic. I stared up at him, transfixed. I stood by the podium, his personal adjutant, while his voice rang through the stadium. "We are not, nor will we ever be, Yankee flag-wavers!" The roar that followed drowned out the whole world.

The following day, I sat in my seat, ignoring Miss Colon as she neatly drew triangles on the board with the help of plastic stencils. She was using colored chalk, her favorite. Edwin, sitting beside me, was beaning girls with spitballs that he fired through his hollowed-out Bic pen. They didn't cry out. They simply enlisted the help of a girl named Gloria who sat a few desks behind him. She very skillfully nailed him with a thick wad of gum. It stayed in his hair until Edwin finally went running to Miss Colon. She used her huge teacher's scissors. I couldn't stand it. They all seemed trapped in a world of trivial things, while I swam in a mire of oppression. I walked through lunch as if in a trance, a prisoner on death row waiting for the heavy steps of his executioners. I watched Edwin lick at his regulation cafeteria ice cream, sandwiched between two sheets of paper. I was once like him, laughing and joking, lining up for a stickball game in the yard without a care. Now it all seemed lost to me, as if my youth had been burned out of me by a book.

Shortly after lunch, Mr. Rios appeared. He talked to Miss Colon for a while by the door as the room filled with a bubbling murmur. Then, he motioned for me. I walked through the sudden silence as if in slow motion.

"Well," he said to me as I stood in the cool hallway, "have you thought about this?"

"Yeah," I said, once again seeing my father on the podium, his voice thundering.

"And?"

"I'm not saluting that flag."

Miss Colon fell against the door jamb as if exhausted. Exasperation passed over Mr. Rios' rodent features.

"I thought you said you'd think about it," he thundered.

"I did. I decided I was right."

"*You* were right?" Mr. Rios was losing his patience. I stood calmly by the wall.

"I told you," Miss Colon whispered to him.

"Listen," he said, ignoring her, "have you heard of the story of the man who had no country?"

I stared at him.

"Well? Have you?"

"No," I answered sharply; his mouse eyes almost crossed with anger at my insolence. "Some stupid fairy tale ain't gonna change my mind anyway. You're treating me like I'm stupid, and I'm not."

"Stop acting like you're some mature adult! You're not. You're just a puny kid."

"Well, this puny kid still ain't gonna salute that flag."

"You were born here," Miss Colon interjected patiently, trying to calm us both down. "Don't you think you at least owe this country some respect? At least?"

"I had no choice about where I was born. And I was born poor."

"So what?" Mr. Rios screamed. "There are plenty of poor people who respect the flag. Look around you, dammit! You see any rich people here? I'm not rich either!" He tugged on my arm. "This country takes care of Puerto Rico, don't you see that? Don't you know anything about politics?"

"Do you know what imperialism is?"

The two of them stared at each other.

"I don't believe you," Mr. Rios murmured.

"Puerto Rico is a colony," I said, a direct quote of Albizu's. "Why I gotta respect that?"

Miss Colon stared at me with her black saucer eyes, a slight trace of a grin on her features. It encouraged me. In that one moment, I felt strong, suddenly aware of my territory and my knowledge of it. I no longer felt like a boy but some kind of soldier, my bayonet stained with the blood of my enemy. There was no doubt about it. Mr. Rios was the enemy, and I was beating him. The more he tried to treat me like a child, the more defiant I became, his arguments falling like twisted armor. He shut his eyes and pressed the bridge of his nose.

"You're out of my hands," he said.

Miss Colon gave me a sympathetic look before she vanished into the classroom again. Mr. Rios led me downstairs without another word. His face was completely red. I expected to be put in my corner again, but this time Mr. Rios sat me down in the leather chair facing the principal's desk. He stepped outside, and I could hear the familiar clack-clack that could only belong to Miss Marti's reptile legs. They were talking in whispers. I expected her to come in at any moment, but the principal walked in instead. He came in quietly, holding a folder in his hand. His soft brown eyes and beard made him look compassionate, rounded cheeks making him seem friendly. His desk plate solemnly stated: Mr. Sepulveda, PRINCIPAL. He fell into his seat rather unceremoniously, opened the folder, and crossed his hands over it.

"Well, well, well," he said softly, with a tight-lipped grin. "You've created quite a stir, young man." It sounded to me like movie dialogue.

"First of all, let me say I know about you. I have your record right here, and everything in it is very impressive. Good grades, good attitude, your teachers all have adored you. But I wonder if maybe this hasn't gone to your head? Because everything is going for you here, and you're throwing it all away."

He leaned back in his chair. "We have rules, all of us. There are rules even I must live by. People who don't obey them get disciplined. This will all go on your record, and a pretty good one you've had so far. Why ruin it? This'll follow you for life. You don't want to end up losing a good job opportunity in government or in the armed forces because as a child you indulged your imagination and refused to salute the flag? I know you can't see how childish it all is now, but you must see it, and because you're smarter than most, I'll put it to you in terms you can understand.

"To me, this is a simple case of rules and regulations. Someday, when you're older," he paused here, obviously amused by the sound of his own voice, "you can go to rallies and protest marches and express your rebellious tendencies. But right now, you are a minor, under this school's jurisdiction. That means you follow the rules, no matter what you think of them. You can join the Young Lords later."

I stared at him, overwhelmed by his huge desk, his pompous mannerisms and status. I would agree with everything, I felt, and then, the following week, I would refuse once again. I would fight him then, even though he hadn't tried to humiliate me or insult my intelligence. I would continue to fight, until I. . . .

"I spoke with your father," he said.

I started. "My father?" Vague images and hopes flared through my mind briefly.

"Yes. I talked to him at length. He agrees with me that you've gotten a little out of hand."

My blood reversed direction in my veins. I felt as if I were going to collapse. I gripped the armrests of my chair. There was no way this could be true, no way at all! My father was supposed to ride in like the cavalry, not abandon me to the enemy! I pressed my wet eyes with my fingers. It must be a lie.

"He blames himself for your behavior," the principal said. "He's already here," Mr. Rios said from the door, motioning my father inside. Seeing him wearing his black weather-beaten trench coat almost asphyxiated me. His eyes, red with concern, pulled at me painfully. He came over to me first while the principal rose slightly, as if greeting a head of state. There was a look of dread on my father's face as he looked at me. He seemed utterly lost.

"Mr. Sepulveda," he said, "I never thought a thing like this could happen. My wife and I try to bring him up right. We encourage him to read and write and everything. But you know, this is a shock."

"It's not that terrible, Mr. Rodriguez. You've done very well with him, he's an intelligent boy. He just needs to learn how important obedience is."

"Yes," my father said, turning to me, "yes, you have to obey the rules. You can't do this. It's wrong." He looked at me grimly, as if working on a math problem. One of his hands caressed my head.

There were more words, in Spanish now, but I didn't hear them. I felt like I was falling down a hole. My father, my creator, renouncing his creation, repentant. Not an ounce of him seemed prepared to stand up for me, to shield me from attack. My tears made all the faces around me melt.

"So you see," the principal said to me as I rose, my father clutching me to him, "if you ever do this again, you will be hurting your father as well as yourself."

I hated myself. I wiped at my face desperately, trying not to make a spectacle of myself. I was just a kid, a tiny kid. Who in the hell did I think I was? I'd have to wait until I was older, like my father, in order to have "convictions."

"I don't want to see you in here again, okay?" the principal said sternly. I nodded dumbly, my father's arm around me as he escorted me through the front office to the door that led to the hallway, where a multitude of children's voices echoed up and down its length like tolling bells.

"Are you crazy?" my father half-whispered to me in Spanish as we stood there. "Do you know how embarrassing this all is? I didn't think you were this stupid. Don't you know anything about dignity, about respect? How could you make a spectacle of yourself? Now you make us all look stupid."

He quieted down as Mr. Rios came over to take me back to class. My father gave me a squeeze and told me he'd see me at home. Then, I walked with a somber Mr. Rios, who oddly wrapped an arm around me all the way back to the classroom.

"Here you go," he said softly as I entered the classroom, and everything fell quiet. I stepped in and walked to my seat without looking at anyone. My cheeks were still damp, my eyes red. I looked like I had been tortured. Edwin stared at me, then he pressed my hand under the table.

"I thought you were dead," he whispered.

Miss Colon threw me worried glances all through the remainder of the class. I wasn't paying attention. I took out my notebook, but my strength ebbed away. I just put my head on the desk and shut my eyes, reliving my father's betrayal. If what I did was so bad, why did I feel more ashamed of him than I did of myself? His words, once so rich and vibrant, now fell to the floor, leaves from a dead tree.

At the end of the class, Miss Colon ordered me to stay after school. She got Mr. Rios to take the class down along with his, and she stayed with me in the darkened room. She shut the door on all the exuberant hallway noise and sat down on Edwin's desk, beside me, her black pumps on his seat.

"Are you okay?" she asked softly, grasping my arm. I told her everything, especially about my father's betrayal. I thought he would be the cavalry, but he was just a coward.

"Tss. Don't be so hard on your father," she said. "He's only trying to do what's best for you."

"And how's this the best for me?" I asked, my voice growing hoarse with hurt.

"I know it's hard for you to understand, but he really was trying to take care of you."

I stared at the blackboard.

"He doesn't understand me," I said, wiping my eyes.

"You'll forget," she whispered.

"No, I won't. I'll remember every time I see that flag. I'll see it and think, 'My father doesn't understand me.' "

Miss Colon sighed deeply. Her fingers were warm on my head, stroking my hair. She gave me a kiss on the cheek. She walked me downstairs, pausing by the doorway. Scores of screaming, laughing kids brushed past us.

"If it's any consolation, I'm on your side," she said, squeezing my arm. I smiled at her, warmth spreading through me. "Go home and listen to the Beatles," she added with a grin.

I stepped out into the sunshine, came down the white stone steps, and stood on the sidewalk. I stared at the towering school building, white and perfect in the sun, indomitable. Across the street, the dingy row of tattered uneven tenements where I lived. I thought of my father. Her words made me feel sorry for him, but I felt sorrier for myself. I couldn't understand back then about a father's love and what a father might give to insure his son safe transit. He had already navigated treacherous waters and now couldn't have me rock the boat. I still had to learn that he had made peace with The Enemy, that The Enemy was already in us. Like the flag I must salute, we were inseparable, yet his compromise made me feel ashamed and defeated. Then I knew I had to find my own peace, away from the bondage of obedience. I had to accept that flag, and my father, someone I would love forever, even if at times to my young, feeble mind he seemed a little imperfect.

OPTIONS FOR DIALOGUE

- Discuss all the things you think were going on in the narrator's mind from the time he first refused to salute the flag until the end of the story.
- What were some of the things the narrator's father had said and done to give him the idea that he would support this act of rebellion?
- Why do you suppose the father reacted the way he did regarding the incident?
- If you had been the father, what would you have done?
- Discuss the teachers and the ways they did or did not support the narrator.

SUGGESTIONS FOR ACTION

- Review at least two historical accounts of the relationship between Puerto Rico and the United States. Report back to the class the factual information you learned and an attitude you have that either changed or was strengthened by your research.

- Read the other stories in *Tales of the South Bronx: The Boy without a Flag* by Abraham Rodriguez, Jr.
- Review the work of a Puerto Rican artist—a painter, musician, or songwriter; a poet; a writer; a dancer or sculptor. Report to your class about the work and discuss some relationships you see between the sociopolitical history of Puerto Rico and this work.
- Review "Understanding Bilingual/Bicultural Young Children" by Lourdes Soto (1991) in *Young Children, 46*(2), 30–36. Relate some of the points made in the article to this story.
- Read about Juan Bosch and Albizu Campos and answer the following questions:
    1. What are examples of how an attitude that you have about some of the issues in this reading have changed, been broadened, or been reinforced through this experience?
    2. What are some things you have learned about political history that influence your understanding of the Rodriguez story?
    3. Describe some factual information you have learned that is important to you.
- Read one of the following books (or one with a related theme):

    Golden, M. (1992.) *Long distance life.* New York: Ballantine.
    This novel focuses on the lives of three generations of a black family in Washington, D.C.

    Haynes, D. (1993). *Right by my side.* Minneapolis: New Rivers.
    Black teenager Marshall Field Finney is doing his time at a suburban St. Louis high school when life gets complicated. Marshall decides to write down what has happened and "run it by again" to figure things out; the result is this book.

    Haynes, D. (1996). *Heathens.* Minneapolis: New Rivers.
    This collection of short stories involves students of color in school contexts.

    Jordan, J. (1992). *Technical difficulties.* New York: Pantheon.
    These are African-American notes on the state of the Union.

    Kozol, J. (1991). *Savage inequalities.* New York: Crown.
    Jonathan Kozol movingly and persuasively documents the devastating inequalities in American society. He recognizes the millions of American children living in poverty who do not get enough to eat or have adequate living conditions.

    Kozol, J. (1995). *Amazing grace.* New York: Crown.
    This book is about the hearts of children who grow up in the South Bronx—the poorest congressional district in our nation.

Answer these questions about your reading:

1. In a few sentences, summarize the reading(s).
2. Why did you read this? What relationship to your personal or professional life does it have?
3. Do you feel an accurate picture of the information was presented? Why or why not?
4. Which points from the reading did you *not* agree with? Why?
5. Discuss which information or opinions presented here were new to you.
6. Discuss any conversation about this subject that you may have had.

Home: Resilience in Varied Forms

There is magic in what families across cultures do best—care for, attend to, and love each other, regardless of conditions. Magic is made when educators are informed by families' knowledge. Knowledge can come from many sources, and alternative ways of knowing can only add to our vision of issues, influences on development and schooling, and understanding of curriculum and pedagogy. It is useful to hear different voices tell stories about how they experience family and the relationship of that experience to schooling (Bloch, 1991, p. 106). Once again, it is our hope that listening to the authors' stories will add to the readers' knowledge.

Through the listening, dialogue, action process in the activities and readings, and the reflection that is built in, we believe the reader is participating in a complex form of autobiographical narrative. Combining both literature and critical theory allows the readers to use autobiography as a way to move beyond a neutral conception of culture in discussions of the relationship between schools and families and toward a more well defined conception in a pluralistic, multicultural society (Willis, 1995). The students' participation in this method is autobiographical in two senses: the student reader is constantly encouraged to reflect on her or his own experience, and the authors of the selections are giving us glimpses into their own autobiographies. Personal narrative lets us listen to the voices of the participants—students and authors in their cultural contexts—as they tell about their experiences and explain ongoing efforts at agency and transformation. Bloch (1991) explains that this type of symbolic science "focuses on intersubjectivities that are created through interactions between people, their discourse, and the interpretations of meaning within specific contexts" (p. 97). This relational theory sees experience as central to theorizing and to understanding practice.

In this section we have chosen stories and suggestions for possible responses to them that focus on aspects of family important to teachers and all human service workers: literacy in the home, sibling support, how family relationships support learning, family access to information, individual voice in family context, judging public policy through the lens of family concerns, and a broadening awareness of what configuration of relationships constitutes family.

LITERACY IN THE HOME

Earlier in this book we referred to an interview study of diverse teachers. We refer now to this study to see how these artisan teachers describe the strengths of their families. It is important for us to be aware of the presence of teachers in the family. The teachers in the study, like many well-known writers and visionaries (Allen, 1991; Walker, 1990) talked about the importance of having mothers and grandmothers who passed on stories. Vicki Brathwaite smiled as she reported that her West Indian grandmother passed on teachings through folk tales. She also spoke at length about her mother's influence on her reading—in terms of modeling, interest, and actually providing trips to bookstores and libraries. Likewise, Pam Russell's mother was part of Pam's first memory of reading. Her mother brought home an illustrated book about a ballerina and read it to her. Pam then read it over and over again as a precursor to her own reading and her dance. Wayne Wazuko talked about both his grandfather and grandmother. He noted that in his youth passing on stories in his American Indian community was done orally. People would gather around a camp-fire, and the eldest would talk—often the grandmother.

The positive modeling through family—in many cases, mother and grand-mother—did offset negative school experiences. For example, even though Del Tide-man had a difficult time with reading in elementary school, reading was a central part of her family life and a source of nurturance from the time she was very young. Her early school experiences in reading were very negative, yet she was a self-described book worm. Her grandma lived with her family, and she read to the children while both parents worked. A similar thing happened with Donn Morson-McKie and her stepmother, who encouraged Donn to read.

David Haynes, teacher and author, whose stories are in this book, told us: "I think the gift of teaching is that you really are around lots and lots of dynamic lives, which if you don't look carefully, they may not seem like they are dynamic. But if you look carefully, and particularly if you listen, you hear that there really are things going on and very often important and interesting things" (Haynes, in press, p. 73).

David believes in strengths. He joins Beth Swadener and others who insist upon naming children and families "at promise" rather than "at risk" (Swadener & Lubeck, 1995). These visionary teachers live what writer Audre Lorde metaphorically de-scribes: "It is learning how to take our differences and make them strengths. For the master's tools will never dismantle the master's house. They may allow us temporarily to beat him at his own game, but they will never enable us to bring about change" (Lorde, 1984, p. 12).

Unfortunately, the school experiences of many of the teachers we interviewed did not reflect their families' ways of life, values, or language. Raúl Quintanilla had very positive stories to tell about his family as they moved from farm to farm doing migrant work; but as far as school was concerned, he talked about the old basal readers with Dick and Jane family stories. He said he couldn't understand the situations where Mommy dropped Daddy off at the airport with a suitcase. Nor could he relate to Daddy's always having a tie. He said he and his siblings would go home and say, "My father never wears a tie," and "We didn't know anything about airports." Even the food was out of context for him and his community. The books presented a breakfast of eggs, milk, toast, and orange juice. The breakfast he knew was a cup of coffee and a piece of Mexican sweet bread. He could make no relation between school and home settings.

Heath's (1983) research explores the practice of bedtime story reading and fam-ily language use. David Haynes, who has written several acclaimed novels, doesn't re-member his parents' ever reading to him specifically as a very young child.

> I don't remember that they did or that they didn't. I do remember that when I started school in kindergarten, at that point getting read to was a regular [by his teachers]. These were teachers that did it daily and spent a lot of time reading to kids. I have very fond mem-ories of being read to. I have another third grade memory that really sticks with me. There was this teacher, she loved books and she loved reading to students and the last day of school she had packed up all of her things and we had our daily reading time and there wasn't much left to do because everything was packed up. She had a *Reader's Digest* that hadn't been packed away so she started reading this story about this family whose car broke down in the

desert. They were off the road where no one could see them. They were stuck for days and days. The last section she read before the bell rang was, "Color Crayons for Breakfast" and she sort of left us there with them still in the desert. All of these years I have wondered how that family ever got out of that desert. (Haynes, in press, p. 80)

SIBLING SUPPORT

In many cases, the schools do not recognize or use families' strengths, such as sibling support. Bill Simpson remembered that everyone in his family read a great deal. His parents read all the time, even his mother, who never graduated from high school. He already knew how to read when he entered first grade. He remembered that the nun was surprised. She handed him some letters, and he read them; and then she handed him a book, and he read that too. He remembered going to school with his sister, two years older than he was; and because he could already read, he was motivated and excited.

Donn Morson-McKie's career choice was initially affected by her younger brother. After her brother was born she thought about teaching because she was 12 and really loved being with him and his little friends, teaching them the alphabet and new songs and watching them grow. Judith Borer talked about her older siblings reading. Her sister was always getting yelled at because she was hiding in a book instead of helping with the dishes or cleaning. Today in her professional life, Del Tideman notes the support of her sister, saying that she and her twin sister talk about books a lot.

Raúl, whose family context was very different from Judith's, described similar experiences with siblings. His story is important because there is a lack of information about the strengths of poor families in migrant communities. He explained:

We were so many. There wasn't a big house, so there wasn't a lot of space. I would read outside. I wasn't the only one. There were two little ones that I read with. We would play school. I would read inside even though my brothers and sisters would look at me and wonder, "What is he doing?" Well, reading. Or if I had a project to work on for school I would practice a speech or a presentation with them, but they couldn't understand. They would laugh . . . . They didn't understand. (Quintanilla, in press, p. 205)

FAMILY RELATIONSHIPS SUPPORT LEARNING

Another family strength that affected the teachers was parents' reading practice. While families didn't always read bedtime stories, people read what they were interested in. This reading, combined with the relationship among family members, seems to be what matters. It often differs from much traditional literacy development advice, which stresses the importance of the bedtime story. These teachers were affected as children, not usually by having storybooks read to them, but by the positive relationship of parents and children and exposure to parents who were reading what they wanted and needed to read for themselves.

Del talked about her mom and dad reading at night. The children would read with them and try to be like them. Her dad would read the newspaper, and her mom would always be reading a novel. Bill also noted that his mother read mostly novels. Both parents read the newspaper avidly, so to this day he is a newspaper junky. Wayne said his family didn't really have a lot of books. But he read the Sunday newspaper, *Life* magazine, and *Look* magazine. His parents read very little. Raúl said that his parents never read to the children, but the children saw the parents reading novels and magazines such as *Superman* in Spanish, comic-book form. When he visited cousins in Mexico, he saw that they had many magazines lying around. He remembers reading *La Bruja* and many others. Spanish seemed really easy to him.

Some of the teachers did have storybook reading at home. Pam Russell told us about her mother, an educator who worked with young childhood and read a lot. Pam saw a lot of books about people of color for adults, works by writers such as James Baldwin and Richard Wright. Those were in her home, "but I didn't see a lot of children's books with people of color, so I became interested in the adult books and would read them."

Tracy Montero reported that her mother always read to her and her brother, and her father tucked them in. Lisa Boehlke explained that "Dad associated books with riches. Because after he had read all of his books in his library he would try to borrow books from neighbors. . . . Before I had reached five years of age there must have been more than five hundred books in the house" (Boehlke, in press, p. 97).

Raúl pointed out the ambiance of his migrant farm worker family: "Everything was very positive. Your father is there, your mother is there, and your brothers and sisters are there too. You are all working together and your father is saying good things all day, every day for a long time. I didn't know at that time, but it was a close family unit. They talk about supporting a family now with two incomes. With the migrant families we were doing that long ago" (Quintanilla, in press, p. 209).

FAMILY ACCESS TO INFORMATION

In almost all of the interviews the teachers talked about the importance of the library in their early literate lives. Pam remembered going to the library:

> You know, it is so funny because my friends look at me now and say, "We're not surprised you're a teacher" because I would arrange for the children in my neighborhood to go on trips to the library and I would go there all the time! Anyone who knows me would say, "Pamela was always a reader." I always used my imagination. Books took me places and I always enjoyed that. (Russell, in press, p. 66)

Raúl pointed out that the library was not only his friend but also a bridge for him to the side of town where the white kids lived. Mary said that she was lucky that the library was on the same side of the street as her house so she could walk there alone, at will, as a child. Lisa remembered in detail going on walks, in her town, to the library. She remembered being told that one of the first words that she said was "berberdy," which was her word for going to the library.

Access to information is very important. If federal and state funds are continually whittled away and libraries disappear, where will the children learn about other worlds of information and how will attitudes grow toward tolerance of the unfamiliar? As we hoped, the teachers' stories about their families and their experiences growing up showed us the importance of sociocultural context and images of place in childhood. This is also true for the stories in this section.

INDIVIDUAL VOICE IN FAMILY CONTEXT

Another theme illuminated by the stories in this section is the individual family member's struggle with self-identity and the acceptance or rejection of beliefs and traditions that are important in the family. Many women representing diverse cultural and class experiences document the painful processes of assimilation and socialization in the United States, often in the context of voice. Diane Glancy (1988) writes of her trouble with the spoken word, an often "macaronic breach of two languages," English and Cherokee: "a bifurcation of thought not only from within / but also pressed inward from the out" (p. 38). Rita Dove (1995) tells of the shock of recognition and relief she discovered when, in graduate school, she came across Toni Morrison's *The Bluest Eye*. "As soon as I started reading it . . . you still can't tell if the author's black or white. But I just knew. I remember standing there and leafing furiously through the first few pages of the book because I was trying to figure out where she came from. I thought, 'This is my country she's talking about' " (p. 56). Maxine Hong Kingston (1989), in *The Woman Warrior*, writes that "when my second grade class did a play, the whole class went to the auditorium except the Chinese girls . . . . Our voices were too soft or nonexistent" (p. 167). She compares this to the education she experienced in the evening Chinese school: "there we chanted together, voices rising and falling, loud and soft, some boys shouting, everybody reading together, reciting together and not alone with one voice" (1989, p. 167). This classroom sounds like the one teacher Judith Borer envisions.

> I don't like the way boys are so loud in the classroom. They dominate, shouting out answers, and I have trouble ignoring them, and bright girls are quietly sitting there. I had a very bright girl this year. Her parents were concerned that she was too bossy. The bossy label is a way of keeping girls down. Parents are changing too. Parents don't want their girls to be really compliant. . . . I still get this image that I am sticking out too much when I speak up for something or question. I think it's like that for girls—how to be heard, to speak out in the classroom, and not feel that they are sticking out or be afraid to stick out. (Borer, in press, pp. 246–247).

JUDGING PUBLIC POLICY THROUGH THE LENS OF FAMILY

According to Hite (1994), "there are many more advances we are on the threshold of achieving: naming and eliminating emotional violence, redefining love and friendship, progressing in the area of children's rights and in men's questioning of their lives" (p. 34). We believe that the readers of this book can be involved in these advances, and we hope they can gain insight from the authors' stories.

In *Right by My Side*, a novel by David Haynes, Rose writes to her son, perhaps as David would write to all students: "You'll have that power over people, too. That power to hold on come what may. The power to make people believe that, no matter what else comes along, there will never be anyone like you. I will that power to you. Like me, you will always be loved. Use your powers wisely. Enjoy yourself" (Haynes, 1993, p. 158).

In an address given at the 1996 American Educational Research Association conference in New York, Maxine Greene spoke of how Hannah Arendt titled one of her

books *Men in Dark Times,* borrowing the phrase from Bertold Brecht. In her introduction Greene made the point that dark times are no rarity in history, and even in the
darkest of times we have the right to expect some illumination. She continued: "and
when I think of our times as dark in that sense, I think of the violations and erosions
taking place around us: the harm being done to children, the eating away of social support systems, the savage inequalities, the inter-group hatreds, the undermining of the
arts in the schools" (Greene, 1996). Yet Greene believes that each person (each
teacher) in his or her distinctive voice can speak "of the capacity of human beings to
reach beyond themselves to what they believe should be, what might be but something of which they never can be sure" (Greene, 1996).

We can learn ways to do this from children and their parents. Suggestions for in-
creased parental involvement in schools have been surfacing at conferences and in fo-
rums discussing state and national standards. However, new approaches are needed
that represent an understanding of the strengths of families, not more admonitions for
parents to "read together" or "use T.V. wisely" and for schools to "make parents feel
welcome" (p. 19).

What about parents such as the Haitian mother described in Edwidge Danticat's
Krik Krak! (1996)? "My mother . . . never went to any of my Parent-Teacher Association meetings when I was in school." Her mother explained: "You're so good anyway. What are they going to tell me? I don't want to make you ashamed of this day
woman. Shame is heavier than a hundred bags of salt" (p. 154).

TOWARD A NEW UNDERSTANDING OF FAMILY

Teachers, other human service professionals, and others who write to form public
opinion and affect government decisions need to understand that "children do not
need the archetypal family model. What they do need are warm and mature people
around them. We should construct positive new families which meet children's
needs, not close our eyes because the world is not fitting our icons. We should begin to reach out to one another in new ways, to groups wider than our own nuclear
families, and think of the whole society as part of our family too" (Hite, 1994,
pp. 362–363).

Wholeness in our own lives is inevitably tied to the well-being of others, particularly the ones who have been set aside as "other" because of their color, class, sexual
orientation, or frailty of mind or body and those children and parents who do not have
input into the public policies that affect their lives. It is time to greet every piece of
policy or media onslaught with the same urgent question: what does this mean for
children and families?

STUDENT-GENERATED PROBLEM POSING ABOUT HOME

We hope the literature chosen for this section helps readers question the resilience
of family and home. We have chosen selections in which several critical aspects of
home and family are presented. These issues are told through the story and poetry
selections, not often the format of psychological discussions in the media or the aca-

demic press. We maintain that, with the help of the authors of the literature, the reader can reflect on the issues surrounding home in a profound way. Again, we do not want to impose our interpretation of the individual pieces for the reader, but we do encourage listening, dialogue, and action that consider the student as an individual who is part of family and community. We create the context for readers to pose questions and encourage consideration of the strengths of students and their families and the barriers they face daily. We also believe the literature presents human and soulful aspects of home not often captured in other reports. In this section we have chosen stories and suggestions for possible responses that focus on aspects of family important to teachers and all human service workers. Critical questions that readers may consider as they journey through this theme web include, What kinds of family interactions truly enhance a child's literacy development other than storybook reading? What is a family? What types of families are portrayed in the books that children read? Whose agendas are carried out in parent-teacher organizations? What kinds of strategies could teachers suggest to parents who do not speak English in order to share storybooks with their children? How can classroom contexts support the teaching power of siblings? How do the media portray poor families? What are the motivations underlying this portrayal? What would a society that truly supported children and families look like? How can teachers and other human service workers best learn to work with diverse families?

In "Steps to a New and More Wonderful You," David Haynes (1996) continues the story of Ali from "Busted" in Theme Web II. The stereotype of a mother in jail is one of neglect and poor role modeling. Instead, Haynes's character LaDonna shows her creative strengths with a family of women as well as with her own nuclear family. She crosses boundaries to mentor others so they can use their own strengths.

"But You Don't Look Chinese" by Demian Hess (1995) is the story of a Chinese-Jewish-American young man who struggles with issues of identity in both his immediate and extended family. "Distant Touch" by Ellen Hawley (1995) focuses on a young woman's relationship with her family in a time of crisis—in particular, her family member's acceptance of who she is, including her lesbian identity. In "Sour Rice" by Nhien T. Nguyen (1995), a young Vietnamese-American woman breaks family-imposed silences.

"Women Like Those" by David Haynes (1994) addresses stereotypes in issues surrounding abuse in terms of race, ethnicity, and class. "The Peace Terrorist" by Carol Masters (1993) is the story of a young boy who faces family conflict. The story, set during the Gulf War, encourages the reader to connect family conflicts with conflicts in a more global political arena.

"And Say Good-Bye to Yourself" by Susan Williams (1991) juxtaposes hurtful family secrets and collective and individual resilience. Tom Peacock (1993), in "The World of Chili Peatoad" illustrates the continuity of tradition passed on in American Indian families. "A Selkie Story" by Mary Kay Rummel (1996) retells a traditional Irish tale that suggests issues about gender role and individual freedoms in family.

"New York City Mira Mira Blues" by Gloria Vando (1990) brings together our themes of resilient family and community in a poem that sings the praises of a New York City neighborhood.

REFERENCES

Allen, P. G. (1991). *Grandmothers of the light: A medicine woman's source book*. Boston: Beacon.

Bloch, M. N. (1991). Critical science and the history of child development's influence on early education research. *Early Education & Development, 2*(2), pp. 95–108.

Boehlke, L. (in press). Lisa Boehlke. In M. K. Rummel & E. Quintero (Eds.), *Teachers' reading/teacher's lives*. Albany, NY: SUNY Press.

Borer, J. (in press). Judith Borer. In M. K. Rummel & E. Quintero (Eds.), *Teachers' reading/teachers' lives*. Albany, NY: SUNY Press.

Danticat, E. (1996). *Krik Krak!* New York: Vintage.

Dove, R. (1995). Rita Dove. In B. Moyers (Ed.), *The language of life* (pp. 109–128). New York: Doubleday.

Glancy, D. (1988). *Offering*. Duluth, MN: Holy Cow.

Greene, M. (1996, April). A conversation: Imagination, possibility, and curriculum. Speech to the American Educational Research Association National Conference, New York.

Haynes, D. (1993). *Right by my side*. Minneapolis: New Rivers.

Haynes, D. (1994). Women like those. Unpublished story.

Haynes, D. (1996). Steps to a new and more wonderful you. In *Heathens*. Minneapolis: New Rivers Press.

Haynes, D. (in press). David Haynes. In M. K. Rummel & E. Quintero (Eds.), *Teachers' reading/teachers' lives*. Albany, NY: SUNY Press.

Hawley, E. (1995). Distant touch. Unpublished story.

Heath, S. R. (1983). *Ways with words*. Cambridge: Cambridge University Press.

Hess, D. (1995). But you don't look Chinese. *Sticky Rice, 1*(1), 26–28.

Hite, S. (1994). *The Hite report of the family: Growing up under patriarchy*. New York: Grove.

Kingston, M. (1989). *The woman warrior*. New York: Vintage.

Lorde, A. (1984). *Sister outsider*. Freedom, CA: Crossing.

Masters, C. (1993). The peace terrorist. In *The peace terrorist*. Minneapolis: New Rivers Press.

Nguyen, N. T. (1995). Sour rice. *Sticky Rice, 1*(1), 12–15.

Peacock, T. (1993). the world of Chili Peatoad. Unpublished story.

Quintanilla, R. (in press). Raúl Quintanilla. In M. K. Rummel & E. Quintero (Eds.), *Teachers' reading/teachers lives*. Albany, NY: SUNY Press.

Rummel, M. (1996). A selkie story. Unpublished story.

Russell, P. (in press). Pam Russell. In M. K. Rummel & E. Quintero (Eds.), *Teachers' reading/teachers' lives*. Albany, NY: SUNY Press.

Swadener, E. B., & Lubeck, S. (1995). *Children and families "at promise."* Albany: NY: SUNY Press.

Vando, G. (1990). New York City mira mira blues. In D. Keenan & R. Lloyd (Eds.), *Looking for home: Women writing about exile*. Minneapolis: Milkweed Editions.

Walker, A. (1990). *The temple of my familiar*. New York: Harcourt Brace Jovanovich.

Williams, S. (1991). And say good-bye to yourself. In J. Agee, R. Blakely, & S. Welch (Eds), *Stiller's Pond*. Minneapolis: New Rivers Press.

Willis, A. I. (1995). Reading the world of school literacy: Contextualizing the experience of a young African-American male. *Harvard Educational Review, 65*(1), 30–49.

STEPS TO A NEW AND MORE WONDERFUL YOU

OPTIONS FOR LISTENING

- Remember a situation when you made a decision to take some sort of action and other people around you thought you were wrong. Maybe they thought you made a mistake about information or ethics. Maybe they sort of thought you were right in one sense but that you would get into trouble in some way. Write about the situation. How did you stand up for yourself? Whom did you have to defy?

- Reflect on a situation in which you were distressed about something and found yourself telling someone you didn't know very well the whole story. Write in your journal about what happened and why you think you were compelled to explain it to this person.

- What things do you do to feel better when you are upset? Where did you learn these strategies? Did they come from someone in your family or a friend? Did you read about them? Did the advice come from a professional, or is it in the form of passed-down advice? Write about this.

- Think of an example of television advertising in which you or a family member was tricked or misled. What was being advertised? What was the misunderstood message? What was really going on? Write about this.

- Listen to a television advertisement aimed at a certain population or age group. What was being sold? What were the explicit messages? What were the messages not clearly stated? Write about your personal opinion regarding the ethics of this particular incident.

- Read the selection, write down any questions that come to your mind, and note any personal connections to the story.

Steps to a New and More Wonderful You
by David Haynes
(from Heathens)

Step One: Keep a Positive Outlook

In the Cool Whip container the mixture of Noxema and dried basil resembles lumpy potato chip dip. She mashes, she stirs, she whips. As hard as she tries she cannot get the dry gray-green flakes to dissolve.

What LaDonna needs is a mortar and pestle, but that is not the sort of thing they provide you with at the Shakopee Women's Detention Center.

She thinks she might ask one of the guards to help her, but doesn't expect that to get her anywhere. These women are so . . . functional. They walked around looking down on people just like high school gym teachers. They insisted on being called Miss Sherman and Mrs. Ekdahl and Ms. Supelveda. In return they called you by your given name. LaDonna has no time for such foolishness. She calls all the guards Shultzie, believes most of them are named that in real life and have made up names so they can detach themselves from working here. After calling a skinny, drab one Shultzie, she got hauled in front of the prison director, a square, pinch-faced woman, supposedly named Mrs. Indahar, whose clothes and skin were all the same washed out color of gray.

"You understand from your orientation we have rules here," this Indahar woman said. "For the protection of the staff, and for your protection as well."

LaDonna rolled her eyes. If she'd heard this speech once, she'd heard it a million times.

"You are expected to be out of your room and to your job on time."

Right, like she was going to spend all day in some smelly steamy laundry, washing a bunch of other women's underwear.

"You will be treated the same as the other women. If you are sick, report to the Dispensary. If you have a problem, report it to the guards."

"No problem," LaDonna had said.

"Also, you will address our staff in the way you were instructed. I hope that's clear. Despite your incarceration, you are encouraged to do your best. Our model girls earn extra privileges, you know. If there are no more questions. . . ."

LaDonna had plenty of questions. First, why so many rules? Rules on when to get up, rules on when to go to bed, rules on whom you could talk to, rules on when you could talk to them. And where. For heaven's sake, they even had a line painted down the floor you had to walk on when you traveled the halls. They made you wear blue denim jumpers. In her real life LaDonna never wore blue, denim, nor anything remotely resembling a jumper. And you couldn't dress it up with a scarf or anything, and they took away all your jewelry at the gate. It was worse here than any of the jails she'd been in before. It was no wonder the girls here were so . . . tense and cranky. No wonder they looked depressed.

LaDonna knew their problem. These girls lacked dignity and self respect. They had never been allowed to achieve their full potential.

They had never unleashed the goddesses within themselves. That was why she was developing Madame LaDonna's Herbal Beauty Care Products. If only she had a mortar and pestle, she could test her first product—Madame's Neutralizing Facial Flush. She could test it on the girls in the recreation room.

There was one guard who might help her. The blond one with the big behind— she was a nice person, a regular person just like out in the real world. She wouldn't stand in the way of these girls becoming the best they could be.

LaDonna goes to the TV lounge to find her. There she is—pacing the back of the room, trying to look as if she isn't listening in on people's personal conversations, which is, after all, what she gets paid to do.

"Excuse me, Shultzie?"

The blond turns her back from the others. "LaDonna, please. My name is Mrs. Resnik. If you don't stop calling me Shultzie, I'm going to have to report you."

LaDonna sighs. "Whatever. Look: do you happen to know where they keep the mortar and pestle around here?"

Mrs. Resnik just looks at LaDonna with her mouth open. "The what?" she asks. She is a pretty pink-cheeked woman with yellow curls around her head like an angel.

She isn't fat, but she has a big butt which isn't helped by the ill-fitting uniform all the officers wear. Charcoal gray, which LaDonna thinks is a disgusting color, fit only for the upholstery in bus depots.

"You know," LaDonna says. "A cup thing with a post thing with a knob on the end. For grinding aspirins and stuff. You *know* what I mean. Where do you keep it?"

"If you're sick. . . ."

"Never mind. How about . . . do you have a mini food processor? Yay big." LaDonna indicates the size of a bowling ball.

"LaDonna, I don't know quite where you think you are, but this is a women's prison. You ask me for the most outrageous things. Baby oil, dried rose petals. Cucumbers. Do you have any idea what cucumbers go for in a place like this? You need to get real."

"You know, Shultzie, just because a person makes one little mistake doesn't mean her life comes to an end."

Just then a commotion breaks out by the TV. One of the prisoners has buried her head in her hands and is sobbing. The other girls have gathered around to comfort her. Shultzie rushes over to investigate. It is the new girl who is sobbing. The one in the room next to LaDonna. She is thin enough to see the outline of her bones and has wispy hair the color of rat's fur. LaDonna has noticed her. She is a girl who could use a lot of improvement.

Step Two: A Fresh Start Each Day

LaDonna watches as the other girls gather up the weepy one and help her to her room. She steps out of the way—some of these girls are big and mean-looking. They keep razor blades in their cheeks, know karate, Kung Fu, and more ways to hurt you than a month's worth of Friday the 13th movies. They are the kind of girls who like to give orders. LaDonna knows better than to mess with them. Shultzie, who stands there doing nothing, would be of no help should LaDonna get into it with one of them. The girls are saying comforting things such as "Come on, honey," and "We understand." It doesn't do much good. The new girl weeps harder.

LaDonna knows what the poor creature needs. She needs a boost, needs to feel better about herself. She needs to realize the full potential of her womanhood. She needs Madame LaDonna's Neutralizing Facial Flush.

These girls wouldn't know that. Big, horsey, coarse gals. Shoplifters, pickpockets and whores. They were the sort of girls who hid your bra while you were in the shower in gym class. The whole herd steamrolls by, practically carrying the weepy one away. LaDonna presses close to the wall. It is unfair, she thinks. There should be separate prisons for girls like me. One prison for the criminals and one for the nice girls. Girls who have only made a little mistake.

And the truth of the matter: it was not she who made a little mistake. If only those banks had more integrity. Cash a check and they charge your account before you fold the bills and put them away, but try depositing a check, well, then it's three weeks before they get around to crediting your account. The president of the bank: he's the person who should be locked up. And that judge.

Really, it was a perfectly legitimate business deal. And, if you were to believe the people on cable television, absolutely foolproof, and there was no reason why LaDonna oughtn't be ten thousand dollars richer today rather than cooling her heels in some squalid women's prison.

LaDonna did everything just the way the man on the TV show, Kent Worthington, had said to do it. She found a house on Dayton Avenue that any fool could tell was going for cheap. She heard from her friend Cassie who heard from another friend who worked in the city planner's office that a cartel of Japanese businessmen was looking for real estate investment in St. Paul. The right buyer, the right seller, the right price. That was what Kent Worthington called the golden triangle. Kent said all you had to do was to activate the golden triangle, and money would pour into your pockets like water from a bottomless well. And all it was supposed to cost her, according to Kent, was the one dollar that the city wanted to get rid of the abandoned duplex, and a promise to pay the back taxes. Kent said that no-down-payment real estate was fool-proof, and LaDonna knows she is no fool. She had the Japanese businessmen sold on the property before they even saw it. She took them by on a sunny March afternoon, just after a snowfall. The snow covered the garbage, and the sun created flashes of bright light which blinded their eyes to the superficial flaws on the exterior of the building. She chose two P.M. so that the loud, filthy urchins of the neighborhood would be at school and not lower the value of her property with their presence.

"Gentlemen, here it is," LaDonna had said. They had given LaDonna their names, but LaDonna is not good with names. She called them "gentlemen" or "my little friends." She let them in through a side door which she had pried open with a crowbar earlier in the day. The man at the city assessors office told her she could have the key at closing time—details, details, details.

The place was a mess. There were holes in the walls, holes in the ceilings. The floors in many places were rotted clear through to the joists. LaDonna talks that to her advantage.

"Really, my little friends," she said. "Think of the possibilities. You can make this place into anything you want it to be. And, of course, I'll give it to you dirt cheap."

In the car the Japanese businessmen offered LaDonna fifteen thousand dollars. Despite her inclination to talk them up to twenty, she took it, savoring the fact that after the one dollar to the city, and the five thousand dollars in taxes she was nine thousand nine hundred and ninety nine dollars richer than she had been that morning. She asked for five thousand dollars—earnest money she called it, because that is what she had always heard it called before. She rushed to the bank with the check so that she could cover the check for five thousand which she'd written to the tax assessor earlier that same day in order to get the key, which he still wouldn't give her until the check cleared the bank.

In court LaDonna tells Judge McDonald pretty much the same story.

"So, technically speaking, your honor," she said, "having been the person who activated the golden triangle, I am entitled to whatever profits come from the transaction."

Over his glasses the judge gave LaDonna a look of disgust. How rude and unprofessional, she thought. For court she had worn her flowing crimson skirt, the one that is dotted with berries and bees. She had a wide black-fringed shawl wrapped around her waist.

At his disgusted look, she wheeled away from him dramatically and flounced to her seat. She grabbed her man Marcus's hand.

"I don't think that judge likes me very much," she said. "I think he may be prejudiced. We may have to call the human rights commission."

Marcus's sweaty hand petted hers. He shook his head. He had been nervous and apprehensive for days. He thought it a bad idea for LaDonna to act as her own attorney, and suggested that maybe she shouldn't come to court dressed as a gypsy girl. "A simple business suit would do," he told her, as she wound another length of gold chain around her neck. He was an old fuddy duddy. She ignored him. That's why she loved him—because he was a fuddy duddy and because he was easy to ignore. And also because he was the sexiest man on earth. And she would take bets on that.

"Just one minute, Miss," the judge said. "Step right back up to this bench."

LaDonna sighed and rolled her eyes. "What is it?" she said. She stood with her hands on her hips.

"Just a few words before I pass sentence. First: you are aware that it is illegal to write checks against funds which do not exist?"

There was some snickering in the courtroom. LaDonna knew it was her snooty significant-other-in-law, Verda. She'd make that old bitch pay for that snicker. If it was her last act on earth, she would.

"Ah, hah," she said, raising a finger in the judge's face. "But, is it illegal to write a check for money which you know will be or ought to be in your account?"

The judge was not impressed. He made a note with his pen and removed his glasses. "One other thing," he said. "You are also aware, I assume, it is illegal to transfer title to property that you do not own?"

LaDonna pursed her lips. "But, once again, your honor, is it illegal to transfer title to property which you, in fact, intend to own? I rest my case." She said this and spun with a flourish to face the gallery and bowed. Her son Ali, parked back there next to that bitch stood and applauded her. LaDonna waved and started for her seat.

"Get back up here," the judge said.

Marcus put his head in his hands.

The judge looked at LaDonna and shook his head. "You are a piece of work," he said.

"I am shocked, your honor. I am involved in a monogamous, stable, sexually very fulfilling relationship. That's my man right over there. Cute, light-skinned fellow. Whatever it is you're implying. . . ."

The judge raised his hand to stop her. He squeezed his eyes closed and pinched the bridge of his nose. "I have your record here. Let's review a few key items, shall we: operating a bawdy house. Running an unlicensed and illegal gambling scheme. Trafficking in stolen goods. Haven't you learned anything, young lady? You can't get something for nothing."

LaDonna crossed her arms. She turned her back on the judge. It was no use explaining: she'd tried before. These judges just didn't listen. Throw a rent party and they call it "running a bawdy house." What was a person supposed to do? Get thrown out on the street? And she had no way of knowing that those watches were stolen. As if all those big department stores got receipts from all their suppliers, too. And she'd even lost money on that Three Card Monte game. Stupid white folks in Rice Park . . . they always knew just where the damn queen was.

"Turn around and face me," the judge ordered.

"Honestly," LaDonna mumbled. She had no intention of turning around. America had gotten so bad. How was a business woman supposed to make a decent living anymore. Look at poor Mrs. Hillary Rodham Clinton. Try to make a few bucks for yourself and they nail you to a cross.

"Turn around," the judge shouted.

LaDonna faced him and gave him the evil eye.

Judge McDonald's jowls shook. "Despite the fact that no one lost money or property, it seems to me you show no remorse nor any real understanding of the possible harm that could come from such activity. I'm sentencing you to twenty days. Your time begins today."

LaDonna reared back into a horse stance, squinched her eyes, and pointed a finger at the judge. She dropped her voice to a guttural growl.

"May the stench of a thousand dead chickens afflict your every hour. May the dandruff from your eyelashes seal your eyeballs shut, blinding you forever."

"Five extra days. Contempt of court."

"May cats in heat circle your house every night for a year."

"Get her out of here."

The matron pulled LaDonna to the door. Through her fury she could see Marcus making slash marks at his throat, mouthing the words "enough already." In the back of the room, Verda dabbed at her crocodile tears, and, next to her, Ali stood, whistling and applauding, almost doubled-over with glee.

LaDonna interrupted her curses long enough to blow Marcus a kiss. "Call you from jail, honey," she shouted.

Marcus had his head in his hands. He looked afflicted. She knew that he hated her gypsy routines. He said they were kinda silly and undignified, said he wasn't sure that was how a black woman ought to behave. He told her once that despite her full black hair and olive skin, in her babushka she looked more like Aunt Jemima than Maria Ospenskia. She had punched him in the stomach when he said that, and then felt so badly about it she treated him to a weekend in bed at the Crown Sterling Suites. Poor baby. There he was, exhausted, demoralized. The trial had been worse on him than it was on her. That was the problem with these sensitive, safe types. They were easily bruised, skittish. They didn't understand that you had to take chances to get anywhere in life, that you could be whatever you wanted to be if you just believed. They looked askance at big ideas, they distrusted schemes. LaDonna knew that secretly Marcus was as much invested in her plans as she was. Sometimes more so. It was the way he got his kicks. He was a vicarious sort of guy. She blew him one last kiss which he acknowledged with a feeble wave and with his shy sexy smile.

She pointed one last time at the judge. "May your wiener grow warts and fall off, you old crow."

Even the matron laughed at that.

Damn that judge, LaDonna thinks. Damn the bankers, damn the Japanese and damn Kent Worthington, too. LaDonna knows what her mistake has been. She's been too reliant on others. She hasn't used her own resources. She has been a fool, but no longer. Madame LaDonna's Herbal Beauty Care Products would see to that. She had a golden triangle all her own. The right woman with the right idea at the right time. She'd give American women what they wanted—high self-esteem and a clean complexion to boot. Stand back Avon. Watch out Elizabeth Arden. Mary Kay, you can eat my dust.

A shadow blocks the light from the hall, making the Noxema look ashy.

"Can I come in?" It is the mousey weepy girl from next door.

"Sure," LaDonna says. She offers the girl the chair by the window. The room is narrower than a car is wide. LaDonna has to roll back on the bed to let her by. The girl perches on the edge of the chair demurely. It is as if she has been called in for an interview with the warden—her back and her legs are held straight and stiff, and her hands are on her knees.

LaDonna dribbles some baby oil in a bowl. She watches the girl out of the corner of her eye. The girl stares at her hands or at the floor. Flanks of hair hang parallel to her head like blinders.

"Smells nice in here," the girl says. She has a small voice and a small smile.

"Does it really?" LaDonna bubbles. She has no idea. She has lived with the herbs and creams for so long she is immune. "Thanks," she adds. "What does it smell like? You know the smell is really important."

"I don't know. I couldn't describe it."

"Oh, come on. What would you say? Is it like a floral bouquet? Like lemon mist? Like an English herbal garden?"

"I'm not very good at this. I guess . . . maybe . . . maybe the latter. I guess."

"English herbal garden. Exactly what I thought. Don't sell yourself short, girl. You're very good at this. Now try this one." LaDonna removes the top of a round Rubbermaid container. "What do you think?"

"That's the Lemon Mist?" the girl asks.

"Well, actually it's just lemon juice now, but it will be Lemon Mist when I'm done with it."

"What exactly are you making in here?"

"I'm not quite prepared to say as of yet. And don't blab about the lemon juice. It's like an illegal substance around here. That, and the cucumbers. What's the story on that? Are they afraid a person might make a salad or something?"

The girl smiles, and that makes LaDonna relax. The gloom this girl carries surrounds her like a cloud of gnats.

"You always seem so busy," the girl says. "Carrying around bowls and jars and all kinds of things."

"Oh, yes, girl. LaDonna is always busy. Have to be. My mama says even as a baby I had something going in that crib all the time. Life's too short. Got to keep moving."

"So you're LaDonna. My name is Nancy."

"Nancy? Like Nancy Drew? I loved Nancy Drew. I read all those books. I have the whole set. I saved them. Was gonna give them to my little girl. But, then I didn't have any little girl, I had a little boy, Ali. That's his picture over there. He's twelve. Handsome, just like his father, of course. I love him. But what am I gonna do with those Nancy Drews? Ali, all he ever reads is skateboard magazines and comic books. He's a funny kid. Really. You should call him up. He'd have you cheered up in no time bustin a gut. And it's not like I'm gonna have another baby on the chance it should be a girl just so I can pass some books along. It was so horrible that first time. I'm sure you know what I'm saying. Do you have any kids?"

Nancy nods. She looks at her feet.

"One kid? Two kids?"

"Two. A little boy and a little girl."

"Well, imagine that. A little thing like you. You left them with their daddy, I bet. Don't you worry one bit."

Nancy shakes her head.

"My Marcus—he's my man, that's his picture right there, that's what I call him—my man—we're not married or anything. He's just my man—he's a natural born daddy. Other people pay him to take care of their kids. He's a teacher, you know. Is something wrong, honey?"

"It's not fair," Nancy sobs. "I shouldn't be here."

"We have something in common then."

"I'll stay here forever. I don't care. He'll never get my kids. I'll never tell where they are. Damn that judge."

LaDonna rises. Though she isn't sure why, she feels vindicated and triumphant. "Yes, damn him," she says. "Damn that judge. Damn them all, all the judges everywhere."

Step Three: Make the Most of What You've Got

LaDonna dumps another giant-sized clothes basket into the industrial drier. She heaves it up with a loud grunt, lets the basket crash to the ground, lets go a loud whiny sigh. Such torture. She drops to the floor by the machine. It is all she can do to press the button which starts the clothes tumbling. Some of the other women in the laundry give her dirty looks, but she doesn't care. It is hot in here and the machine is filled with sweat-stained jumpers and fat women's panties without any elastic. Just touching them makes her feel faint. LaDonna does not do laundry, not even at home. The Pentecost lady next door—Dr. Ione Wilson Simpson—does it for her. LaDonna never asks her to do it. She just barges in at nine-thirty every Wednesday morning like clockwork, sets on the table her stack of papers from the Mid-North Bible College to be graded, and puts in a load of wash. She has done this for six years since she and her husband Mitch and their son Butchie bought the house next door to Marcus and LaDonna in the Tangletown neighborhood of St. Paul. She takes LaDonna to the Rainbow Foods and makes her buy products such as Spray 'n Wash and fabric softeners. She seems to know what to do with such products—when to spray what on, and during which cycle. It is like some magical technological rite as far as LaDonna is concerned, and she tells Ione she just doesn't get it. Patient loving Christian woman that she is, Ione tells LaDonna that there are no secrets. It is all spelled out for you on the labels of clothes, on the boxes of detergent and inside the lid of the washer. LaDonna resists. She suspects a trap in there somewhere. While the clothes wash, she fills out sweepstakes letters and completes contest applications. Ione fluffs and folds, corrects papers for her course on the Christian Tradition in English Literature. They work right through *The Price Is Right* and the first half of *The Young and the Restless.* Ione impresses LaDonna with her efficiency. While it might take LaDonna all morning to do her Publisher's Clearing House Sweepstakes entry, in that time Ione does two loads of laundry, copies all the new recipes out of *First* magazine onto three-by-five cards which she keeps in a box on the counter for Marcus's use, and grades thirty-five essays on the topic "What Jesus would say to Charles Dickens." And she is a whiz at *The Price Is Right*'s Hi/Lo game. She always knows the exact price of the Dustbuster and the Wurlitzer organ with the burled cherry finish. LaDonna tells Ione that she should fly to California and be a contestant on *The Price is Right,* but Ione says that a Christian woman does not display herself in such a fashion. They both think, despite his animal rights convictions, Bob Barker should go back to brown hair. He was much cuter before.

The dryer vibrates through LaDonna's backbone. She cannot believe this is happening to her. The big gray-haired woman who runs the prison laundry comes over. She wears a white tunic and slacks and has a gray moustache. Her name badge says Shultzie—which just confirms LaDonna's theory.

"Let's go, Miss. This ain't a resort, you know."

"*Isn't* it time for a break yet?"

"You been working for twenty minutes. Let's go. I got a basket of hot sheets over here got your name on them. Up and at 'em, sister." She offers LaDonna a hand and LaDonna takes it. She aims LaDonna toward a rolling laundry cart of white sheets still steaming from the dryer.

"Let's get 'em folded before they wrinkle."

LaDonna sighs.

"These sheets wrinkle, girl, and you'll be down here ironing till the second coming. Get on the other end." Shultzie dangles a cigarette from the corner of her mouth and tosses LaDonna the other end of the sheet.

"What you in for, honey?" The cigarette dances at the corner of her mouth.

"There was some confusion about the balance in my checking account."

Shultzie shakes her head. "Yeah, that'll happen I hear. You got a man?"

Oh, yeah. I got me a man, LaDonna thinks. Quite a man indeed. She misses Marcus so, it has turned into a pain—a pain she feels in her chest. It burns as if she has swallowed a glowing charcoal briquette.

"Yes, there is a man," she answers.

"Don't let that sheet drag, girl. We're not doing this laundry over on account of you."

LaDonna raises her end of the sheet as high as her shoulders. It might be light as down, but weighs on her arms like lead. It is she who must walk her end of the linen over to match Shultzie's—Shultzie won't budge. When the sheet is folded small enough, Shultzie slaps it on the table as if it were a steak, and then irons it with the flat of her hand.

"So, this man," she asks LaDonna. "What was it he done to you got you in here?" She snaps another length of hot cloth in LaDonna's direction.

LaDonna flinches, but catches the sheet before it hits the cement floor.

"Nothing. He didn't do a thing."

Shultzie stops to stub out the cigarette. "Come on, girlie. There's a man in there somewhere. Gotta be. What he do? Steal your kid's milk money? Hide some crack in your purse? Pretty gal like you: Bet he had you out on the street."

LaDonna is incensed at the woman's regressive attitude. It is the 1900's: Where was this woman's head? Had it never occurred to her a woman might be able to get into prison without the help of a man?

"You got it all wrong, Shultzie. My man's completely innocent."

"Girlie, there aren't any of them innocent, not a one. You in here doing time for some man's crime. He's out there got his peter stuck up every piece of snatch he can find."

"Never," screams LaDonna. She balls up her end of the sheet and throws it in Shultzie's face. Never ever. Not her Marcus. He wouldn't. He loved her and she him. And, furthermore: she owned him. Not just his heart and soul, but him, all of him. She bought him. Outright. Paid good cash money at a charity auction at the University of Minnesota.

She hadn't gone there to shop, really. It was back during her student radical days, and she and the sisters from Imani—the African Women's consciousness-raising group—had gone to the annual fraternity row "slave auction" to protest the trivialization of the greatest tragedy in American history, as well as the general racism of the campus Greek system. LaDonna, in a floor-length red, black and green skirt, carried a sign reading "Save Our History." She had hand-lettered it herself between her art history and her marketing classes. Her plan—all the sisters' plans—was to turn that farce out. Get up on that stage and show their behinds if necessary. The field house was dressed for spring carnival in balloons and crepe paper, the stage framed with fake columns and pilasters. Center stage one of those Nordic frat types posed in front of a platform for display of the merchandise. He was dressed as a southern gentleman, riding crop and all.

LaDonna remembers rage souring her stomach. She wanted to kill every damn honky in that room.

Just as she and the Imani sisters made ready to charge the stage, they brought him out.

"Fine looking specimen we got here now," the slave master drawled, his round Minnesota accent sifting through a poor imitation of Southern speech. Marcus, stripped to the waist, had one of those cheap hippy tapestries wrapped around him. "Haven't had a buck like this one on display for many years," the auctioneer continued. Marcus primped and flexed his muscles. He strutted around the block. The next day he told LaDonna he was so stoned he didn't know where he was. Up under the field house lights his oiled brown body had sparkled like patent leather.

LaDonna remembers biting her hand.

"What am I bid for this brown beauty?"

"This is an outrage," yelled sister Aisha.

"You should be ashamed," yelled sister Folani.

"Fifty dollars," yelled LaDonna.

"Sister Yaguama," the others scolded. LaDonna was going by her African name full-time back then. Yaguama El Hakim. These days she only used that name when she wanted to intimidate Ali's teachers or the people at traffic court.

"I have fifty dollars from the young lady right back here. Can I get fifty-five dollars?"

LaDonna bought Marcus for seventy dollars. She could have had him for fifty had it not been for sister Yasmin, who bid Marcus up through the fifties and sixties at two dollar increments. And despite the judgmental look on her face, LaDonna knew Yasmin really wanted him. Wanted him bad, too. Why did black women have to be so damn competitive? If she wanted one she should have waited until the next one came up, but no, she had to bid against a sister, take hard earned dollars out of LaDonna's pocket. LaDonna put Marcus on her Mastercard and said good-bye to Imani forever.

"Get your ass off that dryer and get over here and pick up this sheet," Shultzie orders.

LaDonna sits on top of a large machine, her back to the room. There is no place to hide in prison. All the rooms are locked and everywhere there are guards. The dryer is oversized—all out of proportion like doll house furniture. She knows she looks foolish up here, but she won't let them see her cry, not ever. Not these coarse heifers. How many of them had what she had? How many of them had nice houses in good neighborhoods? How many of them owned their own businesses? How many of them owned their own man?

"There'll be trouble for you, girl, and I mean it. Get down now."

Not her man. Not Marcus. Not ever.

As punishment LaDonna must sit through the prison's evening group therapy sessions. They meet next to the TV lounge in a cinder block room which is decorated to look like a poor person's living room. The sofa and chairs have been upholstered in brown and green stripes. They look soft, but are hard as if they were made of bricks. On one wall a bad seascape has a ketchup stain—or is that the sun—and there is an enormous orange wall hanging opposite it. LaDonna has no idea what it is supposed to represent.

A man who looks like Jimbob Walton runs the group therapy sessions. He places the furniture in a circle and encourages the women to bring their coffee and knitting. The group meets every night at seven-thirty, and about ten women show up. A few like LaDonna and Nancy have been ordered to do so, but some, LaDonna knows, come to lust over Dr. Jimbob. She hears how they carry on about him in the dining room. They speculate on how big he is and how long he might last. LaDonna doesn't know what the attraction is—but then skinny redheads never did do anything for her. And, of course, she had Marcus at home. She couldn't wait to show him off to these crones. That would really give them something to talk about.

"Shall we begin, ladies?" LaDonna sits with Nancy on a love seat. There are knitters and rug hookers and tappers and twiddlers. She and Nancy are the only ones with idle hands.

"I thought tonight we would just have a general bull session. Let's get out what's bothering us. Who wants to begin."

LaDonna rolls her eyes. This is her third meeting. They never got anywhere here. It was one hard luck story after another. How this one got caught up in drugs and how that one wished she'd paid more attention in school. And, of course, everyone's man done them wrong. No wonder that old witch in the laundry was so cynical. Twenty years of listening to this shit.

Tonight there are no takers. The women rock and twiddle and knit in silence.

"Anyone?" Dr. Jimbob prompts.

"We ain't heard from them two." A hard-looking blond indicates LaDonna and Nancy.

"Strictly volunteer here," Dr. Jimbob says. "No coercion in the group."

"Just trying to make 'em feel welcome," the blond says. She gives LaDonna and Nancy a gap-toothed smile. Her hair has been treated with chemicals until it is just lifeless straw on her head. "It's really helped me to open up, these sessions. I feel like I'm getting my shit together. Dr. Lallaburton here is a great listener."

LaDonna had been there the night the blond "opened up." She had told a lurid story which involved being the only female companion of a Puerto Rican motorcycle gang from Chicago. She apparently still loved the leader, a Manuelito, who, according to blondie, was "an all right dude if he would just cut out some of the funky shit he was into." LaDonna has been horrified by all these women's stories. She realizes that, despite the fact she does not do laundry, cook, nor do housework of any kind, compared to most of these women she is the ideal middle American housewife. And, in addition to her general disdain for such public confessionals, LaDonna finds herself shamed into silence. She is ashamed to admit how relatively ordinary and decent her life is. Their lust after her story sickens her. They want to know all about her—what horrible things she's done and who she's done them with. She is tempted to make up a tale, make herself a Mafia gun moll, voodoo priestess, queen of the gypsies. They would have no way of knowing what was true. She could be whatever she wanted. She had always heard about honor among thieves, but she had never imagined it included competition to see whose life was the most immoral.

She is saved by Nancy. "I guess it's just that . . ." she begins, "you can talk about it and talk about it and it doesn't do any good. It doesn't change anything." She trembles and tears roll down her checks. LaDonna pats her arm.

"Nancy is right," LaDonna says. "All this dredging up the past is no good. How do you expect to get anywhere?"

The older black woman who has been knitting speaks up. "Well, baby, sometimes it just helps to have someone listen to you. Dr. Lallaburton says we can't deal with our own troubles until we face them. Talking about them is the first step."

LaDonna isn't sure how to react to the woman. Her name is Mattie. She means well, reminds LaDonna of her mother, and in fact they have committed the exact same crime, except Mattie, unlike LaDonna, was actually buying things with her checks. But unlike LaDonna, she had no intention of rushing to the bank with a perfectly good check drawn on the Bank of Tokyo which ought to have more than adequately covered her expenses.

And all of these women—so impressed with Dr. Jimbob. What did he do but sit there with his mouth open and nod his head? Sure, you can sit there and make notes on your little pad, but can you make Swiss steak with mashed potatoes and creamed peas? Her Marcus could, and he scrubbed a toilet like nobody's business, was great in bed, and meanwhile, here sat this fraud pretending to help people with their problems.

"So," LaDonna says. "We talk and we talk and we talk. And then, what? What happens next? You wave some magic wand and the problem goes away? That's bullshit and every one of you knows it. You want to fix a problem, you make a plan. You figure out what you need to do, you go out and do it."

The women look from LaDonna to Dr. Jimbob, waiting for him to do something. To scold her or encourage her or pat her on the back or slap her on the face. He smiles and nods.

"There's not a plan anywhere to help me," Nancy sobs.

"You mustn't say that," LaDonna says, grabbing both of Nancy's hands. "Never say that. There's always hope. It's like drivin'—what they tell you in driver's ed: Always look for an out. Sometimes it's hard to see, but it's there. You make your plan and you stick with it. If it doesn't work, you go on to your next plan. And the next one and the next one. Until you get where you need to be."

Nancy sniffed. "You really believe that will work for me?" She looks at LaDonna and her eyes fill with hope.

"Your friend is very wise," Dr. Jimbob says.

Yes, wise, LaDonna thinks. I am wise. And, the flash in her brain is what she thinks they must be talking about when they show light bulbs going off above your head in cartoons. Madame LaDonna's Herbal Beauty Care Products are not enough. There must be a book. A book to tell these woman how to release their inner beauty, just as the creams and lotions enhance the surface. A step by step plan. The man says she is wise, and the man is a doctor.

There must be a book.

Step Four: Pay Attention to the Details

LaDonna has found that if she peels cucumbers and removes the seeds, then whips them up with baby oil and egg whites, she has a cream as light as sea foam. Rose petals turn the mixture a pale pink and makes it smell sweet and irresistible. Unfortunately, leave it on the counter overnight and it turns black. Refrigeration should solve that, and surely American women are willing to give up a little space in the ice box for a chance at a whole new life.

Nancy comes in and plops on the bed. The swelling around her eyes has decreased—she must be crying less—but she has taken to biting her thumbnail. Perhaps she has run out of tears.

"I've been thinking about what you said. At the session the other night."

"I was just talking," LaDonna says. "Those people get me so upset."

"No. It was great. I needed to hear that. I want to believe you, too. I do, really, but I just don't know."

LaDonna sits facing Nancy on the edge of the bed. She feels a pounding in her chest. She had been heard and listened to. She has the power, the gift. She knows she can do this.

"I believe there is a way out of almost anything," she says. "Sometimes it doesn't seem that way—I know that I've been in some tough jams. But I never give up."

Nancy takes her thumb from her mouth, folds her hands on her lap. "My husband is a powerful man," she says. "I was attracted to him because he was powerful. He had money and charm, as well. I fell into his trap. Let myself be led around by the nose. He was good to me. He gave me whatever I wanted. You can lose your soul with such a person. I guess that's what I did. I lost my soul because I wanted what he offered. I thought it was such a good life. I never expected to want for anything.

"We had our kids and they were perfect. My boy and my girl. Life was sweet. I imagine I could have continued like that for another fifteen or twenty years. I kept busy. Looking after him and the kids. And I joined committees and served on boards. All of that activity and money is like a drug. It has a way of numbing your mind. It obscures what is really going on around you.

"When my daughter told me that her daddy had hurt her, I didn't really understand what she was saying. She was only six and she didn't have the words to talk about it. And the person she was telling me about was my husband, after all. A man I thought I knew. I wasn't equipped to hear what she was telling me. Who would be?

"The pediatrician was quite good at her job. She didn't pull any punches. She talked about penetration, ruptures, abrasion. All those sorts of things. She tried to warn me what I was about to go through.

"From that moment I operated on instinct. Do you believe in instinct, LaDonna? I sent the children to my mother in Illinois. The bastard denied everything. Of course. First he said it must have been someone else. Then—on his attorney's advice—he claims that his own daughter is a liar. That nothing of the kind has ever happened. That the doctors are frauds. I was given an ultimatum. Go along with his defense or get out. Call my own daughter a liar in court in front of all those people, or get out. Great choice, huh?

"I left and he came after me with everything his money and power could muster. Restraining orders, subpoenas, divorce papers. He closed all the joint bank accounts, canceled all my credit cards. I hardly had bus fare, let alone money to hire a lawyer.

"I don't know how he did it. With money you can do anything. He made a liar out of her. Despite the evidence. Made his own daughter—a six-year-old child—into a liar, right there in court. They ordered her returned home. To his home. But that will never happen. Not as long as I'm alive. There's a network of us out there. Mothers who are sick of the bullshit from the social workers and the judges and the lawyers and the courts. They are supposed to be looking out for the children, and they send them back to something like that? Not as long as I'm alive. I've sent my children away to keep them safe. To be honest I don't even know where they are. I know they are safe and with people who care for them. I know how to find them when I need to. The judge says I'm to stay here until I produce my children." Nancy shakes her head.

"I believe you, LaDonna. I mean, I have to believe you that there is a way out of this. A way I can keep my children safe. I can't go on feeling hopeless. I'm ready to make a plan. Will you help me, LaDonna?"

In the jar LaDonna has mixed lemon juice, Ivory liquid, and yogurt. She stirs with a long wooden spoon. The mixture has the consistency of glue. She knows she must make it thicker.

"I just need a sensible voice. Someone to shake me up. Someone like you, LaDonna. You can help me."

She thinks about her man, Marcus. A man she thinks of as belonging to her. A man who has often to her been like a joke—a joke that she could tell people and they would laugh and she would feel good because the joke was a joke that she made, and because the joke made it like it wasn't real and she did not have to take him seriously. Did not have to imagine that he might be another kind of man other than the kind of man he was. A man like the man this woman chose. Her Marcus. Her man. A man who had only ever confirmed what she knew the first time she saw him, there, shining, under the lights in the field house. That she would melt into the story of his life like butter into warm bread.

Nancy hops off the bed and starts pacing the narrow room. "I'm getting my kids back," she says, and LaDonna feels blessed. She has a man and she has a son and they are good to each other and they are good to her. They bring her herbs and gels and inedible cookies they have made with their own hands. They listen to her stories and her plans and her schemes. They tell her it will all come true just as she says. They tell her she is beautiful. They sit with her on the ugly plaid couch in the cinder block room and hold hands.

"You're gonna help me, aren't you LaDonna."

LaDonna keeps thinking about Marcus and Ali. It is something she knows how to do. "Yes," she says. "I'll help you. Yes."

Step Five: Never Give up Hope

LaDonna writes the final formula for Madame's Neutralizing Facial Flush in her journal. It is a secret. On one page she has sketched possible designs for the label. On another page she has begun outlining her book: *Ten Steps to a New and More Wonderful You*. Each chapter will be one of the ten steps, but so far she has only been able to think of five of them.

Nancy appears in the door. She is laughing and tears are dripping off her chin.

"Not again," LaDonna says.

"I'm a mess," Nancy laughs.

"Come on in. I'm all ready for you."

"You've thought of something. You have a plan."

"Come over here," LaDonna says. Using a spatula she smears Madame's Neutralizing Facial Flush around Nancy's face. She smears extra on the cheeks where the tears keep washing it away.

"How does it feel?" LaDonna asks.

"It's cold," Nancy says. "So cold."

"We leave it on for just a second. It's only the first step. Go ahead and rinse."

Nancy pats her face with a towel, just the way LaDonna instructs. "What if it doesn't work?" she asks.

"Look," LaDonna says. She frames Nancy in the mirror and stands behind her. She outlines Nancy's jaw with her hands. "Look. Can't you see? You're positively glowing."

"Yes," Nancy says. Her eyes are shining and alive. "Yes. I see. I see."

OPTIONS FOR DIALOGUE

• With your small-group members create a character map of LaDonna. Put her name in the center of the page in a circle. Around it write words that describe her. Does she remind you of anyone you know?

- Discuss with one partner examples of LaDonna's strengths.
- Lappé and DuBois (1995) list the hallmarks of active listening as
  1. Staying engaged
  2. Being supportive of the speakers' efforts, whether or not there is agreement
  3. Searching for underlying meaning
  4. Being nonjudgmental
- Do you and your partner believe LaDonna is an active listener?
- Lappé and DuBois (1995) say that the art of creative conflict is constructive, honest confrontation. They suggest several how-to's:
  1. Value and incorporate diversity.
  2. Create an environment safe for difference.
  3. Leave labels at the door.
  4. Agree to disagree when there's no common ground.
  5. Focus on the present and on solutions.
  6. Allow some venting but limit reactions.
  7. Use self-discipline in expressions of anger.
  8. Be well prepared.
  9. Make no permanent enemies.
  10. Model the surfacing of conflict.
- Do you and your partner believe LaDonna was creative with conflict?

  Lappé, F. M., & DuBois, P. M. (1994). *The quickening of America: Rebuilding our nation, remaking our lives.* San Francisco: Jossey-Bass.

SUGGESTIONS FOR ACTION

- Think of three scenes—with your co-workers, for example, or with a friend—that are likely to occur within the next week in which you want to listen very, very well. Write them down. Now imagine yourself in each situation and plan what adaptations you can make to be a more active listener. In each case, how will you know you've been successful? (adapted from Lappé & DuBois, 1994, p. 247).
- Find another LaDonna in your family, in your reading, or in your community. This should be a person who believes that there's a way out of almost anything and who never gives up. Write a description and tell a story about this person to your small group.
- With a partner, devise a ten-step program for feeling better. Promote your program to your classmates. Organize a discussion afterward in which you explore which ideas were jokes, which were serious, which were surprisingly effective, and which were not effective.
- Do a research project about how fair and accurate the media are. Choose a topic of your choice (for example, women in homeless situations, children who are leaders, the environmental impact of a new industry in your community) and look for coverage in several media sources for several weeks. What information is included? What is left out? What assumptions are made by the choice of inclusion? Report your findings in a chart or graph and report to the class.

BUT YOU DON'T LOOK CHINESE

OPTIONS FOR LISTENING

- Reflect on when you were a child and adults talked about who you resembled or looked like. Write about what you remember. Who did you want to look like? Why?
- Write in your journal about whether or not your thoughts and convictions about your identity (or other peoples') differ from your parents' thoughts on this subject.
- What have you seen in popular magazines that tell you how you should look? Write a few thoughts about how you see yourself fitting (or not) in with the image that is perpetuated. Are your feelings about this issue different from when you were ten years younger? Why or why not?
- Read the selection, write down any questions that come to you, and note any personal connections.

But You Don't Look Chinese
by Demian Hess

I've never felt particularly "oppressed." Or outraged. Or angry or upset or down-trodden or victimized. Well, maybe not "never." But I've never carried a grudge about it. I've never had an ax to grind. I've never felt I had a statement to make about the RACISM in our SOCIETY or the OPPRESSION of the DOMINANT CULTURE. Capital letters give me a headache, I guess. And I guess my friends would be surprised if I did make a fuss.

"But what have you got to complain about?" they would say to me, "You're not a minority." And when I point out that, in fact, I am a minority: "Oh, but, well, yeah, your *mom's* Chinese, but you're not. I mean, you don't *look* Chinese."

Yeah, I don't look Chinese. I've heard that before.

I remember this one time when I lived in Rhode Island. I was taking the bus home from the beach and, somewhere between Newport and Providence, this old woman got on board. The bus was half empty, but she chose to sit down right next to me.

"You're Jewish, aren't you?" she said, peering at me closely. I stared at her for a second and then admitted that, yes, I was Jewish. I have no idea how she knew. Maybe it was the nose. I had this tiny, little bean-shaped nose until I was about 12, and then a huge mass exploded out of my face. The family nose. The Jewish stigma.

"You can always tell," the old woman said, and patted my knee. "It's so nice to have someone to talk to, I hardly ever see anyone. My children, they never call, they never visit. It's so hard when you're old. You'll see."

Then she stopped and squinted at me. "But you're not all Jewish, are you?" she said. I shook my head and explained that my mother was Chinese. "Oh," she said, and paused. "Well, don't worry. It doesn't show."

She was right, it doesn't show. And I guess I'm lucky that it doesn't show. But I wasn't born lucky. I was born looking Chinese, and I grew up looking Chinese. When I was six, I had straight black hair, this tiny, little bean nose, almond-shaped eyes and yellow skin. I was very slight, not stocky-tending-to-fat like other kids. I seemed to speak differently, too, although I'm not sure whether that's actually a Chinese trait or not. Did it have something to do with the size and shape of my Asiatic larynx and nasal passages? I don't know, but to my ear I had a strange pitch to my voice, a sort of high, lilting, whistling quality that made me cringe to hear it on tape. I'm probably crazy to think there's anything Chinese about this part of myself.

Whether or not my voice was really different, my appearance certainly was, and none of the other kids in school ever let me forget it. When I was five, my folks moved to a little farm in the Born-Again Bible Belt of Minnesota. Hicksville, the Boonies, Red Neck City. Everyone was white. Germanic or Scandinavian, maybe a little English, but white. And Christian. My family wasn't any of those things. My parents were hippies, atheists, graduate students. And not white. Well, OK, so my father was white, but my mom definitely wasn't. The neighbors didn't exactly know what she was. Chinese? Indian? It didn't matter. She was brown, and so were her kids.

"Chin Chan China man, gets his meals from a garbage can." I heard that nearly every week from the other kids, as they danced around me during recess, making slanty eyes with their fingers. Actually, this was from the more enlightened bigots. The ones who had taken the time to study the issue and determine which racial category I belonged to and which slur was appropriate. Most didn't bother with such distinction.

"You see this?" a student asked me one day, pointing to a small, green country on the globe. I peered at it. It was Nigeria. "See that? That says 'nigger.'" Not only bigoted, but illiterate as well.

But the Chinese thing was only a phase. I grew out of it. One of those unpleasant things you need to get out of your system, like gawkiness, or acne, or a breaking voice. You know, growing pains. Sometime around the age of 12, my nose exploded, my eyes grew round, my hair lightened and took on a bit of a wave. Voilà, instant white.

Well, not quite white. Maybe Mediterranean—anathema at one point in history as well, but pretty much accepted, nowadays, in polite society.

It seemed natural that I should turn white. My parents never encouraged me to be Chinese. Well, I should say that my mom never did. That was her job, right? To teach me to be Chinese? My father was more than willing to spread his Jewishness around. He wasn't religious himself, but he loved the idea of being Jewish. The history, the culture, the jokes. "Oy, the goyim," he'd say, "They got no chutzpah."

But my mom was silent about her heritage. It was the family secret. Although she'd been raised in Chinatown in New York speaking Chinese, she never uttered a word of it in the house. She said she couldn't remember any. And she let us kids bust up her Chinese heirlooms, like the dowry swords made from old coins that came from her grandparents' wedding. My sister and I smacked them together in sword fights, the coins tinkling down around us like a metallic rain shower with each thrust and parry.

The only hint of her past came from food. We ate a lot of Chinese food. Stirfry for dinner. Soy sauce-braised carp, or grouse, or pheasant, whenever we caught any.

And chopsticks. But she cooked and served it up without comment, whereas my father went through this big Jewish routine whenever he opened a box of matzo. "Ba-ruch a-ta Adonai eh-lo-hei-nu," he'd intone, ripping off the cellophane.

After I started looking white, I never thought much about being Chinese. It was out of sight, and I pretty much pushed it out of mind. This lasted until I started applying for colleges. I had to fill out all these forms and check boxes specifying which race I was. All of the schools took pride in touting the "diversity" of their students, so I immediately identified myself as Chinese American. I thought it was an advantage—a unique feature that made me stand out from an anonymous sea of applicants. I checked those boxes for "Asian/Pacific Islander" proudly. It was my most Chinese moment.

But when I got into school, being Chinese didn't seem like a good idea after all. On the one hand, believe it or not, there was guilt. Guilt for not looking Chinese. This came up right away. During orientation week my freshman year, the minority students' center held a big get-together for its "community." I felt like I should go, having checked all those boxes on my admissions forms. I felt sort of like I'd used the organization. Already the guilt was setting in.

As soon as I walked into the students' center, I knew I'd gone to the wrong place. Just about everyone there looked really ethnic—African American, Asian, Native American, Latino. And there I was, this white-looking guy. A few other students looked kind of white, too, but at least their name tags made up for it: last names like "Chan" or "Lee" or "Wong." What was my last name? Jewish. Great.

I stood around feeling really out of place until this other student began talking to me. He was African American. "So what are you?" he asked me, right away. I was relieved to tell him that my mom was Chinese, like I was explaining myself. "Oh, OK, yeah, you can sort of see it," he said after eyeing me carefully. "But would you look at some of the guys here? I don't know what *they're* supposed to be." I left a little later and never went back.

It was just as well that I wasn't welcome at the minority center, because I found out that the other students on my freshman hall frowned on minorities. It wasn't a matter of racism. They weren't racist. Everyone on my hall welcomed diversity. Everyone went to rallies on the Green to protest the university's investment in South Africa. It was a question of style, of fitting in, of dressing like everyone else, going to the same movies, being laid back, sociable and cool. Foreign students, the ones straight from China or Korea, weren't bad because they were Chinese or Korean. African American students had every right to eat by themselves in the dining hall and have their own frats. But those students just weren't that cool. They didn't fit in with what was normal. You never saw that behavior in the *Breakfast Club*—a film all the students on my hall tried to emulate. Well, OK, maybe in *Sixteen Candles*—from that weird, geeky Chinese guy.

Don't misunderstand. I didn't pretend that I was white. I still admitted that I was half Chinese to everyone. But I avoided doing anything that would make me stand out and get labeled "Asian American." There were a few close calls all the same. I remember the worst incident.

The summer before my junior year I was working in Pennsylvania. Every now and then I had a long weekend and would go up to Providence to hang out with a house full of friends. Quite often, I'd get there to find that all my friends had ditched me to take off for New York or Boston or Maine. So it would be me alone in the house along with this Taiwanese student who was subletting a room. He didn't fit in too well. He had a bad haircut and wore sneakers and black socks all the time. He spoke with an accent and studied engineering and economics. I talked to him a little, and we went to some movies. One time his mother came up from New York, and I took the two of them to the beach in my beat-up VW bug. She cooked us dinner later. She seemed really happy that her son had such a good American friend.

One thing that really drove me crazy was that this Chinese guy was sleeping in a lawn chair because he hadn't realized that his sublet would be unfurnished. I knew that an old roommate had left a bed in the last apartment I'd lived in, and I still had a key. She had arranged to sell the damn thing to the next people moving in, but I didn't care. I hated her guts. So I went over there, tied it down to the top of my Volkswagen and drove it back to the Chinese guy. He was really grateful.

I didn't see him much after I gave him the bed. I went back down to Pennsylvania and didn't return until the start of school. I ran into him halfway through the first semester in the dining hall. He was still wearing those awful clothes and was with a big group of foreign students. He came right up to me in the middle of the dining room, grinning like an idiot. He was still thanking me for the damn bed. He turned to the foreign students. "This is my friend," he says, really loudly. I smiled nervously, conscious of everyone watching and listening. "He's Chinese, too," he explained. The foreign students all gave me an odd look—I couldn't read it. Surprise? Confusion? I thought it was admiration. I went crimson from head to foot. I didn't see him after that, although he gave me his phone number in Providence and in New York.

Whenever I think about that incident, I still blush. I'm embarrassed by the way I acted, embarrassed for even thinking they admired me because they couldn't tell I was Chinese. I guess, even though I don't look Chinese, I can't escape it. It keeps coming back in the way I worry and in the way I treat other people. You know, sometimes the problem isn't what others do to you, it's what you do to yourself.

On the whole, though, I feel pretty lucky that I don't have to look Chinese and deal with all that other crap as well. I know what the alternative would be. I only need to look at my uncle. That's my mother's brother. He lives in the Northeast, has a professional job and drives a Porsche. He's always rushing around, going to the club, the office, the gym. He got married my last year in college and I went out for the wedding. I didn't know his wife, I'd only met her once: vague impression of blonde hair and blue eyes—the type my uncle always goes for.

As soon as he sees me, it starts. "God, you're lucky," he says. "I wish I looked like you." My uncle, he's always going on about being Chinese, like it's the worst thing in the world. I guess he's really just like me. He only wants to feel sure of himself and fit in. But in addition to the normal human burden of insecurity is added the extra weight of being Chinese. This does not help his self image. It's not that society is "oppressing" him or that he's being turned down for jobs or that he's being snubbed at parties or anything really important. It's just that he's not white, so he's not quite "normal."

Whenever he goes to a bar, he's never that "guy standing over there," or the "guy in the expensive suit," or the "guy with the black hair," or the "good-looking guy" to any of the women. He's always that "Asian guy." As in: "Yeah, look over there at that Asian guy looking at you." It drives him crazy.

My uncle's telling me all this while we're whipping down the highway in his Porsche. We're going to get something to eat. We're heading for this Yuppie bar and restaurant he goes to a lot when suddenly he hits the brakes.

"Shit," he says. "We can't go there, I'm not dressed. Whenever I go there I try to look really nice. Good suit, tie. I can't go looking like this."

So he screeched down the next exit and heads the Porsche the other way.

"Maybe we'll go over to Wong's, this Chinese place." he says. "Yeah, that'd be good. It's open late, service is fast, it doesn't matter how I'm dressed. Yeah, maybe Wong's'd be good."

But then he hits the brakes again. No, no, no, not Wong's. Not tonight. He's getting married tomorrow (my God, why is he getting married?), he can't deal with Wong's tonight. Can't deal, I guess, with the Chinese ambiance. Can't deal with the fact that he blends in there, that it looks like he belongs. Can't deal with it because he doesn't want to belong. That's Chinese, it's not white, it's just not normal.

So we're off at the next exit and heading back in the direction we were first going. Yeah, we'll go to the other place. It'll be OK. We'll sit at the bar. You don't have to dress up at the bar.

"You're lucky," he says to me, "really lucky."

OPTIONS FOR DIALOGUE

- How did the main character feel about being called a minority and Jewish?
- Discuss any thoughts or experiences you or friends of yours have had about being labeled "minorities," "feminists," "intellectuals," "jocks," and so on. Why does this often become such an emotional issue?
- What layers of complexity in terms of his identity affected this character? What do you learn about the complexity of identity from this discussion?
- Do you remember any ethnic-bashing jokes or rhymes from your childhood experiences? What about in the halls of your college?
- Is it possible to welcome diversity and frown on minorities at the same time? Discuss.
- Please discuss the paragraph in which the main character describes blushing after being introduced to the Taiwanese student's friends.
- The main character's uncle believes that he is lucky because he doesn't look Chinese. What do you think the main character thinks? Discuss.

SUGGESTIONS FOR ACTION

- Read the following selection from the novel *R.L.'s Dream* by Walter Mosely. It discusses the complex effect of identity, race, and political history on family and child rearing.

"I'm not a Negro. My father was pure Arab and my mother was from Brazil. A lot of people think I'm black but I'm not. Not at all."

Soupspoon just stared, dumbfounded by Randy's claim.

"That's why I have such light eyes," Randy went on.

"That's from the Arab or the South American?"

"Some Arabs have blue eyes, it's considered a blessing to have them. There was a whole blue-eyed Semitic tribe in the eleventh century. They were great warriors and scientists."

"Yo' momma come down from them?"

"My father. He was a tradesman."

Soupspoon had known many Negroes who'd passed for being white. Some would just get dressed up and go out to white restaurants and white churches for a hoot. Some, who couldn't bear being what they were, moved into white neighborhoods and lived like they really were white. They'd marry, raise children and explain their curly hair as coming down from Greece or Ireland or some other exotic Caucasian land. They belonged to the Junior League and the Ku Klux Klan, voted for conservatives, some even ran for office. They spoke the white man's language better than he did, because nobody knows white people better than blacks. A black man knows the white man inside out. And why not? They took old clothes, old cars, old books, and old food from white people. They lived in a world where they had to be better than white. White men never had to worry about how they talked or walked or laughed. They took being white for granted. Anything a white man did was okay because it was a white man doing it. But a black man was different. No matter how hard he studied or how righteous he was, a black man still had the mark of Cain on him. All you had to do was look. (p. 128)

How does this segment relate to the story? Write a skit or a poem about this complexity. Share it with your class.

- Conduct a computer search regarding ethnic identity. Abstract two articles, write a critical response to the articles, and relate the articles to the story.
- Conduct an in-depth interview with a person who you know has definite ideas—one way or another—about his or her identity. What did you learn? Report the interview to your class.
- Bill Moyers (1995, p. 67) describes Marilyn Chin as "a fiercely lyrical writer whose life straddles two cultures. [She is] a first-generation Chinese American born in Hong Kong and raised in Portland, Oregon." Read a few of her poems and relate her thoughts about her bicultural situation to that of the author of this story. Report your findings to your class.

   Moyers, B. (1995). *The language of life: A festival of poets*. New York: Doubleday.

- Read the Oryx American Family Tree Series, available from Oryx Press, 4041 North Central Avenue, Suite 700, Phoenix, AZ 85012. Make a recommendation to your school library about whether or not this 12-volume series, which shows readers how to research their family tree, would be useful. Please note the inclusion of a chapter in each book that helps adopted students or students from nontraditional families trace their roots.
- Read *Life on the Color Line* by Gregory Williams, the autobiography of a mixed-race man who is now Dean of the College of Law at The Ohio State University.

DISTANT TOUCH

OPTIONS FOR LISTENING

- Think back to a time when you believed your sibling (or cousin or other close family member) didn't understand you or appreciate you. Describe what happened and why you felt this was true. What questions do you still have about your relationship with this person?
- Remember the time in your life when you felt most supported and understood by your sibling (or cousin or other close family member). Write about this. If you could ask this person anything now, what would you ask?
- Think about a time when you wanted to speak about something to a family member but were afraid to break the silence. Write about the incident.
- Describe in your journal a time when a family member was very ill or dying. How did the other family members support this person and each other? What were the most difficult incidents? What were the easy, even surprising, incidents that you remember?
- What questions do you have about the complexities of a same-sex relationship and how it affects each partner's extended family? Write about your questions in your journal.
- Read the selection, write down the questions that come to your mind, and note any personal connections.

Distant Touch
by Ellen Hawley

Cath sits in a hospital coffee shop watching a woman in scrubs walk toward her. The woman's blond, athletic looking, and she knows she's being watched. Her face goes blank and her eyes fasten on some spot beyond Cath, at the far end of the room. Cath looks away, but a second later she's watching the woman walk again. She needs the motion. She needs a steady flow of people to keep her from joining one thought fragment to the next, from connecting *My father's dying* to whatever would naturally follow that.

Sooner or later a thought will have to follow, but Cath's in no hurry to find out what it is. It's enough to know that she'll remember sitting in this place long after she's forgotten more important things. She'll remember the off-white of the walls and the sixtyish couple sharing a sweet roll at the next table. The woman pulls tiny pieces off the roll, eating some of them herself, urging some of them on the man, and he accepts them gently, almost reluctantly. Birds court like this, or a few species do—goldfinches, cardinals, canaries. With birds, though, the male does the feeding. The people are stout and mild-featured, and Cath tries to imagine the person they've been sitting with upstairs, but she can't connect them with another person, only with each other, with this moment, with how fondly she'll remember them long into the future.

She'll remember her brother less fondly but also just the way he is right now, coming toward her with a plastic tray in his hands, and on the tray two styrofoam cups and two sweet rolls in individual cellophane bags. He's filled out since she saw him last—or else he filled out years ago but she's gone on seeing him the way he used to be. His face has the look of someone who once thought hard work and initiative would take him somewhere and now thinks he was a damn fool. Charlie sells sports equipment, and he's stalled out somewhere below the suit-wearing level. It's been years since Cath felt comfortable asking about his job, and even longer since he talked about it without being asked.

He sets his tray down and unloads their coffee, along with a handful of plastic cream containers and packets of sugar—more of them than any two people could use. Charlie's heard of finite resources and wants to make sure he gets his share.

He pulls out the chair across from her and sits.

"So the doctor doesn't expect much," he says, not asking as much as tossing out a statement to see if she'll argue.

Cath shakes her head.

"He kept using the word *massive*. Massive damage. Massive this, massive that." She runs one finger around the lid of her coffee cup. "He didn't want to do any more than make him comfortable. It was Mom—."

Cath waits for Charlie to pick this up but he doesn't. He's seen the tubes and monitors and machines that anchor their father to his life. He doesn't want to hear how they got there. He says, "I've been thinking about Mom."

Cath nods. Their mother's upstairs, waiting until she can go back into their father's room. She told them to walk around, to get some coffee, to not feel like they had to sit with her every minute, and they left together as quietly as kids who are old enough to behave well in a strange place but not old enough to know what they should do there unless someone tells them.

Charlie pries the lid off his coffee.

"The question is, what's going to happen to her afterwards."

Cath opens a container of cream and pours it into her coffee. She pushes the foil cover into the container, sets it down and picks up a plastic stir stick. Even with these, Charlie's taken more than they need. They lie on the tray like a Rorschach test. *I see excess, doctor. I see waste. Is that within normal parameters?* She flexes the stick between her hands. She should nod here, or say *Yes?* or dig her heels in and argue with she's not sure what yet. Instead she puts the plastic stick into her coffee and stirs. On the other side of the corridor, a man sweeps a table clear of empty sugar packets and styrofoam cups, then sprays the table down and wipes it.

"The house is going to be too much for her. It's not just the yard and the snow, but maintenance, repairs—." He nods his head to the side as if the list is much longer but too obvious to need spelling out.

Cath shakes her head. She takes the stir stick out of the cup and the coffee goes on circling without her help.

"What's that mean?" he asks.

"It's too early to think about it."

"We've got to think about it." His voice is solid, responsible. He wants to take care of their mother. Cath's being sentimental. "You're not going to show up every Sunday and mow the grass, are you? You're not going to reroof the house."

"You're not going to reroof it either."

"Exactly."

"*Dad* wasn't going to reroof it."

"That's not the point."

"It doesn't *need* reroofing."

Charlie pinches the skin above each knuckle methodically. This is their father's gesture. Cath can't remember whether Charlie's always done it or whether he's trying to move into the space their father hasn't quite moved out of yet. She looks away to keep from snapping at him. The couple at the next table have finished their sweet roll and are talking slowly and quietly to each other—a few words, an easy silence for the words to land in, a few more words.

"You're not listening to what I'm saying," Charlie says, "An old house always needs something—if it's not the roof it's painting, plumbing. You know how to snake out a drain, or rewire a light fixture? If it isn't one thing it's another. All I'm telling you is it'll be more than she can keep up with."

Cath runs her fingers through her hair.

"I'm not having this conversation, okay? Nobody's dead yet."

Charlie makes a disgusted sound, pours two containers of cream into his coffee and stacks the empties inside each other, then inside the container she's emptied.

"You're not being realistic."

Cath's braced for him to say more, but he's not being realistic either. He doesn't want to talk about what's coming any more than she does. They look away from each other. Cath thinks how odd it is that they're not crying, but there isn't a tear in her, and she can't imagine where one would come from. All she can imagine is what's in front of her: the white top of the table, their hands, their coffee cups, this dry bone of a woman, her even drier brother.

She breaks her sweet roll out of its body bag. It's almost square, with squiggles of icing across the top. The thought comes to her, fully formed and in words, that if she were anywhere else in the world she wouldn't eat this. She breaks off a corner and chews. It tastes of sugar, of oil, of something long ago descended from apples.

"When do you have to be back at work?" she asks.

He hesitates before he answers—just enough that she can hear him decide not to argue.

"I'll call on Monday and see what I can negotiate."

It's not until they're on the elevator and he's punching buttons for the sixth floor, and for the door to close right away, without waiting for anyone else, that she thinks of what she should have said: that she doesn't want to make plans for their mother unless their mother's part of the discussion; that it isn't up to them to decide for her. For a second she wonders who she might have been if Charlie hadn't been in her life from the moment she was born, always placing himself next to the elevator buttons, the TV controls, the levers that choose the time, place and subject of every conversation.

Their mother's not in the waiting room anymore, and Cath calls the intensive care desk to ask if they can see their father. The rules allow two visitors for twenty minutes of every hour, but when she and Charlie walk past the desk together no one looks up to count heads, add their mother's and come up with a total of three.

Their mother's head is nodding, but she raises it automatically when they get close to the door. After all these years, she's still tuned to the vibrations of their shoes on the floor.

"I must've been asleep," she says, but already she's shaken off any trace of haziness. She's as alert as Cath's ever seen her—a guard dog disguised as a sixty-year-old woman. She'd snap death himself in half if she could get her jaws around him. It's the role she's been training for all her life. She'd be the same way if Charlie needed her. Or Cath. She'd tear them away from carjackers, cops, drug-crazed Hell's Angels with assault weapons. She's never had a crisis worthy of her till now.

Cath holds out the sweet roll and coffee they bought. Their mother didn't ask for anything, but it seemed important to bring something back, even if it was only this— food you eat not because you want it but because you don't know what else to do, and because you remember, in an abstract sort of way, that the living have to eat.

"Did you bring sugar?"

Cath nods at the cup.

"It's in there."

"Good girl."

Something catches in Cath's throat. A host of green lights draw lines across the monitor above her father's bed. A machine forces air into him through his lungs. Her mother takes the lid off her coffee and sets it on the bedside table to cool. She won't drink it until it's almost cold, when it holds just the faintest memory of heat. She toys with the wrapper on the sweet roll.

"I could get you a sandwich instead," Cath says.

"I can't even think about food."

Cath nods as if she understands, although in fact she could eat again right now, without hunger and without end. The taste of sugar lines her mouth and she wants something to replace it—tuna fish; a hamburger with pickles and ketchup; a ham sandwich with mustard. She's standing by the head of her father's bed. Tubes disappear into his mouth. The thick one is air; the green one, food. Each time the pump pushes air through him, his chest bucks under the blanket like he's trying to push it back out. With each breath, the machine ticks, then sighs. Cath touches his forehead with two fingers. In the next glass-walled room, liquid gurgles inside a tube, making a sound like a kid sucking the last drops of Coke through a straw, only thicker.

"We're all here, Dad. Charlie's here. Mom's here."

She wants to say her own name but can't. The machine forces air into his lungs. At the nurses' station, a phone rings. Cath tries to believe that he hears her but she doesn't quite. He's sedated heavily, and there's no telling how much damage the heart attack did to his brain. Still, she wonders if there's anything she wants to tell him— any last message to shoot after him into the void, some human sound she can send with him. He played in a jazz band before Charlie was born, and she hates the idea of him sliding out of the world to the tick-sigh of an electronic metronome.

"Charlie," their mother says, "go see if you can find your sister a chair."

"I'm okay, Mom. I'm fine."

Charlie's been leaning against the doorway and he pushes himself upright, waiting for them to make up their minds. Their mother nods at him and says, "Go."

"Mom—" Cath says.

"It won't hurt to let someone do something for you once."

"I should go home anyway. I need a shower."

Cath's mother softens visibly.

"What kind of mother am I anyway? Of course you should go."

This is an old family joke—what kind of mother am I anyway?—and Cath smiles. She notices that she can do this and it strikes her as overwhelmingly odd that she's smiling at a joke she always hated while her father lies beside her dying.

"I could drive you home if you want to change or something."

"Later. After visiting hours."

Cath's father and his machine breathe. Charlie lumbers back with a chair and sets it beside their mother's.

"I'm going home in a minute," Cath says. "I'm too grubby to be out in public."

Charlie shrugs—he's not responsible for his sister's whims. She wants to remind him that she spent last night in the waiting room with their mother, curled up on the floor with her jacket bunched under her head, only Charlie knows this already. He spent most of last night driving up from Chicago, finally stopping to grab some sleep when he realized that the lightning he was seeing had nothing to do with the snow clouds and everything to do with exhaustion.

Cath touches her father's forehead again. His skin's oily. Maybe it always has been. She can't remember touching his forehead before today, although she must have when she was little.

"I'm going home for a few minutes, then I'll be back," she tells him.

The machine breathes. He resists.

"I won't be long," she tells her mother.

"We'll be fine."

Cath touches her mother's shoulder. On her way past Charlie, she touches his arm and he pushes away from the doorway and says he'll walk her out.

At the nursing station, a man's telling two women something so full of medical language that all Cath understands are the pronouns and prepositions. *I, out, you, him, off.* Along the wall, someone's parked a tank of compressed gas and a pair of machines with dials all over them. Everything's on wheels, as if the whole unit's made to be rolled away. All they're waiting for is some financial wizard to decide they can make more money from a cafeteria, or a theme park.

"I'm glad you were with her last night," Charlie says when they reach the elevators.

He sounds unsure. He's not used to saying this sort of thing and can't tell if he has the accent or the order of the words right.

Cath glances down, nods, shrugs.

"How do you think she's doing?"

"I'm not sure any of us know how we're doing right now."

He laughs, not because she's funny but by way of agreement. She touches his arm again and says she really should go.

Outside, the sun's blinding and there's fresh snow on the ground. When she drove to the hospital last night, she watched this same snow fall. She's fond of it as she is of the couple in the cafeteria. It floated down gently, almost weightlessly. About two inches, all told. The radio predicted four.

She calls Maggie from her apartment. In the background, a woman's voice is paging someone. Maggie works at Riverside and Cath's father was taken to Lutheran, but the voice is the same one she's been hearing all morning—soothing, bland, letting everyone know the situation's under control, there's nothing to get upset about.

Maggie asks about medications, about the oxygen level in Cath's father's blood, and Cath says she's not sure, she doesn't know, she didn't ask. She remembers a doctor leaning against the wall to talk to her and her mother. She remembers the metal frames on his glasses, a single white hair growing wild out of his black eyebrows. She remembers knowing that her mind was reaching overload. All she really understood was that her father was dying. She remembers her mother saying she didn't give a damn about the odds, she wanted him to have every chance, as if there were still chances to be had.

"I'll stop by as soon as I get off work," Maggie says.

"Mag, my uncle's coming by, we're in and out of the room—I don't even know where to tell you to find us."

"Trust me, I know how to find people in a hospital."

"It's not the best time for you to meet them, that's all."

"So tell them I'm a friend—you don't have to explain your whole life to them. A doctor'll sometimes talk differently to another medical person, even if it is just a lowly nurse. At the very least, I'll be able to translate for you."

"They're doing everything they can already. Christ, they're doing more than they should."

Maggie doesn't say anything.

"Let me think about it."

"Fine. Think. What hospital is he in?"

"I said let me think about it. I'll call you."

"Cath—."

"I'll call you. I promise."

Cath hangs up and stands by the phone, half expecting Maggie to call back, but the phone doesn't ring. She tells herself this isn't what matters right now, her family's what matters, but her mind keeps picking up the argument again. In the middle of her shower, suddenly she's clenching her jaw and telling herself Maggie has no idea what it's like.

Cath has no idea what the words mean. What *it* does she have in mind?

Cath turns off the faucets and runs her hands over her hair, pressing out streams of water. She dresses, dries her hair and makes herself a slice of toast, then knocks on her landlady's door to borrow a shovel, explaining about her father, about last night's snow, about her parent's sidewalk. It feels false somehow, as if she were playing a role: dutiful daughter helping out in a crisis; isn't she admirable?

When she gets back to the hospital, her uncle's in the waiting room between Charlie and her mother, looking like he's been there all night too. He's gray, diminished, older than he was at Thanksgiving. She pulls up a fourth chair and they go silent so she can ask, "Any change?"

They shake their heads.

Cath has lost track of whether no change is good or bad. He's no worse; he's also no better. More than she's afraid of him dying she's afraid of him coming only halfway back, with a mind that's not the same one he had when he left them, with a body that gives him nothing but pain.

Her uncle pats her hand and says he's glad she's here, "You and the big fellow over there, both of you." He nods toward Charlie. Some part of Cath begins the old complaint; no one ever pays attention to what she does. She notices it the way she'd notice a TV playing across the room with the volume turned down.

"Have you been in to see him?" she asks her uncle.

"I only got here a few minutes ago."

Cath turns to her mother.

"You want me to call?"

"It hasn't been an hour but go ahead and try them—sure."

The nurse says they can go in, and Cath tells her mother she'll wait—even if they can get by with three people, four's pushing it.

She calls Maggie from a phone near the elevator. The man who answers puts her on hold, then comes back and says she's with a patient. Cath leaves her name, the name of the hospital and the letters ICU. As soon as she hangs up she wants to call back and tell him it's important, can he promise Maggie will get the message or does she need to call back?

Not that asking would reassure her.

She adds hiding Maggie from her family to the list of everything she's done wrong in her life and rides the elevator downstairs to buy a newspaper. While she's there, she browses through the magazine rack and looks at the flowers in the cooler—skinny bouquets of daisies, single roses padded out with fern and baby's breath, each cluster wrapped in cellophane. The list of things she's done wrong plays through her mind in more or less random order—which means not in their absolute order of importance. It gives a lot of play to her calling a client by someone else's name because it only happened yesterday and because the client she was talking to and the client whose name she used are both black. She's not sure how it happened: a couple of wires that crossed in her brain; a patch of racism lying inside her like black ice on the highway, imperceptible until the tires lose their hold. She'd blame her father being in the hospital, but he was fine then. She apologized to the client, but she doubts that fixed anything. There's nothing to do now but live with it. She pays for her paper and heads toward the elevator before her mind churns up anything worse.

By the time Cath gets back upstairs, Charlie and her mother and uncle are back, sitting exactly where they sat before.

The waiting room serves three units, and it's filled up since this morning. Each family gathers a group of chairs, turns them inward and keeps its conversation low.

"Any change?" she asks.

They shake their heads.

Cath sets the paper under her chair. Her uncle tells her again that he's glad to see her here. She smiles and tries to look pleased, the prodigal daughter returned, except he has no idea how prodigal and she hasn't been anywhere. He says it means a lot to her mother at a time like this, having her children with her. Cath shifts in her chair.

She supposes this is true; she supposes it should make her happy, but she feels nothing. From the corner of her eye she sees Charlie looking out the window at the south wing of the hospital. She holds her smile as long as she can, then lets it fade.

"It means a lot to your father too," her uncle says. "He knows you're here."

Cath's throat tightens and she shakes her head, not to disagree, just to release the tightness.

"You'll have to take an old man's word for that."

Cath scrapes her chair back and crosses the waiting room faster than she wants to. In the far corner, a woman and a teenage girl look up, and by the door a man's eyes follow her over the top of a crossword puzzle book. She locks the door of the women's room behind her. She's willing to cry here, but nothing inside her wants to anymore. She throws water on her face and dries it.

Her mother's watching for her when she comes back, drawn to any sign of weakness like a shark to blood. Or maybe what she's drawn to is vulnerability. Cath isn't in a mood to sort out one from the other. Whatever it is, her mother never had much of it herself but she expected it in a daughter, and she still wants it. Cath stiffens. If anyone touched her right now, she'd shatter. She sets her hands on the back of her empty chair like a politician puffed up behind a podium.

"I asked a friend who's a nurse to stop by this afternoon. She thought she could get some information for us, or interpret what we've got."

Her mother's face sharpens. She sees surgeries they haven't told her about, tubes, medications, machines that can spin time backward and heal the damaged heart. Charlie's face shows a spark of interest too, but it's a different one. He understands how important contacts are, and influence, and networks. This is a pure interest; he doesn't have to expect anything to appreciate them. Cath has a value he hadn't suspected.

"I'll tell you this about the doctors," Cath's mother says to her uncle. "They'd have been just as happy to let him die. God help the person who doesn't have someone to fight for them."

"It's all about money," Cath's uncle says. "They cut corners anywhere they can."

"Well, they're not cutting any corners here, I'll tell you that much for free."

Cath's still standing, chin out like she wants an argument. She sits and tips her chin down, toward her breastbone, but she can't shake the feeling that it's jutting forward still, doing whatever it can to provoke someone. Her mother leans close to put an arm around her shoulders, shaking her lightly.

"Go ahead and cry if you want to," she whispers. "You'll never have a better reason."

Cath pulls away.

"Mom, leave it, will you?"

"Whatever you want."

Her mother doesn't sound angry. She sounds like whatever's wrong must be wrong with Cath because she hasn't done anything to account for it. She turns away from Cath and refuses to say anything else. The rest of them slip into an embarrassed silence, which her uncle finally ends by saying, "You know, Charlie, I've been having a lot of trouble with my brakes lately. You know anything about brakes?"

"Not much. I know they stop a car. At least, I know they're supposed to stop the car."

The way he says this makes it man-talk—bluff, good natured, not a confession of ignorance, the way it would be if Cath said it.

"Well, mine stop the car all right, but they make the most god awful noises when they do it. Not all the time, just here and there. And never when I take it in."

"That's the way it always works, isn't it?"

Their uncle gives an inventory of the times he's taken the car in, and what the mechanic tried and how much he charged for it and the times when he didn't charge.

"I guess I'll just have to keep taking it in," he says at the end of the list.

"Might ought to try the dealer."

"I don't know. Gets expensive, taking it to the dealer."

"Gets expensive taking it anywhere."

The conversation trails off. Cath should offer some topic from her own life to keep them talking, but her car's holding its own and the rest of her life is a fog—she can't think of anything worth mentioning. With a fingernail on her right hand, she cleans the fingernail on her left. Charlie pats his pockets for the cigarettes he gave up years ago. Their mother stares at the doorway.

"Why don't you two get some lunch?" she says after a few minutes, her eyes indicating Cath and Charlie. "Let the old folks visit in peace."

Cath glances automatically at Charlie and sees that he agrees, although his face doesn't give any outward sign.

"What can we bring you?"

"Just coffee."

Cath's about to argue and reads an invisible signal from Charlie: *Don't worry about it, we'll bring her something anyway.* She has no idea if he's really thinking this or if she's imagining it.

"Uncle Paul?"

"Whatever they have. Nothing with onions, though. I can't take onions anymore."

He puts the flat of one hand on his chest, just below the throat.

Cath follows Charlie out of the waiting room. Her mind shows her a snapshot of their parents' house, exactly the way it stood when she drove up this morning, snow lying clean on the front walk, only the mailman's feet marking a trail across the lawn from the neighbors on the south side to her parents' door and on to the neighbors on the north. Her father would have had the snow shoveled and the walk salted before he sat down to breakfast. Then he would have knocked the snow off the shovel, wiped it down with a rag and hung it in the garage, inside the painted outline on the wall. Cath doesn't understand how someone who once played jazz could have ended up being this fussy, but she doesn't know any musicians to compare him to.

"Did you ever hear Dad play his trumpet?" she asks Charlie.

"Why? Does he still have it?"

They're watching the elevator doors, waiting for one to open.

"I don't know. I was thinking about him giving it up, that's all. About whether he missed it."

This isn't exactly true. What she thought was that he gave it up when Charlie was born, as if it were Charlie's fault more than hers—as if, before their parents had even wrapped a diaper around him, they saw some flaw in his character that would keep him from doing well as a musician's child. Rearranging the thought leaves a ripple in the flow of her words, but Charlie doesn't seem to hear it. He gives her one of those older-brother looks that come from a distance she'll never cross.

"He wasn't getting anywhere with it. He was probably glad he had a reason to quit—you know, the kind of thing that keeps you from having to say, *Well, I busted my ass but it didn't work.*"

A bell chimes behind them and they wedge themselves into the elevator, joining a flock of people Cath doesn't really look at—they're reasons to stop talking, nothing more. She's never thought of her father as a failed musician, only as one who couldn't make a living at it, or not the kind of living he was willing to raise a family on. It shouldn't surprise her that Charlie sees those as the same thing, but it does—it surprises her into a gaping absence of thought.

On the ground floor, they follow a corridor toward the coffee shop.

"You'd think he'd kept playing, though," she says. "If he liked music, you'd think he'd have kept playing."

Charlie shrugs. He understands success and failure and all the gradations in between. He understands money and plans and the rational place for their mother to live. He understands sports. What he doesn't understand, he doesn't see the point of, and it doesn't make sense to talk to him about it. And with that out of the way, Cath's father begins to make sense to her: Once you've played for an audience, and once you've been paid for it, maybe you can't go back to playing in the basement. The hope goes out of it and the pleasure follows.

She walks faster than she would have if she were alone, keeping up with Charlie, moving left to pass a bone-thin woman in dreadlocks, moving back beside Charlie once they're in front of her.

"How are you holding up, anyway?" she asks.

"I could use some sleep. I'll be all right."

This isn't what she was trying to ask, but it's close enough. Information isn't what she wanted anyway, just contact. They follow a line of people into the coffee shop and past stainless steel shelves, plastic-wrapped food, a cash register. Most of the tables are filled now. The noise of talking and the scraping of chairs echo off the walls and ceiling and crash back in on them. The gentle couple with the sweet roll is gone. At the next table are three office workers in their twenties. They're talking about plans for the weekend, and their voices are hard-edged and cheerful.

Cath peels back the seal on her sandwich and extracts it. It's a pale egg salad on light brown bread, and it's cool and soft in her mouth, all texture and no taste.

"Listen," she says, "I've got to tell you something."

Charlie has his own sandwich open and looks up from stirring his coffee. The voices around them overlap and the words lose their shape and meaning. Cath hadn't planned to say this and searches her mind for some bush-league revelation to pawn off on him.

"My friend who's stopping by? The nurse?"

At some point she's looked away from him, and she's staring into her coffee now. She has no idea when she did this. She looks up.

"The thing is—." she runs her hands through her hair, says "Shit" and folds her hands in front of her on the table. "Listen, you're not going to like this, but I'm going to say it anyway. I'm a lesbian."

Time slows down. Invisible lines spring to the surface of her rib cage and gauge the vibrations in the room, the sound level at the next table, the power of her words to override the office workers and force them to hear what she's just said. These are lateral lines, like the ones fish use to communicate, to orient themselves, to sense danger. *A system of distant touch,* her college textbook called it. Evolution is instituting one of its miraculous changes in a species, right here in the hospital coffee shop.

"Yeah," Charlie says, "I pretty much figured that."

At the next table, a woman says, "I know, but he *could* have called," and then her voice goes under, overlapped by other words, other thoughts. Cath's mind reaches back and reassembles Charlie's words, first as sound only, then as meaning.

"You knew that?"

"I wasn't positive, but yeah, I thought so."

"You shithead."

They burst out laughing as if this is what they've been holding back all morning. The women at the next table glance over and look away before anyone can catch them at it.

When Cath can talk again, she says, "Do Mom and Dad know?" She hears the present tense and the plural but doesn't go back to sort them out.

"Probably. I don't know. It's not the kind of thing people talk about."

Charlie's still smiling, expecting her to share this joke too, and she does—her face radiates a three-year-old's pleasure at being in on it. She has a younger sister's rock-solid belief that if she and her brother are laughing together the world's exactly the way it should be, even though stretching ahead of her she can see that he'll never once talk about her being a lesbian unless she brings it up first, and then he won't say anything more about it than he can help. When the time comes she'll be angry about that. Right now, though, she smiles, and she points at the extra cream containers, stir sticks and sugar packets piled on his tray.

"Charlie, you shithead, how come you take all that stuff when you don't use it?"

"In case I need it," he says.

His face is open and innocent. He's willing to talk about this, but he can't think for the life of him why anyone would want to.

OPTIONS FOR DIALOGUE

- Please discuss with a partner Cath's first impression that her brother doesn't approve of her. What does she remember?
- Did this disapproval have anything to do with Cath's sexual preference?
- Do you and your discussion partner have comments about how Maggie may have felt about Cath's fear of including her? Elaborate on this. Were you empathetic?
- Please have a discussion about Charlie.

SUGGESTIONS FOR ACTION

- Interview a hospital employee about hospice care and how he or she work with families whose relative is terminally ill.
- Read a book that focuses on the relationship between gay, lesbian, and bisexual men and women and their family members. Respond to this story by writing a poem or a personal story or creating a work of art. Many bibliographies can be obtained through the World Wide Web on the Internet. Two such sites are Queer Resources Directory (http://www.qrd.org/qrd/) and Gay, Lesbian, Straight Teachers Network (http://www.glstn.org/).
- As a teacher or human service professional, create the beginning of an action plan that would help you include diversity of sexual orientation in your work. For example, if you were a primary teacher, what books would you include in your lessons about family? If you were a middle school teacher? If you were a counselor in a high school?
- Read several poems about the theme of breaking family- or community-imposed silences and write a poem or a personal response to these readings. Some authors you may consider are Denise Chávez, Julia Alvarez, Edwidge Danticat, Mary Gordon, Gloria Anzaldúa, Judith Katz, Marge Piercy, Adrienne Rich, David Mura, and Sharon Olds.
- Read *Sexuality and the Schools: Handling the Critical Issues* by Joan L. Curcio, Lois F. Berlin, and Patricia F. First, available from Corwin Press, 2455 Teller Road, Thousand Oaks, CA 91320. Relate information to the story and make recommendations for curriculum inclusion in high school programs.
- Read *Out with It: Gay and Straight Teens Write about Homosexuality* edited by Philip Kay, Andrea Estepa, and Al Desetta, available from Youth Communication, 144 West 27th Street, Suite 8R, New York, NY 10001. Make a recommendation to your community library about whether or not to include this book in its collection.

SOUR RICE

OPTIONS FOR LISTENING

- Think about the silences within your own family. Are there things you are not supposed to talk about? What are some of your own experiences in breaking family silences?
- How are conflicts resolved or not resolved in your family? How did you, as a young person, respond to family conflict?
- Describe in your journal any novels, short stories, nonfiction essays and articles, or news reports that you have read that are focused on children and young adults who are dealing with parental conflict and divorce. What is a critical question that you had or still have about some aspect of the issue?
- Read the selection, note questions that arise, and write down any personal connections that occur to you.

Sour Rice

by Nhien T. Nguyen

The bowl hit the floor with a crash that resonated throughout the house. Lin looked at the shattered porcelain chips that lay on the floor; bits of them had flown under the brown dining room chairs. Her eyes reluctantly followed up the legs and arms of the chairs and met 11 pairs of eyes staring at her in disbelief. Her body stood frozen in the corner of the room, while her hands shook uncontrollably. She could feel the warmth of anger and embarrassment that came from her guts and surfaced to her head. Her face radiated with heat.

Lin's mother, Mai, released a nervous, forced laugh. She said, "Oh, Lin, you know better than to carry those bowls when your hands are so wet. Now, Charlie, what were you saying about your customer in the restaurant?" Her mother turned her back and slid into the chair next to her uncle.

The heavy silence of the room was slowly broken as Uncle Charlie resumed his long, tedious story as if nothing had happened. Lin thought back to all the times her parents would have one of their furious fights with each other one minute and joke with a friend on the phone the next minute.

The second after she threw the bowl on the floor, she knew that this was the last dinner party that her parents could drag her to. The smell of the fish sauce, the old plastic oranges and apples sitting on the coffee table, the little napkins made into fans. She hated it, all of it. To Lin, it seemed like most of her young life was spent smiling and nodding to her parents' friends as they came through their door for the monthly get-together. They spoke to her slowly in broken English and remarked what a pleasant and smart girl she was. The worst of it was Lou's usual ritual of punching Lin in the stomach.

It was hard to avoid Lin's stomach because it practically lay at eye level for her parents and all their friends. Lin always towered over everybody at these parties at 5-foot-8 and almost doubled everybody's weight at 170 pounds. Lin eventually got to the point where she was used to the playful hitting and expected the same jokes and teases.

The same people came to these parties; the guests were mainly distant friends, acquaintances from years past. Lin had the feeling that her parents were obligated to host these gatherings. Her father's shoe store business had suddenly become successful, and her mother could finally afford to buy nice flower vases, mauve carpeting and a long oak dining-room table, perfect to seat a large group. Mai loved the compliments on how beautiful their house was and how well she kept it. Their friends all loved Lin's parents; they always asked them advice on marriage and admired how happy they looked around each other.

Now, as she stared at the floor, Lin could finally move her legs, careful not to walk on the broken chips. Without thought of what she did, her body automatically went to fetch a broom. As she grabbed the handle, her head could not stop hearing the words over and over that her mother had said to her before the bowl had shattered:

"It will all be your fault if your father leaves."

Lin's mind replayed what had just happened between her and her mother. Her father had asked her to go to the kitchen to get more bowls for the fish soup. When she carried the five white and gold porcelain bowls back to the dining room, her mother stopped her, looked at her intensely and asked, "Have you been talking to Buna?"

"Of course I have, Mom, I see her every day."

Buna was a childhood friend of her mom's who had gotten Lin a job at the bookstore. Of all the people that her mother knew, Buna was the friendliest and the easiest to talk to. She was the only person who understood Lin and her family. Lin never talked specifically about her family, but Buna was perceptive enough to know when Lin was feeling down. Buna also knew her mother well enough that few words were needed for Lin to express any given situation.

"You know what I'm talking about," her mother said, lowering her voice as she realized how loud she was talking. Lin started moving toward the tables as she looked for her father across the black heads crowding the room.

"My own daughter looks at my face and lies to me," Mai said. The music that began in the background was now classical music. The random conversations around the room drowned out her mother's words.

Lin turned her face around to look at her mother. She never really noticed the heavy lines that ran across her mother's face. When Lin was 8 years old she could remember how she would rub her hands across her mother's cheeks; her skin was as smooth as silk and white as porcelain. Lin could still hear mother's voice telling her to come back into the house when she played outside. "Your skin is already black like a prune," she would say.

"Mother, what could I possibly have said to Buna that would concern you?" The corner of Lin's lips curved up, a habit her mother always hated. "Why do we have to talk about this now. Uncle Lou will start his story about killing chickens if we don't get him his soup soon."

Her mother's eyes widened as she raised her pale finger to Lin's face. "You told her that your father and I were going to. . . ." Mai's eyes blinked and her black pupils became glassy. There were few times when Lin saw her mother cry. Even at her aunt's funeral she was too busy arguing with Lin's father to shed any tears.

Lin faintly understood what her mother was referring to. She thought back a week ago when she was working at the store. Lin had come early to the bookstore that day so that she could escape the loud yells and fierce words. Lin remembered how grateful she was that all the dishes had remained intact on the dish rack instead of smashed on the floor.

When Lin entered the bookstore, she was so glad to see Buna sitting behind the cash register, her face buried into a book titled "Pandora's Box." She wore her usual long purple skirt with yellow-flowered top. Her scraggly black hair was bundled up into a clump piled on top of her head. Next to her tiny hands on the counter was her gold-lined bookmark given to her by her husband before he died.

Buna's head lifted up as her glasses fell down to the tip of her nose. "Lin, you're early! Are you all right?"

Lin couldn't tell if her face had shown her distress or if Buna was just surprised to see her early for once.

"Oh, I'm fine, Buna. I'm just worried about this English test that I have tomorrow." Lin looked at Buna's face, hoping to read whether Buna had bought the excuse or not.

"Oh, come now, Lin, you should know that I can see right through you," Buna teased.

Lin paused and said, "I just wonder what it would be like if my parents were separated." Lin caught herself and added, "I mean, I was just reading this book about a boy whose parents were going through a divorce."

Lin almost slipped and broke the cardinal rule. The only other time she was faced with telling her parents' problems was two years ago, when her friend Rebecca came to sleep over at her house. They both had camped out in front of the television set that night in the living room. Her parents had moved their argument to the kitchen, where they threatened each other in Vietnamese, apparently unaware that Lin and Rebecca were within earshot.

"What's your mom saying?" Rebecca asked.

"I don't know," Lin giggled, "I never know what they're talking about when they kid around like that."

Lin could remember how she sank into her musty sleeping bag on the couch and told Rebecca that she was too tired to continue to talk.

The look that Buna gave her was the same expression that Rebecca had before Lin turned off the lights that night. Buna knew Lin well enough to leave her alone at that moment. It finally came to Lin that Buna must have questioned her mother about the comment that she had made at the store that day.

"Mom, I didn't tell her anything, she must have misunderstood what I said," Lin pleaded. "What does it matter anyway? She's your friend. She only wanted to help you and make sure that you and Dad were all right."

Lin knew right then that she had gone too far and had admitted to something that was forbidden. Her mother's face cringed when Lin had said that she needed help.

"You are an ungrateful daughter. How could you tell them that about your father's papers?" Mai lowered her voice and said, "It will all be your fault if your father leaves."

It was at that moment that Lin had slammed the bowls down on the kitchen hardwood floors. The sound was so harsh and sudden that it had startled everyone in the room. Her mother had made her usual safe recovery from the incident and left her to clean up the mess. Lin looked at the beaten up broom that she had in her hand; the wood was giving her splinters in her fingers.

Lin set the broom back in the closet and headed toward her room. As she crossed past the dining room table, all the guests were too busy eating and chattering to notice her; only her mom had looked up in the midst of her conversation. Lin escaped from the room too quickly to see the scowl that swept across her mother's face.

She decided to go to her father's den room to calm her nerves. Lin looked down at her hands and realized that they had not stopped shaking since her outburst.

When she entered the room, the smell of her father's aftershave mixed with the scent of wood wafted up her nose. Lin picked up the statue of the old Confucius-looking man holding his fishing pole sitting on her father's desk. A stack of papers caught her eye as she examined the cracks on the statue. The papers were torn down the middle, the cover sheet laid on top. The picture on it had black silhouettes of a man and a woman standing apart from each other, their bodies facing opposite from each other. Underneath the picture were the words, "When Love Hurts: Divorce at an Affordable Price."

The meaning of the papers in front of her took a moment to register in her head. Lin sank into her dad's desk chair, her eyes mesmerized by the words on the torn pieces of paper.

The sound of the door knob turning interrupted her thoughts as the door of the room swung open. Lin's heart jumped, expecting to see her mother's short, skinny body in front of her. She released her breath when she saw a stout figure standing in the doorway, her father carrying a bowl of soup in his hand.

"Linny, I thought I would find you here. I noticed you left without eating anything." Lin's father smiled and lifted the soup to Lin's face. "You know that you have to eat so that your brain can grow."

Lin laughed at that phrase that her father had said every time she didn't eat anything during dinner. She always failed at her dieting attempts whenever her father commented on how little she ate. Guilt from her father's warm and caring words forced her to eat more than she had planned.

"Your mother did that," he said. His eyes pointed to the torn sheets of paper sitting on the desk. "Those contracts cost a lot of money."

Silence swept across the room. "Dad, why? Why do you guys have to do this? Why can't you just stop arguing with each other?" The tremble in her pleading voice made her close her mouth.

"I don't know, Lin. This is the only way I know how to stop the fighting, for us to stop hurting you." Her father's hand reached out to touch her head, when the door opened.

"The both of you in here?! All these guests are in our house and you two are in here?" Mai's voice was harsh and loud.

"Mai, calm down, there's nothing to get upset about." Her father's hand gently touched Lin's shoulder. "Come on, Lin, Uncle Lou is dying to tell you another story."

"No," Lin said, pulling her shoulder abruptly away. "I can't go out there and smile to everyone like nothing's wrong!" Her words rose to the ceiling.

Her parents both stared at her wide-eyed, their bodies stood stiff. Her mom's gaze rested on the pile of papers on the brown desk. "I thought I told you to throw those away. We don't need them!" Mai said to her husband. Her mother grabbed the stack of papers into her tiny hands, aimed at the trash and threw the papers all over the floor. "Lin, I want you to go out to the dining room right now and talk to everybody. If you don't do as I say, I will do what I did to you when you were 7 years old."

Lin could feel her cheeks sting as the thought of that moment triggered in her mind. She had been eating lunch that day on a humid summer's day; she could still feel her moist shirt sticking to her back. During her summer vacations, her mother would come home from the textile factory so that she could make lunch for Lin and make sure she was all right. Mai was rushed to get to work that day and gave Lin a bowl of leftover rice and vegetables. As soon as Lin put the rice in her mouth, her face crinkled from the sourness of the rice, and she spit out the food in her mouth onto her mother's workcoat. Her mother was standing over her, frantically running around to get back to work on time. When she looked over at the bits of food around her, her mother swung her hand to the side and sent it flying across Lin's face. Lin was too shocked to explain and too surprised to speak any words.

Lin erased the memory from her mind and let out an unexpected laugh.

She said, "Mom, I'm twice as big as you now. I'm not that short little girl you hit 10 years ago."

Mai's face became red and her lips pursed together. Lin could see her mother's hand lift up, ready to swing at anything that was in its path. A loud knock sounded through the room.

"Mai, Lin, Tuan, are you in there?" a muffled voice said. A woman with a pink paisley shirt and matching skirt walked into the room. Lin's anger dispelled as she saw Buna standing in front of her.

Water began to flow uncontrollably out of Lin's eyes as she tried to cover her face with her hands. Buna looked down and noticed the words written on the scattered pieces of paper that lay on the ground.

"What is all this?" Buna asked. "I don't understand. When I asked you if you were having problems with Tuan, you told me that nothing could be better."

"They are, I mean, I don't know where you get the idea that we're having problems." Mai avoided looking at what lay on the ground. "Tuan, you tell her that everything is fine." Her eyes darted straight onto her husband's face.

Lin's father let his head fall to his chest. He hesitated and his voice became solemn. "Mai, it's over. You have to accept it."

The expression on Mai's face was one mixed with astonishment and pain. The words were crisp and seemed to hit her in the stomach as she fell on her knees. Lin stopped crying and stared at her mother. Tears began to fall down Mai's face and sobs of anger rose from her lungs.

The door was left ajar and the sounds of the cries and sobs had filtered into the dining room. Slowly, each person came into the room and saw Mai kneeling on the floor, her face buried in her hands to keep the tears from the view of the bystanders.

Lin looked at all the eyes that stared in bewilderment at the scene in front of them, mumbles of explanation to those who could not see past all the black heads echoed throughout the room. Fingers pointed to the papers on the floor, broken Vietnamese phrases went back and forth across the room expressing sadness for Mai and Tuan, pity for Lin and her lost family.

Throughout this spectacle, Lin's anger disappeared and her sadness from seeing her mother cry subsided. Within that moment, Lin felt lighter, like she could float to the ceiling where no one could catch her. The next time she would see all of her parents' friends, she wouldn't have to smile at them as if nothing was wrong, she didn't have to nod in agreement to how happy her parents were together. Perhaps she would never have to see them again.

OPTIONS FOR DIALOGUE

- Discuss with a partner Lin's reactions to her mother's admonitions and denial of her marriage problems.
- Why did Lin feel lighter at the end?
- Why was Lin's mother so reluctant to acknowledge the impending divorce?
- Connect Lin's experience with another story that you have read, a film you have seen, or an experience of your own or of someone you know.
- Please discuss why an understanding of Lin's experience is important for teachers.

SUGGESTIONS FOR ACTION

- Interview a peer who has a family connection to Southeast Asia—ideally a Vietnamese American or a peer whose family members were involved in Southeast Asia. Report on the results of your interview.
- Prepare an annotated bibliography of books to use in your work with children and their parents. It should include books of fiction for children and young adults in which the members of a family deal with divorce. It should also include books of poetry and nonfiction on the same theme.
- Read *The Hite Report on Family* (1994) by Shere Hite (New York: Grove). Compare it to another book or article about separated families in the United States. What critical questions do you have about the findings in the two pieces? How are they alike and different? Submit your comparisons and contrasts to a newsletter for a family support group.
- What questions do you have about diverse family structures? List these and choose one to research.
- Interview a child from a single-parent family. Ask the child to describe both the positive aspects and the difficulties. Write the results of your interview as an article to publish in a newspaper or newsletter.
- Read *Lives on the Edge* (1993) by Valerie Polokow (Chicago: University of Chicago Press) or *Amazing Grace* (1995) by Jonathan Kozol (New York: HarperCollins). In your responses point out the strengths of the characters as well as the barriers they face. Report to your class.

WOMEN LIKE THOSE

OPTIONS FOR LISTENING

- Have you ever known a family (or known of them) in which physical abuse has occurred? Write in your journal some details about the situation the people lived in, the nuances of their personalities, and the sequence of events as you saw them. What are some questions you have about the whole situation?
- Write a brief, fictional, "up close and personal" newspaper article about a person you see regularly in a public place. What details about the things you see give you information? What details about the person remind you of other people you actually know? What questions would you like to be able to ask the person?

- Listen to your local public media (television, radio, or newspapers) for a week and document any stories you hear about domestic abuse. What specifics are covered? What do you think is left out? Did you already know about this news before it was reported? What other questions do you have?
- Read the selection, write down any questions you think of as you read, and note any personal connections.

Women Like Those
by David Haynes

Bobby and Julie are sitting by the window in "Table of Contents," eating sourdough bread and waiting for their salads. Fresh endive in a vinaigrette.

"You think you're so cute," Julie says. She runs her foot up and down his leg, tilts her head provocatively to one side. "See over there," she prompts.

Bobby turns his head and looks where she has indicated. "Bald guy with glasses?" he asks. "That's professor Herbert Von Hymen. Religion, or at least that's what he teaches. His real field is transcendent ritual sex cults. Little number with him there: she's his sex zombie."

"Bobby!" Julie complains, rolling her eyes, but to no avail. He has her in his thrall tonight and he knows it.

"You see she's wearing his ankle bracelet. . . . Don't look now. Don't . . . try not to be so obvious, would you."

But Julie does look. At the bracelet and at the professor, and at the woman eating behind them, alone, hiding the cover of the book she is reading; at the waiter with five piercings in his left ear; and at the well-tailored middle-aged woman with the young man whose ripped jeans and ponytail obviously make her uncomfortable. And Bobby looks too, and they make up stories about these people over pork medallions and salmon. And more stories while splitting the sautéed orange pound cake.

When it's her turn Julie weaves a family history for the boy and the women as complex as a daytime drama. She imagines characters who have long since died, re-married, or moved on to another city. The men are duplicitous, or rich and wise, and the women, long suffering, but inevitably resilient, the ultimate survivors. Bobby says Julie's stories are generic, that they could be about anyone. And though he has never rebuked her for it, she often repeats herself. Tonight she says the woman with the book is a divorcee from the coast, beginning a new life in Saint Paul, just like the woman with the Monet scarf in "Palomino" last week. Bobby is secretly disappointed at Julie's lack of creativity. He prides himself on inventing whole lives from the smallest details—from a tattoo or a bangle or a scar. He likes his stories concise and simple, like the thirty second news teasers inserted in the evening line-up on ABC. Julie encourages Bobby to add more details to his stories. She accuses him of holding out on her, of going for the cheap laugh like a desperate stand up comic would, but Bobby holds his ground. Like those news teasers, he wants her to stay tuned for more.

It is Bobby's month to do laundry and the washing machine in the apartment building has died. The landlord, Skjoreski, says he'll fix it, but they don't hold their breath. He's got them by the short hairs—cheap rent, long lease and a prime Crocus Hill location he'd turn over in twenty minutes if they had any complaints.

"Think of it as an adventure," Julie says, and encourages him to come back with lots of tales of Laundromat people.

He loads the car and drives over to Grand Avenue, but the machines there are full, and so are the ones on Dale. That's about it for the high rent district. He heads out to the Midway.

Someone has propped open the door, but still the heavy scented air assaults the lungs. He has washed at the Midway Coin Op before, and if he can't get any closer to home, prefers it to the ones down on West Seventh Street which are sometimes full of runaway teenagers and street people.

There are only two customers today: two women. Bobby loads his duffels and basket into three washers and sits back to read a biography of Frederick Douglas.

"I know one thing: Black men sure are dogs," one of the women says. The other woman grunts her assent. Though he can't imagine she means him, she says it loud enough for him to hear. He sees her out the corner of his eyes, doesn't want to give her the satisfaction of looking directly at her. It is the heavy set white girl. She swooshes a pale-colored sheet from the drier which Bobby thinks may have once been white, but is now gray and threadbare, and covered with stains shaped like mushroom clouds and giant amoebas. The black woman picks up a sock that dropped from the bundle and lays it in her basket.

"Lying dogs, everyone of them," she says, in Bobby's direction. He ignores them and goes back to his book.

When it is Bobby's month to wash, it is Julie's month to iron. He helps her fold and stack things in the basket to put away in the bedroom later. The Cosby show plays in the background, but they are not watching. They have seen this episode before.

"So tell me: who was in the laundry today?" Julie asks. "Did you see Flo?" Flo is a bag lady who collects postcards. Julie claims that Flo used to be married to a world famous jazz musician—who she refuses to name—but that he dumped her for an equally famous actress—also nameless—and that now she is forced to live in the third drier from the end in the Midway Coin Op.

"What I saw was better than that old hag," Bobby replies.

"Was it that one Hmong girl—the one who has twenty-six kids?"

"It was Tammi and Tina," Bobby says.

"*Oh*, Tammi and Tina," Julie repeats, intrigued.

Bobby grabs a shirt to hang and adopts his best story telling voice. He says, "I go in, minding my own business, and this Tammi starts right in on me. She says to me 'Them Maytags down on the end work best, hun.'"

Bobby gives Tammi a country accent. He can tell Julie likes all the details he is adding today.

"This gal's waddling all around the place like she owns it. She goes over to her friend whose sitting there, reading 'The Weekly World News.' They huddle together and make some sort of snickering noise about me. They sounded like pigs."

"Oh, so these wenches were flirting with you. Well I just may have to go over there and cut me some Tammi and Tina."

"Tammi, she's this big white gal. She looks like she could take you easy. She's the kind that looks like all she eats is pork rinds and potato chips. You know: the kind my mother calls horsy."

Julie says she knows, and then says, "Let me guess: she was wearing a halter with all this blubber sticking out and so you could see her stretch marks. And shorts and thongs."

"You *have* seen this girl," Bobby says, though he remembers what she was really wearing was a frilly pink blouse with long sleeves, even though it was summer and almost 90 degrees.

"Let's see what else: I bet she had this real long stringy blond hair. . . . No! It was all wound up in those nasty sponge rollers."

"Listen to this," Bobby says. "She actually starts pulling those nasty curlers out of her hair right there on the table where people were sorting their clothes."

Julie makes gagging noises and says, "Tammi. And I bet she signs her name and puts a little heart right over the **I**."

He nods and says, "Now, Tina, she was a black woman. Tall and thin."

Like you, he was going to say, and that she looked a little like Julie, too. But he didn't have time to tell her that, because they were meeting Mike and Deanna for a late dinner down at Fourpaugh's and they were running way behind schedule.

Julie's favorite story Bobby made up was at her office Christmas banquet where they had the misfortune of being seated at the same table with Naomi Shumacher, one of the company's executive secretaries. Everyone feared Naomi—including Julie—and she wore her tightness and authority as if it were a suit of armor. When she excused herself to go to the bathroom, Bobby told Julie that Naomi was really Mistress Helga, a well-known Lake Minnetonka dominatrix, who ran an all night pleasure dungeon in the basement of her townhouse. For the rest of the evening Julie had been unable to look anywhere in the direction of Naomi, and whenever the woman spoke, Julie feigned a coughing fit to cover up her laughter.

She often requested updates from Bobby, and he provided them, picking out Mistress Helga's clients in the most unlikely figures: local politicians, newscasters, even the principal of the school he taught at. Bobby agrees this is his best story—it has all the right elements: pretentious characters, unlikely situations, and even a kinky side—the part of her that thinks it a sin to mock—that stories such as this one appealed strongly to her sense of justice, this notion they both had that there were an awful lot of people out there who probably needed to be taken down a notch or two.

Tina has a little boy. Or the girl he calls Tina has a little boy with her when he next goes to do the wash. Skjoreski hasn't fixed the washer and won't, not at least until after the beginning of the next month, after all the rent checks have cleared the bank. The little boy is about four-years-old and has tiny tortoise shell glasses which make him look precocious and old for his age. Tammi also has a baby with her—a deep cream-colored baby with a head full of woolly sandy hair that indicates to Bobby that this is probably a mixed-race baby. Tammi has on sunglasses, too, and when she takes them off, Bobby sees she has an eye that is black and swollen shut.

"Are you sure it was a black eye?" Julie asks. "You know that type wears a lot of dark mascara and eye liner."

"It was a black eye, all right. Looked pretty new, too."

Julie shudders. "Willie must have hit her," she sighs.

"Who's Willie?" Bobby asks.

"Troy's father, of course," she says, exasperated. "Dude with the Cadillac."

"Oh, *that* Willie. Nigger comes struttin in there today, red silk shirt on, black tuxedo pants, some Stacy Adams. Thinks he's something. He asks her for a twenty so he can get some gas. You should see all the dents on that car. Looks like it was rolled off a mountain."

Julie clicks her tongue. "Lazy bastard. Never had a job in his life. Lives off that poor girl's AFDC."

"What was the other little boy's name?" Bobby asks.

"Troy," Julie answers, and they both laugh. This is funny because they know that women like those name their boys Todd or Troy.

"Too bad about that girl's eye," Julie adds.

Bobby tells Julie that Tina told Tammi that she had better take care of herself. "You know what she said?" he asks her. "She said that if a nigger ever hit her, she'd kill him."

"Good for her, and you know: I'd do the same thing myself." Julie says this and gives Bobby a look that tells him she means it.

Getting ready for bed that night, Julie brushes her hair back over the top of her head, away from the nape of her neck, the hair which is softer there and not as knotted.

"Did that girl have any bruises?" she asks.

"What girl?"

"The one today. In the laundry."

"Oh, her," and he thinks, and remembers and says, "A couple, I guess."

"What did they look like?"

He shrugs. "Like bruises."

"Well, you saw them. I mean, were they purple? Or what?"

Yes, he'd seen them, today, and the other day as well, when they weren't quite hidden by the long sleeve blouse. She was shameless about them, wore them almost as if they were medals. He bet she wore tank tops some days, and things that barely covered her arms and her breasts. And, just then he isn't sure whether he and Julie are still playing the game, but he says:

"They're gross. They're like crushed plums on vanilla pudding. That give you an idea?"

Julie turns away from him. She turns out the light on her night stand and rolls up in the covers. "That girl is crying out for help," she says.

Saturday they have dinner Uptown in Minneapolis. Out the window are fashion plates and pseudo-punks. A man—or a woman—with a tall purple Mohawk skates by. Rarely do they have this much raw material, but Julie seems disinterested.

Bobby tried once. He said, "That woman there, the old one with the Red Cross shoes: She's Bill Clinton's secret lover. She's been hidden here in Minneapolis by the CIA." Julie laughed, but it was half-hearted, so they gave up and ate their Plaza Burgers.

Next week the girl shows up after Bobby has begun his load. She is overburdened with clothes and the baby, and the black woman helps her to get situated. The girl sits at the next table down, opposite her friend and picks in her teeth with a fingernail covered in chipped pink nail polish. Bobby reads his book while the machines rumble and clank. In the cyclical silence he hears things such as, "says he don't want no nigger babies in his house," and "ain't got hardly enough to wash these damn dirty clothes." Bobby looks up at the girl and she catches his eyes with a look as hard as iron, and as cold and strong, too tough for tears.

"How do people get themselves into these things?" Julie asks at home that night. They are balling up socks, quietly in front of "Seinfeld." The game has shifted, and Bobby feels himself on unsteady ground. He wants to make Julie smile, to make things light again, but he doesn't know *what* Julie wants, whether he can, or if this is even a game any more, for that matter.

"Who knows?" is his only answer. All he knows is that the city is full of girls like Tammi—tough little white girls, acting black, a baby or two and no place to call their own. He saw them all the time at school and he'd never given them much thought.

"Hey, maybe she likes it," he ventures.

"Don't ever say that," Julie says. She snatches up all the clothes to be put away. "And don't tell me anything else about this. Ever. You hear?" She stalks away to the bedroom with the laundry basket.

"Why?" he asks, coming up behind her.

She tosses the basket on the bed. "Cause it makes me hate men, that's why."

He hands her some underwear that have fallen from the bed. "I'm a man," he says. And she doesn't say anything at all.

And that was almost the last time they spoke of those women. Skjoreski bought a new machine just when it was Julie's turn to wash, and then it was Bobby's again, and life went on with its usual routines. Yet, he was curious about those women and he knew Julie was too, in the same way they were curious about former child stars and retired politicians. You wanted to know about them, though it wasn't worth investing too much of your time to find out.

They were at "Cafe Latte" having cheesecake and cappuccino. It was about six months later, and Julie brought it up in a way he felt was probably a lot less casual than she intended.

"What do you imagine ever happened to that girl over at the laundry?" she asked.

Bobby knew immediately who she meant, and seized the opportunity. He told her he was glad she'd asked, because it seemed the story had a happy ending after all. He told her how the last time he had washed there, Tammi had appeared, and even though she was still bruised, she acted stronger and more in control. She had brought the baby, and had unloaded from a taxi what were probably all her worldly goods—two cardboard suitcases and three garbage bags, if Julie could imagine. He told her that Tina got on the pay phone with her and called around to some women's shelters until they found her a place, and he bragged that he had even chipped in some change for the phone calls without being asked to.

He painted a picture of Tammi as Scarlett O'Hara, bravely swearing off Willie, black men, and all men for that matter. He raised a bread stick over his head to better help her get the picture. Tammi, with baby Troy, rode off into the setting sun, west to Minneapolis, and Julie could see this, too, he knew, because he could feel her relief, feel the barrier which had stood between them, crumbling, dissolving into the textured tile of the restaurant.

And *he* was relieved too. Because, at last, the waters were still. It had been months since he had invented this story—months since they'd enjoyed any other stories either—and he was happy to at last have the chance to tell it, and be done with the whole episode forever.

The truth: the last time he went to the laundry the black woman came in alone. They nodded at each other, and she put her wash in the Maytags. The little boy was with her, and she read to him from an abandoned "People" magazine.

He had helped her fold a sheet and he had asked her where her friend was. She'd looked at him like she didn't understand.

"Girl that's always here with you," he said. "Big white girl."

The woman just shook her head and shrugged in a way that told him she not only didn't know, she didn't much care.

They finished their laundry and left.

And sitting there, eating his caramel cashew cheesecake, he does not feel the least bit guilty—feels satisfied, in fact, as if the story had had an ending just like the one he told Julie. Who knows what becomes of women like those in places like that? He only knows that he and Julie see all kinds of people all the time, and he knows that a lot of those people are looking right back at them and making up stories just like theirs, or worse. He knows it doesn't matter: the plot of those stories. He and Julie know who they are, separately and together.

They don't talk about those sorts of women, or others like them. They don't have opportunity to run into them much, and they have, anyway, learned their lesson. They save their eyes and their stories for the silly, the absurd, for the fun: the man with celery in his briefcase, the nun with a masculine face, carrying her kitten. Most of the time it is as if the washer had never been broken at all.

Sometimes, though, Bobby sees someone who is too hard to look at. Someone broken by life, ragged or crippled, and he can feel Tammi and Tina's presence, just as if they were ghosts of his own long-dead relatives. And he knows, when he sees such people, that Julie sees them too, and that she remembers Tammi and tries to get them—and her—out of her head. He always hopes that she is able to do just that, and if she is not, he hopes that when remembering Tammi, she isn't thinking of him at all.

OPTIONS FOR DIALOGUE

- Please discuss the following questions in your small groups: was Bobby's account about Tammi's life believable? Why or why not? Why did Julie get mad? Why did Bobby give the story about Tammi the ending he did? What was Julie's reaction to his story? To the ending? Why? Why did they never talk about Tammi again? Do you see any parallels between Bobby's and Julie's reactions and general society's reaction to this situation? What other questions do you and other group members have?

SUGGESTIONS FOR ACTION

- Investigate a center for transitional housing/domestic abuse prevention programs. Report findings to your class.
- Poet laureate Rita Dove said in an interview with Bill Moyers (1995): "Memory is untruthful and inaccurate. The memories that inform and haunt us are actually probably very skewed—they aren't exactly what happened so much as how we felt about what happened. So our sense of ourselves is often rooted in how we felt in certain situations, but that's only a kind of truth" (pp. 123–124). Develop some interview questions and interview a close friend about that quotation. Relate your conversation to the story. Report to your class.

    Moyers, B. (1995). *The language of life: A festival of poets.* New York: Doubleday.

- Rita Dove said in answer to Moyers's question "how do you get into their world and into their emotions?" that "their experiences had to be imagined at some level, and my imagining began with an actual occurrence described in 'The Event.' My grandmother had told me about my grandfather's coming North as part of a song-and-dance team working on a paddleboat, and about his best friend drowning in the Mississippi because an island sank. The question for me was, 'How did this man, who must have been racked with guilt over the death of his friend, come to terms with his guilt?' So as I was writing these poems I was working toward this sweet, wonderful, quiet man that I knew as my grandfather" (Moyers, 1995, p. 124). Relate this imagining and art of poetry to the story. Plan a way to disseminate your learnings to others in your community.

THE PEACE TERRORIST

OPTIONS FOR LISTENING

- Think about recent or past events related to war or the absence of peace in the United States or another country. What do you know or remember about the event? What media images relating to it remain in your memory? What did you read about the issue or hear others say about it? What is a critical question that you had or still have about some aspect of the events or responses of the media and individuals to them?
- In your journal create a word web, a piece of writing or a drawing centered on the word *peace*. What does peace mean to you? Write about a person you know for whom peace has a similar meaning. Write about a person you know who has a very different idea about peace.
- Read the selection, write down any questions that arise, and note any personal connections you think of.

The Peace Terrorist

by Carol Masters

(from *The Peace Terrorist*)

"Nobody loves you when you're eleven years old." Jacob's grandma said it often, but first she would squeeze his shoulder to say she didn't mean it. He was still eleven but now she had a variation. Nobody loves you but Jesus when you're eleven. And she didn't touch him so much; she said hugging him was like snuggling up to a rock. He was Rock Warsziniak, the bruiser, the star linebacker for the Chicago Bears.

Last summer when Jacob and his mom and his brother Jesse moved in with Grandma and Grandpa, Grandpa had welcomed him, pinching his arm: "Brown as a tree branch, not one ounce of fat!" he said.

"Yeah," Jacob's dad said, "Twig is more like it. He's going to be skinny like me." His dad was smiling but his eyes were angry. Nobody was happy packing up and moving Jacob's mom and Jesse and Jacob over to Grandma's for the separation. But Jacob's dad Jim acted like it was an insult he should have to help them move, when it wasn't his idea. Jacob's mom said the only reason he was helping was to make sure they didn't rip him off.

Grandma also used to say things would be better soon. They weren't. The latest blamefest was the peace sign Jacob had shaved into the long crew cuts Uncle Johnny gave them for Christmas. Jacob was going to make something like a Nazi-punk sign but a peace sign was more fashionable at his school. He was going to design it only for himself but Jesse had whined and pleaded until Jacob did one for his six-year-old brother, too. Jesse's was neater and rounder, since Jacob had practiced on himself. But no one liked it.

Grandma believed in peace, she said, but she thought the signs were disrespectful to Uncle Johnny who had to go to Saudi. Johnny didn't give a blip; he just said let's hope I'm home before they grow out. Grandma cried and so did his mother but they couldn't deny there was more room in the apartment when Johnny left. Now there would be even more, because Jacob was leaving.

"A change of scene," Grandma told him. "It'll be good for you." She meant good for everybody else. "It's not like you won't be back—unless you don't want to." His mom told him something different, that she and Jesse might go to live with Aunt Seal in Minneapolis too, if he liked it after a while, or maybe they would find an apartment there if his mom could transfer her Field's job to Dayton's. This way Seal could practice with a family first. Him. It was nice of Aunt Seal to offer, everyone said. They meant she was the only one in the family who got along with Jacob, probably because she wasn't around much.

She'd always been Seal, his Aunt Cecilia, with her slick black hair and her pretty dark eyes like a seal's. She had all the Italian, Grandma said, except for Jacob. Jacob inherited the dark eyes and inquisitive nose, but unlike his aunt's disappearing chin, Jacob's Polish chin stuck out into the world.

Jacob didn't mind being with Seal, except that he worried about being on the losing side. He knew his aunt was sometimes on the wrong end of things, with her letters to the editor and her barking arguments with the family. At Christmas dinner, she went on and on about peace, or she shut up and gloomed into the plates, shaking her head from side to side like a seal. Grandpa said she was always for the underdog and Seal said another war would make everybody underdogs. Grandma said somebody has to be responsible and Seal said believe me I know, with her laugh-bark, so they kind of agreed at Christmas. Grandpa told Grandma, when he didn't think Jacob could hear, that at least Seal was god-fearing and would take Jacob to Lutheran church, big whoop.

No one listened when Jacob said he'd rather stay in Chicago. He even tried to say it to the judge, only she was a lady judge and they called her a referee like on football. "Hush a minute, Jacob," his mother said. "Let her read the letters." He guessed the referee agreed with his mom because his dad never bothered to show up at the hearings. Holding them by the edge as if they'd make her fingers dirty, the judge examined the letters. His dad wrote them, to his mom and her boss at Field's and their minister at church. Jacob had seen only part of the one where Jacob drew a picture of Miss Piggy. His dad wrote his mom's name on it for a joke and wrote some other words that his mom and the judge wouldn't let Jacob see.

Maybe he could have stayed in Chicago, but just after Christmas, a week after Seal went back to Minneapolis, things fell apart. Grandpa said the bathroom night was the last straw; Jacob's dad was using Jacob to mess up the family. Everything was generally Jacob's fault. When they whispered in the kitchen, Grandma and his mom, about Grandpa's silent heart attack, they said it was stress. They meant stress from Jacob.

But it was Jesse who locked himself in the bathroom, not him. After school, they had nothing to do until their dad picked them up for supper. Jacob's mom was working extra hours because his dad wasn't paying support, but inventory after Christmas made lots of hours, so it was okay. She'd be home around midnight. The boys hung around in the apartment, not wanting to play outside in the icy courtyard, and they weren't supposed to go farther than the corner without someone bigger. Grandma said Jesse was too little to go to the playground and Jacob shouldn't go alone. Jesse was six for Christ's sake and big for his age. He'd catch up to Jacob they said if he kept going the way he was. Except he acted like a baby most of the time. Jacob could just pretend to pinch him and he'd squeal.

Their dad didn't come and didn't come and his grandma was tired of Jesse's squealing so she separated them, parking Jesse in Grandpa's chair by the television and leaving Jacob in Grandma and Grandpa's room with just a radio. Grandma told him to take a nap but he noticed his shoes made marks on the bedspread, so he decided to make a strategic circle of the room, bouncing his superball. He was supposed to bomb the targets on the opposite wall, planting one foot only on whatever furniture was in the way. It required agility, precision, and intelligence in picking his targets. He'd scored 29 in only two circles on the room, although he gave himself a 5 for hitting his mom and dad's picture between their heads, and a 10 for missing Jesus' face, catching just the left edge of his long curls. He was careful, aiming only at pictures without glass; and nothing fell. But his grandma slammed into the room, wanting to know what on earth, and confiscated his ball.

Nothing else happened except dinner which Grandma cooked because his dad didn't come but they had stupid stew with cabbage and he didn't feel like eating anyway. Jesse locked himself in the bathroom as soon as their dad rang the buzzer downstairs. Jesse said he had a stomachache. It was almost eleven and his grandma was asleep but Jacob wasn't. He ran to press the buzzer, as Jesse stumbled off the couch into the bathroom. Jacob was all for leaving him there to stew in his own juice. Jacob pictured Jesse stewing, sailing boats of cabbage leaves and paying no attention to Grandpa or anybody else telling him he was in hot water, while the greasy broth mounted to his ankles.

Grandpa tried to talk Jesse out of the bathroom, and Jacob went to wait on the landing with his dad. His dad started asking questions like if Jesse really had a stomachache and was his grandpa mean to him this week and why wouldn't Jesse come out? Patiently answering no, no, and I don't know, Jacob considered his father. Jim's thin light face looked scraped but still unshaven, his beak nose red with the sun from the loading dock, though his mother said it was drinking. He'd rather be with his father when he was quiet, just smoking and not asking questions, and when his dad's girl-friend wasn't around at his dad's place. But that was hardly ever anymore. She had to sleep with his dad and Jesse got the only couch. Jacob didn't care about that, though. He'd rather sleep on the floor anyway, the couch smelled of Jesse's pee.

He decided to go inside and say good-bye to Jesse. He leaned on the door, putting his mouth to the crack, "So long, Jesse, we're leaving now! Dad's waiting for me in the car, so good-bye!"

Naturally Jesse started yelling, but he unlocked the door, as Jacob knew he would. Jacob was going to lean against the door just until he heard the click and then jerk it open when the knob started turning, so Jesse would come out fast like a Jesse-in-the-box. He wasn't going to hurt Jesse. But Grandpa misinterpreted; he yelled, "Jacob get away from that door!" and grabbed Jacob's arm hard, as though Grandpa wasn't the one who wanted Jesse out of the bathroom in the first place.

That was when his dad went completely crackers, hollering "What's he doing to you, Jacob!" and though he stormed in and could see nobody was doing anything to anybody, he went marching up and down the hall waving his cigarette with the ashes snowing and talking to the walls calling God to be his witness. Jacob guessed he wanted the neighbors to be witness, because Mrs. Zitkowski downstairs started knocking her broom handle on the ceiling underneath their apartment, dah dah de dah dah! Jacob grabbed the Comet can from the tub and answered her on the floor tiles, dah dah! Only a little Comet spilled out and a small green cloud went up to Jacob's nose, making him sneeze once, but it was enough to make Jesse laugh, so his stomach must have got better. His dad never saw it, just kept yelling at Grandpa. Grandpa was pissed enough to tell him to shut up, Grandma was sleeping, which was a lie because they could hear her opening and closing windows, a weird action in the middle of January even to air out the place. Jacob assumed she wasn't coming out.

Grandpa gave his dad's shoulder a small shove, or maybe Grandpa grabbed it to wag it in a friendly way.

"Back off, Jimmy, can't you? The kids. . . ."

But his dad slapped Grandpa's hand down and pushed on his chest and looked like he'd do more. Jacob himself was flaking out by this time; he grabbed Jesse's hand to pull him back in the bathroom until his father left. Unfortunately someone grabbed at the knob just as Jacob was closing the door and Jacob's finger was the one that got jammed. He couldn't help shrieking.

His dad said it was Grandpa's fault, and Grandpa didn't know. Grandpa stopped looking angry and looked old. He asked Jacob to move the finger, which was red as hell, so he didn't want to. His dad said the finger was probably broken. It wasn't though. His dad said it was too late to go out now, and he had to leave, he wasn't feeling well.

Grandpa said, "Go on, you already started making a night of it, to judge by your breath; go on home!"

Jacob's dad stood there with his fists clenched as though he'd like to start up the fight again, but he finally turned and went out. As soon as the apartment door banged, like magic Grandma appeared with ice cubes wrapped in a towel and told Jacob to hold it. He didn't want to, but he had to admit the cold helped a little. Jesse just kept sucking his own thumb as though he was the one who got hurt.

That was the way Jacob's life went that winter, picked up one place and put down in another, like mail. He had to go to Aunt Seal's. That was the way it was, he had no say in the matter.

Aunt Seal met him at the airport the day after the real war started, the day after we bombed Baghdad. It was a strange feeling, being in the air and thinking of bombs. The night the bombs dropped, Mrs. Zitkowski even came to their door during supper. It was the first time he's seen her in person and she didn't look like a shriveled prune, the way he'd pictured her. She was fat, or anyway coming out of her clothes in places where a serious-looking baby on her hip pulled at them. "Turn on your television!" she said, "It started." He didn't know she had a baby either, and maybe it was Mr. Z who pounded on the ceiling all the time. Only the mailbox just said Mrs. Zitkowski. Grandma didn't let the boys stay up to watch the bombs, she said Jacob had a long trip tomorrow. Jacob was thinking maybe his flight would be canceled, but Grandma said she hardly thought so, the war was a long way away.

It was Thursday night, January seventeen, and Jacob was flying, aimed at Minneapolis. He watched the lights sliding below, on and on, bright stones spaced evenly on a dark table. Most were pale yellow, a few sulfurous orange. Baghdad must have looked like that from the air, except maybe they had blackouts. He wondered. They didn't know when it was going to be, but our president warned them. He told them it was going to happen. Jacob couldn't see any tall buildings; it must be neighborhoods below.

"Hey, you want to trade seats, or what?" the man next to him groused. To see, Jacob had to lean over the lap of a large man who had hogged the window. It was a dumb question, Jacob thought, because the seatbelt sign was on. But the man took charge; he unsnapped the belts, lifted the hinged arm between them, hitched himself up and let Jacob scoot under his legs to the window seat. The stewardess never saw them.

Jacob was most interested in the blue moving necklaces, especially a long curving one whose jewels winked on and off, automobile lights under spiky shadows of trees. The long necklace was the road next to the dark Minnesota River, or maybe it was the Mississippi there. Near the airport, the Minnesota joined the Mississippi in a Y whose right arm climbed into St. Paul, before the Mississippi swooped down to meet the St. Croix from the north and made the border of Minnesota and Wisconsin and Iowa and even Illinois and way down to New Orleans. He looked at the map last night when Grandma didn't let him watch the war. He could be a pilot, he had a great sense of direction: Jacob Warsziniak, decorated bomber pilot of World War III. He narrowed his eyes at the necklace below and aimed carefully.

Then the necklace of cars rushed toward him, the noise accelerating until his ears could hardly stand it. For a brief moment he imagined the metal roof of a car and heads oblivious to the missile racing down to meet them, the parents in the front, arguing about where to go, a couple of kids in the back seat. There was a muffled shriek as the plane's engines reversed, then a calm drift past the focused lights of the runway. They made it, they were down.

Jacob hadn't had time to imagine an enemy. At first, it seemed like there were no people, only lights—nobody cooking late dinners or going to the movies or Burger King or to meet someone. Of course he knew they were real people under the plane, under the winking lights, under the roofs of cars. Maybe one of the blue jewels had been Aunt Seal. A little dizzy from concentrating so hard, he stood shakily on the seat to pull down his backpack from the overhead compartment. His seatmate had stood up before the plane stopped rolling, and was gone; everyone was in a hurry tonight. The stewardess at the door gave him a bright good-bye, staring at some point over his eyes. He looked behind himself but the plane was empty.

Grandma told him Aunt Seal couldn't come to the concourse because of security. The airlines were afraid of terrorists. That was wise, he thought, he could be a spy from Chicago bringing in stuff, some message from headquarters.

Aunt Seal would wait at the baggage claim on the bottom floor, and the crinkle of the claim check in his shirt pocket reassured him. Still, he wished, as his feet felt the wobble and creak of the metal of the accordion gangway, for a glimpse of her head craning over a crowd looking for him. The concourse was nearly deserted, and of the people bored or busy walking past him, none suspected his name, Warsziniak the Spy. They wouldn't even look at him, unless he shouted hi! to startle them. He didn't.

He forgot to ask directions to the baggage claim, absorbed in counting the number of bars on this concourse. Every other waiting area seemed to be next to a bar or snack shop. Of course he'd been in bars with his father, but not such fancy ones, with blonde counters and red leather high seats with backs. His father's bars were noisier, too. Here, the television wasn't showing any sports, just news. The people stood around staring, with drinks in their hands or forgotten on the bar, at the screen, and listened like they were in church. No one spoke.

Outside one lounge, Jacob watched as the television image shifted from a serious announcer in a suit to a monster, some kind of humanoid or droid with a huge insect head with goggle eyes and a snout. It was obviously a mask, but somehow he knew he shouldn't laugh. Then the monster lifted his head off and he was a regular reporter talking about nerve gas. The reporter was actually in a bomb shelter. The shelter was really an ordinary room; the camera panned to tape on the window and door. Two kids played on the floor in a corner. Then one of the kids looked up at the camera and his mouth drooped and he looked kind of like Jesse; the other kid was even smaller.

"Jacob!" Aunt Seal was trying to pick him up and squeeze and yell at him all at once. With her was a man in an airport police uniform, so Jacob didn't know if they were under arrest, or what.

They didn't let him watch any more television, but he didn't mind—his eyes were scratchy and watery from watching too much. It turned out that a steward was supposed to hand Jacob over to his aunt like he was a package, but someone had got the wrong flight number and he'd escaped. Then they both had to go with the policeman through a metal scanner. The man mumbled into a little radio, but then he let them go to the baggage claim by themselves. "Don't get lost any more, sonny, hear?" he said. As if Jacob really was lost, instead of ignored in an airport screwup, he was going to say, but Seal kept squeezing his hand.

Jacob's red suitcase rode lonely around the carousel inside a fence, waiting for him. No one even checked his pass when he went through the barred turnstile. "Some security," he grumbled, "I could have *anything* in here." Aunt Seal ruffled his hair, but he noticed she looked around quickly.

By the time they pulled up in Aunt Seal's driveway, it was near midnight. He was supposed to be registered the next day, Seal said, so she scooted him into his room next to the kitchen, with the covers turned back on one twin bed. Jesse could have the other one when he came. Great, he thought, just get my own room and look forward to having Jesse in it. But the picture of the taped room in his mind faded a little, and he drank some milk with Seal.

He liked the way the snow lit up his bedroom, after Seal clicked off the kitchen light. Seal's house was small, one story with three tiny bedrooms, just enough. His window faced a back yard, with a spruce tree that was gathering white by the minute, from fat flakes that glittered like sidewalk mica when they landed. The snow didn't do that in Chicago. Or maybe it did on late cold nights without wind or so much pollution. He'd have to check sometime. If they lived here they'd probably visit Grandma and Grandpa pretty often. That would be okay. When the flakes filled up Seal's footprints by the bird feeder, then he'd get in bed. But it took too long; his eyes were scratchy again.

No wonder he was crabby the next morning. Even though it was Friday and the semester had just begun, you think they'd let him sleep in for one day? No, he had to be wrapped up and shipped off to school so he wouldn't miss any of the stupid lessons. He had to go through his stuff and pick out the least dorky sweatshirt and then change because Seal said it was hot in the classrooms and he should layer, wear a thin one underneath. After school, she said, he could shop for some nonholey socks and boots.

It was too much. He threw himself face down on his bed; no way. No way was he going to drag along behind Aunt Seal in some stupid suburb mall, full of yuppie banners and crude boxes of ferns and fertilizer, which was shit anyway, wasn't it? He worked himself up to tell her so, but when he looked up she wasn't there and he smelled the hot sharp smell of pancakes.

Seal must have ripped off a funhouse mirror for the bathroom; the nerd looking back at him looked swollen as an apple under his skin. He looked like he was about to whine or say something snotty to someone who'd want to at least hit him like his dad or even once or twice lately his mother. He could make her cry just like his dad did by the things he said. He had a way with words lately.

Maybe Seal would too if he was snotty enough. Probably she'd just send him back, like a package. "I'm a goddamn package!" he yelled at the mirror, astounded at the red-apple ferocity of his face.

"What?" Seal was at the door, and their eyes met in the mirror. He looked away, then back, horrified as Seal pushed her nose flat with two thumbs and with her little fingers pulled her eyes into slits and stuck out her tongue. "Hey Jake, can you do that?" He couldn't help giggling even if she did think he was some kind of baby, needing to be entertained for Christ's sake.

Breakfast wasn't bad though the cakes were a little black around the edges, from the fooling around in the mirror. But then Seal informed him that she expected him to do the sock shopping. It wasn't far, she said, just three blocks down, and not a mall, it was a funky seconds store. She said she hated shopping, every time she passed a mirror she wanted to do this—she pushed her nose in—and he couldn't help laughing until his stomach hurt. And then she gave him a pair of sunglasses to be incognito if he wanted. He'd cruise with the glasses and if a saleslady pestered him he'd say not just yet, ma'am. Should he say ma'am? Not just yet, thanks, that was better.

But at school the teacher asked him to take off the glasses while she introduced him so everybody could see his eyes.

"They're pink," he cracked, "I'm an albino!" and there were a few laughs. The black kid Phil at the next desk got more laughs when he said, "Yeah, so am I."

Phil and another black kid and Jacob were the only three who had relatives in Desert Shield. Everybody in the class was supposed to write to somebody in Desert Shield. Only now it was Desert Storm, Ms. Ward the teacher told them; Jacob thought the name was stupid because it probably meant a sandstorm, and how could you bomb in sandstorms? On the television before the bombs fell, the land looked like snow, like a white empty beach at night. Anyway the bombs were probably like lightning and there was no lightning in desert storms. Or was there? He'd have to write and ask Uncle Johnny.

Except that he gave the job of writing to Uncle Johnny to the girl Abby. He hadn't meant to say anything about Johnny; it was the teacher's fault. This teacher was a jerk sometimes, as most of his teachers had been. She made such a big deal that Abby would have to write to a senator, because Abby's mother had called the school and said she was a social worker and she was worried that her daughter and other young children were writing and forming relationships with soldiers. So Abby was the only one who had to write to a senator, while the rest of the class got to write to soldiers.

So Jacob announced that Abby could have his Uncle Johnny; maybe her mother wouldn't mind her writing if it wasn't to a stranger, and Jacob would write to the senator. Jacob had a couple of things to say to a senator, anyway. Abby had red-brown hair and looked mad all the time she was in the classroom.

"Don't you want to write to your uncle, Jacob?" He told Ms. Ward he'd written already, which was half a lie but he'd been thinking about what he'd write him on the plane.

"Abby. Would you and Jacob work on a joint letter to the senator." She didn't make it a question. "And you could think, too, about what you might write to Jacob's uncle." Abby didn't look at her, but she muttered something out the window.

"Abby, we speak out in this classroom." Ms. Ward's voice had prickles in it that made Jacob want to grit his teeth. Abby said, fairly loud for a girl, "I said my mother said they could die. The people we're writing to could die."

"They're not the only ones," Jacob said, but not very loud, because Ms. Ward just went on talking to Abby. He stuck his hand in the air, waiting for the teacher to stop talking.

"We know your mother has strong beliefs about peace and that's important to all of us, even though we may not agree with them, isn't it class? And we protect those freedoms, don't we? Yes, Jacob?"

"Bombs kill kids, too," he informed her. He meant in Iraq and maybe Israel, where the taped-up room on television was, but a nerdy girl in front of him waved her hand in his face and said, "Teacher, are we going to die?"

Ms. Ward spent the rest of the time until recess explaining with maps how far away Iraq was, and that the bombs couldn't reach Minneapolis, for Christ's sake. Jacob was paired up with Abby for most of the day, which he really didn't mind because she fit his mood. She was mad at everyone especially her mother and Ms. Ward. If her mother or Ms. Ward said the P word once more to her she'd spit in class.

"What P word, piss?" It was all he could think of but he couldn't imagine Ms. Ward saying it. He and Abby were standing in a snow fort on the playground that they'd fixed up with new snow from last night. The temperature had risen so that by mid-morning the snow was decent for packing. Abby told him they weren't supposed to throw snowballs during school, but sometimes people did. He scooped and packed some spears, just in case. Abby's cheeks were so red they looked chapped, but she really looked better when she laughed.

"Nooo. It just *sounds* like a bad word. PEACE!" she shrieked. A bunch of kids waiting in line to go inside looked over at them. A big kid, an eighth grader, yelled back, "Okay, okay, we surrender!" Then the kids walked inside holding their hands in the air, making fun of them.

But Abby thought it was cool. "We're peace terrorists!" And she wouldn't go inside until they had stomped out a peace sign in the snow under their room's windows. They kept up the peace theme all day. At lunch, Jacob ordered peace soup when he saw the putrid pale green mush that was the choice du jour, though he hated peas. The cafeteria lady glanced at him suspiciously; "It's broccoli," she told him. He took it anyway. Abby selected the vegetarian plate, mounding mashed potatoes and vegetables to form another peace sign. They shared the food; Jacob was hungry.

In the afternoon they had to write to the senator. They wrote, "We are two eleven-year-olds from Chicago and Minneapolis who don't want the war to continue. Too many people on all sides will be killed." Jacob wanted to put in, "Bombs kill kids, too," but Ms. Ward was monitoring them and she didn't think the tone was respectful. She gave them a B for the letter, though. All in all, it wasn't a bad day.

Sunday was the best, though, even if he and Seal had to go to church. On Saturday Jacob said he'd rather not, if Aunt Seal didn't mind. He admitted Grandma wanted him to go and pray to Jesus, but if Grandma thought you could pray anywhere, what was the point? It wasn't for kids anyway. He hadn't thought Seal would pressure him, but she did. She said he might not understand now, but later he could take comfort from church. She said *she* took comfort, especially when the world didn't make sense. He said he would be more comfortable staying home and he didn't mind.

But she informed him that he was going to stay home for a little while today, because she was going to visit some friends of hers in jail who were in because of peace demonstrations.

"I'd rather go with you today," Jacob pleaded, "couldn't I go there instead of to church?"

Absolutely not, she told him, kids weren't allowed unless they had a parent inside, and then only special hours once a week. He couldn't even wait in the car for Christ's sake, even if he hid under a blanket so the guard at the gate didn't see him.

"Would they let me in if you were in jail? And how come you're not, didn't you demonstrate?"

Seal didn't know about the first question. Then she told him: "I've already been in jail, Jacob. Right after the sit-in, after Christmas, I pleaded guilty because I knew you were coming and I couldn't risk more time. See, you get more time if you go through a trial and say what you did was right. I wanted to get the sentence out of the way."

He didn't understand. She didn't tell Grandma or anyone. Seal didn't even send him a postcard from jail. Then she said it was no goddamn adventure, she even used the swear word. They didn't have a good relationship on Saturday morning for goddamn sure.

Saturday night was a little better. In the afternoon while Seal was gone, he stomped out stuff, m-f war, damn Saddam and other words on the sidewalk in front of the house, then shoveled, dribbling the massacred hate words onto the snow banks along with the dog pee. He was going to finish it off with a peace sign on the lawn, but the snow looked swept clean, not even a wind ripple, so he decided to leave it.

Seal told him he'd done a great job—even the driveway! Which she hadn't asked him to do. He shrugged, admitting he had pretty good arms. They were aching, though; he wasn't used to it. After dinner, he let her beat him once at Chinese checkers, and she told him a few things about jail without his asking. She said almost everyone in there was young and skinny but her. He asked about the food; she said it was all right if you liked white bread and potatoes, which of course he did. So he wondered what the bad part was for her.

"Not having any choices, I guess. No, the worst part was being with women with less choice about what they do."

"Kids don't have any choice," he told her. Her dark eyes were bright for a second, and she looked away.

"They do, Jacob. They still do—only it's hard to see what the choices are, sometimes."

"Not important ones," he mumbled, looking down at his new socks, which were an interesting shade of green the saleslady tried to talk him out of. He could tell Seal liked them because she asked to borrow his sunglasses to look at them. But he knew she was humoring him, and he knew kids didn't have any say about what mattered, like whether a bomb was going to be sent at them. You just had to be on the right side.

By Sunday morning, he was resigned to spending a boring hour. Seal promised that after church he could vegetate and watch the Super Bowl, though what, she said, a nice peace terrorist like him could enjoy about a bunch of cauliflower heads making themselves into chopped liver she'd never understand. Actually, he never did watch the game. He couldn't wait to tell Jesse what happened.

Ten minutes into the service, the pastor said, "I ask all the children and anyone who's a child at heart to gather around." Since Seal had told Jacob what to expect, he wasn't too surprised that a few kids and no adults ambled up the nave and sat down around the skirted minister. Jacob wasn't thrilled about it, but Seal said the pastor sometimes gave the kids little presents, like chewing gum or a Bible card. He wondered if there was a choice, but from the looks of Pastor Nusswandt, he doubted it.

Pastor Nusswandt was large, blond, and kind of young for a minister. Jacob thought he wouldn't want him falling on him, as the pastor leaned forward from the altar step to pin each kid in the circle with his pale blue eyes, scowling as he did.

"Do any of you think Jesus was a wimp? You've seen the pictures, haven't you—the long hair, the gentle expression?"

Jacob didn't particularly think long hair was wimpy, but he didn't feel like bringing that up at the moment. In fact, nobody admitted they thought the Jesus pictures looked wimpy. Only about five kids had come up and most of them were small.

The pastor leaned back, satisfied. He talked about driving bad men out of the temple with a whip and how in His day that took anger and courage, too. Then he was talking about Saddam, and Jesus giving his life and our soldiers risking their lives and the minutes stretched on. Jacob arranged his brain to be back in the airplane, thinking about Johnny. It was a half hour before they landed, and the evening came quickly. Night deepened over farms and highways as he watched. Clouds slid under the plane and hid the land, clouds turning blue and deeper blue, like lumpy snow, then like blue-tinged hills to shelter the soldiers, then nothing, black, nothing but his own scared face reflected in the window.

The pastor told them to stand up for Jesus, and released them. By this time, bulletins crackled, and the congregation was generally coughing and moving its feet. Back in their pew, Aunt Seal's face was white, and her hands clenched the seat like it was about to take off.

Fortunately, no adult sermon was scheduled, only a hymn sing. Pastor Nusswandt suggested—his nod to the organist made it not a suggestion—that they begin with "Onward Christian Soldiers." Seal groaned, but she opened her hymnal. She whispered, "Remember, it's *spiritual* foes!" Jacob knew the song. It was about taking action, and Jesus leading with banners and all that.

But the pastor stopped them after the first verse and made them sing it again. He said he knew it wasn't their tradition to be rousers with hymns but they shouldn't sit on their dignity now, they should remember the boys—and girls—over there and "Get into it, people. Show them how, children!" He started with a low and off key "FORward into ba-attle," marching his feet up and down and staring straight at Jacob, who swallowed something between singing and a throat lump that tasted terrible. He understood then that Aunt Seal was wrong: they weren't singing about spiritual foes at all. Pastor Nusswandt's congregation sang against a real enemy with human faces.

Bombs kill kids too, didn't they know? He thought about the kid in the taped-up room, a kid like Jesse and Abby and even himself, waiting for something to fall. Jacob knew beyond any teaching that he didn't want to sing that song.

He decided what to do; it was his choice. Clicking loud on the linoleum floor, Jacob tramped down the nave and up the side aisle, swinging his arms, goose-stepping enthusiastically past the pastor, who stared and dropped a couple of notes. Still marching, but faster, Jacob paraded back to his aunt. There he marched in place, holding out his hand as if to share the peace but looking desperately at the back door. As he knew she would, Aunt Seal grasped his hand and walked with him out of the church. The last notes they heard, "the cross of Jee-sus," stretched thin and reedy behind them, as one by one the voices dropped away.

OPTIONS FOR DIALOGUE

- What images of peace and war on both a national and personal level are interwoven in this story? Compare these images to the personal images you explored in the "listening" section.
- Compare your images for peace with those of others in your group. Please discuss the origins of your images for peace. What images were established in childhood? How did this happen?
- How does the title "The Peace Terrorist" relate to Jacob and the world in which he lives?
- What does this story show about the creation of other people as enemies? What role does the media play in this process? How do you see this happening today?
- What other diversity issues that you have explored throughout this book also enter into this story in more subtle ways?
- What other questions do you have about any aspect of the story?

SUGGESTIONS FOR ACTION

- This story brings into focus the issues involved in the responses of young children to violence. Some have tried to control children's experiences through censorship of books or media. How do you feel about censorship? Who should decide what children should read, view, or hear? Should art be censored? What should be censored? Take an anonymous class poll in response to the previous or related questions; then analyze the results. What does this mean?
- Interview some parents. Find out what families do to instill values in children. What about outside influences? If you don't censor, what do you do? How does this occur in other societies?
- Investigate what child psychologists and others who have studied this issue have to say about the effects of violence in the media or literature on children.
- Conduct a research study on the topic of censorship in the schools. What materials have been censored? Why? What groups promote censorship? What guidelines have the state in which you live or professional organizations such as the National Council of Teachers of English set up to help teachers, librarians, and school administrators make curriculum choices and respond to would-be censors? What is the difference between censorship and selection of materials?
- Talk with a member of the American Civil Liberties Union about school censorship cases in which he or she has been involved in your state.
- Read the chapters in part 1 and part 3 of *Battling Dragons: Issues and Controversies in Children's Literature* edited by Susan Lehr (1995) (Portsmouth, NH: Heinemann). What is your response to the issue of book censorship after reading these chapters?

- Read Edward Said's "Declaring War on Islam" (1996) in *The Progressive, 60*(5), pp. 30–33, or other writings by Said. Compare his analysis of anti-Islamic propaganda with Jacob's experiences in "The Peace Terrorist."
- Interview a group of children about images of peace and war in their own lives and families. Help them explore ways to become peacemakers in their own contexts. What questions do you have about this activity?
- Write a personal story about a time when you solved a serious conflict with another person in a nonviolent way. What did you learn from this experience?
- Watch the video "Spirit and Nature" (from Video Finders, [800] 343-4727) and create your own response. How does this video relate to ideas in "The Peace Terrorist" and other works you have read in this chapter?
- Read one or more works of fiction for children, young people, or adults. Note particularly the ways in which human beings are framed as enemies during times of conflict and the effects of violence on families. Explore the following books or one of your own choosing:

Books for Adults

Alvarez, J. (1994). *In the time of the butterflies.* New York: Algonquin.
  The book explores issues of family, culture, and politics as Alvarez explores historical events in the Dominican Republic during troubled times under dictator Trujillo.

Guterson, D. (1994). *Snow falling on cedars.* New York: Harcourt Brace Jovanovich.
  Japanese American Kabuo Miyomoto is arrested in 1954 for the murder of a fellow fisherman, Carl Heine. Miyomoto's trial stirs memories of the grief, loss, and prejudice triggered by World War II.

Picture Books

Baillie, A. (1992). *Adrift.* New York: Viking.
  This exciting survival adventure is set in Australia.

Baillie, A. (1994). *Little brother.* New York: Puffin.
  This is a children's story about Vithy's journey to a refugee camp in Thailand.

Books for Older Children and Young Adults

Ho, M. (1991). *The clay marble.* New York: Farrar, Straus, & Giroux.
  In the late 1970s 12-year-old Dara joins a refugee camp in wartorn Cambodia and becomes separated from her family.

Lowry, L. (1993). *Number the stars.* New York: Harper & Row.
  Anne Marie, a Danish child, helps a Jewish family escape from Nazi soldiers.

Myers, W. D. (1988). *Scorpions.* New York: HarperKeypoint.
  Jamal Hicks is a seventh grader who becomes the new leader of a gang called the Scorpions. One of the gang members gives Jamal a gun. He knows it is a bad idea, but he is looking for a way out of all his home and school problems.

Uchido, Y. (1985). *Journey to Topaz.* New York: Bantam.
  A Japanese-American family is forced to go to an internment camp.

AND SAY GOOD-BYE TO YOURSELF

OPTIONS FOR LISTENING

- Think back to an important historical event (either tragic or joyous) and describe in your journal where you were when you became aware of the event. Describe other aspects of the context such as the emotional dynamics of the setting, who was with you, and how those people were moved by the news. What is a critical question you had or still have about some aspect of the event?
- Describe in your journal any novels, short stories, nonfiction magazine articles, or professional reports you have read regarding an incident of sexual abuse within a family setting. What is a critical question you had or still have about some aspect of the story?
- Listen to a media-produced report about sexual abuse either on a documentary or a news program. What information was included? What was omitted? What would you like to ask the producers of the report?
- Read the selection, write down any questions you think of as you read, and note any personal connections.

And Say Good-Bye to Yourself
by Susan Williams

Most people my age remember where they were when Kennedy was shot. I remember where I was when I found out about Judith Campbell Exner. It was in a bait shop outside White Bear Lake. A Saturday. I was coming from my friend Mary Kaye's place on the lake, trying to get back on the freeway, and there was the *St. Paul Pioneer Press* on a crate of tackle with the headline and her picture—Liz Taylor as Vegas showgirl.

How Sinatra or Peter Lawford or someone had introduced them. How she'd phoned him hundreds of times in the Oval office and met him at the Carlyle Hotel in New York. How they'd made love, she said, in every major bedroom in the White House—in spite of Jack's bad back—when Jackie was out of town, or in town. How she was Sam Giancana's girlfriend at the same time (and maybe Sinatra's) and how that somehow implicated the Mafia in the assassination. Or meant the President was being blackmailed by the Mob. Or by J. Edgar Hoover, who had bugs in every second bedroom in Washington. Or Jack was leaking Justice Department secrets in the sack. Or she was spilling Giancana's nasty business. Or the President tried to use the Mafia to get Castro but they finally got him instead because Bobby was closing in on them. Or something. And the other girlfriends. Students and starlets and heiresses and hairdressers. Out of the woodwork. More than he'd have had time for if he'd been a stockbroker or mountain climber. Or a movie star.

I don't remember driving home. I found my way without directions. Some things you know are true because of how much you don't want them to be true, so I made up arguments against it and argued with people about it. It wasn't true, or it didn't matter. But I knew it was, and it did.

The thing that really bothered me about the story was Jack telling a friend—I don't remember who—how beautiful she was and how she could have sold it but here she was giving it away. Okay, so he was no romantic. A little fucked up about women. That old he-goat of a father of his—it was him. Bringing women to the house. Hitting on his sons' dates. ("Try me when you get tired of him. I'm twice the man he is.") Gloria Swanson showing up on family vacations. All that screwing around under Rose's holy Roman nose. But I didn't know about all that when I heard about Judith Campbell Exner.

I was on a bus to New York when I heard about Marilyn—August 5, 1962. On my way to take a ship to Rotterdam to be an American Field Service exchange student to Belgium. Sixteen. Thirty-six seemed almost old enough to die.

My Belgian family lived in a pretty river village in the French-speaking south between Liège and Namur and we didn't like each other very much. The father was a dentist with bad breath and his wife rarely spoke to me. The children were shy and so was I. And homesick. When the mother got sick they used it as an excuse to pack me off to Brussels to another family, which was okay with me except I was in love with a boy in the town who looked just like James Dean—Etienne. But that's another story.

But before I could go to my new family in Brussels (they were on vacation somewhere) I had an interim family. A rich family. Aristocrats with a country estate about half the size of Belgium near a town named after their family, with stables and tennis courts and peach orchards and a wine cellar and private art gallery and a mile-wide library.

The first morning, after a four- or five-course second breakfast, I went for a walk with Ione, the oldest daughter. She had been an exchange student in New Jersey the year before and lived with a CBS cameraman and his family and fallen in love with a boy who looked like Marlon Brando in *The Wild One*. She had three albums of snapshots of him and said she was going back to America to marry him but I knew she wouldn't because his father was a longshoreman and Cordonnets were stone snobs.

Ione's father, Jean, was in Brussels but from his picture he looked a lot like her mother, Jeanne: tall, thin, chilly people with chiseled nose and lobeless ears and pointy little teeth and tan, leathery skin and clothes in rich fabrics and subtle colors that all matched and matched their hair and skin and upholstery. And generations of money behind them. There was no one like them in Blooming Prairie. Or Hollywood.

I loved the country house. I felt like Jane Eyre turned loose in Mr. Rochester's library. Acres of Morocco-bound classics in dark oak bookcases with sliding glass doors and a ladder that ran around the room to a deep cream windowseat that turned gold in the sun. I wanted to stay in that room forever.

But we left for Brussels the next day. Saturday. To join Monsieur. The women went to mass first and I stayed home—they were careful about not inflicting their religion on me—and read *Portrait of a Lady*. After mass we arranged ourselves in the long tan Mercedes that matched their matching luggage and Madame's cashmere sweater and swirly skirt and ran so quiet it made you want to whisper and drove through the matching woods to Brussels to the Avenue des Americains, where they owned the most of a handsome old red brick building.

Inside everything matched, all white this time and cream and peach and shell pink and pale yellow and colors I didn't even know the names of. My hair, which everyone had always said was beautiful, was about seven shades too red for this setting.

It was Saturday but everybody had appointments anyway—Madame to have her legs waxed, Ione for a haircut, and Vincienne, the younger daughter, who I loved for her knotty knees and elbows, to be fitted for a first communion dress. Monsieur would be home for dinner, for which we would, of course, dress. I scrunched up in the softest chair I could find, overlooking the Avenue, with a copy of *Catcher in the Rye*. The maid brought me cream soda. I felt like I was in a movie. If only, somehow, they would each meet with a separate, painless (I didn't hate them), but fatal accident and I could stay here alone forever. Or the women would die and Monsieur would come home and fall in love with me and marry me and come home once a month or so to bring money to keep all this going and leave me to read and look out on the Avenue forever. And then after awhile he'd die (painlessly), leaving me plenty of money and I'd send for Etienne, whom I truly love.

But he came home before I'd even finished my cream soda. He looked like his pictures. He was in a snit about something. He asked where Martine, the maid, was. He didn't appear to be in love with me. The women talked to me in English for practice but he steamed away in French without moving his lips or giving me time to translate, much less answer. He was so taut and tan, his skin stretched so close across his cheekbones, his nose so impossibly thin (how did he breathe?), ankles so slender under his skinny socks, he made me feel thick and pasty and mid-western. He got bored with my stumbling French in about a minute and went to find a drink.

Next time I saw him, after Madame and the daughters had come home, he was, as my father would say, "three sheets to the wind." He seemed to be in better humor at least, teasing Ione about her gamin haircut, making her pirouette so he could see it from all sides, teasing me about drinking milk instead of wine. "And I suppose you eat corn in Minnesota also," he said in precise English. "In this country we save that stuff for the pigs."

We sat down to dinner. Cold clear soup and a fragile fruit salad and three colors of rice and bite-size potatoes and thin strips of carrots and another vegetable I didn't recognize and little twists of tan bread and trout with heads on. I wasn't used to eating so much at a sitting (how did they stay so thin?). Or so late. At home we ate supper at six, not dinner at eight. Vincienne's chatter danced too fast for me to follow. I was nodding off into my fish when Monsieur Cordonnet's voice jerked me awake. "Et Kennedy? Your President Kennedy? This species of rich boy you have chosen? What about *him?*"

What *about* him? I loved Kennedy more than I loved Montgomery Clift! Monsieur was slashing away in French again, stabbing the air with his fork, his face suddenly red and clenched. Had I fallen asleep and missed something? His eyes shot around the table, daring anyone to speak, then locked on me. "Cet mauvais espèce de. . . ." I couldn't follow. Vincienne was quiet, twisting her napkin in her lap. Madame was trying to swallow her lips.

"*Qu'est-ce que vous dites?*" I squeaked, finding my French and nearly spilling out of my chair at the same moment.

"This rich kid doesn't know how to be President!" he snapped, slapping the table. The trout jumped off his plate. "He will run us all into disaster—he and his companions."

"You object to his money?" My voice startled me. His eyes tightened on me. My stomach bunched up.

"And you? What do you know? An infant from a baby country. What does your father do in that country?"

I looked around. Madame's mouth was twitching. Martine appeared and hustled Vincienne out of the room. Ione studied her trout. Mine was rising up in my throat. Cold came off Monsieur Cordonnet's face at me. He was three chairs away but I could feel it. I wondered about the etiquette for throwing up.

"*Mon père est un* . . . salesman," I choked. "He sells water softeners. He voted for Kennedy." He hadn't. "I rang doorbells for him." I didn't. "Everybody works for their man in America. Everybody votes." I was panting. I'd told my first family, when they asked how fast Americans drove and seemed disappointed when I said seventy miles an hour, that this was the *slowest* speed the law allowed. Monsieur was playing with his knife. The weather had changed around his mouth. Was he smiling? Martine had slipped back and was refilling his wine glass. Without looking at her he closed his hand around her wrist. "What do you think?" he said to the far end of the table. "Do you think our young lady from America is ready for a drop of Beaujolais now?" No one answered. His fingers ticked on the table. "Ione will pour," he said. "Come, Ione."

"It's really time Ione turned in also," her mother said with a little twisty smile. "She must study tomorrow for her mathematics exam."

"Ione will pour," her father said. "Come, my dear." Ione had been piling up the fingers on her left hand—1-2-3-4-3-2-1. She looked at her mother with no expression, then at her father, then slowly backed her chair away from the table, still looking at him, and walked around the table. He handed the bottle to her, neck first. His other hand spidered over the small of her back. She didn't move until he took his hand away, then she walked to the end of the table with an empty face but with her long vanilla throat thrown back and poured me a glass of wine.

At first I couldn't sleep that night and when I did I dreamt about his voice. Talking to Ione. Just loud enough so I could hear. Telling her not to cry. One of them was crying.

She looked fine at breakfast—beautiful in a lemon dress with yellow lace braided into the pockets and her new short haircut. She looked like Audrey Hepburn in *Green Mansions*. Audrey with breasts. The two of us ate breakfast alone. After breakfast she asked if I would take a walk with her. She had to borrow a book from a friend who lived beyond the park. As we walked, she talked about Jimmy, her American boyfriend. She showed me the last letter she got from him, half English and half high school French. She wanted to be a writer and live in New Jersey with Jimmy. I told her about Etienne, embroidering a little. She thought I should run away with him. She was sure my second family would be even worse than the first, who never even *tutoied* me in seven weeks. We didn't talk about the night before or her father except when we stopped to watch a man throwing a stick for his dog. She said her father was a champion dog trainer. She liked to watch him put his prize collie through her paces—heel, three steps, turn, sit, wait. One day he made the dog wait, frozen in her show pose, eyes on him, for twenty minutes. "And I watched," she whispered. "I couldn't move. It was like a dream." The pulse jerked in her neck.

I didn't see her father that day and the next day he left for Zurich on business and I never saw him again. The next month, when the Cuban missile crisis happened, I wanted to phone him and ask him what he thought of Kennedy now but I didn't.

By then I was living with the Joufflus at 22 Rue Van Campenhout. They were comfortable as overstuffed chairs. They braided my hair and counted my freckles and giggled at my French and took me to tons of American movies. They *tutoied* me immediately. They thought I was skinny and tried to fatten me up with peanut butter and banana sandwiches which their daughter, an AFS student in Seattle, had written them about. They would have got me bushels of corn on the cob if I'd asked for it. We partied for three days around my birthday in November and three weeks later, when I had to go home, we all cried and hung on each other and we wrote once a week for about a year and then sent Christmas cards.

Last month, just before Christmas, I went to a hypnotist to try to get over the married man I thought I was in love with. He had me hypnotized, I guess, finishing sentences to reveal my "psychic history," and the last sentence was "I'll never get over _____" and I said, "Kennedy's murder." I wonder.

We lived all over south Minneapolis, my son and I, and one time we lived next door to this black guy who was a decent guy—he took Josh fishing—and a good neighbor except he drank too much and carried a gun. One Saturday night he got thrown in jail in Eden Valley for carrying a gun and being drunk and black in the suburbs. He phoned me the next morning and I went out and bailed him out and on the way home he told me about this white guy he ran into in the drunk tank who was bragging about screwing his baby daughter—four years old. Said there was nothing like it except he couldn't do it too often because it took about two weeks for her to heal every time. Fred, my friend, said this with a straight face but I figured he was making it up—he was always coming up with stories about kinky honkies who did things black folks would never even think of—or the white guy had lied to him.

I dreamt about it a few nights and then a few months later we moved away and I forgot it. A few years later they started arresting people in Eden Valley for having sex with their kids. Unemployed pump jockeys who lived in trailer parks first and then shoe clerks and shopkeepers and schoolteachers and cops and doctors. Even grandparents with their grandchildren. It made the CBS evening news about a week in a row. A whole freaking sex ring. I'd never heard of such a thing. Then I remembered Fred.

They say Marilyn was molested as a little girl, for years, by half a dozen foster brothers and fathers. Now they're saying she was in love with the Kennedys—Jack first and then Bobby. Somebody puts out another book about it every other month or so. Somebody wrote that she called Peter Lawford after she took those pills that August afternoon and told him to say good-bye to Jack. "And say good-bye to yourself," she said, "because you're a good guy too."

When somebody told me, in front of the freshwater fish tank on the fourth floor of the old zoology building after psych. 101 that Friday afternoon that the President was shot, I knew he was dead, no matter what they said. Some things you know are true.

OPTIONS FOR DIALOGUE
- What did you learn about the main character in the story?
- Describe to your partner what you found out about Ione's family? What details in the story confirm your opinions?

- What did you learn about the Joufflus?
- Do you and your partner agree on your opinions about the two families? What details support each of your opinions?
- Who was Judith Campbell Exner?
- The author said, "Some things you know are true." Do you and your group members believe that she was referring to the news about Kennedy only or to other issues in the story? Why?
- What other questions do you have about any aspect of the story or any issues raised by it?

SUGGESTIONS FOR ACTION

- Investigate some of the known facts regarding sexual abuse of children in family situations. Explore some of the following sources or others of your choosing to obtain information:

  Armstrong, L. (1983). *The home front: Notes from the family war zone.* New York: McGraw-Hill.

  Armstrong, L. (1987). *Kiss Daddy goodnight: Ten years later.* New York: Simon & Schuster.

  Bass, E., & Davis, L. (1988). *The courage to heal: A guide for women survivors of sexual abuse.* New York: Harper & Row.

  Blume, E. S. (1991). *Secret survivors: Uncovering incest and its aftereffects in women.* New York: Ballantine.

  Davis, L. (1991). *Allies in healing: When the person you love was sexually abused as a child.* New York: HarperCollins.

  DeSalvo, L. (1989). *Virginia Woolf: The impact of child sexual abuse on her life and work.* New York: Ballantine.

  Miller, A. (1990). *Banished knowledge: Facing childhood injuries.* New York: Doubleday.

  Wisechild, L. M. (Ed.). (1991). *She who was lost is remembered: Healing from incest through creativity.* Seattle: Seal.

- Interview an elementary teacher about the frequency or infrequency of information provided by support staff regarding abuse. Ask about information the teacher has accumulated over her or his years of teaching about observable effects of abuse on a child's life.
- View one or more of the following audiovisual materials and choose a means of reporting your learnings to your class:

  Breaking Silence, (1985), a film on incest and the sexual abuse of children. 58 minutes, 16-mm film/video. Available from New Day Films, 121 West 27th Street, Suite 902, New York, NY 10001, (212) 645-8210.

  Still Killing Us Softly, (1987), a film about images of women in advertising; explores violence and stereotyping. 30 minutes. Available from Cambridge Documentary Films, P.O. Box 385, Cambridge, MA 02139.

- Contact organizations in your region that advocate for victims of abuse and request information. Choose a method of reporting to your class.

THE WORLD OF CHILI PEATOAD

OPTIONS FOR LISTENING

- What is the history of naming in your family? Where do the names come from? Are names in your family connected to ancestors? What is the history of your name? In your journal trace the history of your name.
- What is the history of a tradition or a celebration in your family? Where did it originate? In your journal write or draw a past/present "snapshot" of a tradition in your family. What questions do you have about your family?
- Write about a story that has been retold in your family or in a group of your friends. How has this story changed during its retelling. What are the underlying meanings or truth in this story? What have your family members or friends learned from it over the years?
- Who are the storytellers in your family or group of friends? How did they get this role? Describe them in your journal.
- Read the selection, write down any questions you have, and note personal connections.

The World Of Chili Peatoad
by Tom Peacock

Northern Lights

I. To many Ojibwe people the northern lights are said to be the souls of the old people who lived long ago as well as those who have recently completed the circle of their time on this earth.

A particular time many years ago my family attended a fall ceremonial in Sawyer. We brought my mother with us and I remember she had said that was the only time she had gone to a ceremonial because she had been brought up Catholic and had always been told the ceremonies were pagan. We had a wonderful time because the event was held with great dignity and our own unique brand of Indian humor. During the evening there was a great feast where venison, ducks, and bear were served along with wild rice and fry bread. Later one of the male participants played a trickster, dressing like an old woman and entering the dance area trying to get the old men to dance with her. There she (he) danced in all her glory, in a long dress, the heavy nylons and laced black boots of old Ojibwe women, a wig and shawl. Many wondered about this old Indian woman. "Who is that old woman over there," they would say.

Returning home late that night the northern lights danced and it seemed they were more brilliant than I can ever remember them because they covered the entire sky.

II. Sometimes we spend our entire lives waiting for a miracle to confirm our faith and in doing so we completely ignore the everyday miracles that occur around us— the rising and setting sun, the smell of sweetgrass, seasons, the northern lights. I am reminded of a story I read some years ago about a great Micmac chief, Ulgimoo:

Because he had once before known death . . .
now he knew that joy
came from the earth, from
slow moving shadows and the
sweet scent of grass. He marvelled
that he had lived one hundred and three
years and had not known these things
were sweet and good in themselves

III. She had come again to dance
in the shadow of the tree
away from the weight of books
and mindless teachers, stones
she danced
whirling, spinning
laughing within herself
the many stones

She had come again to dance
in the shadow of the tree
away from the children with pencil teeth
and taunts that brought tears to her eyes

She was the stonecatcher
a child of feathers and timeless chants
she danced
whirling, spinning
laughing within herself
the many stones

Faster she danced
whirling, spinning
rising above the earth
laughing tears on the pale children below

She is a star
she is the northern lights
at night she dances

Owls in Early Winter

On several early winter evenings returning home at that time of near dark there came from the woods behind my house the song of an owl.

"ko-ko-ko-oh! ko-ko-ko-oh!"

I wondered then of its deeper meaning, this bird messenger that visited me only at the cleave of light and darkness.

On a particular evening I returned to the cold quiet, to the accompaniment of snow crunching beneath my feet, and to breath. And this particular evening there sat in the shadow against the deep red and dark northern sky in an old dead elm that had succumbed to some malady—there on top of that tree was the owl.

Ancestral fear and neo-traditional anger welled up in me and I walked to the base of the tree and talked to him for what seemed like the longest time.

"What are you doing here, owl? Why have you come to sit in my tree? Who are you here for, owl? Who are you here for? If you are here to tell me of death I need to tell you I still grieve from past losses. What right have you to be here?"

But mostly our conversation was not of a spoken kind because silence is the deeper language between owls and men, quiet accentuated by cold.

I finally left him to sit in the tree, satisfied he was there only to look for a meal.

I have not seen or heard of him since that time.

> The Chippewa gave much attention to the training of their children. Odinigun said, "In summer the children could play out of doors, but in winter they had to be amused indoors." It was hard to keep the little children quiet in the evenings so they would not disturb the older people. The mother often said, "Keep still or the owl will get you." If they did not keep still she went to the door of the wigwam, held back the blanket, and said, "Come in, owl; come and get these children, who won't keep still." Then the children put their heads under the bedding and were soon asleep. In the daytime they constantly wanted to run outdoors. Some had no moccasins and were barefoot. The only way to keep them in was to frighten them. So the older people made a birch-bark mask of an owl and put it on a stick where the children would see it if they were outdoors.
>
> Densmore, Frances. *Chippewa Customs.* Washington: U.S. Government Printing Office. p. 59. 1929.

Naming

When it was time for my children to receive their Indian names my wife and I asked their uncle, who was from Inger. And we offered him tobacco and asked him if he would give names to them and he said he would.

"I'll come down in a few weeks and we can do it then," he said.

Now in the language of elders a few weeks can mean anywhere from a week to a month, or more, and it is part of our learning these things to know that. Never once have I heard one of the old people say, "I'll be there next Sunday at 2:00 in the afternoon."

We saw him again when he was in town and he said he would be over to see us in a week. My wife prepared a feast of meat, wild rice and fry bread and we got a pouch of tobacco. And he came over that day and gave the children their names. I remember him sitting there in the living room and asking the children to come over to him and he took them separately by both hands and talked to them in Ojibwe and in English. He talked about his dreams and gave them their names. We set out a separate plate of food with some tobacco which later was brought out into the woods.

Later I said of my boy's name, "What does it mean?" and he said, "You are walking in the woods and out of the corner of your eye you see a wolf. And you look over toward where it should be and it is not there."

Good thing that name is in Ojibwe.

A long time ago Anishinabe children were given names by a namesake, or way'ay', because it was believed that if they died without a name they would not be able to make the journey west into the land where our ancestors have gone. Moreover, the Great Spirit (Gitchi Manito) could not answer the prayers of those who didn't have their name because he would not know who was speaking to him.

Usually the person selected as namesake was an old person, and always an old person who had not been ill during his or her life. This was because it was believed the child would then be healthy. Children who were sickly were sometimes given two or more names from different namesakes for this same reason. Namesakes could be either men or women and there did not seem to be a limit on the number of children that they would name; however, the namesake always gave a different name because each name was dreamed.

There was always a feast held when a child was named in which venison and wild rice were prepared by the parents. Guests were often invited to the naming ceremony.

Pantomimes of Frozen Rabbits

In those early days my family would often spend its evenings sitting in the living room of our old house which stood where the Fond du Lac Housing Compound now stands. Because there were so many of us, we often had to bring in chairs from the kitchen so everyone had a place to plop their bodies. The boys would turn the chairs around and sit on them backwards, using the back rests as arm rests, sort of like the way kids nowadays wear baseball caps.

A particular Sunday evening we sat there watching the Ed Sullivan Show and were entertained by a mime. I had never seen a mime before and was both humored and fascinated with his black clothes and derby and pancake white face.

As he moved about in graceful silence, I could only think about how wonderful it would be if he would perform a pantomime of frozen rabbits in various states of run. You see, when we would go out to check our rabbit snares we always encountered frozen rabbits in various states of run. In jump. In trot. In half and full leap. Always frozen in movement like pictures.

And I think maybe someday a shinob will become a mime and my dream will be fully realized. . . .

In the old days the Anishinabe would catch rabbits in snares made of nettle fiber twine. With the coming of the white race nettle twine was replaced with metal wire. In my childhood days we used no. 11 picture wire. You just weren't a traditional rabbit choker unless you snared rabbits with no. 11 picture wire.

Several years ago the science teacher at the Ojibwe school was teaching the kids how to snare rabbits and it seemed that all the rabbits were able to escape the wrath of their snares. And I remember asking about the snares and it seems they were using the wrong kind of wire. They were using muffler wire, the kind we use to hold up our mufflers. "No wonder they aren't choking any rabbits," I laughed, feeling just righteous and traditional.

Any one who knows rabbits knows the heads were eaten with special delight and I remember my grandmother reminding us as we went out the door in the winter to check our rabbit snares, "Save the heads. . . ," she'd say.

I hope their next lesson is to learn to save those heads.

Two Woodland Crows

Once in the fall when it was crisp I went hunting, something I always did alone because it gave me time for solace and reflection. And I remember walking down an old logging trail into a large field. It was dark and so quiet the only sound for miles was the sounds of leaves beneath my feet.

There at the cleave of field and trees I stood and watched first light break across the sky, and darkness became light blue and red. There was no wind. There was only the cold and the sound and sight of my breath.

And when the sun first shone across the plane of the earth there was a mist that rose and hung low across the field.

To the east I heard a sound of wings and as I listened it became louder, this sound of wings. It seemed to go on the longest time. And just over the tree line breaking into the open field were two crows and it was so quiet I could only hear the sound of their wings. They flew the contour of the land to the far edge of the field and the sound faded. Before they entered the woods they half cawed to each other. Not full caws, but more leisurely half caws. Crow slang.

And I imagined that these two woodland crows were saying, "Did you see that guy down there?"

"I sure did."

All that day I could only think of those two crows.

In the days before my grandfather the Anishinabe considered all animals our elder brothers because they were third in the order of creation before humans. Animals lived according to the Great Laws of Nature. All possessed a precognition of events. Each individual creature had a purpose for being. You will notice that crows (Andig) are often in the companion of wolves. One of their tasks is keeping the earth clean. The other is to remind us that life should be honored.

Many generations ago the deer, moose and caribou vanished and it was found that they were willingly being held captive by crows. And a great war was fought between the Anishinabe and the crows in which there was no victor. It seems the animals were content with the crows and angry with the Anishinabe because they felt the Anishinabe had wasted their flesh and desecrated their bones. Only when the Anishinabe promised to honor them in life and in death did the animals willingly return to the land of the crows to remind the Anishinabe that life must be honored, that life for one means death for another and that life must not be taken in anger.

a rendition from Basil Johnson's *Ojibway Heritage*

The B-B Gun and Red Rubber Slingshot War

The only war I am aware of between the Fond du Lac Band of Lake Superior Chippewa and the white settlers occurred in the early 1950's just west of Leach School in the city of Cloquet. What began as a slight disagreement between two rez and town boys quickly escalated into a slight disagreement between several rez boys and an equal number of boys from town.

It was quickly decided that a war would be held to determine which group would reign supreme over the Leach School playground. Dates and times after school were agreed upon and both sides began preparations.

On the day of the great battle the town kids came prepared with B-B guns and an abundance of ammunition they had gotten fresh from the five and dime store. The rez kids showed up with their red rubber slingshots and pockets full of rocks they had picked from the road. Little did the town kids know these slingshots were deadly weapons. Made from the crotches of maple, strips of rubber cut from the inner tubes of tires, and pouches from boot or shoe tongues, they were used by rez kids for hunting purposes. In those days it wasn't unusual to see rez kids in school wearing shoes without tongues. Shoe tongues served several useful purposes.

No one knew who fired the first shot but someone did and it soon became apparent the B-B guns were no match for the red rubber slingshots. It was one of the few wars the Indians ever won. Rumor has it the battle ended when a town kid lost a tooth as a result of a well-aimed rock.

Occasionally we still have B-B gun and red rubber slingshot wars with town kids but nowadays they are held in court rooms, board rooms and legislative hallways.

I wonder what ever happened to that kid who lost his tooth. My guess is he's working at a casino.

> In the time of my great grandfathers the warriors were typically young men of the bear, wolf and lynx dodaim (totem), animals disposed to being fierce. To the young warriors the fights were not done for any economic or political reasons, as is the case in modern warfare. Nor were the fights intended to commit genocide or enslave or take away property or land. Fighting was a way to show and gain courage. That was its only purpose.
>
> Johnston, Basil. *Ojibway Heritage*. Lincoln, Nebraska: University of Nebraska Press, 1990.

Chili Peatoad

In my bib overall, big hook shoes and red rubber slingshot days (when I was a young boy), it was my brothers' and cousins' practice and chosen professions to be golf ball hunters, just like our grandfather. In those days our grandfather made his summer living as a golf ball hunter, scouring the woods and pastures of the nearby all white country club, a private course built on land taken from my grandfather's grandfathers. With the earnings from selling golf balls, our grandfather bought tobacco and rolling paper and wine. Especially wine.

So it was his grandchildren's mission in life to emulate their grandfather and it seemed that as we tried to do just that we could only find a fraction of the golf balls as him and our meager earnings were quickly consumed through the purchase of life's necessities—candy bars, seven-up and barbecue potato chips.

A particular summer came to us young golf ball hunters and season in which we practiced a unique ritual out on the golf course I can only refer to as chili peatoad. No one knows or remembers where the term came from. It is one of life's little mysteries. Chili peatoad had to be proclaimed whenever someone would vent gas from the lower extremity. We call it bugat. Some call it farting. And when some-one would bugat, the fox (the person who bugated) would proclaim to the world, "Chili Peatoad!"

All the young golf ball hunters would rush to touch a piece of wood because the last one to touch wood would be the loser. "You ate it," we would say. So it soon be-came common practice for all of us to carry a piece of wood in our pockets just in case a call would echo through the woods and pastures that overlooks the river that flows through Nagajawamong.

"Chili Peatoad!"

Several years ago at the ground breaking ceremony of Fond du Lac Community College, the reservation's tribal college, I stood there surrounded by formerly young golf ball hunters, who had long since left their chosen professions to become coun-selors, teachers and tribal politicians. And as we thrust our golden spray painted Hard-ware Hank shovels into the earth and proclaimed a new vision and time on the rez, a little boy in me was yearning to proclaim to all the dignitaries, politicians, political has-beens, power junkies and television cameras "Chili Peatoad!"

In the time before my grandfather, children often had little choice in who would be their companions, and more often than not they were members of the extended family consisting of brothers, sisters and cousins. These companions were life-long friends, and no matter what would happen in the circle of their lives they could always count on their companions in times of need. Small groups of young relatives always played together and parents had no need to worry about negative peer pressure. As they would age and en-ter the fall and winter seasons of their lives they would continue to get together for story telling, playing games, gambling and dancing. And at their feet their children, and their grandchildren would play. It was this way for many thousands of years.

OPTIONS FOR DIALOGUE

- Please discuss why the author, Tom Peacock, ends each story segment with a con-nection to the past history of the Anishinabe people? He has said that his stories are about continuity. What does he mean by this? For whom is he writing these stories?
- How many different generations can you find in "The World of Chili Peatoad"?
- Did any of the author's boyhood memories remind you of your childhood experi-ences. Tell your memory to a partner.
- In what ways were your childhood and family experiences like those of the author? In what ways were they different?
- Why is storytelling important to you as someone who will teach or work in hu-man services?

SUGGESTIONS FOR ACTION

- Abenaki storyteller and author, Joseph Bruchac, said in an address at the Interna-tional Reading Association meeting (New Orleans, 1996) that the real truths of Amer-ican Indian traditional stories are in the beliefs that are in the layers of meaning in the stories. The truth is in the lessons in the story, not in the belief that the events happened in a literal fashion. Find one or more collections of stories or poems either written by or gathered by Joseph Bruchac. What are some underlying truths in these stories? Here are some of the more than 40 books written or retold by Bruchac:

Four ancestors: Stories, songs and poems from native North America. (1996). New York: Bridgewater Books/Troll Communications.

The girl who married the moon. (1994). New York: Bridgewater Books.
(with J. London) *Thirteen moons on turtle's back.* (1992). New York: Philomel.

- Explore family stories with a group of students. Ask them what they have learned from those stories.
- Listen to a group of children or adolescents tell stories about their lives. What can you learn from these stories?
- Learn more about storytelling in American Indian tribal cultures. Listen to an elder tell stories. Attend a powwow and listen to the stories.
- Write an essay about your experience in listening to stories.
- Prepare a story to tell and share it with others in the class. This could be a traditional tale or a family story. Tell the story to a group of children. How do they respond?
- Critically analyze programs for young children on TV. What stories are being told in the media? What are some of the meanings or messages being taught by these stories? Write an article for parents to publish in a newsletter.
- Go back to your "snapshot" of a tradition in your family. Trace the history of a tradition in your family. How has it changed over the generations? What have you learned from this tradition in your life? Create a story, audio or videotape, a piece of visual art, or a chart that shows these changes or the importance of the tradition to you.
- Read *Krik? Krak!* (1995) or *Breath, Eyes, Memory* (1993) by Edwidge Danticat (New York: Soho). Compare the storytelling of Haitian mothers and grandmothers to the storytelling in "The World of Chili Peatoad" and the storytelling in books by Joseph Bruchac. What are the connections between these stories and your own life? Document your thoughts in the form of a letter to a family member.

A SELKIE STORY

OPTIONS FOR LISTENING
- In your journal describe a time when you had to leave home in order to do something you wanted to do. What was difficult about this? How did you maintain relationships even though you were gone?
- Remember a time when you had to do something because it was right for you even though others close to you did not want you to do it? Write about this experience.
- Write a short journal entry that describes your family members and their roles and responsibilities. Do you see any patterns of expectations for males in your family? Do you see any patterns of expectations for females? Write any thoughts you have related to the issue of roles within families.

- What are some questions you have about roles and responsibilities within family contexts?
- What are some questions you have about the issue of leaving home?
- Read the selection, write down the questions that come to mind as you read, and note any personal connections.

A Selkie Story

retold by Mary Kay Rummel

Today, my grandmother said, *would make a fine day back in the islands. I have a great desire to go, for it was an airy place.*

"How would we get there?" I asked.

Musha, child, we could row, she said, *toward the west, pull alongside the big island and see between us and Slea Head nothing but light. As soon as I'd pass the Horse's Mouth westward, a cloud would rise from my heart, born as I was in the Inish.*

There on the rocks above the reefs crying and keening are the seals. They're like people, you would think, and you'd be thinking right. Long ago on the south side of the Inish many people were put under magic. My grandfather went hunting seals there, about the month of Samhain it seems, because a young seal was born. He went up after the young seal stick in hand, but the cow-seal lept straight at him with open mouth snarling. He clambered up to a ledge on the side of the cove and when he had reached it the cow-seal spoke to him. "If you are wise," she bellowed, "you will leave this cove now, for you will not easily kill my young daughter." My grandfather was so frightened. "For the sake of the world," he called to his brother, Sean, in the boat, "back in here as quick as you can." And Sean untied the bottle of holy water that they kept in the prow of the boat, as was the custom in those times, and sprinkled it toward the rocks to protect him from the magic, but from that day on my grandfather was a quiet man and quite unlucky.

They are part human all right—not all, just some—and one of them has your name.

"How could one have my name?"

Musha, child, and you will let me tell the story. You think you are named Maura because it is your mother's name and my name and my mother's before me. And you think we are named after the Holy Mother of God, but that is not how it happened. Your name was in the land from the time before Columba and his priests came to the Islands. Your name is a Blasket Island name and one of the seals has it.

"Tell me the story."

A fisherman named Tomas was in his curragh in the deep waters beyond the Inish. He heard from the island a noise which took an echo out of the coves. Gurla-gu-hu-hu-golagon! Gurla-gu-hu-hu-golagon! He looked in and saw up to thirty seals; then in the path of the rising sun he saw a beautiful young woman on the rocks and began to row toward her. The olagon from the seals was so loud anyone would think the living and dead were gathered there. But when he landed and climbed over the rocks, they raised their heads. Then away they slid into the water. Not a spot of the strand but was hidden by the spouts of foam they sent up into the sky. And soon not a seal was to be seen, the sea still again save only the rings they had left in their wake. He looked down through the water and could see the bottom clearly and the seals rushing out below. But he could not leave that place until he saw the girl again, so he hid in the rocks. Och, he had to climb up high, for the strand doesn't wait for milking time.

Tomas knew it was Samhain when the women change form. He knew the girl was a Selkie, a seal maiden, and that this was no place for him to be, but he waited the night. The next morning at sunrise the seals clambered back on the rocks. He watched, and five of them slid out of their skin and lay there. One of them was the most beautiful woman he had seen. Her long hair shimmered like fire around her. It was like yours, child, deep red as the winter sun when it meets the western waters. And her eyes, like yours, brown as the bay in the wake of a storm. The seals made a great moaning and keening, but she was silent. No wonder they sound human, he was thinking, they are human; and slowly he moved quietly toward the woman.

Before the seals saw him he grabbed the arm of the beautiful one, and as the others lept into the water she was held. Such a moaning and keening was never heard in that place as the seals cried for their daughter, but Tomas would not let go. Musha, he said I won't hurt you. I want you to come with me and be my wife, for I love you. Please let me go, she said, for I cannot belong to you or any human. My home is beneath the waves and I belong to the spirit of the sea. But Tomas would not let her go and took her to his home, married her, and called her Maura. She was a quiet one, and her eyes always sought the west, the rocks, and the water. Soon she had children, four sons, and she cared for them well. The fifth year she had a daughter, and Tomas said she too should be named Maura after her beautiful mother. The sons as they grew older fished with their father, and the young Maura helped her mother with the cooking and gardening and weaving of the clothes.

Maura took her daughter to the shore where they gathered red tubes of rubbery bladder verach and dried seaweed the color of blood, and when they were alone in the hut she taught her to weave a tough red-black skin. Together they worked and at night hid the skins beneath a pile of straw.

It was Samhain when the skins were finished and Maura, laughing now, brought her daughter to the rocks at the western edge of the island. "Musha, don't be frightened, daughter. It is time for us to return home." The seals began their moaning when they came, but the girl was not frightened. Quickly the mother slipped the reddish seal skin over her daughter and then put on her own. Then away with them, the two of them, with all of the other seals into the sea spouting foam. It was this way a half-human daughter was born to the seals.

When Tomas and the four boys returned in the evening the hut was empty. There was no meal waiting for them. Without a word he ran to the shore, and there lined up in the waves were the heads of seals, two of them a black red shining, and he knew sorrow in his heart. He looked around him then, as is the habit of a man in a strange land.

That winter Tomas was full of sorrow, but he had always known he could not keep her. He was grateful to her for staying with him and giving him sons. Now the sea was home to the two women he loved, and the sea was his life. When the winter came and the great sea was coming on top of him and the strong force of the wind helping it, he was safe. The sea gave him food and comfort and finally took him to itself.

Maura's great-grandchildren are in the sea and on the land to this day. On the Blasket Island, that lies in the mist looking like a sleeping bishop from the mainland, there

were always mothers and daughters named Maura. And now that the humans had to
leave, only the seals are left; and if you go there in the curragh and listen to them, on quiet
days in the mist, you will hear them call your name, "Maura, Maura, Maura." And you
will see some that are deep red, the color of the verach and blood weed and your own head.
       "Can we go there? I want to hear them."
       Musha, child, I would take you there if I could, but it is a far country from America.
I am old and a spool is no faster turning than my life. Someday you will go there and you
will know the truth of my words more lasting than the wealth of the world.

A Story She Wraps around Herself

The boot marks of the unfortunate
are to be seen on the grey stones
of the beach.

                                                                    —*Peig Sayers*

Here on Clougerhead waves crash
on granite cliffs, steaming shafts
of rock shatter the Atlantic.

Three miles out the deserted green hills
of the Blasket Islands mourn the lost
civilization of the tongue.

I imagine your black skirt
slicing through wind out there
your rosary dangling from your
large red hands.

It was this sea that gave
you stories
for your neighbors
and later for the scholars
who came to hear your words
songs foreign to their ears.

You carried your dead son
from the cliff bottom.
With unshaking hands
you rearranged his skull
for burial. Once—
you allowed yourself to cry
then clapped the end of mourning
and found the words to pray.

And you made the men pray
those who came to listen.

Made them kneel on the cold flagstone.
They had to say the rosary with you,
the angelus, blessings for sick
and non-sick, for sinners and non-sinners
and you kept them at it
as long as you could.

You talked with your hands
as well as your tongue
a clap of the palms for urgency
a flash of thumb over your shoulders
your hand over your mouth
to show a secret.

It's hard to be growing old you said
but I'll be talking after my death.
A woman's tongue is a thing
that doesn't rust.

—*Mary Kay Rummel*

OPTIONS FOR DIALOGUE

- At the end of the story why did the selkie woman decide to return to the sea?
- How do you feel about her decision?
- Fantasy has roots in reality. Is there anything about this fantasy that relates to reality for you? For example, are there events from your own life that connect with the story?
- How does this story relate to themes in any of the other stories or books you have read for this class? How?
- Analyze your individual response or the group's discussion. What differences did you see in individuals' interpretations of the story? How would you explain this?

SUGGESTIONS FOR ACTION

- Conduct a survey of realistic picture books and chapter books for children. What is the role of the mother in these books? In picture books how are mothers of different racial and ethnic groups portrayed in illustrations? In stories of separated families, does the mother leave the children? In how many books? In what ways are the individual needs of mothers considered in these books? Share the results of your survey with others in the class or in an article for a literacy journal or newsletter in your area (such as the newsletter of your local council of the International Reading Association).
- Find versions of the selkie woman story in other cultures. What are the truths carried by these traditional stories? Begin with *The Selkie Girl* (1986) by Susan Cooper (New York: McElderry). Then watch the film *The Secret of Roan Inish*. Compare the story in the film to the selkie stories you have found. Read "The Star Fisher" (1991)

by Lawrence Yep (New York: Morrow). Compare this traditional Chinese story with the selkie tales. Why is the theme of a mother who has to leave to go where she belongs an important theme of many tales across cultures?

- Find versions of the Cinderella story from at least five different cultures. Create a chart comparing and contrasting these stories. What are the underlying teachings about women in these stories? How are these traditional teachings like or different from the teachings in the selkie stories? Compare traditional Cinderella stories with stories in contemporary media such as the films *An Officer and a Gentleman* and *Pretty Woman*. What is the underlying message of Cinderella stories presented to girls in the media? Present your findings to the class or in a written report for the media or a newsletter.

- Write your own version of a folk tale focusing on the roles and messages about women in the tale. Share your tale with the class or with a group of children. How does your audience respond? Document the experience and report to your class.

- What does the folk tale mean to you? Portray your learnings from this project through writing, art, or storytelling in a way that can be shared with others.

- Gloria Steinem has said, "[Marilyn Monroe] was a female impersonator; we are all trained to be female impersonators." What does she mean by this? How does this statement connect with your own life and with the selkie story? What does this mean for a teacher of children or someone who will work with young girls and women?

- Read the children's book *Journey* (1991) by Patricia MacLachlan (New York: Delacorte) or *Walk Two Moons* (1994) by Sharon Creech (New York: HarperCollins). What do these books tell us about the role of women in the family? Respond to the book you chose in some way.

- After doing one or more of these actions, what critical questions do you have about human service work and the perceived or promulgated role of women in our culture? What can you do in your work to break stereotypes created by society?

- Read *In a Different Voice* (1982) by Carol Gilligan (Cambridge: Harvard University Press) or *Sounds from the Heart* (1995) by Maureen Barbieri (Portsmouth, NH: Heinemann). Then visit a school and observe how girls are treated. How many times are they called on? Which jobs are they assigned? How many times does the teacher say, "Boys!?" Actually count the times girls are called on. Compare this to the times boys are called on. Report your results.

- Attend a lecture or seminar. How many times are women in the audience called on? Who are the "experts"? Are they male or female? Report your findings.

- Tales written for children such as Hans Christian Andersen's "The Little Mermaid" were stories of female silence. The little mermaid had her physical ability to speak cut from her mouth. She surrendered her feminine voice in order to have a chance for success in the patriarchal world of air, sun, and legs. Brown and Gilligan's 1992 study addresses the ways in which women's voices have been trivialized and dismissed. They record how girls progressively give up voice in order to be in relationships. Read this book and connect it with your own life.

- Read copies of *New Moon* and other "zines" written by and for preadolescent girls. Compare these to popular magazines designed for the same market. What differences do you see? Write a report about places in which young girls can find voice.

NEW YORK CITY MIRA MIRA BLUES

OPTIONS FOR LISTENING

- Go back to the journal writing about your neighborhood that you have done for other selections in this book. Make a chart describing this neighborhood in the past and future as well as the present. Place your neighborhood in a historical context. Who lived there in the past? How has it changed? Who will live there in the future? Imagine a return visit to this neighborhood after a time away. What social, political, and cultural forces have influenced the history of your neighborhood, the families there, and your personal history within it? Share these reflections with a partner.
- Listen to a representative from a local or regional media organization describe the effect of homelessness on families in the region that he or she has learned about.
- Listen to an invited representative from a county social service agency discuss some of the causes of homelessness in all their complexities in the region.
- Reflect and write in your journal about any personal responses to the previous information. Do the information, the people, or the societal ramifications relate to you in any way?
- How have you been enriched by immigration?
- Read the selection, write down any questions that you think of as you read, and note any personal connections.

Glossary

mira   look; also used as an exclamation to call attention, like "hey!"

jíbaro   hillbilly, peasant; now a national symbol

Isla Bonita   pretty island; refers to Puerto Rico

El Fanquito   San Juan squatters' slums

todo el mundo   everybody

mancha de platano   stain from viscous secretions of the plaintain; refers to a native Puerto Rican

abuelita   little grandmother

coquí   tree frog indigenous only to Puerto Rico; it cannot survive elsewhere

music   beginning of the popular song "Puerto Rico"

New York City Mira Mira Blues
by Gloria Vando

From the freeway you can almost
hear them screaming in their
red brick coops
    HELP ME, HELP ME
through glass grids silhouetted
like chicken wire against the
skyscrapers of Madison, Fifth,
Park, and lately Third Avenue,
where the old el used to shield
the homeless, now homes the shielded.
O Marcantonio! What did you do
to this city in your urgent need
to sprinkle liberalism like holy
water on the heads of the oppressors?
You should have played fair, hombre:
you should have left the jíbaros
in the mountains of their Isla Bonita
perched like birds of paradise
on Cerro Maravillas observing
the rise and fall of the earth's curve
as it slumbers beneath the sea;
left them in El Fanguito, squatting
on squatters squatting on the land
that once was theirs; left them
in Borinquen, where there was no cool
assessment of who owned what,
no color line splitting families
in two or three, where everyone,
todo el mundo, was tainted
with la mancha de plátano—but no,
you needed votes. Sure votes.
Had to buy them, fly them in by
planeloads, skies darkening thickly
with visions of barrios to come.
Since it was so easy getting in, you'd
think it would be easy getting out, but
where to go, and who'll take you in?
Take you in, yes; but give you shelter?

The Triborough Bridge, 50 years old
in gold cloth 50 feet high spanning
its towers, waves greetings to us as
we cross the East River, where I swam
as a child, running home as fast as
I could to stash my sopping clothes
in the hamper before Abuelita found
out and exiled me to my island bed.
Now dressed in punk colors, FDR Drive
shouts SAVE EARTH: GIVE A SHIT and
raises a SHAKER-KLASS-AMERICA fist
to the inmates on Welfare Island
whose view of the newyorkcityskyline
is optimum, while the rich on Sutton
Place and York only get to see slums.
Welfare Island whose one aesthetic
function is to spew enough smoke and
soot into the air to obscure Queens
and itself, if the wind is right,
in a merciful eclipse. Welfare Island,
where poet Julia de Burgos was confined,
forgotten, all her protest silenced
with yet another 2 c.c.s of thorazine.
On 110th Street, my concrete manger
overlooking Central Park, only Spanish
signs remain to remind us of the second-
to-the-last immigration wave: Cubanos
seeking refuge when corruption takes
a backseat to red slogans, red tape.
The Bay of Pigs non-invasion spurs
them on to invade us, Miami first, then
slowly up the coast like a spreading
thrombosis that ruptures in Nueva York,
where all Hispanics blend into one
faceless thug, one nameless spic.

The cab cuts like a switchblade
across the park; I try to hear Ives'
marching bands meeting in noisy combat
on Sheeps Meadow, but later sounds
intrude, reintroduce themselves
like forgotten kin—midnight, a baby
carriage, my mother crossing the park
from her sitter's on the Eastside

to her husband's on the West. And she,
loving the leaves' black dance against
the night, recalls her mother's warning
that she not try to blot out the sky
with one hand, but oh! there beneath
the trees, the immensity of space is
palpable—she feels safe. And lacing
the earth, a fragrance she cannot discern
causes her to yearn for home. She hums

half expecting the *coquis* to sing along.
It is that time of night when muggers
are out—even then before the word
was out—blending into shadows, bushes,
trees, like preview footage of Vietnam,
waiting to assault whatever moves,
whatever breathes. She breathes hard
but moves so fast they cannot keep up.
Westside Story before they learned
that death set to music could make
a killing at the boxoffice. With one
Robbins-like leap up a steep incline,
we escape; I sleep through it. Now
I'm wide awake watching every leaf quake
in the wind as her young limbs in flight
must have then, fifty years ago
on that moonless night in Central Park
where fifty years before that
sheep grazed and innocence prevailed.
We exist on 86th Street, head down
Central Park West, past the Dakota
to our safe harbor in the heart
of Culture and Good Manners with
Lincoln Center only steps away.
Next door a flop house. Old people
with swollen legs sunning themselves
on folding chairs, used shopping
bags with someone's trash,
their treasure, at their feet.
The buzzards of the human race

cleaning up other people's droppings.
We walk around them, as though
proximity could contaminate. Nearby
those less prosperous prop themselves
up against their own destruction.

I see my children stepping carefully
between them, handing out coins
like Henry Ford. I see them losing
faith, losing hope, losing ground.
But I am home, I tell myself.
Home from the what and the corn
of Middle America, where whole-
someness grows so tall you cannot
see the poverty around you, grows
so dense the hunger cannot touch you.
Home to the familiar, the past; my
high school moved comfortably closer,
renamed LaGuardia for the Little Flower
who captured our hearts with Pow!
Wham! and Shazam! on newsless
Sunday mornings during the war.
Home to my Westside condo with free
delivery from columns A to Z,
a xenophobic's dream come true.
Home to the city's long shadows
casting tiers up, across, and down
skyless streets and buildings,
an Escher paradox turning a simple
journey to the corner into a fantasy
in Chiaroscuro. Yes, I'm home.
Home, where my grandmother's aura
settles softly and white like
a shroud of down, stilling, if only
for a moment, the island's screams.

OPTIONS FOR DIALOGUE

- In groups create a chart describing the past, present, and future of the neighborhood described in the poem. What are the historical, political, and social forces making an impact on this neighborhood? What are the strengths of the people and places described in the poem? How does the writer feel about them?
- Analyze a history textbook that you have used recently for its perspectives on immigrants and immigration.

- Make a chart that puts into perspective events in history that effect immigration. How do these events relate to immigration quotas in the United States?
- What are the origins of anti-immigrant feelings? What are your critical questions about the lives of immigrants?
- What is wrong with the statement often seen on editorial pages of the popular press: "Why can't they just pull themselves up by their own bootstraps?"
- Research proposition 187 in California. What is the history of this proposition?

SUGGESTIONS FOR ACTION

- Research the history of Puerto Rican immigration to the United States, especially New York. Share this information with the rest of the class.
- Read the memoir *When I Was Puerto Rican* by Esmeralda Santiago (1993; New York: Vintage). What supportive family experiences did the author have in Puerto Rico? How did this help her overcome adversity when she was taken to New York? How did she learn about U.S. colonialism in Puerto Rico? How does this story connect with "New York City Mira Mira Blues"? How does it connect with your own life?
- Read poems from the anthology *Looking for Home: Women Writing about Exile* (1991) edited by D. Keenan and R. Lloyd. (Minneapolis: Milkweed), in which this poem was first published, or other collections of poetry. Find other poems that describe the immigrant experience such as *This Same Sky* (1994) edited by Naomi Sahib-Nye, New York: Harcourt Brace Jovanovich). What are the universal aspects of the experience? What are the things that bring comfort and strength to the immigrant?
- Read a novel written for adults or young adults that focuses on the experience of immigration. Share your response to this novel with another person.
- In small groups create a scenario that dramatizes a kind of escape from an oppressive situation. In the following ways create meanings around the word *immigrant* that bring to light many social contexts:
  1. Students share scenarios with other class members.
  2. The observers brainstorm words that the scenario brings to their minds.
  3. Class members look for connections among the words that are listed.
- Interview someone who has left oppressive conditions or poverty in one country and emigrated to another country or someone who has moved from one part of the United States to another to create a better life. The person could be a grandparent or a neighbor. Share the results of the interview with the rest of the class or create a work of art or a story based on the interview.
- Share books on the theme of homelessness with a group of children or adolescents. Provide a context in which they can develop an action plan to advocate for the homeless.
- Investigate organizations that advocate for the homeless both locally and nationally. Share this information with the class. Here is one organization: National Coalition for the Homeless, 1612 K St. NW, #1004, Washington, DC 20006, (202) 775-1322.
- Investigate ways in which you can help children understand economic injustices, identify stereotypes, and dispel myths about homelessness and prepare them to deal with important social problems instead of sheltering them from the concerns of society. Decide on a way to share this information with others.

⟐ INDEX